"What this book brilliantly documents is that Latin American liberation theology introduced a new method of doing theology, relating theory and practice in an original way, a method that came and continues to be applied in all parts of the Christian Church as the theological approach that explores the emancipatory power of the Christian Gospel."

Gregory Baum
McGill University, Montreal

"Theologians in Latin America, Asia, and Africa, where two-thirds of the world live in poverty and oppression, are crying out in agony for liberation. They have generated the movement for liberation theology, one of the most significant, aspiring, and awesome developments in both the contemporary church and in the entire post-colonial and post-Communist world. Father Hennelly has described and analyzed their surging aspirations of the spirit in which almost 4 billion people are involved in a global pursuit of justice.

"This important book is well researched and compelling. It will be an indispensable guide for everyone who desires to comprehend more fully one of the most important theological developments in the modern world."

Robert F. Drinan, S.J.
Professor, Georgetown University Law Center

"This invaluable compendium of writings will correct the false impression that liberation theology is an isolated Latin American phenomenon. The book clearly demonstrates that liberation theology, in its essentials, knows no geographical or cultural boundaries. Highly recommended."

Msgr. George G. Higgins
The Catholic University of America

"Alfred Hennelly is already a familiar name among the interpreters and exponents of liberation theology. In *Liberation Theologies* he augments and interprets the most significant liberation voices world-wide. Readers will find already significant names and writings, but will also meet many more for the first time. All are given sympathetic and helpful hearings."

Robert McAfee Brown
Professor Emeritus of Theology & Ethics
Pacific School of Religion, Berkeley, California

"*Liberation Theologies* is at once a survey of a vast theological output and a proposal that its point of unity is a worldwide struggle for justice. Through a judicious commentary on representative theologians, Hennelly connects the tributaries to a mighty river."

Phil Berryman

"Alfred Hennelly's *Liberation Theologies* is an important contribution to an appreciation of the significance and impact of liberation theology. Hennelly's work demonstrates the reach of this theology and the extent to which liberationist theory has penetrated Christian theology as a whole."

Roger Haight, S.J.
Weston Jesuit School of Theology

"Alfred Hennelly follows in the mold and spirit of all the major schools of liberation theology in their global pursuit of justice. His pellucidly clear survey is the finest book yet written in the many-splendored area of liberation theology."

Deane William Ferm
Author, *Profiles in Liberation*

"Theology should be exciting, if it is trying to deal with the major issues of our time. As Fr. Hennelly demonstrates, theologians are asking the important questions of life, death, justice, and ecology. From this remarkable assemblage of writers, well-known and less known, a global picture emerges of the struggle of Christians to be faithful to the Gospel of Jesus Christ, and to be responsible in their particular contexts.

"Justice, poverty, ecology, feminism, ecumenism, liberation, political theology, freedom, racism—the range of topics is broad, the seriousness of the issues beyond question. Hennelly helps Christians, in colleges or universities or in their armchairs, to enter into the exciting work of key theologians of our day, writing from all corners of the globe."

Peter Schineller, S.J.
Regional Superior of the Jesuits of Nigeria and Ghana
Author, *A Handbook on Inculturation*

LIBERATION THEOLOGIES

The Global Pursuit of Justice

Alfred T. Hennelly, S.J.

TWENTY-THIRD PUBLICATIONS

Mystic, Connecticut 06355

Twenty-Third Publications
185 Willow Street
P.O. Box 180
Mystic, CT 06355
(203) 536-2611
800-321-0411

© Copyright 1995 Alfred T. Hennelly. All rights reserved. No part of this publication may be reproduced in any manner without prior written permission of the publisher. Write to Permissions Editor.

ISBN 0-89622-647-6
Library of Congress Catalog Card Number 94-62051
Printed in the U.S.A.

Dedication

To all liberation theologians
Christian laity as well as scholars
in every corner of the world
from every race, gender, class, and nation
united in solidarity against oppression and poverty
companions with all persons who seek a just society
I dedicate this book

Acknowledgments

A truly indispensable opportunity for beginning the writing of this book was a year-long Faculty Fellowship (1992-1993) from Fordham University in New York City. The Fellowship also allowed me to complete the editing of two other books during that time. Thus, I am deeply indebted to the administration of Fordham University and its President, Rev. Joseph A. O'Hare, S.J., for granting me this auspicious occasion.

A second indispensable blessing was provided by the directors and staffs of several libraries throughout the United States, especially the Fordham University Library, the Maryknoll Library at Ossining, N.Y., the Woodstock Library at Georgetown University, Washington, D.C., and the Library of Congress in Washington, D.C. Too numerous to mention are the many universities and colleges throughout the nation that provided a large number of interlibrary loans with great courtesy and efficiency, thus saving much valuable time. My colleagues at the Woodstock Theological Center in Washington, D.C., also provided me with their usual hospitality and fine conversation during the year.

Again, too many companions throughout the Americas have acted as helpful interlocutors during my work for me to list them all without omitting someone. My colleagues in the Department of Theology and Jesuit community at Fordham University have borne my labors with forebearance and sometimes amusement, as have my relatives in the Carolinas, especially my brother and nieces and nephews.

Finally, I acknowledge my immense debt to the perceptive editors and excellent staff of Twenty-Third Publications. Without their commitment and acumen in publishing liberation theologies and similar works over the past few decades, this book could never have been written.

CONTENTS

PROLOGUE

BLAZING NEW TRAILS

IN A SCIENTIFIC ERA LIKE THE PRESENT, WE have all become accustomed to immense spans of time. We can imagine going back millions of years to the reign and fall of the dinosaurs, to the billions of years that our planet has sped around the sun, and, perhaps with greater difficulty for our imagination, to the existence of other racing planets, suns, galaxies, and black holes that are millions of light years away from us. From this perspective, the fact that Christians have lived for just two millennia on mother Earth is hardly startling. The Christian church itself is often referred to as ancient, laden with the burdens, the joys and sorrows of history, as it trudges through the centuries, with its footsteps slowing, the creases on its visage deepening, and its vision dimming as it trudges along its ancient roadway. But in this book I will envision its two millennia of existence as a mere beginning, a prelude, compared to the age of the universe. The church, then, may best be hypothesized as a young and vivacious child, peering ahead with unfailing hope and brio at the bright paths that beckon him or her.

This youthful and vibrant church, as in the centuries of the past, has created a theology to express its experience of the God of Jesus

Christ, an experience that has erupted in every continent and every corner of the world, and has touched the hearts and minds of persons of every race, sex, class, nation, and creed upon Earth. It has been called the theology of liberation (or the theologies of liberation), but the name is not that important. One of the best known theologians of liberation, the Uruguayan Jesuit Juan Luis Segundo, has written from the context of his own continent of Latin America and the Caribbean:

> It is my opinion that the "theology of liberation," however well or poorly the name fits, represents a point of no return in Latin America. It is an irreversible thrust in the Christian process of creating a new consciousness and maturity in our faith. Countless Christians have committed themselves to a fresh and radical interpretation of their faith, to a new re-experiencing of it in their real lives. And they have done this not only as isolated individuals but also as influential and sizeable groups within the church.[1]

I agree with Segundo's reading of the situation in Latin America, but my goal in this book is considerably more expansive in its scope. For the point of no return, the irreversible thrust, of liberation theology is not only characteristic of Latin American theology, but also of other theologies that have sprung up in every part of the planet.

Some time ago I published a documentary history of Latin American liberation theology.[2] As a result of that research, I was led to envision a book that would be not historical but strictly theological, and would include a description of and evaluation of all the major schools of liberation theology. (There would be neither time nor space for the minor schools, minor in size but not in vitality and commitment.)

I also wished to test a hypothesis that has occurred frequently during the course of my research, namely, that all of the liberation theologies share a very profound unity, a unity that actually *demands* very diverse contexts, different cultures, different races and sexes, different forms of oppressions, nations, and ethnic communities, as a constitutive part of the profound unity.

To test this hypothesis, I intend to reflect upon and, I hope, comprehend more profoundly the continuities and discontinuities, the valleys and peaks, the similarities and dissimilarities, the *luces y sombras* of these continuously developing and creatively expanding theologies. My method, if it can be called that, will not be an attempt to *survey* everything in these theologies. Rather, I have selected authors (one or several) in each of these theologies who in my judgment are the most profound, most creative, and most influential leaders who are blazing new trails for their churches and society.

Undoubtedly, then, my approach cannot be designated as systematic theology, in any strict sense, but it certainly can be called theological reflections. At any rate, it is entirely possible that the production of systematic summas, such as the works of Aquinas, Barth, Tillich, and von Balthasar,[3] will become extinct (or are already extinct) with the terrible swiftness that ended the dominion of the dinosaurs. Elizabeth Johnson, who has written with some astonishment at the enormous diversity of feminist theologies,[4] is quite lucid on this point:

> Rendering insights into systematic speech about God may be premature, for the experiences of women continue to grow, generating an ever-expanding naming. We are still at the stage of building, finding, forming, thinking, and feeling our way ahead. No doubt too, the design of theological systems and their contents will change with continued feminist discourse. *The very concept of a system may be too restrictive.*[5]

Also, in this book I do not choose to enter into dialogue with the prodigious number of classical theologies that might be marshalled into service as interlocutors with the liberation theologians. This could possibly be a praiseworthy endeavor if someone found it interesting. My own interest and the interlocutors with whom I will interact will be the myriad liberation theologians of today and tomorrow with their visions, dreams, struggles, and celebrations of a new creation, with a just, sustainable, and truly democratic society and with a world community of all human beings and all God's creatures. It will be, as the bygone song expressed it, a "many-splendored thing," a many-splendored family of God. And this new

world community of liberation represents the vanguard, the pioneers, the spearhead, the cutting edge of a new Christianity for a
new millennium.

Most of the multitude of theological books that are published
each year either explicitly or implicitly are directed to the same
goal. Each of them strives to make a contribution to the never-
ending task of *fides quaerens intellectum,* that is to say, of a faith that
searches for understanding. This task, indeed, has a venerable and
treasured tradition, extending back through the centuries to the apostolic age of the Christian churches. In this book, I certainly do not
propose to jettison this tradition, but I do intend to change it in a
very important sense. What I seek and what I believe to be essential
to all contemporary theology is not merely faith searching for understanding, but rather *fides quaerens liberationem,* that is, "faith
searching for *liberation."*

This is not, to be sure, a total reversal of the tradition of faith
seeking understanding. Understanding is an essential element, but
understanding that is inextricably locked in dialectical tension with
Christian *practice,* which consists fundamentally of profound and efficacious love in history.[6] I would also emphasize that Christian understanding that purports to avoid the Christian practice of love,
either directly or indirectly, must be seen to be tangential to authentic Christianity and, at best, a waste of intellectual time and energy. At its worst, such evasion must be understood as the
theological equivalent of blasphemy, that is to say, of using
Christian understanding as an implicit or perhaps explicit legitima-
tion of and alliance with the social sins or crimes of injustice, domination, and oppression, especially when these are visited on the
weak and the powerless.

This practice of Christian love, then, must be seen as the acid test
of any Christian understanding. In this book I will discuss the views
of a number of theologians who have a Christian faith that is searching for liberation along many different paths and in many different
parts of the world. These theologies have often been viewed by other theologians as superficial or at best peripheral, thus not meriting
the status of serious theological discourse. They are often attacked,
also, because they create disunity and disorder in academic theol-

ogy, and do not concentrate on the great theological syntheses of the past. To some extent, these last accusations have a kernel of truth; all of the liberation theologies are continually open and searching for new and better understandings and avenues of practice. In this sense, they understand themselves as "*compañeros* of history," always open to the new challenges and new visions that history continually presents.

Regarding the charges of being peripheral or superficial, the liberation theologians are more than willing to wager that their work represents the future and will win the verdict of history. Within that history, they apply the "Gamaliel test," taken from the Acts of the Apostles (5:33–42). According to this book, the Pharisee Gamaliel was a member of the council that was questioning Peter and his companions. The council members became enraged at their answers and shouted that they should be put to death. At this point, Gamaliel, who was also a doctor of the law, called upon the council to remember and reflect upon the recent cases of Theudas and Judas the Galilean. Each of these men had gathered together a few hundred disciples, but they ended up being put to death, while their movements disappeared entirely. Then Gamaliel continued: "So in the present case I tell you, keep away from these men and leave them alone; for if this plan or this undertaking is of men, it will fail; but if it is of God, you will not be able to overthrow them. You might even be found opposing God."

At this point, it may be helpful to provide at least a general outline of what is meant by the theologies of liberation. In this book, I will treat them in the following order, which are not necessarily the most important or the most extensive: 1) the Latin American liberation theology; 2) the feminist theology of liberation; 3) the black theology of liberation in the United States; 4) Hispanic-American liberation theology; 5) African liberation theology and South African liberation theology; 6) Asian theologies of liberation; 7) liberation theology in the first world; 8) an ecotheology of liberation for the whole world; and 9) a liberation theology of the world religions.

As mentioned earlier, I have selected the major theologies, that is, those with the greatest number of adherents and with the greatest development in their theological reflections. The numbers are easily estimated, and I have included a *selective bibliography* for each theology which demonstrates its theological productivity and which, it is hoped, will lead readers to a deeper draught than I could include in each chapter. And I repeat that there are many smaller liberation theologies, such as Asian-Americans and native Americans in North America, that are deserving of much greater attention, study, and articulation.

In this prologue, also, it is helpful to be aware of problems that confront liberation theology but do not usually affect other theologies. In many areas of the world it has been and is a political crime to publish or disseminate these theologies. This has meant imprisonment, torture, and death for many Christians, bishops, clergy, and thousands of lay persons.[7] At times, too, the churches themselves have persecuted in less lethal ways liberation theologians who have criticized the church for placing itself on the side of the oppressors. As Harvey Cox has pointed out, the silencing of theologians is a form of blasphemy, a way of denying God.[8]

A second problem concerns the problem of co-opting the language of liberation theology and emptying it of its content. This has been described as follows:

> Classical Catholic education describes itself as an education in liberation, and even the most right-wing ideology makes frequent use of the idiom of liberation. And so we are confronted with a paradox that is readily comprehensible in ideological terms: on the one hand authentic theology of liberation is persecuted as subversive; on the other hand its terminology is adopted in watered-down form to front for ideas and attitudes that have no connection whatsoever with truly liberative changes.[9]

A third problem concerns the fact that liberation theologies arise out of real life situations that deeply affect people's lives. So it had to move forward without the erudition and attention to every detail that occurs when a new European or North American theology is introduced. And the result was that it "clearly evoked a certain amount of academic disdain from the great centers of theological thought around the world."[10]

Despite these difficulties, all the liberation theologians are gifted with the indomitable virtue of profound hope in the future. Jon Sobrino of El Salvador (a country wracked by poverty, torture, and murder for decades) summarizes their Christian hopes eloquently:

> As Paul puts it, it is a "hoping against hope" (Rm 4:18). Christian hope is not a hopeful optimism which looks *beyond* injustice, oppression, and death; it is a hope *against* injustice, oppression, and death. When the New Testament asks Christians to give an account of their hope (1 Pt 3:15), it is in the context of persecution. . . . Hope arises precisely at the moment when it would seem obliged to disappear, at the moment when love and goodness fail to triumph.[11]

In summary, the liberation theologians comprise one far-flung global brotherhood and sisterhood, with an unquenchable hunger and thirst after justice for all. Here I present some of the most articulate leaders among them, that they may animate and stimulate to action the Christian churches, the world religions, and all those women and men who search passionately for justice. May their tribe increase!

CHAPTER ONE

THEOLOGY FROM THE UNDERSIDE OF HISTORY

Latin American Liberation Theology

An early death for the indians, and sin on the part of those who oppress them. It is the context in which Bartolomé [de Las Casas] receives the call to denounce these conditions, and to proclaim the Reign of life in its stead. The liberation of the "Indian oppressed" looms before his eyes as a colossal exigency. In the Indians, he sees Christ himself, humiliated and scourged. It is within this christological perspective that Bartolomé reaches the great intuitions of his life.

Gustavo Gutiérrez
Las Casas: In Search of the Poor of Jesus Christ 67

This is my hope: The day will come when all people, lifting their eyes, will see the earth shining with brotherhood and sisterhood, mutual appreciation, true complementarity. . . . Men and women will dwell in their houses; men and women will drink the same wine, and dance together in the brightly lit square, celebrating the bonds uniting all humanity.

Ivone Gebara
With Passion and Compassion:
Third World Women Doing Theology 134

THE FIRST QUOTATION ENCAPSULATES the entire zealous and truly indefatigable life (1484-1566) of the Spaniard Bartolomé de Las Casas: Dominican friar, preacher, amazingly prolific writer, lawyer, bishop, and jack of all tasks as he helped to midwife the vast New World that was being born in the West, for better or for ill. Five centuries later, a Peruvian Indian priest, Gustavo Gutiérrez, has been living in the footsteps of Las Casas, as may be seen in the Centro de Las Casas in Rimac, a slum of Lima, which is entirely dedicated to the study and welfare of the many native Indian tribes in Peru and contingent nations. Moreover, Gutiérrez has over several decades written a book on Las Casas that is a colossal monument of scholarship and passionate interpretation, so that Gutiérrez too sees Christ himself in the Indians. I will turn again to Gutiérrez.

In this chapter it will become evident that the innovative theological ideas and strategies of Latin Americans have transformed the lives of persons, communities, nations, and the world's Christian churches, as well as a host of non-believers who previously paid little heed to the life and words of Jesus Christ. As worthy representatives of what is now a vast library of articles and books, I have chosen to interpret and evaluate the work of Gustavo Gutiérrez of Peru, and of Juan Luis Segundo of Uruguay, in whose writings I have long been interested.[1] Gutiérrez is a diocesan priest in the diocese of Lima, Peru, while Segundo is a member of the Jesuit order, the Society of Jesus. One reason for selecting these two men is the fact that they are not only extremely productive and profound in their theological reflections, but also that they represent *different contexts* for their work. Thus, Gutiérrez devotes his labors to communities of people in the constantly expanding slum community of Rimac, while Segundo theologizes in intellectual and professional dialogues with communities in Montevideo, both Christian and non-Christian.

More important, these two men are the two most significant leaders in the genesis and evolution of the Latin American liberation theology, and their influence continues to this very day. Ana María Bidegain, also, stands out as a leader among many other women who are now destroying the many forms of sexism that have plagued their continent. She too is a personification of a passion for justice, with regard to sexism but also to racism, classism, and militarism. We now turn to these three leaders and their visions of the future.

GUSTAVO GUTIÉRREZ

In the summer of 1991, Gustavo Gutiérrez embarked on one of his frequent voyages to the United States. Although racked by a severe cold, he gave a series of lectures on liberation theology to a packed audience at Boston College that anticipated new insights from a founder of this new theology. A ripple of surprise was visible, however, when he was discussing his poor parish of Rimac near Lima, Peru. He emphasized that in the parish he had never once used the term "liberation theology," and spoke with great conviction that "I preach Jesus Christ; I do not preach liberation theology." In an earlier periodical interview, he clarified this by noting that theology was for his free time, while his primary vocation was as a pastor for the poor. He continues: "In Peru no one would think of calling me Professor Gutiérrez. . . . The pastoral work is what I enjoy most. This is my primary function. . . . *I was ordained not to 'do theology' but to proclaim the gospel. I consider theology only a help toward that, nothing more."*[2]

It is clear from his words that the author's theology has been enriched with great vitality and prophetic power, precisely because of his life with the poor and for the cause of the poor. I do not know of any other liberation theologian that has been daring enough to end his *chef d'oeuvre, A Theology of Liberation*, with words such as these:

> To paraphrase a well-known text of Pascal, we can say that all the political theologies, the theologies of hope, of revolution, and of liberation, are not worth one act of genuine solidarity with exploited social classes. They are not worth one act of faith, love and hope, committed—one way or another—in active participation to liberate humankind from everything that dehumanizes it and prevents it from living according to the will of the Father.[3]

In this chapter I will devote most of my attention to his book on a theology of liberation, although he has published other useful volumes.[4] In my opinion, this book is not only one of his best works, but is also an excellent survey of his major ideas.

The Preamble at Chimbote

As a fitting prelude to his book, attention should be given to a talk Gutiérrez gave at Chimbote, Peru, to a group of priests and laity at the end of July 1968, just one month before the epoch-making event of the conference of Latin American bishops at Medellín, Colombia. His talk was entitled "Toward a Theology of Liberation" and it is no secret that the ideas in it had a profound influence on the final document of Medellín, especially in the three sections on justice, peace, and the poverty of the church.

His address made it clear that the Peruvian was already deeply influenced by the theme of liberation three years before the publication of his book. Thus he affirms that there "is talk today of a theology of human liberation. Using this or other expressions, the theme has become a major preoccupation of the magisterium of the church in recent years."[5] He then proceeds to an even stronger approbation of the term:

> If faith is a commitment to God and to human beings, it is not possible to believe in today's world without a commitment to the process of liberation. That is what constitutes a commitment today. If participation in the process of human liberation is the way of being present in the world, it will be necessary for Christians to have an understanding of this commitment, of this process of liberation.[6]

It should be evident that the author's basic themes, in all his writings, are intended not only for Latin Americans but for all Christians, especially those in the United States and the rest of the first world. Since the three "worlds" no longer exist, with the demise of the Soviet Union and Central Europe as a bloc, I will henceforth refer to the two main protagonists in the world as the "first world" (the developed nations) and the "third world" (the developing nations). At any rate, if Christians in the North accept the enormous challenge laid down by liberation theology, they may provide a key role in the long march that will lead to what Martin Luther King, Jr., referred to as "the beloved community," although his community now refers to solidarity in the north and south, that is, the entire planet.

A last text is one of the most important in Gutiérrez's address, since it concerns the problem of method, which, as we shall see later on, provides the keystone for all the edifices of liberation theology. In the talk Gutiérrez points to three characteristics of his liberation theology. First, he sees it as a *progressive and continuous understanding*, but the understanding of "a commitment in history concerning the Christian's location in the development of humanity and the living out of faith."[7]

Second, he presents his tentative description of *theological method*, which I believe is the best paragraph in the entire talk. I quote it in full:

> Theology is a reflection—that is, a second act, a turning back, a reflecting, that comes after action. Theology is not first; the commitment is first. Theology is the understanding of the commitment, and the commitment is action. The central action is charity, which involves commitment, while theology arrives later on.[8]

There is no doubt that the author is fully aware of the immense pastoral consequences of his statements. In a sense, as in the efforts of Hegel and Schleiermacher in the nineteenth century, he "stands theology on its head" and audaciously proclaims that it "is not the role of theology to tell us what to do or to provide solutions for pastoral action. Rather, theology follows in a distinctive manner the pastoral action of the church and is a reflection upon it."[9]

His third characteristic rightly stresses the absolute necessity of pastoral *action*, which will be accompanied by a theology that provides continual orientation and inspiration. Finally, a very important statement clarifies the dialectic of action and theory in a brief but striking manner: "Every action of ours must be accompanied by a reflection to orient it, to order it, to make it coherent, so that it does not lapse into a sterile and superficial activism."[10] To stress even more the centrality of action, Gutiérrez notes that theology is a science and, like all sciences, has only a modest role in human life. He then caps his argument with the famous words of Blaise Pascal: "All the things in this world are not worth one human thought, and all the efforts of human thought are not worth one act of charity."[11]

The Book That Roared

The Spanish original edition of *A Theology of Liberation* appeared in bookstores around the entire continent in 1971, to be followed by the English edition in 1973, which soon turned into a "bestseller" as theological volumes go. In the book, Gutiérrez very shrewdly planned his structure to follow the three characteristics that we have just seen in the Chimbote conference, with special emphasis on the method. I will begin, then, with an analysis of that structure.

The volume is divided into four major divisions: 1) Theology and Liberation, 2) Posing the Problem, 3) The Option before the Latin American Church, and 4) Perspectives. The theological core of the book may be found in Part Four, on the perspectives, while the first three parts provide an essential but less important introduction. This is analogous to the structure of the gospel of Mark, which some scripture scholars refer to as "a passion narrative with an introduction."

It is illuminating to see the first part as a definition of the terms "theology" and "liberation," a technique employed by theologians for centuries. The terms, however, are not merely information, but provide the foundation of the entire book, although the author emphasizes that as "we progress, various shades of meaning and deeper levels of understanding will complement this initial effort."[12]

Before entering a discussion of the meaning of theology, the author boldly advances a view that may not be acceptable to many in the academy:

> There is present in *all believers*—and more so in every Christian community—a rough outline of a theology. There is present an effort to understand the faith, something like a pre-understanding of that faith which is manifested in life, action, and concrete attitude. It is on this foundation, and only because of it, that the edifice of theology—in the precise and technical sense of the term—can be erected. This foundation is not merely a jumping-off point, but the soil into which theological reflection stubbornly and permanently sinks its roots and from which it derives its strength.[13]

As in the case of the quote of Blaise Pascal, Gutiérrez attempts to strengthen his position by a quotation from outside the field of theology, this time from a well-known text of Antonio Gramsci.[14] It must be emphasized that Gutiérrez has spent his entire pastoral life with and on behalf of the poor; thus he has had ample experience of the scope and profundity of "knowledge of God" manifested by poor laborers and *campesinos*. It is also evident that their knowledge of God and spirituality far outstrips many of those who have acquired degrees in theology, like myself.

Furthermore, as regards the meaning of theology, Gutiérrez in his first chapter clearly opts for an inductive approach rather than a deductive one, as was clear in his Chimbote lecture. The deductive method would start with the learning of a series of doctrines of the Christian faith, which are then "applied" to real life situations and present "answers" to the problems that may arise for people in different contexts. Once again, Gutiérrez turns this on its head when he uses an inductive approach that can be expressed in a brief sentence: *Theology is a critical reflection on praxis in the light of the Bible.*[15] "Praxis" is sometimes considered to be a modern term, but the gospel of Matthew (16:27) places it in the mouth of Jesus: "For the Son of man is to come with his angels in the glory of his Father, and then he will repay everyone according to their practice (in Greek: *katà tén prâxin autoû*). In the letter to the Romans (12:4) Paul also employs the word when he affirms that "all the members [of the body of Christ] do not have the same practice or function *(tén autén prâxin)*." Finally, Luke uses it as the title of his second book, the Acts *(praxeis)* of the Apostles.

It is important to underline that praxis in modern theology must not be understood as practice or action *alone;* rather, the term signifies a constant historical dialectic between theory and the practice of the theory. In brief, action must be constantly tested and refined by theory, while theology must always be put to the test according to the practice or action that proceeds from it. In other words, the Christian churches must express their faith both by ortho-doxy (right teaching, or theory), and by ortho-practice (right action, or living), so that a genuine *orthopraxis* may be the result on a personal, communal, and societal level. In the history of the churches, excessive emphasis was often given to one or other parts of the dialectic, which is a *complete* distortion of true praxis.

In advancing his inductive approach, Gutiérrez briefly discusses the early church up to the medieval period which understood theology as wisdom or spirituality. From the twelfth century on, theology moved beyond the wisdom approach to understand theology as a science or, more accurately, rational knowledge. The author forthrightly states that there has been a "degradation" in the Thomistic concept of theology, and that after the Council of Trent (1545-1563) it became an ancillary agent of the magisterium of the bishops with three fixed functions: "1) to define, present, and explain revealed truths; 2) to examine doctrine, to denounce and condemn false doctrines, and to defend true ones; 3) to teach revealed truths authoritatively."[16] In fairness, it should be noted that his attitude toward theology as wisdom and theology as rational knowledge is somewhat nuanced:

> In summary, theology is of necessity both spirituality and rational knowledge. These are permanent and indispensable functions of all theological thinking. However, both functions must be salvaged, at least partially, from the division and deformations they have suffered throughout history. A reflective outlook and style especially must be retained, rather than one or another specific achievement gained in a historical context different from ours.[17]

As we shall see, other forms of liberation theology will use different terms to express the same inductive approach as that of Gutiérrez; they often use the term "experience" as an indispensable approach to theology, not a vague general experience but one that flows from a specific, concrete *sitz-im-leben*, or context. For example, feminist liberation theology places great emphasis on human *experience* as a source of theology, but an even greater and absolutely indispensable source is the experience *of women*. Another form of experience that will be of great importance later in this book may be found in Gutiérrez's statement that *"the very life of the church* appears ever more clearly as a *locus theologicus* [theological source]."[18]

At the end of the first chapter, the author sums up the new approach to theology in a burst of eloquence that can only be considered prophetic. He insists that critical reflection on historical praxis "is a liberating theology, a theology of the liberating transformation of the history of humankind and also therefore that part of humankind—gathered into *ecclesia*—which openly professes Christ." And in a final glorious burst he sums up his own vision and his own passion:

> This is a theology which does not stop with reflecting on the world, but rather tries to be part of the process through which the world is transformed. It is a theology which is open—in the protest against trampled human dignity, in the struggle against the plunder of the vast majority of humankind, in liberating love, and in the building of a new, just, and comradely society—to the gift of the Kingdom of God.[19]

Called to Freedom

In the second chapter of his book, after defining theology, Gutiérrez moves on to a definition or at least a description of "liberation." The author's views on dependency theory and development after more than two decades must be considered outmoded. Therefore I will concentrate on his concept of liberation considered theologically.

The author emphasizes that the Bible presents the life and teaching of Jesus Christ as a liberation, and focuses his argument on the teachings of Paul in the letter to the Galatians. It is Paul who continuously reminds us "of the paschal core of Christian existence and all of human life: the passage from the old to the new person, from sin to grace, from slavery to freedom. 'For freedom Christ has set us free' (Gal 5:1)."[20] Gutiérrez waxes eloquent on the negative and positive dimensions of how Christ has set us free:

> The freedom to which we are called presupposes the going out of oneself, the breaking down of our selfishness and all of the structures that support our selfishness; the foundation of freedom is openness to others. The fullness of liberation—a free gift from Christ—is communion with God and with other human beings.[21]

Gutiérrez then presents a synthesis of "liberation" on three interdependent levels of meaning of a process that finds its full realization in the work of Christ. Throughout, he attempts to demonstrate why liberation is a much more appropriate term than "development," which was very popular in the 1950s and 1960s and even led for a brief time to a "theology of development."

First of all, Gutiérrez emphasizes that liberation expresses "the aspirations of oppressed peoples and social classes, emphasizing the conflictual aspect of the economic, social, and political process which puts them at odds with wealthy nations and oppressive classes."[22] By contrast, "development" sounds aseptic and does not reflect the tragic reality and conflict that exists in Latin America.

On a second level, liberation can be viewed in relation to a history of human beings who assume conscious responsibility for their own destiny, and create their own selves throughout history. Thus, says Gutiérrez, the "gradual conquest of true freedom leads to the creation of a new humankind and a qualitatively different society."[23] Although he does not mention it explicitly, it is clear that Gutiérrez has in mind the process of conscientization developed by the Brazilian educator, Paulo Freire. This has been adopted as an essential technique for the base ecclesial communities (*comunidades eclesiales de base*), which constitute the grassroots church, especially in Latin America but also in parts of Asia and Africa.

On the final level, the term "liberation" is viewed as much more in harmony with the biblical sources than "development." This culmination of the whole chapter is thus depicted from a biblical perspective:

> In the Bible, Christ is depicted as the one who brings us liberation. Christ the Savior liberates from sin, which is the ultimate root of all disruption of friendship and of all injustice and oppression. Christ makes humankind truly free, that is to say, he enables us to live in communion with him; and this is the basis for all human fellowship.[24]

Grace Is Everywhere

The first part of the book, then, was mainly concerned with a definition of terms. Part Two is concerned with an urgent *cluster of questions* that revolve around the themes of secularization and the "one call to salvation." The correct posing and answering of the questions is absolutely crucial for the construction of the foundation of a liberating theology. Gutiérrez expresses it succinctly:

We are dealing here with the classic question of the relation between faith and human existence, between faith and social reality,
between faith and political action, or in other words, between the
Kingdom of God and the building up of the world. Within the
scope of this problem the classical theme of the Church-society or
Church-world relationship is also considered.[25]

Once again, a number of issues that seemed urgent when *A
Theology of Liberation* was written over twenty years ago are no longer critical, although they may be espoused by various enclaves in
the church, both clerical and lay. The author refers to them in chronological order as the Christendom mentality, the New Christendom
mentality, and the distinction of planes. The latter mentality, he affirms, was eroded by a positive interpretation of *secularization* and
by what we may call universal grace or, in the author's words, *one
call to salvation.*[26]

For Gutiérrez, secularization must not be viewed as an adversary
of true religion, as many Christians see it. Rather, he views it as a
process "which not only coincides perfectly with a Christian vision
of human nature, of history, and of the cosmos; it also favors a more
complete fulfillment of the Christian life insofar as it offers human
beings the possibility of being more fully human."[27] On a more
pragmatic level, this means that "Latin Americans, by participating
in their own liberation, gradually are taking hold of the reins of
their historical initiative and perceiving themselves as artisans of
their own destiny."[28] The intimate link between these two texts is
very significant, for it annihilates the specter of *fatalism* that has so
often dominated religion in Latin America and in other poor nations around the world, and substitutes an understanding of life as
a project both on the personal and social levels in order to advance
the Kingdom of God.

With regard to universal grace, there is no need to trace the evolution of that concept in the present century, which was spear-
headed by such eminent theologians as Henri de Lubac and Karl
Rahner. Gutiérrez states the result succinctly:

Once the way was cleared, however, for the elimination of dualism, the problem took a sudden new turn; a significant stage was

introduced with the recovery of the *historical and existential* viewpoint. In the concrete situation there is but one vocation: communion with God through grace. In reality there is no pure nature and never has been; there is no one who is not invited to communion with the Lord, no one who is not affected by grace.[29]

In a sense, Gutiérrez in this section has jumped out of the introductory mode and entered the august dominion of theology. But this move was essential, since in Part Three, it is necessary to understand at least in outline the changes in theology that have contributed to the changes in individuals, communities, nations, and indeed the whole continent of Latin America. These changes are carefully listed by Gutiérrez in every stratum of the Latin American church, in order that he might put into practice the theological method we have discussed earlier in this book. That is to say, if theology is a reflection on praxis, then it is absolutely necessary to examine and analyze the Christian praxis of Latin Americans in the last few decades. Only then will they be able to forge a creative and liberating theology that will provide illumination for their intellect as well as inspiration and motivation in their actions for the Kingdom of God.

Reflections on Praxis

Gutiérrez has always exuded great confidence and hope in the People of God in Latin America; he is confident that the different sectors of that society are making decisions based on their own circumstances and committing themselves to the process of liberation. It is intriguing that in his investigation of a hierarchical community the author gives first place to the laity, next to the priests and religious, and last place to the bishops. At any rate, we will turn now to his survey.

The author brings together seven of the more important theologico-pastoral questions that arose in the early 1970s when he published his book, which served as a basis for the rest of the book. First, he turns to a fundamental question that kept arising: "What is *the meaning of the faith* in a life committed to the struggle against injustice and alienation?"[30] This is not answered satisfactorily, but it is clear that it will be responded to in Part Four. Next, he observes that many who are committed to the process of liberation are experiencing a serious crisis with regard to *personal and community prayer*, and he calls for a spirituality of liberation. He then concludes with the provocative statement that this is a new generation and in "many areas of their life they are without a theological and spiritual tradition. They are creating their own."

A third important question is concerned with the fact that Latin America exists in a *situation of deep conflict*, and that this fosters problems, since Christians are not accustomed to such situations. The author suggests that it would be very helpful to stress collaboration and dialogue with others struggling for liberation. The next important question is a demanding one, since it concerns the *profound divisions* among its members with regard to classes. However, I would not agree with the author's solution: "Participation in the Eucharist, for example, as it is celebrated today, appears to many to be an action which, for want of the support of an authentic community, becomes an exercise in make-believe."[31] One could rather say that the Eucharist is even more necessary today as an essential step toward overcoming the divisions he speaks of.

There is also some ambiguity in Gutiérrez's fifth question, where he asserts that the church "must place itself squarely within the process of revolution, amid the violence which is present in different ways. The *Church's mission* is defined practically and theoretically, pastorally and theologically, in relation to this revolutionary process."[32] This raises many questions. Can or should there be a nonviolent revolution? Can one theologian define a political option that binds all Latin Americans? The sixth question is merely a repetition of the previous one, although it is much more tentative and diffident than the fifth, which amounted to a ukase: "Should *the Church put its social weight* behind social transformation in Latin America?"

The final question, a perennial one, Gutiérrez phrases thus: "The Latin American Christian community lives on a poor continent, but the image that it projects is *not, as a whole, that of a poor church.*"[33] He goes on to elucidate this point:

The majority of the Church has covertly or openly been an accomplice of the external and internal dependency of our peoples.
It has sided with dominant groups, and in the name of "efficacy"
has dedicated its best efforts to them. It has identified with these
sectors and adopted their style of life.[34]

It must be remembered that this book was written two years after
the Medellín conference in 1968. Since then more than two decades
have passed, and other conferences, at Puebla, Mexico, in 1979 and
in Santo Domingo, Dominican Republic, in 1992, have taken positions that call for a preferential option for the poor, following in the
footsteps of the Medellín meeting. At the present time, significant
numbers of bishops, priests, religious, and laity have devoted themselves with genuine Christian love to the cause of the poor and the
oppressed.

History Is One
As he moves into the fourth and final part of his book, Gutiérrez
emphasizes that his point of departure has been the analysis of the
social praxis of the Latin American church (as in the seven questions just discussed), which he will now use as he presents a fresh
and creative interpretation of Christianity in the world today:

The most important point seems to be the following: the scope
and gravity of the process of liberation is such that to ponder its
significance is really to examine the meaning of Christianity itself
and the mission of the Church in the world. These questions are
posed, explicitly or implicitly, by the commitments that Christians
are making in the struggle against an unjust and alienated society.[35]

In an overall perspective, chapters nine, ten, and eleven are actually expansions and deepening of the themes of "one call to salvation" and the universality of grace that we discussed earlier.[36] The
concluding chapters, twelve and thirteen, are in my view the climax
of the book, since Gutiérrez's major interest has been ecclesiology
and especially the conversion of the church. These chapters appear
to me to be intimately related to the previous three, since the two

major attributes he confers on the church are "the sacrament of history" and the "universal sacrament of salvation." His final chapter on poverty also applies principally to the church. It may be recalled that this virtue of poverty was the one most stressed for the church in his social and pastoral analysis of the Latin American situation.[37]

At this point, it would be impossible to consider all the issues and nuances that the author had delineated in these final chapters in his reinterpreted theology. Thus I will merely point out some of the more significant highlights in his thought.

In chapter nine on salvation and liberation, he expands the meaning of salvation within the entire process of liberation. Retrieving the concept of universal grace analyzed earlier, he concludes that there exists only one history, and summarizes it thus:

> All this means that building the temporal city is not simply a stage of "humanization" or "pre-evangelization" as was held in theology until a few years ago. Rather it is to become part of a saving process which embraces the whole of humanity and all human history. Any theological reflection on human work and social praxis ought to be rooted in this fundamental affirmation.[38]

Further on, speaking about Christ and integral liberation and Christ the liberator, the author then demonstrates that "salvation embraces all persons and the whole person; the liberating action of Christ—made human in this history and not in a history marginal to real human life—is at the heart of the historical current of humanity; the struggle for a just society is in its own right very much a part of salvation history."[39]

The tenth chapter continues the concept of salvation, stressing that human history provides the location of our *encounter with God.* After demonstrating that every human person must be treated as a temple of God, he goes on to stress that therefore we encounter God in our contact with others and in our commitment to the liberation of humankind. Gutiérrez had earlier stressed the urgent need for a spirituality of liberation, and thus presents a brief sketch of such a spirituality. "A spirituality of liberation," he asserts, "will center on a *conversion* to the neighbor, the oppressed person, the exploited social class, the despised ethnic group, the dominated country. . . . To be converted is to commit oneself to the process of the liberation of the poor and oppressed, to commit oneself lucidly, realistically, and concretely."[40]

The strange bedfellows of "eschatology and politics" dominate the eleventh chapter. Eschatology is reinterpreted according to the contemporary "theology of hope," which is especially indebted to the writings of the German theologian Jürgen Moltmann. Although Gutiérrez admires Moltmann's work, he is also critical of the German theologian's tendency to deny the concrete present because of over-emphasis on the Promise, and thus his failure to ground his thought in concrete historical experience. Gutiérrez expresses it thus: "The hope which overcomes death must be rooted in the heart of historical praxis; if this hope does not take shape in the present to lead it forward, it will be only an evasion, a futuristic illusion."[41]

The political dimension of the gospel is also debated here with another European theologian, the Catholic priest Johannes B. Metz, who has encountered acclaim as well as controversy for his espousal of the "new political theology." Once again, Gutiérrez both lauds and criticizes Metz: ". . . because the climate in which his reflections develop is far from the revolutionary ferment of the Third World countries, he cannot penetrate the system of dependency, injustice, and exploitation in which all of humankind finds itself."[42]

As regards the question of "Jesus and the political world," Gutiérrez advances some interesting and nuanced ideas, especially concerning the historical Jesus in relation to the political situation. I believe he makes the right choice when he embraces the position that Jesus was deeply affected by both religion and politics:

> The Sanhedrin had religious reasons for condemning a man who claimed to be the Son of God, but it also had political reasons: the teachings of Jesus and his influence over the people challenged the privilege and power of the Jewish leaders. These political considerations were related to another which affected the Roman authority itself: the claim to be Messiah and King of the Jews. His trial closely combined these three reasons.[43]

A Sign to the World
The final chapters in the book are devoted to the church and the

virtue of poverty, which in Gutiérrez's perspective are intimately linked. He begins by affirming that the teaching on the universal call to salvation (which must be acknowledged as the *leitmotif* throughout the book) has created a veritable upheaval in the church in a variety of ways. First, he proposes an "uncentering" of the church, since after the Second Vatican Council the church is no longer understood as the single, exclusive vehicle for the salvation of humanity. The foundation of his new ecclesiological perspective is also derived from the council, which emphasized strongly that the church should be seen as the "universal sacrament of salvation" (*Lumen Gentium*, no. 48).

As a result, the church finds it necessary to turn to the world, where Christ and his Spirit are continually active in the salvation of all humanity. It could also be maintained that the church should be "evangelized" by the world, with the result that a theology of the church in the world must be complemented by "a theology of the world in the church." The result is succinctly expressed:

> This dialectical relationship is implied in the emphasis on the church as sacrament. This puts us on the track of a new way of conceiving the new relationship between the historical Church and the world. The Church is not a non-world; it is humanity itself attentive to the Word. It is the People of God which lives in history and is oriented toward the future promised by the Lord. It is, as Teilhard de Chardin said, the "reflexively Christified portion of the world."[44]

A very important corollary to this consists in the fact that the church as sacrament or sign must truly signify to the world that its inner structures and all its activities are at least striving to be consonant with the life and teachings of Jesus Christ. Once again, Gutiérrez hits the mark: "As a sign of the liberation of humankind and history, the Church itself ought to be a place of liberation. A sign should be clear and understandable."[45]

The author also includes brief but cogent comments on the centrality of the Eucharist. He emphasizes that the "Eucharist is done within the Church, and simultaneously the Church is built up by the Eucharist."[46] He also establishes the Eucharist not as an individualistic aid to heaven but as a challenge to social justice in the world:

> The bond which unites God and humanity is celebrated—that is, effectively recalled and proclaimed—in the Eucharist. Without a real commitment against exploitation and alienation and for a society of solidarity and justice, the Eucharistic celebration is an empty action, lacking any genuine endorsement by those who participate in it. This is something that many Latin Americans are feeling more and more deeply and they are more demanding both of themselves and of the whole church.[47]

Gutiérrez takes up also the question of class struggle, which is somewhat outmoded in the contemporary world with the demise of Marxism in many parts of the globe. He is certainly correct, however, when he proclaims that social conflict or class struggle (whatever the appellation) is a *painful historical fact* that must be faced squarely and be eradicated. It is evident that the division between classes, between enclaves of opulence and the most horrendous misery, continues to stalk the Latin American body politic like a malignant cancer. Thus, Gutiérrez is correct when he insists that in a divided world, "the role of the ecclesial community is to struggle against the radical causes of social division. If it does so, it will be an authentic and effective sign of unity under the universal love of God." He ends with a plea to all Christian communities to work together and to achieve unity in their commitment to the poorest.[48]

The Legacy of Gutiérrez

The major achievement of *A Theology of Liberation* in my opinion is *not* that it produced a comprehensive and profound synthesis of all the major divisions and themes of contemporary theology, as theology is comprehended and practiced in the North. Rather, to use various metaphors, Gutiérrez succeeded in creating a blueprint for a different kind of edifice, an outline map for a new but perilous journey, a sea chart with enormous promise while sailing in troubled waters, a sketch or outline of a novel and, finally, a creative manner of thinking theologically and putting those thoughts into practice.

Thus, he proposed a theological method that did not start from theological dogmas in a deductive stance; instead he proposed that theology was indicative, a second step, a critical reflection on praxis in the light of the Bible. His whole book, then, was a splendid prototype, an excellent exemplar of what a new and liberating theology looked like in print. For scores of Latin theologians, this was the long-sought and liberating catalyst that produced a flood of new volumes, while they also broke out from the straitjacket of the theology of the North. I will say more about Gutiérrez's work later on, in dialogue with other theologies, both in Latin America and in every area of the world, including North America.

JUAN LUIS SEGUNDO

At various times in his books, Juan Luis Segundo of Uruguay has narrated an episode that encapsulates his entire writing career. The incident concerned a Latin American who was escorting a visiting African bishop on a tour of the Brazilian city, Rio de Janeiro. The two strolled through the city, its luxurious villas, its world-renowned beaches and night clubs, its gigantic statue of Christ looming above the city, and other landmarks. Eventually, however, they came to the hillsides encircling the city, which are also world famous for the fetid *favelas* (slums) that perch precariously on the slopes, whose inhabitants pray daily that rain or mudslide will not destroy their jerry-built hovels. Finally, the astonished bishop turned to his guide and blurted out: "You say that you are a Christian country and that you have inhabited this land for over five hundred years." He then threw open his arms to the hideous obscenities that swarmed over the cliffs and questioned angrily: "Is *this* what you mean by Christianity?"

Segundo, then, has been trying to respond to that question for well over three decades. Born in Montevideo in 1925, he is one of the older liberation theologians. If Gutiérrez is the father of liberation theologians, Segundo must be seen as the dean of them all. Also, it must be kept in mind that Segundo was publishing a liberation theology before Gutiérrez and before the Second Vatican Council, although he did not use the words liberation theology.[49]

He also published an article in 1962 in a French periodical, written before the Second Vatican Council, that anticipated many of his later books and articles.[50]

Let us recall that Gustavo Gutiérrez described liberation theology as "a critical reflection on praxis in the light of the Bible." My first task will be to demonstrate that Segundo has refined and deepened the meaning of these terms, although he certainly agrees with Gutiérrez' definition. The first concept refers to the significance of the word "critical." I believe there is a gulf between the two theologians in this regard. Gutiérrez mentions the word, but provides only a brief description that states that we "refer to a clear and critical attitude regarding economic and socio-cultural issues in the life and reflection of the Christian community. . . . But above all we intend this term to express the theory of a definite practice."[51]

Segundo moves beyond this description in a number of ways, the first referring to his presentation of the "hermeneutic circle," or interpretive circle. This is not a minor concept for him, but crucial for his method:

> It is most important to realize that without a hermeneutical circle, in other words, in those instances where the two aforementioned pre-conditions are not met, theology is always a conservative way of thinking and acting. It is not so much because of its content but because in such a case it lacks any *here-and-now* criteria for judging our real situation.[52]

The first precondition mentioned is that the questions in our real situation be rich and basic enough to "change our customary conceptions of life, death, knowledge, society, politics, and the world in general." The second is that these questions must change our customary interpretation of Scripture, or else the hermeneutic circle is brought to a close. Segundo also emphasizes that most progressive theologians in Latin America are "more interested in *being liberative* than in *talking about liberation*. In other words, liberation deals not so much with content as with the method used to theologize in the face of our real-life situation."[53]

Segundo then proceeds to delineate the four steps of the circle:

First, there is our way of experiencing reality, which leads us to ideological suspicion.

Second, there is the application of our ideological suspicion to the whole ideological superstructure in general and to theology in particular.

Third, there comes a new way of experiencing theological reality that leads us to exegetical suspicion, that is, that the prevailing interpretation of the Bible has not taken important pieces of data into account.

Fourth, we have our new hermeneutic, that is, our new way of interpreting the fountainhead of our faith (i.e., Scripture) with the new elements at our disposal.[54]

Segundo gives four examples of the circle, in the writings of Harvey Cox, Karl Marx, Max Weber, and James Cone, arriving at the conclusion that Cone was the only author to complete the circle.[55] I believe, however, that it will be more helpful for English-speaking readers if I propose some examples that are taken from our own context.

It has been the experience of thousands of people in the United States, young and not so young, to travel to developing nations in the South. I am not referring to tours to Cancún or Acapulco, but to journeys to these countries that will entail work with the people, especially with the poor. These come from college programs, Peace Corps, international volunteer groups, lay missionaries, and many others.

In the first step, coming from a wealthy country to an existence of abject misery, they are almost overwhelmed by the change, which deeply challenges their fundamental ideas. In the second step, in the course of time they develop ideological suspicion concerning the extremely wealthy in these countries, and also about the role of the United States and its foreign policy toward these countries. If they are religious, they also critique the role of churches and theology, which often appear to be insensitive and uncaring before tableaux of such enormous suffering.

In the third step, they apply exegetical suspicion, namely, that the teachings of the Bible are used to conceal or to legitimate this suffering. In the final step, they reread the Bible and discover that

God is on the side of the poor, that the final judgment is based on our actions toward the poor (Mt 25), and many other insights. As we mentioned earlier, Gutiérrez emphasized that all Christians are to some extent theologians, so that both professional and ordinary Christians can make use of the hermeneutic circle.

Another example of this occurred in an entire nation, the United States, from the late 1950s to the 1970s, when the country was caught in a domestic struggle, the battle for black liberation, as well as in the foreign conflict of a cataclysmic war in Vietnam. Both of these events threatened to tear the country apart. Precisely because of this, many people recognized structural evil in their own country and churches, and also became aware of the lies and deceit that sought to hide the evil. Christians, too, were summoned to a re-reading of the scriptures and to the creation of what can only be called a liberation theology. Once more, liberation theology's location is in the streets, not primarily in the universities.

Let me end this discussion on method with what has become a famous statement of Segundo:

> . . . perhaps one more thing has been brought out clearly to the reader, something which is of the utmost importance. It is the fact that the one and only thing that can maintain the liberative character of any theology is not its content but its methodology. It is the latter that guarantees the continuing bite of theology, whatever terminology is used and however much the existing system tries to reabsorb it into itself.[56]

Segundo's Razor: Ideology-Critique

It is a truism that liberation theologians use the social sciences in doing their theology. The reason is obvious: These sciences systematically apply reason to both the personal and communal existence of the human being, and thus possess great importance for the theologian, especially when the theologian is searching for strategies to overcome the oppression and impoverishment of millions. Thus, both Gutiérrez and Segundo make use of the social sciences, but Segundo is the only one to attach great, perhaps the greatest, importance to the sociology of knowledge.

I agree with Segundo that the latter science is of extreme importance, since theology is precisely knowledge. The sociology of knowledge requires that one ask from what social location are you speaking, what group in society are you addressing, who is benefitting from what you say, and whose interests are being served from the topics one chooses—or doesn't choose. It appears transparent to me that most theologians and almost all of the social teaching of the Catholic church do not answer these and many other questions regarding ideologies. For Segundo, however, this is one of the most crucial tasks of a theologian, namely, to uncover the ideologies, disguises, lies, and deceptions that defend or legitimate the interests of the society or of the churches. This *ideology-critique*, therefore, constitutes a truly indispensable weapon in the armory of the modern theologian. For the moment, I should mention that the author uses "ideology" in a completely different sense later on and we will discuss that under the rubric of "praxis."

Some examples of Segundo's may be mentioned referring to the sacraments, unity in the church, and our idea of God.[57] He stresses that the Eucharist, for example, affords an image of *ahistorical* efficacy, with "unvarying liturgical elements, pre-established readings, an unchanging Eucharistic service, and the eternal return of the same feasts on the yearly liturgical calendar."[58] The average Catholic, then, receives the impression that God is more interested in timeless values than in efforts to solve historical problems in this world, and in committed efforts to transform the world and history. He concludes:

> Is it by chance, then, that this conception and practice of the sacraments dovetails perfectly with the interests of the ruling classes and is one of the most powerful ideological factors in maintaining the status quo? Would it be too much to admit that sacramental theology has been influenced more by unconscious social pressures than by the gospel message itself?[59]

More briefly, *unity* in the church also exercises an ideological influence, according to Segundo, since it passes over in silence crucial historical issues that may actually be dividing people. The price paid for unity is that the church must say that "the issues of suffering, violence, injustice, famine, and death are less critical and decisive than religious formulas and rites."[60]

Also, the author devotes prominent attention to the image or idea of God that different Christians adopt, and has devoted an entire book to the subject.[61] Thus he affirms:

> One person pictures a God who allows dehumanization whereas another person rejects such a God and believes only in a God who unceasingly fights against such things. Now those two gods cannot be the same one. So a common faith does not exist within the church. The only things shared in common is the formula used to express that faith. And since the formula does not really identify anything, are we not justified in calling it a *hollow* formula vis-à-vis the decisive options of history?[62]

Further on, Segundo provides a concise definition of key aspects of the sociology of knowledge. The liberation methodology supposes for reasons of convenience that the mechanisms that underlie social life are normally concealed from human consciousness, even though they are active and determine reality. And "among those mechanisms we naturally find those, which, gradually and unbeknownst to us, go on shaping our theology so as to uproot it from its base in divine revelation and place it in the service of social interests."[63]

Expanding the Reflections

In his definition of liberation theology Gutiérrez referred to critical *reflections*. I believe Segundo would be in full agreement with the reflections in Part Four of Gutiérrez's book. I believe, however, that Segundo has moved beyond his friend, and creatively produced a number of reflections on *cruces theologicae,* or very difficult theological issues. I believe, too, that these issues will inevitably arise in all of the many liberation theologies. Thus, these theologies may not accept Segundo's views, but they should possess the theological integrity to propose better solutions for these formidable questions to the theological community. Segundo has treated these issues in detail in two foundational volumes, *The Liberation of Theology* and *Faith and Ideologies.*[64]

The following, in my judgment, constitute Segundo's major contributions. At times he has elaborated his views on all of these at considerable length, but I will have to analyze them cursorily. The issues are: 1) faith and ideologies, 2) scripture and its relation to ideologies, 3) the continuation of revelation, 4) the church after Vatican II, 5) grace in a liberation theology, and 6) religion and politics.

1. Ideologies Spring from Faith In discussing the hermeneutic circle discussed earlier, it became apparent that the circle was also a spiral in a continuous process of change. As Segundo expresses it, "Our hermeneutic keeps moving on to an ever more authentic truth that is to be translated into ever more liberative praxis."[65] In order to continue the process of change, Segundo believes that it is essential to clarify the relationship between "faith and ideologies," concepts that must be considered the keystone, or foundation, of the author's entire theological edifice. He begins with what he calls "human" faith, that is, a faith possessed by all human beings, whether they are religious or not. Using the play of Albert Camus, *Caligula*, and phenomenological analysis, he concludes that all children receive their values from their parents or others, making an act of faith in them and espousing their values. These could be Buddhist, Christian, secularist, or espouse other values, and they can and should change, perhaps drastically. Everyone, then, possesses a system of values, a faith, that provides significance to their life: ". . . we recognize a faith in the fact that it claims to possess an *objectively* absolute value. In his faith a person supposedly comes in contact with an objective font of total truth."[66]

With regard to the concept of ideology, it is most important to emphasize that Segundo is here using the term in a sense that is *completely different* from the one used earlier. There it was used in a pejorative sense; an ideology was to be exposed and if possible obliterated in the course of ideology critique. Here he understands ideology in a more neutral sense as *a system of means to achieve a specific goal,* whether an altruistic goal or a criminal one. A number of authors have sharply reprimanded Segundo for the confusion that this usage brings about, and I am in agreement with them. He could easily have used another term to express the same meaning and avoid the misunderstandings that have occurred; for example, he could easily have used a term such as "strategy," which is defined in the dictionary precisely as "a plan [another possibility] for achieving some end."[67]

At any rate, Segundo continues: We "recognize an ideology in the fact that it has no *pretensions* about representing any *objectively* absolute value. An ideology is worth as much as the reasons or arguments that support it."[68] As a natural consequence, he insists that people can and must change ideologies if they do not achieve their goals:

> When some ideology linked up with my faith proves to be inoperative or grounded on uncertain presuppositions, then the objectively absolute value of my faith should logically prompt me to a new and different encounter with the absolute revelation of my faith. If I am a Christian, for example, my ideological crisis should force me back to the gospel message.[69]

The importance of the concepts of faith and of ideology will become apparent as we consider some of the other theological issues that Segundo has dealt with.

2. *Ideologies in Scripture?* The astonishing pace of change that now encompasses the entire globe, as well as the omnipresent and enormous communications networks that stitch the world into a single community, are phenomena that generate crucial but largely unanswered questions for theology. Or, as Segundo expresses it: "There seems to be less and less sense to look for similar situations in cultural milieus dating back thirty-five centuries, particularly since the pace of history seems to be accelerating every day."[70] Can the Bible, then, have relevance for the massive, complex problems that confront us today and challenge theology for answers?

In attempting to resolve this enigma, Segundo uses the categories of faith and ideologies just discussed. He begins by asserting that there exists a real unity in the entire corpus of scripture that is based on *two elements:* "One element is permanent and unique: *faith.* The other is changing and bound up with different historical circumstances: *ideologies.*"[71]

In attempting, furthermore, to relate the Bible to the accelerating problems of history, we are confronted by two possibilities. The first is to search the Bible for situations that are closest to the present situations, and then to accept the ideology in the Bible as the correct response of faith today. A second approach is the one that Segundo believes is the only valid solution to the question we are discussing:

> The other possible approach is to invent an ideology that we might regard as the one which would be constructed by a gospel message contemporary with us. What would the Christ of the Gospels say if he were confronting our problems today? If the faith is one amid the diversity of history, then there must be some ideology that can build a bridge between that faith and our present-day situation even as there were such ideologies in the past.[72]

It should be apparent that the first approach (which is very common) will nourish a conservative tendency, while the second one (which is generally used by biblical scholars) will foster creativity and originality as totally new ideologies are required and created. The second approach, I believe, will be the cutting edge of the future.

On a human level, then, as regards scripture, we are in a lifelong process of learning how to learn, that is, a *deutero-learning*, where the ideologies in scripture "are responses learned vis-à-vis specific historical situations. Faith, by contrast, is the total process to which the human being submits, a process of learning in and through ideologies how to create the ideologies needed to handle new and unforeseen situations in history."[73]

3. Can Revelation Continue? At this point Segundo broaches another *crux theologica*, that is, the *continuation* of revelation. John the Evangelist obviously believes that the revelation of "all the truth" will continue after the time of Jesus through the "Spirit of truth."[74] On the other hand, classical theology speaks of revelation as a "deposit," one that ended with the death of the last apostle and that now is to be preserved intact and regarded as the definitive revelation. Segundo in these words strongly opts for the teaching of John the Evangelist:

> Jesus clearly affirms that many things remain to be said and that

they will be said, although in a different manner. The Spirit of truth will take many things which Jesus himself had not spoken and will make them comprehensible as obviously belonging to the same divine revelation. Jesus' language is very clear. It points not towards a better understanding of what has already been spoken but towards the learning of new things.[75]

The author believes it appropriate to substitute "ideologies" in place of "things" in the above text. Jesus knows that there will be other historical situations where other disciples will respond in ways (ideologies) that *cannot* be spoken of now. But later, when "they are spoken by the Spirit . . . they will automatically be converted into ideologies associated with a specific historical situation that renders them comprehensible and useful."[76]

The deutero-learning that was discussed earlier is brought in at this juncture and shown to be the exact opposite of the concept of a "deposit" of revelation:

> Jesus is saying that one stage of the process is ending, but he is also promising that the project can continue through its own proper means. And those means are nothing else but a succession of ideologies vis-à-vis the concrete problems of history. In short, after Christ history itself is entrusted with the task of carrying on the process. The Spirit of Christ, that is, the dynamic, intrinsic result of the revelatory education process, ensures a process that will lead to the full and complete truth.[77]

Without ideologies, finally, faith is "as dead as a doornail." Here Segundo is emphasizing the notion of praxis, which Gustavo Gutiérrez also stressed. Revelation, then, and faith are "maturity by way of ideologies, the possibility of fully and conscientiously carrying out the ideological task on which the real-life liberation of human beings depends."[78]

4. *Which Eschatology in the Church?* I believe it is obvious that the deutero-learning process cries out for a community of faith, that is, a church, one profoundly concerned with interpreting the privileged nucleus of historical experience which is the Christian Bible. Segundo, however, surprises the reader by asking shocking questions in this regard:

How capable is the Church of permanently living out the tension
between the dynamic unity of faith on the one hand and the historical plurality of the ideologies to which faith gives rise on the
other hand? Can the Church keep this revelatory process going
without bursting into pieces, since it will take countless ideologies
to make the faith a reality within history?[79]

Part of the problem involved in these questions is that often ideologies stubbornly resist change, that is, newer ideologies do, and
thus become conservative and bastions of the status quo. Other ideologies take an opposite track, and give rise to excessive hopes and,
precisely because they are excessive, to inflexibility and even oppression. At first glance, it would seem that the Christian notion of
eschatology could be an antidote or panacea to these occurrences,
since eschatology points to the transcendence of all historical
events. Unfortunately, though, this is not the case:

> It would seem that this notion [eschatology], linked up with the
> function of the Church, would be destined to keep de-ideologizing
> the human mind, to keep it open and flexible, to liberate it from
> its ahistorical pretensions. Yet there is reason to believe that this
> continuing function of de-ideologizing may in fact oppress our
> ideological creativity. Why? Because it wields the sword of crit-
> icism even before ideologies have time to be effective and to
> arouse real enthusiasm.[80]

With regard to eschatology in the churches, Segundo analyzes a
large number of these and other thorny issues at great length, and
they cannot all be discussed at this point. There is one text, however, that illuminates with stunning clarity how present-day
churches in Latin America are *acutely polarized* in their basic ec-
clesiologies and in their basic eschatologies:

> All Christian churches contain an eschatological element, since
> our faith "gives substance" to the things for which we hope. . . .
> And what we look forward to is the kingdom, or reign, of God.
> Wherein lie the differences in the eschatologies of the various
> Christian churches? I think we can say that basically it lies in their
> differing conceptions between events in history on the one hand
> and the kingdom of God on the other hand.[81]

To go beyond Latin America, I have no doubt that this same division has occurred within the Christian churches throughout the world. It is another one of the touchstones that identify liberation theologies in opposition to other contemporary theologies.

5. *Liberating Grace?* We have already examined the teaching in the theology of Gustavo Gutiérrez that the grace of God for salvation is bestowed on every human being, and that this is both the clear teaching of the Second Vatican Council and also a crucial foundation stone of liberation theology. Segundo, too, accepts and accentuates the significance of this teaching. He adds, however, a further development of doctrine that involves not only the concept of grace but also a possible ecumenical breakthrough for the reunion of the Protestant and Catholic churches.

Segundo begins with an interesting overview of the ecumenical situation in Latin America:

> Liberation theology is a profoundly ecumenical theology. It seems that the Christian's concern to collaborate in the process of liberating mankind unites him more effectively and surely with other Christians than does any attempt to resolve age-old theoretical problems. Liberation poses problems of such magnitude that Christians of whatever denomination feel closer to those who have made the same option in history than they do to other members of their own denomination. This ecumenism extends beyond the boundaries of Christianity, in fact, uniting all [people] of good will in decisive options and separating those of "ill will" wherever they are found.[82]

Despite this agreement on both sides, in Segundo's view, both churches are confronted with another crucial step regarding the contemporary meaning of grace.

To summarize, each of the churches since the era of the Reformation have, with a full measure of aggression, emphasized only *one critical aspect* in what should be a dialectical understanding of grace. A synthesis of the two aspects, consequently, would result in a truly profound and liberative understanding and praxis that would enrich and animate both churches.

We know that Catholic theology has traditionally stressed merit for good works done in accordance with the moral law, and therefore it preserves the principle "that human liberty is liberty *for* something definitive and indeed eschatological: the building up of the kingdom of God."[83] On the other hand, Protestant theology emphasizes that justification comes from faith alone and *not* from good works, in fidelity to the teaching of Paul. Thus, Luther "clearly and correctly pointed out that faith should free the Christian from the law and preoccupations with it. That was his creative intuition, welling up from his own consuming inner problem."[84]

In summary, the Catholic position by itself produced legalism, while the Protestant approach alone promoted passivity. But if we understand that Catholicism was maintaining the necessity of freedom *for* the kingdom of God, and that Protestantism was protecting the obligation of freedom *from* the law, we begin to glimpse the fact that there could have been a fruitful and liberating synthesis regarding the question of grace. Segundo expresses this very succinctly when he asserts that faith "liberates man from the preoccupation of the law so that he can launch out into creative love rather than remain paralyzed by the problem of personal security and individual salvation." Thus we can summarize:

> . . . in entrusting our destiny to God, we should not imagine that God simply wants us to leave him alone because any cooperative effort on our part would somehow diminish his glory. On the contrary, the Christian God is a god who loves and needs to be loved. He needs our creativity for his work, and so he asks us to entrust our destiny to him in faith.[85]

6. Religion and Politics The pairing of religion and politics inevitably raises questions fraught with serious disagreements and even bitter hostilities over the centuries; at this point, then, I intend merely to establish some general but very important principles relating to the Christian religion and politics. First of all, in recent years a phenomenon not generally perceived but of colossal significance in the Catholic church is this:

> From *Mater et Magistra* to *Octogesima Adveniens* all the encyclicals purportedly dealing with what used to be called the "social doc-

trine" of the Church have concentrated on what is really the "political doctrine" of the Church. . . . The fact is that those recent documents have not focused as much on such issues as social classes, wages, and work conditions as they have on national and international political structures.[86]

I would go further and emphasize that this phenomenon is even more manifest in the major so-called social encyclicals of Pope John Paul II, that is, *Laborem Exercens* (On Human Work [1981]), *Sollicitudo Rei Socialis* (On Social Concern [1987]), and *Centesimus Annus* (On the Hundredth Anniversary of *Rerum Novarum* [1991]).

After the entire world experienced profound and almost unbelievable changes between 1987 and 1991, the dates of the last two encyclicals, the pope was certainly perspicacious in addressing the changes and thus creating new ideologies, although he would not have used that word. And these new ideas were overwhelmingly political; in fact, the pope is not only the most political member of the Christian churches, he is certainly the most political pope in the history of the Catholic church. Many contenders for that appellation were not fortunate enough to possess Boeing jets and "Popemobiles" to extend political influence to every nook and cranny of the planet.

At any rate, Segundo agrees with Gutiérrez when the latter states that "human reason has become political reason." Segundo expresses it thus:

> Whatever one may think about the political stance or the political neutrality of Jesus himself, it seems evident that his commandment of love and his countless examples and admonitions concerning it in the Gospels must be translated to an era in which real-life love has taken on political forms. . . . To suggest that almsgiving should continue to be the Christian response to the whole problem of wealth and its relationship to love is also to seriously distort the gospel message. . . . And the same thing applies to any attempt to inculcate an apolitical love today—presuming that love can be apolitical at all in a world where politics is the fundamental human dimension.[87]

Throughout the entire corpus of his work, Segundo has reiterated the truism that to adopt a position of neutrality—an "apolitical" posture—amounts to allowing governments to do whatever they wish without any interference or protest by the churches. Many governments that are oppressive or even murderous with regard to their own citizens would loudly applaud and reward such churches. But objectively the "apolitical" church would stake its claim on the side of oppression and injustice, and that is the ultimate blasphemy for a Christian community.

A summary of the author's principles on politics will serve to bring this section to a close. First, he asserts that every "theology is political, even one that does not speak or think in political terms" and the "worst politics of all would be to let theology perform this function unconsciously, for that brand of politics is always bound up with the status quo."[88] He then proceeds to sketch a summary of what the correct position is: "Liberation theology consciously and explicitly accepts its relationship with politics. First of all, it incorporates into its own methodology the task of ideological analysis that is situated on the border between sociology and politics." And in conclusion, when academic theology attacks liberation theology for becoming involved in politics, "thus ignoring its own tieup with the status quo it is really looking for a scapegoat to squelch its own guilt complex."[89]

The "political theology," or social doctrine, of the Catholic church has been repeated, nuanced, and propagated for well over a century. Yet a number of distinguished theologians seem to systematically eliminate it entirely from their various intricate systems as if it were some noxious plague, like a theological AIDS. Perhaps in the future we will be able to point to this rejection of church social teaching as a form of "social heresy" that should have been investigated by authorities at Rome. At this point, we turn to another and very important interlocutor.

ANA MARÍA BIDEGAIN

Ana María Bidegain stands out as an excellent representative of the rapidly increasing number of talented and committed women theologians throughout Latin America and the Caribbean. This is abundantly evident in a collection of their writings entitled *Through Her*

Eyes: Women's Theology from Latin America.[90] Bidegain's essay in this volume bears the intriguing title of "Women and the Theology of Liberation."[91] She is a native of Uruguay, now a citizen of Colombia, and holds a doctorate in Church History from the Catholic University of Louvain in Belgium. She is at present teaching in the University of the Andes in Bogotá, Colombia, and at Duke University in Durham, North Carolina, and is the author of three books.[92]

As a professional historian, Bidegain proposes a historical view of her topic, rather than the usual systematic approach familiar to theologians. Her focus is on the understanding of sexuality that was disseminated to women by the Catholic church, the role that women played in the creation of liberation theology, and—a new venture for Latin Americans—the pursuit of more human and Christian relations between women and men in a culture notorious for its *machismo* (sexual domination of women).

Sex and Domination

Regarding the understanding of sexuality, I will select key ideas from Bidegain's somewhat long discussion. She notes that Europeans landed on the shores of America at the beginning of capitalism and also at the apogee of their military and economic power. "For them," asserts the author, "women's sexuality was mainly a motive for uneasiness. And their only thought was to curb it."[93] Furthermore, she states that sexuality is not a problem for the individual, but a complex cultural reality, intimately linked to economic forces.

Christian puritanism, moreover, is said to have installed sexuality at the center of its pastoral goals. In short:

> In the pastoral activity of the Catholic Church since the sixteenth century, sexual morality has moved from the peripheral, second class status it had in the Middle Ages . . . to constitute for all practical purposes the principal focus of that activity. The resultant polarization of sexual morality has meant the relegation of politico-social concerns to a secondary status. Hence we have the tendency, since that time, to identify "sin" all but exclusively with a particular sort of sexual behavior.[94]

Bidegain also describes how women became marginalized from public life from two directions: 1) She was treated as a minor "scarcely more than an imbecile," and thus in dire need of a guardian; and 2) she has been exalted, so that activities outside the home are below her dignity. Thus, the only choices for women since the nineteenth century are to become a mother or a consecrated virgin.[95] The author also discusses the role of Catholic Action for young men and women (which was the topic of her doctoral dissertation), and which acted as a conscientizing vehicle, especially for the young women who had somewhat tardily joined that movement.

The Birth of Liberation Theology

A rigorous and puritanical view of sexuality reigned in Latin America until the calamities and upheavals of the 1960s. Amid all this, Bidegain stresses, "we discovered that if we were to live in a genuine Christianity, we should have to become involved in the construction and liberation of Latin America."[96] These experiences also resulted in a sharp break with the prevailing understanding of spirituality. Their new motto has lasted until the present despite continuing conflicts: "to see, to judge, to act." Whether women or men, their new approach sought "to embody the gospel, the sacramental life, and prayer, in our own young lives through the witness we could give in the factories, at the universities, on the farm, and in our families." At the same time, they turned to the church itself and launched into "a struggle for the freedom and rights of the laity, male and female, with a view to being able to act on society in the way that seemed correct to us as Christians."[97]

Bidegain also pays tribute to the commitment of religious women in the movement, who more astutely than the priests understood the meaning of solidarity with the poor during the 1960s. Other sectors of the church, seeking to be servants of the people, concentrated on creating basic Christian communities, leading the author to point to an essential element of the *birth* of liberation theology: "The membership and influence of these sectors grew, and it was on the basis of reflections issuing from the communities they founded that they continued to develop the major themes of the theology of liberation."[98]

An important observation here leads to the conclusion that the birth of liberation theology was not without labor pains. Bidegain expresses her experience in an essentially male dominated church with a patriarchal ideology and a habit of subordinating women:

> . . . we had to, if I may say so, practically disguise ourselves as men. We had to reason like men, act with the same combativeness as men, use men's vocabulary, and live a man's spirituality. In a word, we had to become male, or at least present ourselves as asexual beings.[99]

In such a situation, it was abundantly clear that liberation theology had a serious flaw from the beginning in that it did not address the situation of women in either church or society. Along with this, it had no interest in developing a moral theology on sexuality, nor did it direct any attention to male-female relationships. Only one liberation theologian, she asserts, dealt with the issue, Leonardo Boff, in his book *The Maternal Face of God.*[100]

Perhaps the most important statement in Bidegain's whole essay is the assertion that today in the church a battle is being waged with regard to a new male-female relationship:

> Very timidly, a feminist theology is being sketched within the current of liberation theology. . . . An ever-growing group of women, lay and religious, in Latin America today is doing theology, and related disciplines like religious sociology or church history, from the same perspective, seeking to consolidate, within the popular movement in the Church, a new kind of man-woman relationship.[101]

Another very significant situation that is rarely treated in liberation theology is "the worldwide feminization of poverty," which is borne out in studies by the United Nations Organization, and which is a consequence of sexism in alliance with racial oppression. The author summarizes concisely:

> Racial discrimination, sexism, and capitalist exploitation in Latin America constitute the triad that keeps women in subjection. Latin Americans who dismiss feminism as a "bourgeois issue" are

altogether off the mark. On the contrary, one of the basic tasks incumbent on Christians is to struggle against *all* discrimination—social, racial, and sexual.[102]

The author then devotes several pages to recapturing "the liberating strength of Jesus and of Mary," which brings her reflections to a fitting close on a level of profound spirituality and burning commitment.

Reflections

It is clear in my choice of Gustavo Gutiérrez and Juan Luis Segundo for this chapter that I believe they are the most important figures in the creation and development of liberation theology in Latin America, as well as in countless places around the world. As I mentioned earlier, they have very different pastoral interests and goals, but they were able, quite providentially, to complement each other. Gutiérrez was the right man at the right time in 1971 when he published *A Theology of Liberation*, which provided, as I have tried to show in this chapter, a broad panorama of the method, themes, and other elements of a liberating theology.

On the other hand, Segundo provided the essential foundations and girders for the liberation edifice as he probed more broadly and profoundly into the elaboration of its method and his unique creation of a "social phenomenology." Thus, he fulfilled the essential task of providing a secure structure for liberation theology, protecting it successfully from the many attacks that continue to this day. At present, some theologians (especially in the first world) have continued to knell the demise of Latin American liberation theology. The facts of the matter, however, and not the ideologies of the West, demonstrate the opposite; what is actually burgeoning at present is a type of renaissance, an arrival at a plateau of theological maturity and profundity. Let me, then, focus briefly on some outstanding recent achievements.

After years of research and reflection, Gustavo Gutiérrez has brought to birth his masterpiece, *Las Casas*,[103] following in the celebrated footsteps of the great Dominican friar, Bartolomé de Las Casas, whose missionary zeal spanned the entire sixteenth century.

Although Gutierrez's historical research in his tome of 682 pages is a great scholarly achievement in itself, his pastoral and theological reflections on the contemporary scene also comprise a creative achievement of the highest order. The subtitle of the book, *In Search of the Poor of Jesus,* could stand as a burning emblem that both men had pledged their whole lives to the indigenous Indians and other races throughout the continent.

Juan Luis Segundo continues his prolific and creative work. *The Liberation of Theology,* mentioned earlier, has been united with a companion volume, *The Liberation of Dogma.*[104] In the latter volume, he probes more profoundly into the inner processes of revelation and how it is translated into dogma. Those familiar with the thought of Segundo will recall his emphasis on the "divine pedagogy," which enables the human community "to learn how to learn" and to articulate new truths, even in dogmas. Another recent, untranslated book, *What is the World? What is the Person [hombre]? What is God?* speaks on a secular level and a Christian one. Segundo believes both levels are essential for understanding theology and dogma, and his goal is to reformulate these "in order to achieve a more vigorous clarity, reality, profundity, and richness"[105] for his readers.

Another important work is Jon Sobrino's *Jesus the Liberator: A Historical-Theological View.*[106] This comprises a thoroughly revised and deeply formulated christology, while a second volume (stressing the resurrection) is awaited by his readers. A lifelong friend and colleague of Sobrino, Ignacio Ellacuría, before he was murdered in San Salvador, produced a magisterial and profound philosophical treatise, *A Philosophy of Historical Reality*[107] (not translated). In this 606-page volume he enters into a profound and lasting dialogue with the Spanish philosopher, Xavier Zubiri, who is acclaimed only in Spain.

Finally, Sobrino and Ellacuría edited two volumes similar to and on a par with European encyclopedias such as *Mysterium Fidei* [Mystery of Faith]. They entitled their two large volumes *Mysterium Liberationis* [Mystery of Liberation]: *Fundamental Concepts of Liberation Theology,* which survey the gamut of the fundamental ideas of liberation theology in Latin America.[108] A one-volume edition was published in English, with some articles dropped. In summary, these observations might convince some of my readers that the Latin theologians are the equal if not the better of world theologians today. At this point, however, we turn to a very serious problem.

Ana María Bidegain's article points out glaringly that one of the most crucial building blocks was left out of Latin American liberation theology: the indispensable experiences and contributions of women. Every Latin theologian from now on must enter into that dialogue, to which they have been blind and mute so far. This state of affairs is especially acute, because the continent is known all over the world for its *machismo*, which is entirely more than a series of male peccadillos but a true horror, a real social sin, the systematic oppression of women on every level, personal, social, economic, political, and cultural. Without exaggeration, it can be safely said that Latin American women in Latin America and the Caribbean have their own gilded and not so gilded cage of apartheid. Ana María Bidegain, however, and her myriad sisters throughout the world are harbingers of a different future; the adherents of *machismo* in Latin America (and many other countries, including my own) are already becoming obsolete and doomed to their dinosaurian demise.

Finally, I want to emphasize that throughout this book I am primarily interested in the *dialogues* that must begin, or flourish if they have begun, *among the various liberation theologians.* These dialogues must entail honest constructive criticism, as in the article of Ana María Bidegain, but the liberationists worldwide are basically friends, *compañeros*, and the time has come for them to unite on a *global basis* in solidarity and in their hunger and thirst for justice and peace. Our enemies are also evident and unmistakable; if any one is unsure about who they are, please speak to the poor or the oppressed in any corner of the world or in any corner of one's own nation or city or neighborhood. They will provide you with names, detailed descriptions, and an atrocious litany of unspeakable crimes against the wretched of the earth.

QUESTIONS FOR REFLECTION AND DISCUSSION

1. Did Gustavo Gutiérrez ever use the term "liberation theology" in his parish work? What does this say about the true goals and mission of liberation theology?

2. Describe the theological method employed by Gutiérrez. What does this say with regard to the role of theology today?

3. How does Gutiérrez define "liberation"? Why is the term "liberation" rather than "development" more suitable and appropriate in his theology?

4. Is Gutiérrez's method on "critical reflection on praxis in the light of the Bible" a method that is only meaningful in an area such as Latin America? Does it have implications for theology in all cultures?

5. What is the role of the "hermeneutic circle" in Segundo's theology? Give a concrete example of your own with regard to the "hermeneutic circle" in action. Is the "hermeneutic circle" a step beyond Gutiérrez's method of liberation theology?

6. Describe Segundo's "ideology-critique." Is it necessary for modern theology to use this critique against society? Against the churches?

7. Is the concept of "continuous revelation" consistent with the classical theological perspective on revelation? What concepts does Segundo use to explain continuous revelation in his theology? Are there possible benefits and also possible dangers in this approach?

8. How does Segundo use the contemporary conception of "grace" as a movement toward the ecumenical movement in Latin America and elsewhere? What other elements of liberation theology also provide an impetus toward ecumenism?

9. Is Segundo's claim that a church which is expressly apolitical will necessarily "objectively stake its claim on the side of oppression and injustice" legitimate? Why or why not?

10. In the light of the work of Gutiérrez and Segundo, what are some of the new ideas that Ana María Bidegain has introduced to the task of liberation theology? What are the points of commonality she has with the above theologians?

SUGGESTED READINGS

Aquino, María Pilar. *Our Cry for Life: Feminist Theology from Latin America*. Maryknoll, NY: Orbis Books, 1993.

Azevedo, Marcello. *Basic Ecclesial Communities in Brazil*. Washington, DC: Georgetown University Press, 1987.

Boff, Leonardo. *Jesus Christ, Liberator*. Maryknoll, NY: Orbis Books, 1978.

Cook, Guillermo. *The Expectation of the Poor. Latin American Basic Communities in Protestant Perspective*. Maryknoll, NY: Orbis Books, 1985.

Dussel, Enrique. *A History of the Church in Latin America: Colonialism to Liberation*. Grand Rapids: Eerdmans, 1981.

Ellacuría, Ignacio, and Jon Sobrino, eds. *Mysterium Liberationis: Fundamental Concepts of Liberation Theology*. Maryknoll, NY: Orbis Books, 1993.

Gutiérrez, Gustavo. *Las Casas: In Search of the Poor of Jesus Christ*. Maryknoll, NY: Orbis Books, 1993.

Hennelly, Alfred T., ed. *Santo Domingo and Beyond*. Maryknoll, NY: Orbis Books, 1993.

Míguez Bonino, José. *Toward a Christian Political Ethics*. Philadelphia: Fortress, 1983.

Moser, Antonio, and Bernardino Leers. *Moral Theology: Dead Ends and Alternatives*. Maryknoll, NY: Orbis Books, 1990.

Segundo, Juan Luis. *The Liberation of Theology*. Maryknoll, NY: Orbis Books, 1976.

Sobrino, Jon. *Jesus the Liberator: A Historical-Theological View*. Vol. 1; Maryknoll, NY: Orbis Books, 1993.

Tamez, Elsa, ed. *Through Her Eyes: Women's Theology from Latin America*. Maryknoll, NY: Orbis Books, 1989.

CHAPTER TWO

THE NEW
COPERNICAN REVOLUTION

North American Feminist
Liberation Theology

It is time to take the leap; it is time to change things. It is time to turn our icons and our rebels into saints. It is that for which, with Susanna, we struggle and it is that for which, with Judith, we hope. It is that for which, with Mary, we contend. And contend. And contend.

Joan Chittister
WomanStrength 40

. . . precisely because the feminist issue within the church has re-situated itself in the realm of spirituality, there is some reason to hope that the institutional church may be able to meet this monumental challenge to grow from a male power structure imprisoning the word of God into a fitting locus for the epiphany of the reign of God in this world. Women who are feminists and Catholics bring to the church not only a powerful critique and the very real possibility of massive withdrawal but enormous resources for transformation. . . . They also bring a spiritual strength tempered in intense suffering and a loyalty that has survived twenty centuries of exclusion and oppression.

Sandra Schneiders
Beyond Patching 111

SOME TIME AGO, I FOUND MYSELF INVOLVED
in a heated discussion concerning the relative importance of women's liberation theology vis-à-vis Latin American liberation theology. The women's position held that women's theology is directed toward all the women of the world, reaches out to the very poorest who are usually women, and seeks to eradicate the most insidious, deeply entrenched, and longest lasting enemies of humankind, that is, patriarchism, sexism, and androcentrism.

On the other hand, the Latins argued strenuously that a vast majority of the world's population, women and men, is grossly impoverished, undernourished, and doomed to early death. Thus, the most important task is to begin with the struggle against seemingly intractable misery and to confront the worldwide mechanisms or juggernauts that continue to grind women and men into the dust of the earth.

My own view did not support either of these approaches in isolation, for it is clear that sexism and poverty are interrelated in most of the world in myriad ways. And there are other modern horsemen of the apocalypse such as racism, nationalism, militarism, terrorism, and other cruel scourges that afflict and crush hundreds of millions of human beings. The best liberation theologians, in my view, concentrate on one area of their choice, while trying to integrate their work with different forms of liberation.

To look ahead, however, it appears that the women theologians have been far more successful than the Latin Americans in continuing this difficult and ongoing synthesis and at the same time creating new forms of praxis. Also, the women are unceasingly aware of the quadruple oppression of most of the women of the world, namely, those who are poor and non-white. Thus, these women are first discriminated against because of their gender, then are oppressed because of their race or nationality, next despised because of their impoverished class, and finally given second-class status in the churches and other religious organizations. Any person or community that undertakes "an option for the poor" would certainly have to begin with these, the most miserable and degraded of all and "the least" referred to by Jesus in the twenty-fifth chapter of Matthew's gospel.

Beginning of the Struggles

At this point, I will provide a brief survey of the modern history and theology of North American feminist liberation theology[1] as a necessary prelude for understanding the present and future of the movement. The major advances occurred in the nineteenth century and again in the 1960s. Although the roots of these advances extend further back in the nineteenth century, an organized group arose in the 1840s, more specifically in a Methodist church in Seneca Falls, New York, in 1848.[2] The two leaders of that meeting, Elizabeth Cady Stanton and Lucretia Mott, had considerable experience in anti-slavery movements, which provided them with a theoretical and practical background for a transition into feminism.

Some feminists disassociated themselves from Christianity, but others committed themselves to the admission of women to seminaries and the ministry; along with this they also organized for women's suffrage, abolition of slavery, temperance, the closing of brothels, and women's rights, such as to support of the family, to work, and to an education. Gradually, however, this broad framework narrowed down to an emphasis on women's suffrage. Anne Carr depicts the result:

> Historians today point out that by narrowing their focus to a single issue and by placing their hope in the almost miraculous changes they thought would come about through the vote, nineteenth-century women lost their wider vision of change in all the aspects of women's life. The vote for women was won in 1920, and the women's movement died.[3]

It would take more than forty years before it rose again.

In the twentieth century, the wider secular movement against sexism and for the liberation of women was joined by movements in the churches for women's meaningful participation in ministry, seminary education, participation and power in the structures of society. Even in denominations that ordain women, however, they still have difficulty in being accepted by their congregations and in being considered for the more important and prestigious appointments.

Furthermore, unlike their sisters in the nineteenth century, feminists today have embraced a broad spectrum of issues and have analyzed the close connections between sexism, racism, classism, and other ideologies. Nevertheless, the liberation of women has drawn fire from certain quarters who think it a luxury available or affordable only to white, affluent, middle-class women. Carr has responded to this by insisting

> that there is an acute awareness of the particularities of the situation, for example, of women in black or Hispanic communities, and of the cultural and religious differences when one moves to the global question of women. A wider bonding has begun to take place, and women who are active in promoting the cause of women in church life are likely to be those involved in movements for peace and justice. . . .[4]

As with nineteenth-century feminism, many women today have come to the point where they simply depart from their specific churches or initiate a total break with Christianity. Furthermore, some find in non-religious feminism a form of spiritual home where they experience encouragement, acceptance, and enhanced creativity. On the other hand, many women are determined to persevere and to effect radical changes in their churches; they simply refuse to leave. Carr believes that these are more revolutionary than those who have left, and includes herself among those who "refuse to ignore the liberating, indeed revolutionary, message that the churches bear about the realm of justice, peace, and equality coming in the future but, as the gospel proclaims, even now being born among us."[5]

I have chosen three outstanding *leaders* in feminist liberation theology: Elisabeth Schüssler Fiorenza, Rosemary Radford Ruether, and Elizabeth Johnson. These three women use the same theological method as the Latin Americans, but they operate out of a different *context*, that is, the contemporary *experience of women* and its concomitant forms of sexism, patriarchy, and androcentrism. Although they rightly emphasize the social sin of sexism, they have also integrated it with the scourges of racism, classism, militarism, terrorism, and other spectres of injustice. In the twenty-first century they and their sisters will be leaders in all of the liberation theologies, and the most passionate in their hunger and thirst for justice.

ELISABETH SCHÜSSLER FIORENZA

One of the most important (if not *the* most important) contributions to the feminist theological movement has been the foundational scriptural work of Elisabeth Schüssler Fiorenza—especially in her book, *In Memory of Her*[6]—regarding the role of women in the New Testament. Since my focus in this book is directed at contemporary liberation theologies, I will not attempt to evaluate this scholarly and well-written book, except to point out the sturdy foundations she has provided for those women who are engaged in the construction of the upper stories of the feminist edifice.

Boldly admitting that her reconstruction of women's history means entering "an intellectual and emotional minefield,"[7] Fiorenza begins with a discussion of four models of biblical interpretation, or hermeneutic, which she names 1) the doctrinal approach, 2) positivist historical exegesis, 3) the dialogical-hermeneutical interpretation, and 4) the feminist liberation approach. Obviously, she opts for the last approach, which poses direct challenges to the supposed objectivity and so-called neutrality of academic theology. The basic liberation insight is that theological neutrality is impossible; it is always engaged for or against the oppressed.

Fiorenza then acutely observes that theology, having recently freed itself for the most part from ecclesiastical authority, has jumped from this frying pan into the fire of domination by the academy. Thus, she insists, theology must cater to the interests of the academic institutions, which have a vested interest in the status quo and tend "to serve the interest of the dominant classes in society and church rather than to preserve its allegiance to God's people, especially the poor and exploited women and men of all nations and races."[8] In the academy, also, she stresses that the male is always considered the normative subject of all scholarship, a theme that resounds throughout her book.

The major thrust, however, of the chapter is directed toward a variety of hermeneutical models. The first is the neo-orthodox model, whose hermeneutical process is rooted in a neo-orthodox theology. Fiorenza detects examples of this model in the writings of such well-known feminists as Letty Russell, Rosemary Ruether, and Phyllis Trible. It may be noted here that salutary criticism, as in this instance, appears to be essential in all fields of scholarly inquiry, but this is not always true in other liberation theologies, such as the Latin American version. The only exception to this, to my knowledge, is to be found in the writings of Juan Luis Segundo, whose critiques of theologians led to somewhat inflated attacks from his Latin colleagues.

The second approach is the sociology of knowledge model, which attempts to move from the reading of androcentric texts to the creation of a feminist life center *(Lebenszentrum)* that will generate new texts, traditions, and visions. This is deemed necessary, because the life center of biblical texts are all male. Fiorenza enters into a nuanced critique of the work of Mary Daly at this point which may be summarized as follows: "Although Mary Daly maintains that this model is gynocentric, one must not overlook the fact that it does not have the power to break the androcentric patriarchal model, which situates women on the boundaries and margins but does not allow them to claim the center of patriarchal religion and culture."[9]

The last of the hermeneutic models is the liberation approach, which, again, is the one Fiorenza embraces. Once more criticizing Mary Daly's approach, Fiorenza insists that relinquishing the biblical heritage merely reinforces the androcentric structures and systems, in which the male reigns as the paradigm of human existence and human history.

Thus, positively,

> a feminist reconstitution of the world requires a feminist hermeneutics that shares in the critical methods and impulses of historical scholarship on the one hand and in the theological goals of liberation theologies on the other hand. . . . Feminist theology as a critical theology of liberation therefore seeks to develop not only a textual-biblical hermeneutics but also a historical-biblical hermeneutics of liberation. It challenges biblical studies as "objective" textual interpretations and value-neutral historical reconstructions fundamentally. [10]

Some other characteristics of the liberation hermeneutic accentuate the fact that feminists are concerned not only with analyzing women's oppression in the Bible, but also with changing and destroying the patriarchal forms within the Christian churches. Fiorenza also uses the well-known concept of Johannes Metz regarding the "subversive memory," which "not only keeps alive the suffering and hopes of Christian women in the past but also allows for a universal solidarity with all women of the past, present, and future who follow the same vision."[11]

Also very important for Fiorenza is the need to uncover and to reject *all* the biblical traditions and texts that call upon God to perpetrate violence, war, alienation, and patriarchy. Consequently, the "liberation theologies cannot accord revelatory authority to any oppressive and destructive biblical text or tradition. Nor did they have any such claim at any point in history."[12]

The last sentence in the chapter is a lucid and succinct synopsis of the entire book:

> . . . this theological heritage [feminism] is misrepresented when it is understood solely as the history of oppression. It must also be reconstituted as a history of liberation and religious agency. The history and theology of women's oppression perpetuated by patriarchal biblical texts and by a clerical patriarchy must not be allowed to cancel out the history and the theology of the struggle, life and leadership of Christian women who spoke and acted in the power of the Spirit. [13]

I will comment further on the contribution of Fiorenza to world liberation theology at the end of this chapter.

ROSEMARY RADFORD RUETHER

As a second outstanding feminist liberation theologian and leader, I have selected Rosemary Radford Ruether, certainly one of the most prolific and creative theologians on the contemporary scene. In her book *Sexism and God-Talk*,[14] she surveys a very broad panorama of Christian and non-Christian traditions, searching for illumination, motivation, and praxis for a contemporary feminist theology.

My inquiry will be divided according to the major divisions of the book, which is in two parts: 1) the first four chapters, which are principally devoted to method and foundational issues; and 2) the last six chapters, where she analyzes and transforms the interpretation of traditional Christian themes. In both parts, I will concentrate on those ideas that are germane to liberation method, themes, and praxis. Here and throughout this book my interest is *not* in comparing liberation theology with *other contemporary theologies*, which are concerned with different contexts, interests, and problems than those of the liberation theologians. Rather, I am deeply concerned with an understanding of the diverse liberation theologies and their *relationships* on both *positive* and *negative levels* with the other liberation theologies.

Theology and Women's Experience?

The most important statements of the entire book are clearly and succinctly stated in Ruether's first few pages, where the author treats the connections between theology and experience. She notes a tendency to see "experience" as unique to feminist theology and not germane to classical theology, a tendency which she forcefully rejects: "This seems to be a misunderstanding of the *experimental base of all theological reflection*. What have been called the objective sources of theology, Scripture and tradition, are *themselves codified collective human experience.*"[15]

Extremely significant corollaries come to light as a result of this thesis. First, codified tradition with its roots in experience is continually recovered or rejected through the test of experience:

> "Experience" includes experience of the divine, experience of oneself, and experience of the community and the world, in an interacting dialectic. Received symbols, formulas, and laws are either authenticated or not through their ability to illuminate and interpret experience.[16]

Another important corollary, then, is the relationship of authority to the symbols, formulas, and laws; authority systems, the author insists, try to reverse this relation and "make received symbols dictate what can be experienced as well as the interpretation of that which is experienced."[17] The final corollary provides a summary, stating that if "a symbol does not speak authentically to experience, it becomes dead or must be altered to provide a new meaning."[18]

We may seem to have strayed from the discussion of feminist theology, but this background is essential for understanding a cornerstone of feminist theology. That is to say, the utilization of experience does not comprise the unique feature; it is the employment of *women's* experience that is unique and has been almost completely lacking in the past. Ruether then throws down the gauntlet decisively to classical theology:

> The use of women's experience in feminist theology, therefore, explodes as a critical force, exposing classical theology, including its codified traditions, as based on *male* experience rather than on universal human experience. Feminist theology makes the sociology of knowledge visible, no longer hidden behind mystifications of objectified divine and universal theology.[19]

Ruether also notes that human experience is the starting and ending point of the hermeneutical circle, as was discussed earlier with regard to the hermeneutic circle of Juan Luis Segundo.

At this point, we turn to another foundational thesis of feminist theology, which Ruether refers to as the *critical principle* of feminist theology: "the promotion of the full humanity of women."[20] From a negative perspective, therefore, she insists that whatever denies or diminishes the full humanity of women "must be presumed not to reflect the divine or an authentic relation to the divine, or to reflect the authentic nature of things, or to be the message or work of an authentic redeemer or a community of redemption."[21] From a positive angle, what promotes the full humanity of women is the exact opposite of this quote.

Ruether moves on to assert that the uniqueness of feminist theology is *not* the principle of full humanity in itself, but the fact that women *claim* the principle for themselves. This, however, does not appear to be unique at all, since all the liberation theologies make an identical claim for their own constituencies. That the claim is essential to liberation theology throughout the world will be abundantly illustrated in all the chapters in this book.

As we have seen in the course of this discussion, male theology appears to have been corrupted by sexism, patriarchy, and androcentrism. In response, Ruether is careful to emphasize that fem-

inists should not fall into the trap of reverse racism, affirming themselves in a way that diminishes the humanity of males. The author
avoids the trap with an inclusiveness that could serve as a model
for other liberation theologies. She notes that any principle of religion or society that diminishes one group as less than fully human
diminishes us all: "In rejecting androcentrism (males as norms of
humanity), women must criticize all other forms of chauvinism:
making white Westerners the norm of humanity, making Christians
the norm of humanity, making privileged classes the norm of humanity."[22]

Return to the Sources: Part I

In surveying a panoramic view of the sources or traditions,
Ruether emphasizes that her book is not *the* feminist theology, but
rather *a* feminist theology. Obviously, it is impossible for any synthesis to include all of human experience. Nevertheless, her own approach is based on an extraordinarily extensive historical
background in searching for what she calls "usable tradition" to discover usable foundations for feminism: 1) the Old and New
Testaments; 2) marginalized or "heretical" traditions; 3) the classical
theological traditions, Orthodox, Catholic, and Protestant; 4) Near
Eastern and Greek-Roman religions; and 5) critical worldviews of
liberalism, romanticism, and Marxism.

At the grave risk of oversimplification, I will sketch these sources
briefly, since they form the basic structure of the book. As regards
the Bible, Ruether predictably emphasizes the prophetic tradition,
but stresses that feminism appropriates prophetic thought in different ways than the prophets did, especially in its critique of prophetic patriarchy. She also rightly accents the kingdom preached by
Jesus in the New Testament, in which he profoundly criticized all
domination and power relationships in society. When, however,
"Christianity became a hierarchical and then an imperial religion,
no element in the Gospels was so totally deformed to conceal and
mystify its original meaning."[23] What resulted, according to
Ruether, was a new Christian imperialism, with the church acting
as God's agent to convert and conquer the world.

Feminist theology, therefore, exposes the mystifications of equality and social justice for the poor and oppressed, just as the other liberation theologies do. But it moves one step further than these theologies and applies the liberating principles of the prophets to women, who are the most oppressed. Thus, all "the liberating prophetic visions must be deepened and transformed to include what was not included: women." [24]

As regards the heretical or marginalized sects, Ruether stresses their egalitarian, countercultural approaches, which have been reconstructed by Elisabeth Fiorenza. These, however, were not preserved as the normative tradition in the New Testament:

> The ambiguity of Paul toward this vision, and the patriarchalization of Christianity that occurred in the Deutero-Pauline tradition, suppressed the early vision. The post-Pauline Church all the more vehemently asserted as norms the patriarchal relations of husband over wife, master over slave. [25]

In short, Ruether avers that both orthodox and heretical traditions are necessary in feminist theology, so that by corrections of each other's defects another alternative Christianity may come into being.

In regard to the dominant theological traditions, Orthodox, Catholic, and Protestant, the author is convinced that all of the categories of this classical theology are grievously distorted. This does not entail their complete rejection, but rather their transformation: "As feminist theology systematically corrects the androcentrism of each category of Christianity, it is to be hoped that the alternative possibilities of the Christian pattern of theology for a liberation theology for women will come into focus." [26]

To continue, pagan sources (Near Eastern and Greco-Roman religions) were justified because the Bible was influenced by opposition and conflict with them as well as by adopting some of their thought and their customs of worship. Ruether presents serious problems regarding Feminist Wicca or Goddess religion, but I do not wish to enter into that discussion. In general, then, the positive contribution of pagan sources is stressed: "By entering into the dialectic between the Canaanite and Biblical religions from both sides, allowing Canaanite religion to speak positively to Biblical religion, as well as vice versa, we might discover new insights into the foundation of Western religions and cultural consciousness."[27] In this exchange it is obvious that more data could be acquired regarding the origins of patriarchy.

Finally, Ruether introduces three movements that critique the culture—liberalism, romanticism, and Marxism—and also are opponents of Christian religion and institutions. Once again, these systems are all developed by males and male sexism, tending to ignore women or to incorporate them into the male system of thought. Feminist thought, however, has produced its own versions of the three systems, and these versions have produced their own strengths and weaknesses. Ruether even believes that feminism must not only seek an appropriation of one of these systems, but must advance further and search for a synthesis of all three of them.[28] As a finale in this section, the author explains that her preferred "analytic sign" for God, or the divine, is the term "God/ess" throughout the book. I confess I am not impressed by this choice; also, it does not seem to have appeared in the writings of other theologians, including feminists.

Feminism Transforming Theology: Part II

In this section, I will analyze some of the more significant issues from a cornucopia of theological riches. Perhaps the most significant and difficult theological crux, or problem, is to be found in the chapter on christology and soteriology, as encapsulated in this question: "Can a Male Savior Save Women?"

As a prelude, Ruether discusses briefly the "patriarchalization of Christology" which took place over the first five centuries and in which Christianity was transformed from a marginal sect into the official religion of the Roman empire. In a first period, a Spirit-filled, apocalyptic community arose that entered into conflicts with the developing institution, as prophets and martyrs were pitted against bishops. In a second period, around 70 C.E., the bishops put an end to the prophets speaking in the name of Christ; thus, the sayings and teachings of Jesus were collected in written form as the definitive texts, the "deposit of faith," which were to be passed down unaltered under the tutelage of the bishops.

The last and most decisive step in patriarchalization occurred with the church's union with the empire, resulting in a Christianity that ruled over the world and establishing the reign of Christ the king. Also, Christ is seen as the ruler of the existing social cosmos, while the emperor and church govern the political order, masters dominate their slaves, and men dominate their women.

In medieval scholasticism, the incarnation of God as a male was seen as an ontological necessity, and of course only a male could be the representative of Christ, that is, a priest. Bringing this up to the present, the 1976 Vatican declaration on women's ordination epitomizes this sexism with the statement that there must be a physical resemblance between the priest and Christ. Ruether is rather acerbic as she ends this section: "The possession of male genitalia becomes the essential prerequisite for representing Christ, who is the disclosure of the male God."[29]

Before broaching the elements of a feminist christology, Ruether considers two alternatives, the androgynous and the spirit christologies, which she eventually rejects. Again the question continues to arise: Must women abandon Jesus and search for a new way of redemption in female form?

At this point, the author does not go as far as a more radical wing of feminism, which has totally repudiated the idea of a male savior for women. Rather, her focus is as follows:

> Once the mythology about Jesus as Messiah or divine *Logos*, with its traditional masculine imagery, is stripped off, the Jesus of the synoptic Gospels can be recognized as a figure remarkably compatible with feminism. This is not to say, in an anachronistic sense, that "Jesus was a feminist," but rather that the criticism of religious and social hierarchy characteristic of the early portrait of Jesus is remarkably parallel to feminist criticism.[30]

This is clear in Jesus' subversion of religious status, since he taught repeatedly and consistently that the last shall be first and the first last, and that it was the outcasts of society who would hear and act upon his message. Here women, too, are shown to be the representatives of the lowly, since they are "the oppressed of the oppressed," and the last who will be first in the kingdom of God.[31]

As regards Jesus, his "ability to speak as liberator does not reside in his maleness but in the fact that he has renounced this system of domination and seeks to embody in his person the new humanity of service and mutual empowerment."[32]

Furthermore, Ruether underscores the fact that Christ is not to be confined once and for all in the historical Jesus, since those women and men who have been liberated in his community continue to identify with him in many very diverse ways. Thus, she concludes: "Christ, the liberated humanity, is not confined to a static perfection of one person two thousand years ago. Rather, redemptive humanity goes ahead of us, calling us to yet incomplete dimensions of human liberation."[33]

Mary as Liberator?

It is something of a surprise when Ruether moves directly toward ecclesiology in the next chapter, without developing a feminist theology of the Trinity. Wonderment increases as we discover her approach to understanding the church: a liberation mariology as a symbolic ecclesiology. However, a glimmer of light shines when we see that the key to liberation mariology is discovered through a careful analysis of the gospel of Luke. The salient text, not unexpectedly, turns out to be the Magnificat (1:46–55), where God intervenes to overthrow the power of the mighty and to exalt those of low status.

According to Ruether, Mary's grace and divine favor in bearing the messianic child is seen as a revolution and transformation of an unjust social order. Her actions, furthermore, are deeply significant in Luke's account; for example, she makes her own choices about her sexuality without consulting her future husband. Furthermore, the decision to have the child is between herself and God, and it is stressed that her motherhood is a free choice, emerging from her profound faith. Ruether summarizes:

> This is the key to the new redemptive community of Jesus, as distinct from the old kind of family relationships. In a text that is found in all three synoptic Gospels [Mk 3:34–35], the voluntary community based on mutual choice is seen as the true family of Jesus, as contrasted with the old, unbelieving family.[34]

In short, Luke's mariology reveals an authentic co-creation between God and humanity in the person of the woman Mary. For it is only through such free human responses that God is enabled to transform history on the side of the poor.

Furthermore: "[Mary] herself embodies and personifies the oppressed and subjugated people who are being liberated and exalted through God's redemptive power. She is the humiliated ones who have been lifted up, the hungry ones who have been filled with good things."[35]

With sharp clarity, Luke's language is explicitly economic and political, as well as profoundly partial to the cause of the poor. This is transparent in his many narratives and teachings on social iconoclasm, which relates to a large number of women; indeed, he emphasizes accounts of God's favor and grace on those kinds of people who are despised by the rich, those in power, and the traditionally religious. Ruether's theology here is particularly prophetic and fecund: "It is women especially who represent the Church by calling others out of bondage into freedom. The despised woman as poorest of the poor has symbolic priority in the Church. As such, she also represents the hosts of other oppressed groups in need of God's favor."[36]

Is Conversion from Sexism Possible?

Certainly the most interesting and original chapter in Ruether's book is the one containing a dialectic between "the consciousness of evil" and "the journeys of conversion."[37] She emphasizes that the recognition or consciousness of the fact that sexism is evil and sinful is important, because it leads to the demolition of the widespread and enduring myths of the female as evil. As a result, a true change of heart begins first within the woman herself and afterward demands a change from men in recognizing the full personhood of women.

The author is fully aware of the many difficulties and profound fears that this arouses in men:

Every aspect of male privilege loses its authority as natural and divine right and is reevaluated as sin and evil. This is deeply frightening to males. Consequently, they have been quick to slam

the door on the slightest beginning of such questioning and to
mount counter-revolutionary campaigns of resubjugation of
women whenever feminist movements have begun. But it is also
frightening to women. They have to question all the ways they
have traded a diminished humanity for dependent forms of security.[38]

In other words, the entire ideological framework justifying sexism for thousands of years is now exposed to analysis and critique.
Even the words and symbols that women have used to praise God
become bitter in their mouths as these are seen as tools of a vast ma-
levolent system that negates their very humanity. "Few women,"
asserts Ruether ominously, "have the courage to advance more than
a few steps on this journey of recognition of sexism as evil, so vast
and convoluted are the layers of enchantment, delusion, and seduc-
tion."[39] She then dedicates a number of pages to the present va-
rieties of sexism, including assault or battering, rape and gang rape,
the violence of female "fashions," menial work roles, dis-
proportionate labor in domestic duties and child raising, tokenism
with regard to prestigious jobs, and many other atrocities.

Ruether's approach to facilitating a conversion from the sin of
sexism begins by describing the very felicitous metaphor of "female
and male journeys." Another means of expressing this is to envision
it as a "feminist spirituality" for both women and men. Fully aware
of the enormity of the social sin of sexism and of the need for repentance of all of humanity, it is still possible to launch into the unknown:

> . . . in spite of the reality of systemic evil which we inherit, which
> has already biased us before we can choose, we have not yet lost
> our ability to choose good rather than evil, and hence our capacity
> for responsibility. We can unmask sexism as sin. We can dis-
> affiliate with it. We can begin to shape at least our personal iden-
> tity and then our relationships with others in a new way.[40]

The female journey, as Ruether sees it, has always entailed a network of female communication and of covert resistance. Without
this support, the solitary woman will be terrorized into submission:
"Only where there is a feminist movement that has been able to sur-

vive, to develop networks of communication, and to provide some alternative vision of life is feminist consciousness a real possibility."[41]

As the female journey proceeds, however, all the ways a woman has been taught to be pleasing or acceptable to males must be recognized as a tool of false consciousness:

> We have seen the pretty girl-child who is played with and praised for her cuteness; or the sexy lady who manipulates her physical attractiveness; or the good wife who wins praise by her diligent housekeeping and attentive service to male needs—all these prevent a woman from asking herself who she is as a human person.[42]

Another formidable obstacle to feminism in Christian women is the tendency to identify virtue with humility and self-abnegation, while sin is associated with anger and pride. This ideology succeeds in reinforcing submission and lack of self-esteem: "Women become 'Christlike' by having no self of their own."[43] Thus, their *metanoia* means that they literally discover their own selves, as persons who can create their own identities. In order to achieve this, Ruether warns, one must get in touch with one's own anger, which is understood as "liberating grace precisely as the power to break the chains of sexist socialization, to disaffiliate with sexist ideologies." Along with this is included the necessity of a sense of pride as self-esteem, without which there can be no identity or self.

At this point in the female journey, there is a parting of the ways between those who are willing to experience a deeper anger and alienation and those who draw back from it, inasmuch as their ties of service to men and children are too tightly bound. Ruether clearly states her own choice:

> Unless one is willing to take the journey into that deeper anger, even to risk going a bit mad, one will never understand the depths of the evils of sexism. The great importance of a feminist thinker like Mary Daly is precisely that she insists on taking herself further and further into that journey and insisting that others who wish to be honest follow her.[44]

Only after this phase, then, can a feminist move on to other levels of truth, where one does not lose touch with males, nor does one imagine that women alone are human or that all males are evil. As one gains experience of women's movements, it is readily apparent that women, too, are corrupted by egoism, power, and other vices. In spite of this, women must refuse the egotistic model based on male individualism, and affirm their "grounded self" which relates them to others and to mutual service.

The Male Conversion

Turning to the parallel male journey, the author believes that sexism is not merely a female problem, but is primarily a male problem that men have imposed on women. As one who has observed males in various strategies of response to women's liberation, Ruether has detected two basic stages of the male journey. The first step in the male response is trivialization and the ridicule of women. They cannot believe that women are oppressed; rather, they appear to be happy and well taken care of. They do not admit to a recognition of the stresses and dependency of women in the total system of sexism. Rather, Ruether comments, they "laugh off the silliness of 'women's lib' (a trivializing diminutive used only for female and homosexual liberation movements)."[45]

Co-optation comprises the second stage of the male response to sexism. They see that sexism is a real issue, and immediately jump to the insight that they too have suffered from sexism: "Whole dimensions of their being—their ability to cry, to feel, to relate, to be sensitive—have been repressed in order to shape them for male roles of domination."[46] Soon they become convinced that they are more knowledgeable about feminism than women themselves, and try to be helpful and very sympathetic to feminine oppression. They become angry, however, if their version of feminism is criticized as a male projection and certainly not true feminism. The author somewhat dourly comments: "The male ego is still the center of the universe, which 'feminism' is now seduced into enhancing in a new way. Such male feminists are sometimes worse enemies of women's emancipation than downright chauvinists."[47]

Actually, these stances are covert refusals of conversion from the evil of sexism. Ruether's major contribution is that real conversion will take place if men actually join women in their struggle for liberation. This often occurs through a relationship to a specific woman who is pursuing her own emancipation: "By entering into her struggles, seeing the world of sexism from her eyes, he begins to understand some dimensions of sexism. . . . He begins to feel that he too is recovering a more holistic self in the process."[48]

Finally, the last stage of conversion becomes deeper and begins to involve serious risks, especially from the negative attitudes and attacks of other men. The male experiences his deepest fear as being repudiated and ridiculed as "unmanly," in addition to the probability of economic losses and a general decline in status and prestige. A very important final step is to repudiate male group egotism and the passivity that it engenders as well as to disregard the loss of status or "masculinity." At this point we arrive at the end of the male journey to conversion from sexism:

> At this point, males are able to recognize, without trying to either co-opt or pander to women, that the struggle against sexism is basically a struggle to humanize the world, to humanize ourselves, to salvage the planet, to be in right relation to God/ess. At this point, men and women can really join hands in a common struggle.[49]

Liberating Community and Ministry

This will be the final chapter to be discussed, because of lack of space and because of the intrinsic importance of the topics, community and ministry. The question is how ministry and community can and indeed should function for liberation from patriarchy.

The church, seen as the avant-garde of liberated humanity, should be the support system for the re-creation of all our relationships, the matrix of the regeneration of humanity. It is precisely here, however, that feminists experience their greatest alienation from existing churches, which proclaim the exact opposite message by their language, institutional structures, and social commitments. "The more one becomes a feminist," Ruether states flatly, "the more difficult it becomes to go to church."[50] Women experience, moreover, a starvation rather than nourishment from the sacraments and the word of God. Thus, the question must be asked whether or not the churches will assist women and men who are actively seeking liberation from patriarchy. If so, what kind of ministry, worship, and mission exist or should exist that is compatible with liberation from patriarchy?

A feminist liberation church, the author insists, must be committed to freeing itself from the ideologies and roles of patriarchies and also freeing the social systems and structures which perpetuate such patterns of sexism. Ruether notes that some liberal churches with women pastors or women and men pastoral teams do share an understanding of the gospel as liberation from sexism. This entails inclusive language, of course, but also a real transformation of liturgy to reflect liberation from sexism, and the creation of shared ministry rather than the monopoly of the ordained. Inevitably, teaching and preaching a liberation gospel may drive some people from the church, but there are others who are diligently searching for just such a church and will be delighted to enter a liberation community.

Examples of such groups abound in the base communities throughout Latin America, which have usually been aided in various ways by clergy and bishops, but which are led by lay persons as preachers, catechists, and in a wide variety of other ministries.[51] Ruether has come to a very important decision that the only alternative is to create feminist base communities as the way of creating communities of liberation. The author presents a very precise and graphic description of these communities:

> A feminist base community is an autonomous, self-gathered community that takes responsibility for reflecting on, celebrating, and acting on the understanding of redemption as liberation from patriarchy. Such a community might take on as many or as few of the functions of the church as they choose. They might range from consciousness-raising groups that primarily share experiences, to groups who engage in study and analysis as well, to groups that also worship together. From a study, teaching, and worshipping group, such a community might also choose to share means of livelihood with one another. They might also choose to make their shared spiritual and social life together the base of political action.[52]

Ruether believes that women in such communities would be able to take part in other institutional activities, but they would continue to draw their vision from the more radical approach of the base community. It is to be hoped, moreover, that the liturgies, theologies, and activities of these communities could function as a leaven for the entire institutional church. The author is hopeful that the latter relationship will take on the features of a "creative dialectic" instead of a possible "schismatic impasse," since it is essential that both renewal community and historical institution exist in order that they may be truly regenerated by the Spirit at work in history.

The feminist base communities, Ruether emphasizes, must dismantle clericalism, since this is based on and presupposes patriarchy: "The basic assumption of clericalism is that the people have no direct access to the divine. The clergy monopolize the instrument of mediation between God and the laity."[53] And, although male laity are permitted subordinate functions within the clerical system, women are usually excluded from lay leadership roles and serve as prototypes of the passive recipients of clerical power.

To dismantle clericalism, there must be a stress on the gospel teaching of ministry as service and not as power and domination. "Ministry," Ruether insists, "transforms leadership from power over others to empowerment of others," so that ministry becomes mutual liberation and empowerment of each other.

Ministry, moreover, recognizes that certain people have specific gifts, and tries to draw out and encourage the gifts of each person for the sake of the community: ". . . each gift must cross-fertilize with the others to create a community that truly reflects and acts on the Gospel of liberation together."[54] Along with this, the sacraments must be reclaimed from clericalism and seen as actions that the people are empowered to administer together. They must also be reflected on and interpreted from the common life of the entire community. Once the community has overcome clerical domination, it can rediscover the need for celebrative garments, artistic spaces, and creeds, ritual gestures, chants and songs that distinguish liturgy from ordinary life.

Finally, a feminist community has both internal and external missions, which must be carefully balanced so that one or the other does not dominate. There must be concrete commitments of healing and nurturing to each other both in liturgical expression and in the circumstances of ordinary life. Ruether asserts that the external mission means that "a world without militarism, a world with systems of production and consumption in harmony with nature, is as much a part of the hopes of feminism as are changed relationships between men and women."[55] In short, the base communities are joined with the rest of the church, but what they propose to contribute to it is the overcoming of patriarchy and sexism as well as the creation of true Christian communities of love and liberation.

ELIZABETH JOHNSON

I have discussed key concepts in a feminist approach to *scripture* in a key work of Elisabeth Schüssler Fiorenza. This was followed by a consideration of Rosemary Radford Ruether's *historical retrieval* of feminist elements in a number of traditions, both Christian and non-Christian, in one of her most significant books. It seems appropriate, then, to round out these approaches with a contemporary work of Elizabeth A. Johnson, *She Who Is*,[56] which analyzes the *systematic relationships* between classical theology and modern Christian feminism.

Preliminary Remarks

Professor Johnson stresses from the outset that there is an enormous diversity in feminist theologies, both in the United States and in the other continents, because of the very diverse contexts and experiences of the authors. She is not disturbed by this situation, but rather prizes it, stating that "sensitivity to difference is an intellectual virtue being positively celebrated by feminist thought in resistance to centuries of univocal definition of 'woman's nature.'"[57] Thus, she values all of these contributions, while at the same time stating unambiguously that her "own stance is within the liberation stream of Catholic Christian feminist theology."[58]

Since feminists have been accused at times of speaking only to middle-class white women, it is illuminating to see that Johnson has traveled widely and has been deeply influenced by the plight of poor women of color, especially in her experience of lecturing in South Africa:

For me the goal of feminist religious discourse pivots in its fullness around the flourishing of poor women of color in violent situations. . . . Only when the poorest, black, raped, and brutalized
women in a South African township—the epitome of victims of
sexism, racism, and classism, and at the same time startling examples of women's resiliency, courage, love and dignity—when
such women with their dependent children and their sisters
around the world may live peacefully in human dignity, only
then will feminist theology arrive at its goal.[59]

At this point, the reader may be helped by a brief outline of *She
Who Is*, which is divided into four major parts: 1) the context and
background for speech about God; 2) a selection of resources from
women's experience, scripture, and classical theology for liberating
speech about God; 3) a theology of the trinitarian God from below,
testing the capacity of female images to reveal the action of God in
the world; and 4) female symbols revealing God and searching the
emancipatory potential in speech about God's Trinity, living being,
and relationship to the suffering world.[60]

The author also provides a clear and succinct vision of her feminist theology:

By Christian feminist theology I mean a reflection on God and all
things in the light of God that stands consciously in the company
of all the world's women, explicitly prizing their genuine humanity while uncovering and criticizing its persistent violation in sexism, itself an omnipresent paradigm of unjust relationships. In
terms of Christian doctrine, this perspective claims the fullness of
the religious heritage for women precisely as human, in their own
right and independent from personal identification with men.[61]

Concerning the relationship of feminism and classical theology,
the feminist approach "finds this classical tradition profoundly ambiguous in what it has meant for female well-being." At the same
time, Johnson does propose to listen to classical theology, searching
for wisdom that could be helpful.[62]

Another important aspect of religious feminism is that it not only
articulates speech about God, but it is also a praxis with God that
has great significance for human beings. "What is at stake," says the
author, "is simultaneously the freeing of both women and men

from debilitating reality models and social roles, the birthing of new forms of saving relationship to all of creation, and indeed the very viability of the Christian tradition for present and coming generations."[63] Is that tradition able to take account of, illuminate, and integrate the experience of women today? The rest of the book is dedicated to finding an answer to this "absolutely critical theological question."

Background and Definitions

The second chapter of this book is in my opinion the most important, because it clearly delineates the author's method, whether this is called a "lens of women's flourishing," or a hermeneutic circle, or a preferential option for women. Earlier, we mentioned the great variety of approaches to feminism; a certain unity, however, could be established among feminists (and indeed among all liberation theologies) if there were some form of congruence and cooperation in the area of method.

Another characteristic of all liberation theologies is the experience of domination or oppression. Theology done from such a perspective "is both humanly oppressive and religiously idolatrous,"[64] inasmuch as its concepts and images about God are drawn from male experience and from male domination. Particular criticism is aimed at classical theism and its emphasis on God's absolute transcendence, indifference to human history and human suffering, and the all-pervasiveness of God's dominating power. Johnson then directs some piercing challenges to this classical theism:

> Is this idea of God not the reflection of patriarchal imagination, which prizes nothing more than unopposed power-over and unquestioned loyalty? Is not the transcendent, omnipotent, impassible symbol of God the quintessential embodiment of the solitary ruling male ego, above the fray, perfectly happy in himself, filled with power in the face of the obstreperousness of others? Is this not "man" according to the patriarchal ideal?[65]

Lest we give a sigh of relief that this is merely a relic of bygone ages, the author directs an identical barrage against all of contemporary theology. She insists that there "is not one religious tradition or theological school existing in the world today, nor one atheistic critique of religious tradition, nor one sociopolitical arrangement nor liberating critique of such structures, nor culture of East or West that does justice to the full humanity of women."[66] Thus, we are faced with an enormous juggernaut of "social sin," that is, sexism as it is especially manifested in patriarchy and androcentrism.

At this point, it seems appropriate to define or describe this troika of domination and oppression. Margaret Farley's description of sexism is succinct, calling it the "belief that persons are superior or inferior to one another on the basis of their sex. It includes . . . attitudes, value systems, and social patterns which express or support this belief."[67] Patriarchy (literally, father-rule) is "a form of social organization in which power is always in the hand of the dominant man or men, with others ranked below in a graded series of subordinations reaching down to the least powerful who form a large base." It should be noted that one of the most powerful forms of patriarchy is *religious*, for it claims that its structure is divinely established and therefore beyond all criticism. Finally, androcentrism (literally, male-centeredness) is the "name commonly given to the personal pattern of thinking and acting that takes the characteristics of ruling men to be normative for all humanity."[68]

Although Johnson is usually an admirer of Aquinas, she cites his colossal lapse with regard to female biology as a classic example of androcentrism:

> . . . the active power in the seed of the male tends to produce something like itself, perfect in masculinity; but the procreation of a female is the result either of the debility of the active power, of some unsuitability of the material, or of some change effected by external influences, like the south wind, for example, which is damp, as we are told by Aristotle.[69]

Another bizarre conclusion of Aquinas is that, since the soul informs the body, a woman's soul is likewise deficient, poor in reasoning, and weak in choosing what is good.

Fatal Consequences of Sexism

Throughout her book Johnson takes pains to point out both the social and psychological consequences of sexism. In society, women's political, economic, legal, and educational rights have been consistently violated. Her comments on the fate of women appear to be the fruits of righteous anger:

> . . . while forming more than one half of the world's population women work two-thirds of the world's working hours, own one-tenth of the world's wealth and one-hundredth of the world's land, and form two-thirds of the world's illiterate people. Over three-fourths of starving people are women with their dependent children. To make a dark picture even bleaker, woman are bodily and sexually exploited, physically abused, raped, battered and murdered. . . . Sexism is rampant on a global scale.[70]

This ghastly tableau is merely a fleeting glimpse of the mental and physical carnage that trails women constantly in every corner of the world. It is a credit to the author that she continues to name the horror and to portray the sufferings of women throughout her book.

I have already noted that the churches have often been guilty of patriarchism, staunchly reinforced and legitimated by a patriarchal God. Since Johnson is a Roman Catholic, she manifests a particular interest in that community, where, she asserts, women do not participate fully in the sacraments, in decision making, in law and symbol making, or in leadership roles of any sort, including governance and the liturgy. With characteristic zest, she encapsulates the plight of women as "called to honor a male savior sent by a male God whose legitimate representatives can only be male, all of which places their persons precisely as female in a peripheral role."[71] All of this, of course, is continually reinforced by male-centered language and male-centered symbols, which strive mightily to crush women's self-esteem and self-identity while at the same time inculcating passivity as a splendid feminine virtue.

Finally, these social and psychological factors in sexism are related to all forms of racism, classism, militarism, imperialism, and destruction of the environment, which have been exposed and condemned by other liberation theologians. "The fundamental sin," this gentle prophet insists, "is exploitation, whether it be expressed in the domination of male over female, white over black, rich over poor, strong over weak, armed military over unarmed civilians, human beings over nature." And this spectrum of the colors of domination are closely linked, since they all have the same foundation: ". . . a structure where an elite insists on its superiority and claims the right to exercise dominative power over all others considered subordinate, for its own benefit."[72] Several studies, moreover, have advanced the view that sexism is the original form of domination, and that the suppression of the female is the paradigm for other forms of male power over others. [73]

The Centrality of Method

We have already seen in a number of liberation authors that *experience* is essential for its theological method. Johnson, too, describes the same reality in the different categories of *conversion*, which she views as a "contrast between the suffering of sexism and the *humanum* of women, and confirmation of women's creative agency and power, both mediated through the same Christian tradition."[74] This conversion leads to three tasks that are essential to feminist theology: first, to analyze past oppressions; second, to search for wisdom and history that have been suppressed; and third, to propose new interpretations of the tradition in dialogue with women's experience.[75] Once again, this has all the characteristics of a hermeneutic circle which all liberation theologians employ. Johnson also refers to these as a task of deconstruction followed by a task of reconstruction.

The first step in the circle is an ideology-critique, which "unmasks the hidden dynamic of domination in the Christian tradition's language, custom, memory, history, sacred text, ethics, symbolism, theology, and ritual," certainly a comprehensive panorama for critique. This sexist bias, she continues with a trenchant metaphor, is "like a buried continent whose subaquaceous pull has shaped all currents of the theological enterprise, so that Christian theory and praxis have been massively distorted."[76]

In spite of this quite devastating critique, Johnson moves positively to discover dormant aspects of theology and neglected or suppressed fragments of history. She expresses a poignant hope in this way:

> Although women's words have been censored or eliminated from much of Christian heritage, in the midst of the pain of dehumanization women have nevertheless always been there, in fidelity and struggle, in loving and caring, in outlawed movements, in prophecy and vision. Tracking and retrieving fragments of this lost wisdom and history, all in some way touchstones of what may yet be possible, enable them to be set free as resources for transforming thought and action.[77]

With regard to the level of reconstruction, the third task, it strives to create new articulations of methods and symbols that proclaim the full equality of women, and also gladly employs a new feminist philosophy, literature, and the human sciences as full partners in all this building. Again, a prophetic summary:

> This is a creative moment, typical of all great advances in theology. Life and faith are thought in new ways that promote the equality of women and all the oppressed in a genuine mutuality with those who formerly dominated. A time to tear down, a time to build up; a time to throw stones away, and a time to gather them together—the season of feminist theology involves all of these at once.[78]

We have already seen the text of Rosemary Ruether concerning the criterion of feminist theology: the promotion of the full humanity of women,[79] or, as Johnson expresses it: "the emancipation of women toward human flourishing." Johnson emphasizes that in "choosing the lens of women's flourishing to focus its thinking, feminist theology takes the total personhood of women with utter seriousness, advocating women's well-being personally and corporately in all of these constitutive dimensions."[80]

The passionate *goal* of feminist theology is transformation into a "new community" which reminds one of Martin Luther King, Jr.'s lifetime struggle to achieve a "beloved community" in the United States:

Feminist liberation theology hopes so to change unjust structures and distorted symbol systems that a new community in church and society becomes possible, a liberating community of all women and men characterized by mutuality with each other and harmony with the earth.[81]

In this new community, as Johnson envisions it, only two approaches are ruled out. These include *reverse sexism,* which would entail women's domination to the detriment of men, and *sameness,* which would crush originality, variety, and uniqueness. As a result, feminist theology aims at changing the system, and not making women equal partners in an oppressive system. As Rosemary Ruether expresses it, women are not merely demanding a bigger piece of the pie, but are searching for a new way of baking, a recipe for a new and better pie.[82] Thus, Johnson avers that the "genius of feminist theology has been to see that for the traditional eschatological dream to become historical reality at all, the liberation of women as genuine human persons in communities of mutuality is essential."[83]

This concludes the discussion of method, criteria, and goals and brings us to a consideration of what is the most significant and perhaps most intimidating paragraph in the entire book. Feminist theology's journey of deconstruction and reconstruction is bringing about a colossal paradigm shift in both church and society, a momentous transformation of theology and of religious communities and churches. Johnson's summary is eloquent:

Journeying out of an androcentric world into more inclusive conceptualization shifts the center of the theological universe, much as Copernicus's discovery of the earth's rotation around the sun changed forever the ancient geocentric view. In the process of this major recentering virtually every inherited given comes under scrutiny and is subject to critique, revision, and renewal in the interest of greater liberation in faith and life.[84]

One of the most important "inherited givens" is our understanding of God, to which we now turn.

How Speak About God?

Johnson's major effort throughout the book is to critique language or speech concerning God. It is important to note that she is not opposed to male images or metaphors in themselves, but rather the fact that these terms are used *exclusively*, *literally*, and *patriarchally*.

Prevailing usage in the Christian church is to name God exclusively with male designations, while female terms are forgotten, rejected, or made to appear deviant. A good example is Christian prayer to the Father and the Son and the Holy Spirit, with even the latter addressed in male pronouns.

Other male terms for God are used literally, so that maleness comes to be seen and imagined as an essential characteristic of divine being. As an example of this in learned theological circles, one can hear the statement that God is not male, *He* is Spirit. It grates on people's ears, though, to hear God addressed as "mother" or "she." Thus Johnson asks, "If it is not meant that God is male when masculine imagery is used, why the objection when female images are used?"[85]

The paradigm for the symbol of God is the ruler or dominant man in a patriarchal system; language is used patriarchally. Even if the symbol is benevolent, it is most often depicted as an old man with a white beard: "Imagery of the Trinitarian God most often consists of an older white-bearded man, a younger brown-bearded man, both Caucasian, and a dove."

Dogmatic development in Christology had also led to a dramatic increase in the exclusive and literal masculinization of God:

> The close union between human and divine natures—a hypostatic union—coupled with confession of Jesus the Christ's personal identity as "God from God" has tended to allow the sex of the human being Jesus to be transferred to God's own being. . . .But in spite of Chalcedon's strictures against mixing or confusing the two natures in Christ, the practical effect of this definition has been to promote the viability of male metaphors and the unsuitability of female ones in speech about God. As visible image of the invisible God, the human man Jesus is used to tie the knot between maleness and divinity very tightly.[86]

The Perils of Idolatry

Next, Johnson turns to an analysis of the sociological, psychological, and theological effects of what she terms idolatry. Here I will concentrate on the theological effects of idolatry: "Whenever one image or concept of God expands to the horizon thus shutting out others, and whenever this exclusive symbol becomes literalized so that the distance between it and divine reality is collapsed, there an idol comes into being. . . . Divine mystery is cramped into a fixed, petrified image."[87]

In all of this, the partner of idolatry is oppression. Literal patriarchal speech, then, serves to legitimate social structures of domination, an androcentric world which is hostile to the equal human dignity of women. As a consequence, feminist theology opposes it fiercely:

> Criticism of unjust structures and exclusive world views necessarily entails criticism of the idea of the divine interwoven with them; conversely, questioning dominant religious imagery has potent consequences for reordering the body politic, which is either supported or challenged by prevailing speech about God. Structural change and linguistic change go hand-in-hand. [88]

The burning question for feminist theology, therefore, is this: What new symbols of God should be created that will contribute spiritually and politically to the flourishing of women, in dialogue with other urgent issues?

God, Women, and Equivalence

In response to this question, Johnson selects three basic linguistic options, concerned with God, women, and equivalence, the last referring to equivalent images of God as both male and female. She notes that the dilemma of the word "God" is formidable, since its "effective history has been brutal as well as blessed,"[89] and she even suggests that perhaps we should dispense with the word completely. Finally, however, she decides to take the risk:

> . . . the wager I am making is that at this point in time pouring the new wine of women's hope of flourishing into the old word God may enable it to serve in new ways. "God" in a new semantic

field may restore the word to a sense more in line with its Greek etymology, which, according to ancient interpreters, meant to take care of and cherish all things, burning all malice like a consuming fire.[90]

The strategy that must be followed is to introduce other images that will overcome the exclusive dominance of the male symbols and thus create a more liberating understanding of the mystery of God. Johnson believes that the role of the imagination can hardly be exaggerated: "Far from being peripheral to human knowing, imaginative constructs mediate the world to us."[91]

A corollary of this strategy discusses recent efforts by theologians such as Hans Küng, Yves Congar, Leonardo Boff, and Donald Gelpi[92] to apply female symbols to God. A number of different approaches have surfaced, which Johnson reduces to three main tendencies: 1) granting "feminine" qualities to what remains a male God; 2) uncovering a "feminine" dimension in God, often located in the Holy Spirit; and 3) seeking ways in which both female and male humanity may become a symbol of God in equivalent ways.[93] Without becoming involved in all of the discussions and rebuttals, I merely note the author's conclusion: "Searching the implications of each can show why the first two options lead into a blind alley and why only equivalent imaging of God male and female can in the end do greater justice to the dignity of women and the truth of the holy mystery."[94] The arguments Johnson presents with regard to the first two approaches are closely reasoned and appear to me to be a successful destruction of those theological hypotheses.

The final text of Johnson on the question of equivalence may serve as a fitting conclusion to this issue:

> The mystery of God transcends all images but can be spoken about equally well and poorly in concepts taken from male or female reality. The approach advocated here proceeds with the insight that only if God is so named, only if the full reality of women as well as men enters into the symbolization of God along with symbols from the natural world, can the idolatrous fixation on one image be broken and the truth of the mystery of God, in tandem with the liberation of all human beings and the whole earth, emerge for our time. [95]

JACQUELYN GRANT

Here I turn to a black woman's critique of the first three white theologians in this chapter, Jacquelyn Grant. Generally referred to as a womanist theologian, she is the author of *White Women's Christ and Black Women's Jesus.*[96] Its subtitle expresses more exactly what I will be emphasizing: *Feminist Christology and Womanist Response.* Ms. Grant is an ordained elder in the African Methodist Episcopal Church, and at present is teaching systematic theology at the Interdenominational Theological Center, where she is also founder and director of Black Women in Church and Society.

Grant embarks on her critique of white feminism in her introduction, where she states her thesis: "White feminism does not emerge out of the particularity of the majority of women's experience,"[97] adding in a footnote that it "is significant to note that Black and other ethnic women of color comprise a vast majority of the female population of the world."[98] The final chapter of her book, "The Challenge of the Darker Sister,"[99] presents a much more systematic view of her challenge to white feminism. Beginning with the "limitations of feminist theology," Grant moves toward the jugular, holding that "Feminist theology is inadequate for two reasons: it is *White* and *racist.*"[100]

This whiteness and racism, Grant insists, influence the *nature of the sources* that white women theologians use in producing their theological ideas. As we have seen in the authors in this chapter, a principal source is women's experience. However,

> what is often unmentioned is that feminist theologians' sources for women's experience refer almost exclusively to White women's experience. White women's experience and Black women's experience are not the same. . . . But in this case the difference is so radical that it may be said that White women and Black women are in completely different realms.[101]

Slavery and segregation are said to be responsible for creating the division among these women. Although I do not wish to narrate this history, a few selections will set the tone. During slavery, Grant continues, black women were treated like male slaves but "as a lower species of animals. . . . Brutality was administered not only by masters and foremen but also by mistresses, reflecting the fact that White women were just as much participants in this system of slavery as were White men."[102]

Concerning black women's experience after slavery, Grant points out that, although slavery was abolished, the characteristics of slavery endured. She emphasizes three dimensions of this situation:

> 1) Physical brutality towards Blacks was continued, and even extended to violence outside of the work context. 2) The immediate relationship between White women and Black women did not change; White women were still oppressors and Black women were still the oppressed. 3) As a part of this continuing relationship, Black women were still treated as property. [103]

In short, there is a gulf between the experiences of white and black women.

As regards the charge of racism, Grant admits that to be White does not make one a racist, although it is difficult to avoid being one. She defines racism as "the tendency of a society to degrade and do violence to people on the basis of race, and by whatever mediations may exist for this purpose,"[104] and as "the domination of a people which is justified by the dominant group on the basis of racial distinctions. It is not only individual acts but a collective, institutionalized activity."[105] On the basis of these definitions, even if some feminists were not racist, the feminist movement is thus structured and takes on a racist character. Grant then justifies the "challenge":

> . . . White women have defined the movement and presumed to do so not only for themselves but also for non-White women. They have misnamed themselves by calling themselves feminists when in fact they are White feminists. . . . To misname themselves as "feminists" who appeal to "women's experience" is to do what oppressors always do; it is to define the rules and then solicit others to play the game. It is to presume a commonality with oppressed women that oppressed women themselves do not share.[106]

An article by Brenda Eichelberger continues this line by proposing five categories of reasons that cause black women to reject white feminism. This appears to be an even more trenchant series of challenges than Grant proposed.

1) Class differences mean that while Black women are dealing with "survival" issues, White women are dealing with "fulfillment" issues.

2) Negative imagery of Black women derived from physical and cultural stereotypes has resulted in the debased treatment of Black women.

3) The naiveté, or basic lack of knowledge, of Black women about the women's movement results in their inability to see the relationship between feminist issues and the Black struggle.

4) Black Women perceive White feminists to be racists who are interested in them only to accomplish the White women's agenda.

5) There is a concern that an alliance of Black women with White women in a feminist agenda may be "detrimental to black men" and therefore divisive of the Black community.[107]

Still another hostility, Grant continues, leads many to understand white feminism as a threat to the black family. A sociologist, Iva Carruthers, also refers to feminism as "one of the most serious assaults on African Familyhood," a "White-family affair," and totally irrelevant "to the real needs of Black women."[108]

Before turning to a positive view of black women's consciousness, Grant concludes her challenges in summary and blunt form:

Put succinctly, women of the dominant culture are perceived as the enemy. Like their social, sexual and political White male partners, they have as their primary goal the suppression, if not oppression, of the Black race and the advancement of the dominant culture. Because of this perception, many believe that Black feminism is a contradiction in terms.[109]

She then turns her attention to the beginnings of a womanist theology that will begin with the experiences of black women. Grant uses the ideas of Alice Walker in describing "womanism" as "our being responsible, in charge, outrageous, courageous and audacious enough to demand the right to think theologically and to do it independently of both White and Black men and White women."[110]

Grant also emphasizes that womanist theology must be done out of their tri-dimensional experience of *racism, sexism, and classism.* "To ignore any aspect of this experience," she insists, "is to deny the holistic and integrated reality of Black womanhood."[111] She quotes Bell Hooks:

> Racism abounds in the writings of white feminists, reinforcing white supremacy and negating the possibility that women will bond politically across ethnic and racial boundaries. Past feminist refusal to draw attention to and attack racial hierarchy suppressed the link between race and class. Yet class structure in American society has been shaped by the racial politics of white supremacy.[112]

Because of oppression determined by race, then, black women make up a large percentage of poor, working classes. Therefore, classism along with racism and sexism must be addressed in order to achieve total liberation, and "the daily struggles of poor Black women must serve as the gauge for the verification of the claims of womanist theology."[113]

Reflections

In my reflections on womanist theology I am continually haunted and disturbed by Professor Grant's allusion to the "darker sister." This figure is not a fantasy or daydream, since I have met and spoken with the "darker sister" on five continents and admired their strength and courage despite relentless suffering.

Perhaps Brenda Eichelberger exaggerates when she states that Black women are dealing with "survival" issues, while White feminists are dealing with "fulfillment" issues. Yet it appears if we look at the world panorama that there is a large element of truth in this observation. In Africa, Asia, Latin America, or South Central Los Angeles or the south Bronx in New York City, hundreds of millions of dark sisters struggle for bare existence in living conditions that can only be described as inhuman and barbarous.

Because of its immense significance, I repeat what I said earlier in this chapter. The oppression of poor women of the world is *fourfold.* First, the sister is discriminated against because of her *sex,* ranging from insults to the killing of girl babies and mature women. Next, she is demeaned because of her *race*, since the vast majority of sisters are women of color and therefore viewed by the pure white race as mere objects or animals, open to all forms of maltreatment and even assault. Then, she suffers because of her *class*, because she was born into dreadful poverty, which will accompany her and her children during a life of struggle to live and often to die before their time. Finally, there is discrimination against *religion*, in the Christian churches, which may be overt as in the Roman Catholic church or covert as often in churches which ordain women as ministers or priests. Perhaps a fifth discrimination should be added, *nationality* or *ethnic origin*, as displayed graphically by the murders and mass rapes of Muslim women in Bosnia.

At any rate, it is my dream that the enormous glacier of the women's movement will continue as it moves irreversibly across the face of the world to envelop and care for the "least of our sisters." As women in the first world continue to grow in political, economic, and cultural power, the dream envisions them as the ones who will reach out and share their hard-earned power in helping to humanize the dark sisters of the world. Till now, the males of the world have not achieved this utopian vision, have not seriously attempted to achieve it, and indeed appear to be in the majority of those who have managed to erase these millions of ravaged faces from their consciousness.

I have already emphasized throughout this chapter that the writings of Elisabeth Schüssler Fiorenza, Rosemary Radford Ruether, and Elizabeth A. Johnson, as illustrated in their books cited in this chapter, represent the highest scholarship in their fields and are the acknowledged leaders of feminist liberation theology. Within this theology, Elisabeth Fiorenza has been the leader in feminist biblical studies, while Rosemary Ruether has led the way in historical studies on a very broad scale. Elizabeth Johnson was also on the cutting edge of systematic feminist studies, renowned both for her creativity and her brilliant writing (a rare achievement, in my experience). Their ideas have reached women all over the world, weaving a gigantic web of connections that widens as each day passes. Also, these women in their writings have made many references on behalf of women in the third world, have attended international conferences and visited the highways and byways of the people in their beleaguered countries. I encourage readers to enter their own dialogue with the thought of these talented women, and perhaps to experience a real *metanoia,* or conversion, that Jesus called for. In my own dialogue, I have been greatly enriched by many new insights, and have delighted in the originality, creativity, and boldness *(parhessia*—again as in the preaching of Jesus) in their abundant ideas and projects, all radiant with a passionate hunger and thirst after justice, all enhancing and advancing the ultimate goal of the Kingdom of God.

QUESTIONS FOR REFLECTION AND DISCUSSION

1. Are the feminists who choose to remain in the churches and effect profound changes there more radical than those who leave their churches or break completely with Christianity? Explain your position and your own option.

2. Assess Elisabeth Schüssler Fiorenza's dialogue with Mary Daly. Is Fiorenza's reluctance to relinquish the biblical heritage appropriate for feminists? What is your opinion on the position of Mary Daly?

3. Can Jesus be used as a role model for feminists as Rosemary Ruether suggests? What are her proofs for that assertion? Are there areas in which Jesus' message is consistent with the aims of feminist theology?

4. Can the experience of Mary legitimately be used as a paradigm for feminist liberation theology as Ruether suggests? Are there other ways of interpreting the person of Mary?

5. Describe the phases in both the female and male journeys to conversion from sexism. Can you conceive of people going through these phases? Perhaps you and others you know?

6. What do you think about the future of the base communities described by Ruether? Can you imagine obstacles in their development? Do you know people who have had experience with them? Would you consider joining them?

7. Briefly describe the theological method of Elizabeth Johnson. What do you think of her conception of a "new community"? Can you at least imagine that these communities can come into being and flourish? Or that they are too utopian and impossible to create?

8. Describe some of the issues and problems with regard to the search for female symbols to apply to God. What will happen to the male symbols? Will men accept the new female symbols? Will women accept them? What are your views?

9. Jacquelyn Grant in her final chapter begins with the "limitations" of feminist theology and then declares flatly: "Feminist theology is inadequate for two reasons: it is White and racist." What do you think of her proofs for the latter charge? Can you think of strategies that will help bring together feminist and womanist theologians?

SUGGESTED READINGS

Cady, Susan, et al. *Sophia: The Future of Feminist Spirituality*. San Francisco: Harper & Row, 1986.

Christ, Carol, and Judith Plaskow, eds. *Womanspirit Rising: A Feminist Reader in Religion*. San Francisco: Harper & Row, 1979.

Daly, Mary. *Beyond God the Father: Toward a Philosophy of Women's Liberation*. Boston: Beacon, 1972.

Fiorenza, Elisabeth Schüssler. *Discipleship of Equals: A Critical Feminist Ekklesiology of Liberation Theology*. New York: Crossroad, 1993.

Harrison, Beverly Wildung. *Making the Connections: Essays in Feminist Social Ethics*. Boston: Beacon, 1985.

Hooks, Bell. *Ain't I a Woman?: Black Women and Feminism*. Boston: South End Press, 1981.

Lerner, Gerda. *The Creation of Patriarchy*. New York: Oxford University Press, 1986.

Ochs, Carol. *Behind the Sex of God: Toward a New Consciousness Transcending Matriarchy and Patriarchy*. Boston: Beacon, 1977.

Osiek, Carolyn. *Beyond Anger: On Being a Feminist in the Church*. New York: Paulist, 1986.

Ruether, Rosemary Radford. *Contemporary Roman Catholicism: Crises and Challenges.* Kansas City: Sheed & Ward, 1987.

Schneiders, Sandra. *Beyond Patching: Faith and Feminism in the Catholic Church.* New York: Paulist, 1991.

Suchocki, Marjorie. *God-Christ-Church: A Practical Guide to Process Theology.* New York: Crossroad, 1982.

Welch, Sharon. *Communities of Resistance and Solidarity: A Feminist Theology of Liberation.* Maryknoll, NY: Orbis Books, 1985.

CHAPTER THREE

AMERICAN DREAM— OR NIGHTMARE?

Black Theology of Liberation

Oh Freedom! O Freedom!
O Freedom over me!
And befo' I'd be a slave,
I'd be buried in my grave,
an' go home to my Lord an' be free.
Afro-American Spiritual
Black Power 38

What is logical to the oppressor isn't logical to the oppressed, and what is reason to the oppressor isn't reason to the oppressed. The black people in this country are beginning to realize that what sounds reasonable to those who exploit us doesn't sound reasonable to us. There just has to be a new system of reason and logic devised by us who are on the bottom, if we want some results in this struggle that is called the "Negro Revolution."

Malcolm X
The Speeches of Malcolm X at Harvard 133

If Rosa Parks had not sat down, Martin King would not have stood up.

Delores S. Williams
Yearning to Breathe Free 65

OVER THE PAST QUARTER OF A CENTURY, a number of North American theologians have regularly bemoaned the lack of a North American liberation theology, which would not be the Latin American variety discussed in Chapter One, but one adapted and inculturated to the United States and Canada. As we approach the third millennium of Christianity, it may *appear* that such a theology has not yet been produced. One of the major arguments of this book, however, is to demonstrate that *such a theology (or theologies) is very much alive and positively blossoming* in the churches of North America.

The reason an indigenous theology is seen to be lacking is because *white, male, affluent* theologians have not produced such a theology or at least have not constructed one that has reached a broad audience. *Women*, the *poor*, and *men and women of color* have, in intimate unity with their people, *created the liberation theologies* of North America; it is, perhaps, impossible that white, affluent, males could produce such a theology.

One proof of these assertions has already been given in the previous chapter, with regard to the "copernican revolution" of women liberation theologians in the United States. Their work has not only profoundly influenced the United States, but has touched the hearts and minds of women and men throughout the globe. The major leaders of this movement, moreover, are Roman Catholic laywomen and members of religious orders, and they have been developing their liberation theology in the United States and beyond for over three decades.

The Rise of Black Theology

Another—and just as important—liberation theology in the United States has been the eruption of black liberation theology, which is the subject of this chapter. Like the women theologians, the work of black theologians has profoundly influenced women and men of color in North America and throughout the world, especially in South Africa. I would stress that the *founder and major leader* of this liberation theology was the Rev. Martin Luther King, Jr., and that the beginning of the contemporary black liberation theology can be precisely traced to December 1, 1955, when Rosa Parks, tired from a day's work as a seamstress, sat down in a bus seat reserved for whites in Montgomery, Alabama. When she refused to give up her seat, she was arrested, a bus boycott was begun, and the "civil rights movement" began. I would prefer to call this the "liberation movement"; King's demonstrations, imprisonments, speeches, and sermons were the quintessential model of liberation praxis, practice refined by theory and theory animated by the experience of practice, a strategy that King used consistently for the remaining thirteen years of his life. The similarities between King and the Latin Americans' praxis is obvious from the remarks of Gustavo Gutiérrez and Juan Luis Segundo in Chapter One.

JAMES H. CONE

Much of this chapter will be devoted to King's life and thought; at this point I will move to another person who at the present time is the most influential and commanding figure in black theology, James H. Cone, Charles Briggs Distinguished Professor of Systematic Theology at Union Theological Seminary in New York City.

Background and Influences

In the 1940s and 1950s, Cone grew up in the village of Bearden, Arkansas, an experience that deeply affected him: "Two things happened to me in Bearden that helped to shape my theological perspective: I encountered the harsh realities of white injustice that was inflicted daily upon the black community; and I was given a faith that sustained my personhood and dignity in spite of white people's brutality."[1] The person who affected him most strongly in developing his own worldview was his father, who insisted on his own rights and generally avoided the dehumanizing atmosphere that suffused black-white relations in that era. Cone recalls this key influence:

Growing up with my father and observing his dealings with whites and blacks had a profound effect upon my perspective in the world. He gave me the conviction that survival for black people requires constant struggle, and that no black person should ever expect justice from whites. "How could they treat us justly when they do not regard us as people?" he often asked rhetorically.[2]

The faith that kept his personhood and dignity alive and strong was a prophetic style of black religion in Bearden that was "the source of identity and survival on the one hand and the source of empowerment in the struggle for freedom on the other."[3] He emphasizes the fact that the values of white society were completely the reverse of what was observed in the black church, and that he never saw any member of the black church who used religion as a disguise for oppression or as an escape hatch from suffering and harsh reality. Regarding his own career, Cone states that seeing "so many courageous ministers leading the struggle for justice in the name of the gospel and also seeing the support of the church people undoubtedly had much to do with why I chose the ministry as my vocation, and why I chose *liberation as the central theme of my perspective in black theology.*"[4]

Genesis of Black Theology

With his usual insight and clarity, Cone has delineated three key factors in the rise of black theology. The first involved the civil rights movement, with Martin Luther King, Jr., as leader. Since King's efforts have been somewhat romanticized in the decades since his death, it is important to recall the facts of his struggle:

> . . . when Martin Luther King and other church people began to relate the Christian gospel to the struggle for justice in U.S. society, the great majority of white churches and their theologians denied that such a relationship existed. Conservative white Christians claimed that religion and politics did not mix. Liberal white Christians, with few exceptions (this was during the 1950s and early 1960s), remained silent on the theme or advocated a form of gradualism that denounced boycotts, sit-ins, and freedom rides.[5]

The second factor is a curious one, involving a book on black religion, written by Joseph Washington in 1964,[6] and I find Cone's choice of it as a key factor to be unpersuasive. At that time, in-

tegration provided the dominant ideology regarding white-black relationships, and both races assumed that black people's culture had
nothing to contribute to Christianity or to American culture:

> . . . white liberal Christians understood integration to mean as-
> similation and that meant blacks rejecting their own culture and
> adopting European cultural values. The assumption behind the
> white definition of integration was a belief that African cultural
> values were completely destroyed during the time of slavery.
> Therefore, if blacks were to develop cultural knowledge of them-
> selves, it was claimed that they had to find it in identification with
> white American values.[7]

Although Washington believed that there was a unique black culture and a distinctive black religion, he also held in his book that
they existed only because blacks had been excluded from the genuine Christianity of the white churches. In other words,
"Washington felt that because blacks were excluded from the faith
of white churches, black churches were not genuine Christian
churches. And if there are no genuine black Christian churches
there can be no genuine black Christian theology. Blacks have only
folk religion and folk theology."[8] The white community en-
thusiastically applauded Washington's book, but it was attacked in
the black churches, and *black theology was created partially to refute
Washington's book*. As I have mentioned, I am not convinced that
such a bad book can be considered a source of good theology.

The third key factor for black theology was the black power
movement and the black nationalist philosophy of Malcolm X (certainly a very important influence on the development of black theology), which began to gain influence after the march on Washington
in August 1963. But it was not until the summer of 1966, after the assassination of Malcolm, that the black power slogan began to come
into common usage, principally by the efforts of Stokely
Carmichael.[9] Cone describes the new situation:

> The rise of black power had a profound effect upon the appear-
> ance of black theology. When Carmichael and other black activists
> separated themselves from King's absolute commitment to non-
> violence by proclaiming black power, white church people called

upon their black brothers and sisters in the gospel to denounce
the black power slogan as un-Christian. But to the surprise of
white Christians, black ministers refused to follow the advice.[10]

Instead, the ministers wrote their own statement embracing black
power and published it in the *New York Times* on July 31, 1966, an
event that launched a conscious emergence of a black theology
among many ministers. Their manifesto was named "Black Power:
A Statement by the National Committee of Negro Churchmen."
Furthermore, although Cone does not stress it, he himself is an important *fourth key factor* in the rise of black theology, and he published very significant books for the contemporary black theology:
Black Theology and Black Power,[11] and *A Black Theology of Liberation*.[12]
It is interesting to note that the latter book was published a year *before* Gustavo Gutiérrez's ground-breaking volume, *A Theology of
Liberation*. At any rate, Cone is the acknowledged leader in black
theology at this time, in the United States, in South Africa and other
parts of Africa, and in various nations in Asia and the Caribbean. To
my knowledge, he has not established strong links with Latin
American nations.

Aspects of Cone's Theology

At this time, let us discuss some characteristics of Cone's black
theology before analyzing his latest and most important book. I will
not survey various objections and disagreements with his work by
other writers. Cone has summarized the debates concisely: "While
my perspective on Black Theology was challenged by some black
scholars, they all supported my claim that liberation was the central
core of the gospel as found in the scriptures and the religious history of black Americans."[13]

In the light of the goals of this book, it is illuminating to see that
Cone, in the articles discussed here, has plunged directly, although
briefly, into the issue of sexism. He states that many black male theologians have avoided the subject or, worse, displayed hostility
when black women raised it as a crucial issue. As a result, a black
feminist theology has arisen "in open challenge to the patriarchal
nature of the current perspectives of Black Theology."[14] Cone di-
agnoses the present state of the question:

While they accept the liberation theme of Black Theology, black feminist theologians reject the narrow limitations of that theme to racism, as if sexism is not an important problem in the black community. Because of the urgency of the problem of sexism, black women have begun to insist on doing theology out of their own experience.[15]

A very important aspect of Cone's theology is its early and consistent outreach to theologians from the third world theologians. In 1977, at a meeting of these theologians in Accra, Ghana, he rather audaciously delivered a paper on the future of African theology.[16] Moreover, he acutely observed that a process of cross-fertilization soon broadened many horizons of theologians from each of the four continents:

> Black Theology in South Africa was a natural ally. Black and Latin theologies became copartners in their identification of the gospel with the liberation of the poor, although one emphasized racism and the other classism. A similar partnership occurred with black, African, and Asian theologies regarding the importance of culture in defining theology.[17]

A key event in the institutionalizing of these events had occurred in 1976 with the first meeting in Nairobi, Kenya, of a group to become known as the Ecumenical Association of Third World Theologians (EATWOT), [18] and other meetings have been held regularly since. Cone pointed to the goals of EATWOT in a lucid sentence: "As oppressors band themselves together in order to keep the poor of the world in poverty, so the world's poor must enter into political and theological solidarity if they expect to create a movement of liberation that is capable of breaking the chains of oppression."[19]

Although there have been differences of opinion and at times open disagreements in these meetings, the theologians appear to have a broad agreement on how to do theology, that is, method. The method of "critical reflection on praxis in the light of the Bible" of Gustavo Gutiérrez and the more nuanced "hermeneutic circle" of Juan Luis Segundo seem to be generally accepted, although naturally there are differences in expressions and emphases. On the other hand, Cone emphasizes the major differences between the theologies of the developing nations and those of the first world, which have been deeply influenced by the Enlightenment and the problems of the unbeliever:

> The chief contradiction, out of which our theologies achieve their distinctiveness, is the problem of the nonperson. That is why our most important conversation partners are not metaphysicians and other socially disinterested intellectuals in the university, but social scientists and political activists who are engaged in the liberation of the poor.[20]

At the close of his article, Cone presents a clear description of the method of black theology and that of the third world theologians. A digest of his approach is found in four steps: 1) The liberation theologies reflect upon the meaning of God in solidarity with the poor who are seeking to overcome their domination: "Truth is concrete and it is inseparable from the oppressed who are struggling for freedom."[21] 2) These theologies employ social analysis in order to expose systems of domination, such as racism, sexism, colonialism, capitalism, and militarism, in order to create theologies of liberation rather than theologies of domestication. 3) Flowing from the above, a new hermeneutic is created that enables these theologies to interpret the biblical message that Europeans and North Americans have distorted, and to unleash God's living word as Spirit empowering people to become fully human. 4) Finally, a new language of theology is needed. Instead of the concepts of European and North American seminaries and universities, "truth is imbedded in the stories, songs, dances, sermons, paintings, and sayings of our people."[22] In conclusion, Cone admits that, because these theologies have existed for so short a time, their method is still in need of further development.

The second part of the title of Cone's article focuses on "a vision for where we are going" or a new social order for the black community. Passionately, he argues that freedom has never been given to an oppressed people: "Freedom must be taken, and it involves risk, struggle, and a commitment to stand against those who deny it."[23] The new order has six phases, which can only be sketched.

First, black unity must be achieved by affirming the achievements of black history and culture and also the love of self in a new black future. Second, the new vision will include the "beloved community" of Martin Luther King, Jr., that is, a society that respects the humanity of all, including whites.

Third, the new order must be anti-sexist: "A truly liberated social order cannot have men dominating women."[24] Fourth, it must be socialist, democratic, and protect individual liberties, with all involved in the community. Fifth, it must be a global vision that includes the poor of the third world: "There will be no freedom for anybody until all are set free."[25] Sixth, the new order must affirm the best in black religion and embrace the creative elements in the poor. Cone concludes with an assertion that can serve as an introduction to the next section of this chapter:

> The life and thought of Martin Luther King, Jr., and Malcolm X are the best examples in the black community of the creative role that religion can play in the transformation of society. They combined their religious vision with their political commitment, but they refused to allow either their politics or their faith to separate them from other persons struggling for justice even though those persons held different views.[26]

From this point on I will discuss some of the key concepts, issues, and praxis in Cone's books. Two of these, although decades apart, are central to his work: *A Black Theology of Liberation*, published in 1970, and *Martin & Malcolm & America: A Dream or a Nightmare*, published in 1991.[27] I will also make some references to the other books in his considerable corpus of writings.

Cone's Early Works

Like his predecessors, Martin Luther King, Jr., and Malcolm X, James Cone is blessed with the virtue of openness to change both in his life experience and in his writings. An excellent example of this may be found in his first two books. In *Black Theology and Black Power*,[28] he devotes two-thirds of the book to themes revolving around black power in a way that is almost obsessive; in the following year, 1970, he published *A Black Theology of Liberation*, in which all

seven chapters were devoted to black theology and black liberation,
without any interest at all in the topic of black power. This change
in outlook is evident in the very beginning of the latter book:

> It is my contention that Christianity is essentially a religion of lib-
> eration. The function of theology is analyzing the meaning of that
> liberation for the oppressed community so they can know that
> their struggle for political, social, and economic justice is con-
> sistent with the gospel of Jesus Christ. Any message that is not re-
> lated to the liberation of the poor in society is not Christ's
> message. Any theology that is indifferent to the theme of libera-
> tion is not Christian theology.[29]

In the body of this book, Cone uses the themes of liberation and
black theology to *rethink* the fundamental concepts and issues of
modern theology, which is written from a white, American point of
view. To Cone, this means that it "has been basically a theology of
the white oppressor, giving religious sanction to the genocide of
Indians and the enslavement of black people."[30]

Furthermore, Cone also accentuates the fact that black theology is
a "survival theology," and therefore it must employ a *passionate language,* a discourse not usually tolerated in white academic circles.
There can be little doubt that Cone himself employs an impassioned
style in all his writings, while at the same time pinpointing the lack
of such ardor as a characteristic of white theology:

> The sin of American theology is that it has spoken without pas-
> sion. It has failed miserably in relating its work to the oppressed
> in society by refusing to confront this nation with the evils of ra-
> cism. When it has tried to speak for the poor, it has been so cool
> and calm in its analysis of human evil that it implicitly disclosed
> whose side it was on. Most of the time American theology has
> simply remained silent, ignoring the condition of the victims of
> this racist society.[31]

As a result, the very definition of truth for black theology arises
from a passionate experience of the black reality and of the God of
black existence.[32]

With that background, Cone proceeds to analyze the sources and
the norm of black theology, obviously an absolutely crucial founda-

tion for any theological edifice. The six sources that he displays differ from the sources of white theology in almost every category: 1) black experience, 2) black history, 3) black culture, 4) revelation, 5) scripture, and 6) tradition.

Cone is convinced that revelation is incomprehensible without a concrete manifestation of revelation in the black experience, black history, and black culture of the black community. Thus, he concludes, black theology must take the risk of faith and unequivocally equate God's revelation with the liberation of black people.[33] As regards the Bible, he insists that the "meaning of Scripture is not to be found in the words of Scripture as such but only in its power to point beyond itself to the reality of God's revelation; and in America, that means black liberation." He also adds that the Bible is "inspired" because by reading it a community can encounter Christ and achieve a state of freedom in which it will risk everything for freedom.[34]

A similar criterion is applied to "tradition." Cone stresses that black theology is immediately concerned only with those traditions that are usable in the black struggle for liberation in the United States. Finally, he ends with an unusual articulation of the norm or hermeneutical principle for black theology: *The norm of all God-talk which seeks to be black-talk is the manifestation of Jesus as the Black Christ who provides the necessary soul for black liberation."*[35]

Moving to a chapter on revelation, Cone discusses the views of various European theologians with regard to the concepts of general and special revelation. Beyond that, he reemphasizes what he had stated earlier: "Revelation is God's self-disclosure to man *in a situation of liberation*. . . . God's revelation means liberation, an emancipation from the political, economic, and social structures of the society."[36] Recalling that this is an early book, deeply influenced by the black power movement, Cone needlessly exaggerates when he states flatly that "Christianity and whiteness are opposites." As it stands, this statement is a classic example of reverse racism, an insult to every white Christian in the world. On the other hand, in the later article I quoted with regard to the new social order, he speaks of King's "beloved community" and "the humanity of all, including whites."[38]

Another controversial issue in *A Black Theology of Liberation* is the assertion that God is black:

> Because black people have come to know themselves as *black*, and because that blackness is the cause of their own love of themselves and hatred of whiteness, God himself must be known only as he reveals himself in his blackness. The blackness of God, and everything implied by it in a racist society, is the heart of Black Theology's doctrine of God.[39]

These statements could be understood in the same sense that Asians or American Indians employ symbols of God according to their own features and skin color, or that whites worship a white God with their features and color. But Cone insists that black theologians "must reject any conception of God which stifles black self-determination by picturing God as a God of all peoples."[40] As a corollary to this, he boldly asserts that white Christians "are not capable of perceiving the blackness of God because their satanic whiteness is a denial of the very essence of divinity."[41] This statement appears to combine both racism and chauvinism, with a tincture of demagoguery. It will be taken up again later in this chapter, in the author's more recent work.

Other Key Issues

As regards the human person in black theology, Cone takes an interesting journey through the paths of existentialism and American theology with regard to the meaning of freedom in the human person (he uses the word "man"). Most germane are his theses that freedom means an identification and suffering with an oppressed community:

> To be free is to be black, that is, identified with the victims of humiliation in human society and a participant in the liberation of man. The free man in America is the man who does not tolerate whiteness but fights against it, knowing that it is the source of human misery. The free man is the black man living in an alien world but refusing to live up to its expectations.[42]

These ideas are related to the fallenness of humanity and the theological concept of sin. The author points out that sin is a community or social concept (which is now accepted by many theologians), but more interesting is the notion of sin itself:

> Because sin represents the condition of estrangement from the source of one's being, for black people this means a desire to be white and not black. . . . Sin then for black people is the loss of identity. It is saying Yes to the white absurdity—accepting the world as it is by letting white people define black existence. To be in sin is to be contented with white solutions for the "black problem" and not rebelling against every infringement of white being on black being.[43]

As regards christology, Cone strongly emphasizes that the essence of Christianity is to be found in two words: Jesus Christ. Moreover, the essence of Jesus Christ is his manifestation as the Oppressed One, whose earthly existence was intimately linked to the oppressed of the land. Consequently, to "understand the historical Jesus without seeing his identification with the poor is to misunderstand him and thus distort his historical person. And a proper theological analysis of Jesus' historical identification with the helpless is indispensable for our interpretation of the gospel today."[44]

After reviewing the characteristics of the Jesus of history that confirm the previous statements, Cone arrives at the nucleus of his black christology:

> The definition of Christ as black is crucial for Christology if we truly believe in his continued presence today. . . . Any statement about Christ today that fails to consider blackness as the *decisive* factor about his Person is a denial of the New Testament message.[45]

Cone acknowledges that some whites will reject or ignore this unusual formulation, and others will ask whether black theology really believes that Jesus was *really* a black man. Cone responds by insisting that the *literal* color of Jesus is insignificant, but he insists at the same time that Jesus *was not white* in either the literal or theological sense. Therefore he agrees with those blacks who refer to him as a black Jew or the Black Messiah. The argument for these assertions of a black Christ is that it expresses the *concreteness* of the presence of Jesus today. It should be obvious that other races do the same thing in imagining Christ, and proclaim a yellow Christ or a brown Christ. The point is that the black Christ is only one among many, and they cannot be dismissed from existence by merely theological assertions.

In Cone's theology, the black Christ is intimately related to the realization of the kingdom of God in America. As a matter of fact, the coming of the kingdom in America is the liberation struggle of black people, and he ventures a prediction in this regard:

> . . . what white America fails to realize is the explosive nature of the kingdom. Although its beginning is small, it will have a far-reaching effect not only on the black community but on the white community as well. Now is the time to make decisions about loyalties, because soon it will be too late. Shall we or shall we not join the Black Revolutionary kingdom?[46]

As we come to the end of this book, there is a certain whiff of gunpowder in the air, and one wonders if it will be the theologians who will man the barricades. Moreover, statements like "looting, burning, or the destruction of so-called white property are not primary concerns. Such matters can only be decided by the oppressed themselves . . ." is a very irresponsible statement, whether it is voiced by a white, yellow, or brown person. Cone's method and many of his themes are very similar to those of the Latin American and women theologians. A serious dissimilarity, however, lies in his aggressive and threatening style, both in his concepts and expressions. Although this may be more effective than the rather reserved and timid styles of the academy, it may also lead to a rejection by whites and even by blacks who could see his strategy as suicidal. Again, it must be remembered that these books were published more than two decades ago in the midst of a general ferment of revolutionary rhetoric.

MARTIN LUTHER KING, JR., and MALCOLM X

I now turn to Cone's most recent book, arguably the best he has written: *Martin & Malcolm & America: A Dream or a Nightmare.*[47] The book is without a doubt very different both in style and in content from *A Black Theology of Liberation*. It retains the structure of a commonplace systematic theology, albeit his concepts and language are at times startling. It is certainly a theological work *sui generis*, intermingling biography, narrative, and theological concepts in a truly creative and original achievement. It contains, also, a prodigious amount of detailed research concerning their lives, writings, and speeches. The structure of the book, too, is brilliantly organized, as the tracks of the two men converge and part in various ways in their historical and theological journeys. Perhaps the best way to describe it is to call it a theological narrative or novel, one that is quite readable and based on an intriguing true story.

In discussing it, I will not mine the rich veins of biography in Cone's research, but confine myself to the many theological themes and the religious praxis that are involved and linked in the lives of the two men. The subtitle itself—a dream or a nightmare—appears again and again as an ecstatic or lugubrious symphonic *leitmotif* throughout the book.

The Cruel Contrasts

Martin Luther King, Jr., whose father was a minister, had a fine family background, a decent middle-class existence, and the opportunity for a fine education and career in the ministry. The dream, therefore, is King's vision of the "beloved community" of blacks and whites, and his goal of struggling for the integration of blacks into this community.

Malcolm Little, on the other hand, adopted a new name, Malcolm X, which was conferred on him by Elijah Muhammad, the leader of the U. S. Muslims, with the X signifying that he had been stripped of his real African name. Also, his experience in early life comprised an almost total antithesis of King's youth, since it was dominated by scattered episodes of poverty, drugs, crime, and imprisonment. As a consequence of this cruel odyssey, he perceived American society as almost totally antagonistic to black people on every level and element, so that his vision of the society was unequivocally a "night-mare." For almost all of his life, too, he opposed integration into white society and propagated a form of segregation that was created and led by blacks. The two leaders represented in their lives the two horns of the great dilemma: to be integrated into the American society (Martin) or to be segregated into Africa or its equivalent in America (Malcolm).

To continue on a general level, Martin's faith and theology pointed him to the basic theme of "We Must Love Our White Brothers" (and Sisters). Malcolm, on the other hand, adopted as his slogan a prophecy of "Chickens Coming Home to Roost" in American society or, in another version, as "White America Is Doomed!" In his last year, after leaving the Black Muslims and journeying to the shrines of Mecca, Malcolm somewhat mitigated his views on America, since he was profoundly touched by the panorama of the races from all over the world in the same white garments intermingling in unity and solidarity on the sands of Arabia.

Martin's course, however, changed radically in the three years between Malcolm's death and his own (1965-1968), which Cone summarizes as a period of "Shattered Dreams."[48] This interval was dominated by King's historic and prophetic stance in criticizing American society and government, a time symbolized by his angry and trenchant critique of the war in Vietnam. This move, of course, alienated many of his black supporters, including some of his best friends, as well as most white Americans. We might say that his dream was shattered but unbowed.

Two Roads to Freedom?

Bringing together many of the threads and colors of his giant tapestry, Cone ends his book with a depiction of their *two different roads to freedom*. Neither man actually realized that the two roads actually led to a complementarity that each man needed, and also to evaluations and criticisms that both men deeply needed, but of which they were not fully conscious. To rectify that, Cone himself turns prophetic and honestly points out in detail the most serious lacunae and deficiencies with regard to sexism and classism. At the present time, it is clear that these blind spots were extremely serious, since sexism

and classism are clearly as despotic and malignant as is the ubiq-
uitous plague of racism.

In an intriguing last chapter, Cone focuses on the positive leg-
acies, especially with regard to their impact on culture and politics,
with Malcolm achieving his major impact on northern blacks, while
King attained his greatest victories in the south. Overall, Cone eval-
uates both men as master critics of North American Christianity,
with Martin as an internal critic while Malcolm delivered his biting
messages from the outside. He also assiduously sketches the characteristics of both men, their legacy and, most important of all, their
challenge. These include qualities of leadership, self-criticism and
humility, nonviolence and self-defense, militancy mixed with humor, solidarity with the masses, and their powerful links with other
liberation movements, not only with those throughout the United
States, but also with others throughout the world.

As a grand finale for what is certainly Cone's masterpiece, he
ends his book with a resounding challenge to all the members of the
human family:

> We must declare where we stand on the great issues of our time.
> Racism is one of them. Poverty is another. Sexism another. Class
> exploitation another. Imperialism another. . . . Human beings are
> meant for life and not death. They are meant for freedom and not
> slavery. They were created for each other and not against each
> other. . . . For Malcolm, for America and the world, and for all
> those who have given their lives in the struggle for justice, let us
> direct our fight toward one goal—the beloved community of man-
> kind.[49]

Liberation in Martin and Malcolm

I will now examine in greater detail the major lineaments of
Martin's liberation theology, its influence on Malcolm X, and vice
versa. It is abundantly clear that King, from his very first action in
Montgomery in 1955 until the day of his death in Memphis in 1968,
employed a dialectic of practice versus theory as well as theory versus practice, which together were called praxis, as we have seen in
the earlier chapters of this book. His practice consisted of the various demonstrations, sit-ins, boycotts, imprisonments, and many

other versions of nonviolent direct action. His theory was refined in his eloquent and fiery sermons, speeches such as the famous "I Have a Dream" oration at the March on Washington in 1963, manifestos such as the Letter from Birmingham Jail, a succession of books, and other forms of communication. Thus, he was constantly growing and maturing as he reflected and searched for more effective language and ideas to motivate and inspire his followers, as well as for more efficacious policies and strategies to accomplish both immediate and long-range goals in the struggle for justice and freedom. In short, then, his theory was continually being honed and reshaped in the light of his searching critique and social analysis of his action and practice, and of course the other way around. This, once more, is at the heart of all theologies of liberation.

Justice or Love?

We have already referred to the crucial importance that King allotted to his vision of the American dream. His reflections on this, according to Cone, were solidly buttressed by the core element of his faith: the God of *justice, love,* and *hope.* But there were significant differences in the *emphasis* that he accorded to each of these attributes in the two major periods of his public life: 1) from the Montgomery bus boycott in 1955 to the enactment of the Voting Rights Bill in August 1965; 2) from the autumn of 1965 to his death in April 1968, a time when he began to analyze in greater depth and scope the racism, poverty, and militarism that suffused the politics of the U.S. government, and finally to proclaim boldly and even fiercely his proud opposition to those policies.

In the first phase, then, social justice was the focal point of his attention, in opposition to the patently unjust system of segregation. Also at this point, justice meant "white people treating Negroes with the dignity and respect accorded to other human beings."[50] As regards his first speech in Montgomery, and contrary to King's own report as well as the interpretations of scholars, he was not primarily concerned about blacks *loving* white people. Thus, the major proposition of his message was not love, but justice, which entailed having the moral courage and fortitude to stand up for their rights, as is clear in the original speech of King:

I want to tell you this evening that it is not enough to talk about love. Love is one of the principal parts of the Christian faith. There is another side called justice. . . . Justice is love correcting that which would work against love. . . . Standing beside love is always justice. And we are only using the tools of justice. Not only are we using the tools of persuasion but we've got to use the tools of coercion.[51]

This issue should not be viewed as a mere academic discussion. Cone is bent on analyzing the developments in King's thought, and he stresses the fact that no interpreter has focused on justice as the primary theme in his first speech. "Most are so eager," he maintains, "to stress love as the center of his thought and actions (as King himself did when he reflected on the event) that they (like King) fail to note that this was a later development in his thinking."[52]

Another text from the Montgomery speech is important to show that King had to demonstrate clearly to his audience that protest against oppression was not wrong, and that on the contrary it was a constitutional right as well as a biblical principle. It must be remembered that this marked the very *beginning* of the Civil Rights Movement in this century:

We are not wrong in what we are doing. If we are wrong, then the Supreme Court of this nation is wrong. If we are wrong the Constitution of the United States is wrong. If we are wrong God Almighty is wrong. If we are wrong Jesus of Nazareth was merely a Utopian dreamer and never came down to Earth. If we are wrong justice is a lie. . . . And we are determined here in Montgomery to work and fight until justice runs down like water and righteousness like a mighty stream.[53]

Another reason for stressing this is to show that at the beginning of their careers King and Malcolm X shared the same belief that black people should stand up and demand their rights, but they were far apart on other issues.

A Wider Vision
During the 381 days of the boycott, days of suffering, harass-

ment, bombings, and continual threats, King and other black leaders began to glimpse the larger symbolic meaning of the boycott that extended far beyond the borders of the black community in Montgomery. In January 1956, he insisted that the Montgomery movement "is a part of a world-wide movement. Look at just about any place in the world and the exploited people are rising against their exploiters."[54] King also began to envision the oneness of humanity, informed by creative divine love; as a consequence, he saw that justice within a segregated system was no longer acceptable, and that the major goal of the movement had to become integration. In a sermon delivered in February 1956, he spoke eloquently of his broader vision and worldview as well as his turn toward desegregation:

> Integration is the great issue of our age, the great issue of our nation and the great issue of our community. We are in the midst of a great struggle, the consequences of which will be world-shaking. But our victory will not be a victory for Montgomery's Negroes alone. It will a victory for justice, a victory for fair play and a victory for democracy. Were we to stop right now, we would have won a victory because the Negro has achieved from this a new dignity. But we are not going to stop. We are going on in the same spirit of love and protest, and the same dignity we have shown in the past.[55]

At this stage in King's career, then, justice was shaped by a higher goal of love, that is, justice became the means of achieving love. Expressed in more concrete terms, "love, expressed in nonviolent protest, was the only means of achieving justice, which he equated with desegregation."[56]

I referred earlier to the second phase in King's development, one that was deeply influenced by Malcolm X and his indictment of America as well as by King's own experience of his dream turning into a nightmare. A crucial turning point for King occurred five days after the Voting Rights bill was signed on August 11, 1965, when the Watts black ghetto in Los Angeles erupted in a volcano of violence, leading to the worst race riot in decades. King, deeply shaken by the unexpected disaster, walked through the shattered streets and talked to many of the inhabitants, an experience that began a critical watershed in his career. He began to glimpse the terrible truth that the economic issues based on class relations comprised a catastrophe for blacks that eclipsed the problems of racism, and that the achievement of human rights did not automatically create changes in the *material conditions* in the lives of blacks. For example, King commented at one time to Bayard Rustin: "You know, Bayard, I worked to get these people the right to eat hamburgers, and now I've got to do something . . . to help them to get the money to buy [them]."[57]

New Directions

This new and revolutionary attitude grew even stronger when he tried to call attention to economic needs in the slums of Chicago in January 1966. In a speech at the Chicago Freedom Festival, he bluntly stated that the "purpose of the slum is to confine those who have no power and perpetuate their powerlessness. . . . The slum is little more than a domestic colony which leaves its inhabitants dominated politically, exploited economically, segregated and humiliated at every turn."[58] Many people believed that the Chicago Freedom Movement was a failure because it did not succeed in passing an open housing law, but Cone certainly believes it was a success in that King changed his approach drastically and began to speak of America as a morally "sick society" and of his dream turning into a nightmare.

Another momentous step occurred when he adopted a global vision and began to link the freedom of blacks in the United States with the liberation of billions of their brothers and sisters in the third world. Thus he proclaimed:

> However deeply American Negroes are caught in the struggle to be at last at home in our homeland of the United States, we cannot ignore the larger world house in which we are also dwellers. Equality with whites will not solve the problems of either whites or Negroes if it means equality in a world society stricken by poverty and in a universe doomed to extinction by war.[59]

As a result, King began to incline toward a species of separatism in the sense that he began to encourage a powerful affirmation of black self-esteem and self-determination in the realms of politics, economics, and religious institutions. There can be no doubt that he was profoundly stirred by the Black Power movement and Malcolm X; it is also evident that he had begun to lose faith in the willingness of white people to provide him with support for any form of authentic integration.

Hope in God Alone

Connected with this were his experiences of racism, black empowerment, and finally the war in Vietnam, which eventuated in another shift regarding his central theological themes of love, justice and, especially, hope. In his first period, his hope was at least partially based on the civil rights movement and the support he received from the oppressed black people in their marches and demonstrations as well as the white majority and their commitment to formal equality. In his last years, his hope was no longer based on blacks or whites but, as Cone writes, it "was grounded almost exclusively in the God of the biblical and black traditions, which told him to stand up for right even if it would cost him his life."[60]

In a certain sense, then, King had abandoned hope in America or at least in his government, but was slow and cautious in speaking against the war in Vietnam. Once the fateful die was cast, however, he never wavered and was not to be deterred by anyone, friend or foe. In an address delivered in May 1967, he spoke about his experience: "I want you to know that my mind is made up. I backed up a little when I came out in 1965. My name then wouldn't have been written in any book called *Profiles in Courage*. But now I have decided. I will not be intimidated. I will not be harassed. I will not be silent and I will be heard."[61]

On April 4, 1967, exactly one year before his assassination, King chose the pulpit of Riverside Church in New York City as the venue to deliver his "Beyond Vietnam" speech, an address that resounded throughout the world. As Cone asserts, "In terms of moral courage it was his greatest hour, as he proclaimed America to be the 'greatest purveyor of violence in the world today.'"[62] From that moment on, in the last year of his life, he continued his assault on militarism, pointing out again and again and in great detail its links with those other monstrous evils, racism and poverty. Unfortunately, he was still blind to the end to the evil of sexism.

Many of the blacks in the civil rights movement sharply chastised King for his views on Vietnam, which they felt was diverting attention from the needs and problems of blacks at home. When Whitney Young reprimanded him for his views, he replied heatedly: "Whitney, what you're saying may get you a foundation grant, but it won't get you into the kingdom of truth."[63]

Comparisons and Contrasts

Sexism We have already noted that there existed a certain unique complementarity in the teaching and actions of Martin and Malcolm, and that they drew much closer to each other toward the end of their lives. At the same time, Cone is cautious not to glorify or romanticize these human beings, with all their strengths and weaknesses. The most glaring and harmful was their blindness to sexism, every bit as evil as the horror of racism. As Cone expresses it succinctly:

> While both differed sharply with most white men regarding racism, they shared the typical *American* male's view of women. Martin's and Malcolm's views regarding women's place were not significantly different from those of men of other races. Both believed that the woman's place is in the home, the private sphere, and the man's place was in society, the public arena, fighting for justice on behalf of women and children.[64]

Cone admits that their views on women could be partially explained by the fact that they lived before the flourishing of feminism in the 1970s and 1980s, while it was just beginning in the 1960s. However, he cautions very strongly that this not be used as an excuse or a camouflage for accepting the terrible affliction of sexism:

> While we black men may understand the reasons for Martin's or Malcolm's or our own sexism, *we must not excuse it* or justify it as if sexism was and is not today a serious matter in the African-

American community. As we blacks will not permit whites to offer plausible excuses for racism, so we cannot excuse our sexism.[65]

In her book *My Life with Martin Luther King, Jr.*, Coretta King relates that her husband expected her to be a homemaker and a mother for his children, and was very definite that he expected his wife
to be home waiting for him. Soon after their marriage, he told
Coretta: "I want a wife to respect me as the head of the family. I *am*
the head of the family."[66]

On the other hand, Malcolm X had an even more rigid view of
women as a result of the teaching of the Black Muslims. He went so
far as to say that "the true nature of a man is to be strong, and a
woman's true nature is to be weak, and while a man must at all
times respect his wife, at the same time he needs to understand that
he must control her if he expects to get her respect." Also, because
of his contacts with women in the ghettos, he became something of
a misogynist and expressed his views bluntly: "I'd had too much
experience that women were only tricky, deceitful, untrustworthy
flesh. I had seen too many men ruined, or at least tied down, or in
some other way messed up by women."[67]

Even the Black Muslim women, with all their restrictions, were
moved to complain to Elijah Muhammad because of his outrageous
language against them, while other women hurriedly left the temple when he began his charges that women were responsible for the
miseries of black men.

King also went along with the dominant mood among blacks that
there was a pressing need for strong, assertive black males. As a result, black leaders fashioned their primary objectives as assisting the
black male to get a job and achieve status in the community. In a na-
tionwide interview on "Face the Nation," King strongly accentuated
this focus on "manhood":

> The Negro man in this country . . . has never been able to be a
> man. He has been robbed of his manhood because of the legacy of
> slavery and segregation and discrimination, and we have had in
> the community a matriarchal family . . . in the midst of a patriar-
> chal society . . . and I don't think any answer to that problem will
> emerge until we give the Negro man his manhood by giving him

the kind of economic security capable of supporting a family.[68]

As a result of this emphasis on manhood, there was a lack of *visible* women leaders both in civil rights groups and black nationalist organizations. On the other hand, a large number of women were quite active in the movements, but they were not listened to and extended their due recognition by the male leaders and by the media. A striking example of this is Fannie Lou Hammer, who played a major role in the civil rights movement in Mississippi and also endured attacks on her life by night riders and cruel beatings when she was jailed. King never even mentioned her name in any of his speeches and books.

Another woman, Dorothy Cotton, was one of only two women on the staff of the Southern Christian Leadership Conference (SCLC), beginning in 1960. When an interviewer questioned her on King's attitude to women's rights, she laughed as she responded: "I think that he, too, comes right out of the same society, and he would have had a lot to learn and a lot of growing to do as the Women's Movement took on the momentum that it has taken on."[69]

It is important to note that after his conversion on the "road to Damascus," that is, to the Middle East and Africa, Malcolm X transformed many of his views as a result, especially, of his contact with world Islam. This is obviously true in this text:

> . . . one of the things I became thoroughly convinced of in my recent travels is the importance of giving freedom to the woman, giving her education, and giving her the incentive to get out there and put that same spirit and understanding in their children. And I frankly am proud of the contributions that our women have made in the struggle for freedom and I'm one person who's for giving them all the leeway possible because they've made a greater contribution than many of us men.[70]

Cone's final judgment on this issue of sexism is that both men did change their views regarding women because of the influence of their wives and of women collaborators. However, their efforts were still minuscule compared to earlier champions of women's rights, such as Frederick Douglass and W.E.B. Du Bois.

Classism The second major lacuna in the activities of King and

Malcolm X was to be found in their failure to recognize that classism had proven to be just as baneful and lethal as the other scourges of racism and sexism. Their emphasis on integration and segregation led them to assume that the American polity and economic system was essentially benign and that its *only* problem was the exclusion of blacks and other people of color from its cornucopian prosperity. Thus, there was little attention paid to radical questions about the system and to the class system in American society, primarily because of the pernicious twin spectres of anti-Communism and McCarthyism that had dominated American political culture until quite recently with the demise of Communism.

In the South, anyone who suggested change in the structure of white supremacy was automatically labeled as a communist; because of this, King went to great lengths to separate himself and his movement from radical or leftist persons and organizations. In 1964, he stated somewhat testily that "I'm getting sick and tired of people saying this movement has been infiltrated by Communists. There are as many communists in the freedom movement as there are Eskimos in Florida."[71]

In the beginning, Malcolm X was even more antagonistic than King to the Communists. As a Black Muslim, he obviously condemned them because of their atheism, but he also suspected them because they were white and had no real interest in the liberation of black people. Moreover, in view of the fact that Communists lacked political or economic power in America, Malcolm paid little attention to them in his talks and writings. In short, then, both men first saw racism as *the* most monstrous evil in the world, and this blinded both men to the parallel evils of sexism *and* classism both in the black community as well as in the whole world.

Fortunately, however, both men experienced a very significant metamorphosis in this regard. For Malcolm, it was his break with Elijah Muhammad and his trips to Africa, the Middle East, and Mecca. For King, the conversion was triggered by his voyage to Sweden to receive the Nobel Prize for Peace, followed almost immediately by the astonishing eruption of the Watts riot in Los Angeles. Both men, once more, began to realize that the basic structures of capitalism, in America and elsewhere, were established on the basis of exploitation by the rich classes of the poor classes or underclasses.

Malcolm X knew very little about Marx or socialism, yet he was an avid student. His contacts with socialist leaders in Africa, such as Kwame Nkrumah in Ghana and Julius Nyerere in Tanzania, impressed him profoundly, and he concluded rather cavalierly that "all of the countries that are emerging now today from under the shackles of colonialism are turning toward socialism" or in other words: "It's impossible for a white person to believe in capitalism and not believe in racism. You can't have capitalism without racism. And if you find one . . . that makes you sure they don't have this racism in their outlook, usually they're socialists."[72] Although he considered socialism an alternative to capitalism, he firmly believed that black people had to find their own answers to their problems, without relying on their former colonizers. And "Marxist ideas, as the panacea for the black situation of oppression, did not sit well with him, even though he saw some truth in them."[73]

King himself had done some reading of Marx over the holidays in 1949. He admired Marx's passion for social justice, but it was not until much later after his visit to Sweden that he began to consider European democratic socialism as an alternative to the American system. Added to this was his realization that both black and white poor were getting poorer and the rich much richer, despite the Civil Rights Act and President Lyndon Johnson's War on Poverty. He began to speak more about economic equality, but remained cautious about the dangers to the movement of appearing to approve of "democratic socialism." In summary, then, both men had begun to see glimpses of classism as an enormous evil, tantamount to racism and sexism, but they found it very difficult to fully integrate this social analysis into their writings, speeches, sermons, and actions. Unfortunately, then, both men had these burgeoning ideas and plans terminated forever by the bullets of assassins.

DELORES S. WILLIAMS

In all of the worldwide liberation theologies, a new phenomenon is occurring which might be described as a global "rising of the women." This includes, of course, feminists in the United States, who are predominantly middle-class whites, but the real novelty is the rising of women who are feminists and women of color and feminists who live in the world of the poor. The latter feminists, obviously, combine the characteristics of color and poverty, and they are in the still initial stages of articulating and integrating their own challenging, complex, and often dangerous experience. And these feminists, realizing that they are speaking for the vast majority of all the women (the women of color) in the world, are breaking new ground with great speed and depth to reach out to these often despised and suffering sisters.

In this section, then, I will discuss some examples of this in the context of the *black* men and women we have heard in this chapter. The black women feminists now refer to themselves as "womanists," and their reflections as a "womanist theology;" thus, I will use the terms that they prefer to use. The example I have chosen is a dialogue on womanist theology conducted by Alice Walker and Delores Williams, in an article written by Williams: "Womanist Theology: Black Women's Voices."[74]

Williams begins by defining terms, which she has adapted from the book of Alice Walker, *In Search of Our Mothers' Gardens*,[75] and other writings of this Pulitzer Prize-winning novelist. A womanist theology, writes Williams, is one that affirms women precisely as *black*, while at the same time appropriating their connection with feminism and with the African-American community, both male and female. The name is derived from black folk culture and is a designation, according to Walker, that describes the kind of woman who at the same time displays "outrageous, audacious, courageous and willful behavior" as well as acting "responsible, in charge, serious."[76] Other names for a womanist are a "black feminist" or a "feminist of color," but womanist is the preferred appellation.

In order to develop womanist theology, Williams notes the importance of "cultural codes":

These are words, beliefs, and behavioral patterns of a people that must be deciphered before meaningful communication can happen cross-culturally. Walker's codes are female-centered and they point beyond themselves to conditions, events, meanings, and values that have crystallized in the African-American community *around women's activity* and formed traditions.[77]

Examples of these codes include especially mother-daughter advice, but also female slave narratives, folk tales, black poetry and prose, autobiographies, testimonies of black church women, and many other genres. As regards womanist theology, the codes and traditions "are valuable resources for indicating and validating the kind of data upon which womanist theologians can reflect as they bring black women's social, religious, and cultural experience into the discourse of theology, ethics, and biblical and religious studies."[78]

Another important point is that a womanist theologian locates her understanding in the context of *non-bourgeois* black folk culture. This may smack of elitism, but the choice is based on the fact that the latter culture has traditionally "reflected more egalitarian relations between men and women, much less rigidity in male-female roles, and more respect for female intelligence and ingenuity than is found in bourgeois culture."[79]

Williams traces some of the historical characteristics of blacks, their communitarian sharing of goods after emancipation, their participation in "rent parties" during the depression, and a general togetherness and closer connection to nature. Of great significance, too, was the role of folk heroines such as Harriet Tubman, who was referred to by her followers as "Moses." In what may be the most significant statement in the article, the author says:

> This allusion to Tubman directs womanist memory to a liberation tradition in black history in which women took the lead, acting as catalysts for the community's revolutionary action and for social change. Retrieving this often hidden or diminished female tradition of catalytic action is an important task for womanist theologians and ethicists. Their research may well reveal that female models of authority have been absolutely essential for every struggle in the black community and for building and maintaining the community's institutions.[80]

Quite appropriately, the author quotes a more modern folk expression closely connected with the paragraph just quoted: "If Rosa Parks had not sat down, Martin King would not have stood up."[81]

Again following the lead of Alice Walker, Williams emphasizes that two principal concerns of womanist theology should be sheer survival as well as the building and nurture of communities. Positively, these communities are aimed at creating a deeper quality of life on both religious and secular levels for black women, men, and children. On the negative side, there is an admonition to love themselves and to avoid, *regardless,* the self-destruction that occurs if they take on too much of the task of community-building.

Regarding the relationship between womanists and feminists, Williams and Walker cautiously suggest a close relationship, but also accentuate the *deep differences* between them. The goal of this tentative approach is to give "womanist scholars the freedom to explore the particularities of black women's history and culture without being guided by what white feminists have already identified as women's issues."[82] This statement appears to me to constitute a very important backdrop for any fruitful dialogue between white and black feminists in the future.

Other very important tasks for womanists are mothering and nurturing, first of all to their own children but also to nurturing many others in the struggle for liberation. We may bring these threads together:

> . . . the clues about community from Walker's definition of a womanist suggest that the mothering and nurturing dimension of African-American history can provide resources for shaping criteria to measure the quality of justice in the community. These criteria could be used to assure female-male equity in the presentation of the community's models of authority. They could also gauge the community's division of labor with regard to survival tasks necessary for building and maintaining community.[83]

The Method of Womanism

A sign of maturation in any theology is the careful attention to method, which is to any theological structure what girders are to an edifice. The Christian womanist method, then, contains at least four characteristics: 1) a multi-dialogical intent; 2) a liturgical intent; 3) a didactic intent; and 4) a commitment to *reason* and to the validity of female *images* and *metaphors* in the articulation of theological statements. I will comment on these individually.

The *multi-dialogical* intent aims at allowing "Christian womanist theologians to advocate and participate in dialogue and action with *many* diverse social, political, and religious communities concerned about human survival and a productive quality of life for the oppressed."[84] A major task for womanists is resisting Western white groups or governments in their attempts at genocide and "omnicide" (nuclear extinction). But in this dialogue and action "the womanist should also keep her speech and action focused upon the slow genocide of poor black women, children, and men by exploitative systems denying them productive jobs, education, health care, and living space."[85]

With regard to the *liturgical* intent, womanist theology attempts to be relevant to and to reflect the worship and action of the black church, but also to challenge it with the prophetic messages it has assimilated from multi-dialogics:

> This means that womanist theology will consciously impact *critically* upon the foundations of liturgy, challenging the church to use justice principles to select the sources that will shape the content of liturgy. The question must be asked: How does this source portray blackness/darkness, women, and economic justice for nonruling-class people? A negative portrayal will demand omission of the source or its radical reformation by the black church. The Bible, a major source in black church liturgy, must also be subjected to the scrutiny of justice principles.[86]

In a short space, the womanists here provide all of the other liberation theologies with ideas that bridge what are often fissures between action for justice and liturgy in the churches.

In womanist method the *didactic* intent justifies the teaching function of theology, which should provide new moral insights that support justice for women, survival, and improving the quality of life. The womanist theologian is called upon to give authority to black folk wisdom such as Brer Rabbit literature and to black women's moral wisdom as found in their literature, and from these sources "teach the church the different ways God reveals prophetic word and action for Christian living."[87]

The final intent concerning female *images and metaphors* as well as *reason* should be quite helpful, since the language of black women is drenched in female imagery, metaphor, and story. Williams then provides an apt finale on womanist method:

> The appropriateness of womanist theological language will ultimately reside in its ability to bring black women's history, culture, and religious experience into the interpretive circle of Christian theology and into the liturgical life of the church. Womanist theological language must, in this sense, be an instrument for social and theological change in church and society.[88]

As a final note, Walker and Williams make the interesting assertion that womanist theology has always had a great reverence for the Spirit, and is now creating a theology of the Spirit that is based on black women's political action. This also enables the women to retell and reflect upon the Bible narratives where poor, oppressed women had a special experience of the Spirit as in the story of Hagar. Moreover, black women are able to refocus the Bible so that it stresses the beginning of revelation with the Spirit coming upon Mary (Lk 1:35). This tradition is said to have been traced back to the nineteenth-century abolitionist and feminist, Sojourner Truth, who once confronted a preacher who taught that women could not have rights equal to men's because Christ was not a woman. Sojourner's response illustrates the black folk traditions of the time: "Whar did your Christ come from? . . . From God and a woman! Man had nothin' to do wid Him!"[89]

Williams admits that responses about who God is will come from many sources and not be exhausted by the womanist predilection for the Spirit. Therefore she continues:

> The integrity of black church women's faith, their love of Jesus, their commitment to life, love, family, and politics will also yield vital clues. And other theological voices (black liberationist, feminist, Islamic, Asian, Hispanic, African, Jewish, and Western-white-male traditional) will provide insights relevant for the construction of the God-content of womanist theology.[90]

Williams ends her précis of womanist theology fittingly, with a provocative narrative concerning each womanist's special contribution or gift to the understandings of God. It is taken from the work of Bess B. Johnson, who describes the difference in the play of male and female children in the black community where she grew up. The boys were enthralled by the game of tug-o'-war, where two groups would pull on the rope in opposite directions until one group won.

The girls were not allowed to play in the tug-o'-war, so they constructed their own rope—a chain of dandelions—and anyone, even the boys, could add to the chain until play time was over and they were all called home. Williams ends with a prophecy on the story: "Like Johnson's dandelion chain, womanist theological vision will grow as black women come together and connect piece with piece. Between the process of creating and the sense of calling, womanist theology will one day present itself in full array, reflecting the Divine Spirit that connects us all."[91]

Coda of a Black Liberation Symphony

At the beginning of this chapter, I emphasized strongly that Martin Luther King, Jr., was the founder and the major leader of a liberation movement and a liberation theology that was inaugurated in December 1955, in Birmingham, Alabama, and that tragically ended with his death in Memphis, Tennessee, in April 1968. In his brief public life, King immediately appeared to sense the need of praxis, that is, he combined the *theory* of books, speeches, and sermons, together with a *practice* of boycotts, demonstrations, marches, and imprisonment to advance the cause of civil rights, or what others called civil disobedience. King also intuited the enormous power of early television, and employed it brilliantly in theory and practice. The television pictures showing the "authorities" attacking African American adults and children with nightsticks, stunning them with fire hoses, and releasing savage dogs on them stirred the conscience of the nation and indeed the entire world in an image that was burned into their psyche. Throughout all this, King continued, despite the advice of others, to use the approach of nonviolence.

It is most important, then, to recognize that in the mid-1950s he was the pioneer, the forerunner, of *all the other liberation theologies* that began only in the late 1960s and 1970s. It is entirely fitting, then, that United States citizens devote a national holiday to celebrate his lasting impact on the nation and his liberation theology that strove to liberate both African Americans and white Americans in what he termed "the blessed community."

But King belonged to all of humanity, and inspired hundreds of thousands who were attempting to overcome poverty and oppression all over the globe. Many of those who hungered and thirsted after justice gave their lives, knowing all the while that they might die at any moment. With King and all those others, then, it is fitting to say that they now belong to the ages.

QUESTIONS FOR REFLECTION AND DISCUSSION

1. In what ways were the actions of Martin Luther King, Jr., the quintessential model of liberation praxis, practice refined by theory and theory animated by the experience of practice? Does this resemble the methods presented in the previous chapters? Can you give some examples in his life of the dialectic of theory and practice?

2. What does James Cone see as the different problems addressed by theologians in the first world and those in the third world? How would these problems affect their respective theologies? Although it is not generally accepted, this may be the most important issue in the world both for church and society. What is your viewpoint?

3. Cone states unequivocally that he is attempting a new language of theology. Where does he find the truth embedded? Why is this his choice? What is your position on this key issue?

4. A new world order is presented by Cone, with six stages in the struggle. Which of the stages do you think is most important? Which do you think will not be achieved in the foreseeable future? Can you make any contribution to this struggle?

5. Is Cone's approach and language different than those in previous chapters? Does he still use the method of liberation theology

as do the theologians in the previous chapters? Does he try to create a "beloved community" along the lines of Martin Luther King, Jr.?

6. Analyze the shifting relationship between "love" and "justice" in the thought of King. What do you think the proper relation between these concepts should be? Have you ever had to relate them in your experience?

7. In what manner does the life experience of King embody the "heart of all the liberation theologies"? Is he accepted as a great leader by all Americans or rejected by many because of his race? Can you think of strategies to overcome this form of racism?

8. What were the two issues that King and Malcolm X ignored in their early careers? How would you contrast their careers? Do you think that they both still have an impact on people today?

9. What does Delores Willams designate as the two principal concerns of womanist theology? She also encourages the ideas of "cultural codes," non-bourgeois black culture, and the emphasis on togetherness. Can you think of ways in which the white feminists can create closer relationships to the womanist theologians?

Suggested Readings

Cone, James H. *A Black Theology of Liberation.* Philadelphia: Lippincott, 1970.

Cone, James, and Gayraud S. Wilmore, eds. *Black Theology: A Documentary History, Volume Two: 1980-1992.* Maryknoll, NY: Orbis Books, 1993.

Garrow, David J. *Bearing the Cross: Martin Luther King, Jr. and the Southern Christian Leadership Conference.* New York: William Morrow, 1986.

Hopkins, Dwight. *Shoes That Fit Our Feet: Sources for a Constructive Black Theology.* Maryknoll, NY: Orbis Books, 1993.

Jones, Major J. *The Color of God: The Concept of God in Afro-American Thought.* Macon, GA: Mercer University Press, 1987.

King, Martin Luther, Jr. *A Testament of Hope: The Essential Writings of Martin Luther King, Jr.* James Washington, ed.; San Francisco: Harper & Row, 1986.

Roberts, J. Deotis. *Black Theology in Dialogue.* Philadelphia: Westminster, 1987.

Walker, Theodore, Jr. *Empower the People: Social Ethics for the African-American Church.* Maryknoll, NY: Orbis Books, 1991.

West, Cornel. *Prophesy Deliverance! An Afro-American Revolutionary Christianity.* Philadelphia: Westminster, 1982.

Williams, Delores S. *Sisters in the Wilderness: The Challenge of Womanist God Talk.* Maryknoll, NY: Orbis Books, 1993.

Wilmore, Gayraud S. *Black and Presbyterian: The Heritage and the Hope.* Philadelphia: Geneva Press, 1983.

CHAPTER FOUR

WE ARE A PEOPLE!

Hispanic Liberation Theology

The theological viewpoint of Latina women seeks to respond to the real needs of those who suffer the consequences of this "world order." As such, it overcomes the conciliatory and abstract character of liberal-progressive theology to embrace *oppressed women*—as women, as poor, and as a subordinate race—as the locus from which to shape its reflection . . . from this locus it calls non-poor Latina women who suffer some form of oppression (cultural or sexual) to join the majority and thus share in the gospel promises.

María Pilar Aquino
Frontiers of Hispanic Theology in the United States 27

Indeed, we are living in a time of vast changes in the church's self-understanding, and it is possible that the consequences of these changes will be more drastic than those which took place in the sixteenth century. Hispanic theology, whose first steps we now witness, is but one element of that vast reformation and can be properly understood only when viewed within that larger context.

Justo L. González
Mañana: Christian Theology from a Hispanic Perspective 43

I looked at Brew [Piri's black friend] who was as Black as God is supposed to be white.

"Man, Brew," I said, "you sure an ugly spook."

Brew smiled. "Dig this Negro calling out 'spook,'" he said. I smiled and said: "I'm Porty Rican."

"Ah only sees another Negro in front of me," said Brew.

Piri Thomas
Down These Mean Streets 121

IN THE COURSE OF THE PAST QUARTER century, Latin American liberation theology has penetrated to all corners of the world and continues to have a profound impact, especially in the developing nations. It has already been considered at length in Chapter One, and I will not repeat its characteristics.

What I do want to discuss at this point is a close relative of Latin American theology, Hispanic American theology in the United States. This movement is still in its infancy compared to its highly developed forebear, but it continues to flourish at an astonishing rate throughout the United States. I treat it here because it is related to black theology and to feminist theology, which we have seen as very dynamic movements of liberation theology in the United States at the present time. Another reason is that my own context, or *realidad*, as a liberation theologian is situated in the United States, and I want to give special attention to my Hispanic colleagues—or comrades in arms—in this country. Finally, the Hispanic people in our midst will certainly have an extraordinary impact on all the Christian churches in the coming century, especially on my own Roman Catholic church, on my religious order, the Society of Jesus, and on my country.

Background of Hispanic American Theology

Hispanic theology has not yet become well known in the United States, and is far less known outside its borders. Thus, some background information is in order, with special emphasis on theology.

"Hispanic American" is by now the most accepted term for persons of Latin American descent who have now settled for the foreseeable future in the United States. Persons from Spain who have settled in the United States are not referred to as Hispanics, but as Spaniards.

Other frequent appellations are Latinos, which would include Portuguese in the U.S., and Chicanos, which is favored by some Mexican Americans. Hispanic Americans, according to census figures, comprise between 20 and 22 million inhabitants, or between 11 and 12 percent of the population. Because of a flood of immigrants and high birth rates, they will become, some observers believe, the largest minority group early in the twenty-first century. Further information will be provided later in this chapter when discussing the book of Allan Figueroa Deck.

An important beginning and an increasingly influential source of leadership in Hispanic American theology may be found in the Mexican American Cultural Center (MACC). Located in San Antonio, Texas, it was founded in 1972 by Rev. Virgilio Elizondo, who is also rector of San Fernando Cathedral in that city. In the years since then, he "has provided a paradigm for theological scholarship rooted in a love for the Hispanic communities."[1] Author Figueroa Deck provided further details on his work:

> Elizondo's bibliography includes more than seventy items. He is the only U.S. Hispanic theologian with wide recognition in the U.S., Europe, and the Third World as well. While producing a regular stream of books and articles, Elizondo has always been more than a scholar. He is an extraordinary activist. He founded the Mexican-American Cultural Center in San Antonio, participated in numerous national and international conferences, became a famous lecturer, and served on the board of several national and international theological associations.[2]

The Center celebrated its twentieth anniversary by sponsoring a forum for Hispanics, with emphasis on the Mexican-Americans or Chicanos. At the meeting, its vice president emphasized that MACC "continues to gather the memory of a people whose history was buried. Mexican history was unknown, even by Mexican Americans. Then, through MACC, people became aware of the religiosity of the Mexican people."[3]

Two other significant institutions that have been created very recently are the Academy of Hispanic Theologians in the United States (ACHTUS) in 1988 and La Comunidad of Hispanic American

Scholars of Theology and Religion (CHASTR) in 1989. The first organization was founded by Mons. Arturo Bañuelas, who trains lay
leaders in El Paso, Texas, and Rev. Allan Figueroa Deck, who is co-
ordinator of Hispanic Studies at Loyola Marymount University in
Los Angeles. In the June 1992 meeting at San Diego, the Virgilio
Elizondo Award for outstanding contributions to Hispanic theology
was presented to these two men. A very interesting development
for feminists at the meeting was the election as vice president of the
academy of Professor María Pilar Aquino, who will also become
president. The positions of secretary and treasurer were also accepted by woman members.

The other group, CHASTR, was founded with the support of the
Fund for Theological Education, and thus is under the umbrella of
the American Academy of Religion. The ACHTUS organization has
been active with a distinctively Catholic thrust in such organizations as the Catholic Theological Society of America, while
CHASTR has been more involved in the activities and meetings of
the American Academy of Religion. Both organizations, however,
enjoy very cordial and ecumenical relations.

Another important organization, the National Catholic Council
for Hispanic Ministry (NCCHM), was also recently founded, in
January 1991. In August 1992, it hosted a national gathering of
Hispanic Catholic leaders at Loyola Marymount University under
the title *Hispanic Congress '92: Roots and Wings.* This was the first
time Hispanic Catholics held a meeting that was not convoked by
the bishops but by a group of about 30 Catholic organizations. The
leaders viewed this as a sign of maturity for Hispanic lay persons,
but it caused some alarm within the Bishops' Committee for
Hispanic Affairs. At any rate, Cardinal Roger Mahoney of Los
Angeles gave the group an enthusiastic reception, and six other
bishops attended. "Roots" referred to 500 years of Hispanic cultures
rooted in the Americas, and "wings" to the soaring vitality of these
cultures as they look forward to the future.[4]

ALLAN FIGUEROA DECK

Although a number of interesting books on Hispanic theology have
appeared in the past decade, major importance must be given to

Alan Figueroa Deck's book, *The Second Wave: Hispanic Ministry & the Evangelization of Cultures*,[5] which I will discuss at length. Before that, I want to point out a significant statement he made on Hispanic theology in the introduction to his latest book.

Deck refers to the fact that theology and the "data on which theologians reflected were often suspended in the air, in some eternal realm of ideas. Reality, especially in its socio-economic, political, and cultural dimensions, has too often been *terra incognita* [an unknown land] for theologians."[6] But Vatican Council II had called the church and its theologians and social scientists to a profound dialogue with the world in these areas, precisely where they were called to seek out God and God's will for humankind. However, this conversion, which it certainly was for the church, has not yet happened in the first world. As Deck views it:

> . . . theological production and curricula, with some notable exceptions even twenty-five years after the Second Vatican Council, are limited to a dialogue with the Anglo-European world, its philosophical categories and burning issues, not necessarily with the concerns of the vast majority of human beings, the Third and Fourth Worlds. These worlds are in important ways more representative of the human, of the "real," world, than is the First World itself.[7]

The articles in Deck's book are said to bring these viewpoints into the heart of North American culture. But Deck makes another assertion that will have to be tested throughout this chapter, namely, that there is something *qualitatively different* about U.S. Hispanic theology. "It is a theology," he insists, "which certainly contrasts with mainstream U.S. theology, but also with the theology of liberation. That difference emerges from a simple glance at the origins and trajectory of this theology."[8] At this point, we will turn to those origins and trajectory.

Deck's book, it must be emphasized, is concerned with Hispanic pastoral theology and ministry, but this is also seen as at least an equally important catalyst of change for the *entire North American culture.* As we have noted earlier, the awesome task is the evangelization of the world superpower, the United States. The following text, then, may be seen as the linchpin of the entire volume:

> The key to effective Hispanic ministry, as the very core of today's challenge to evangelize the Hispanics, is the evangelization of North American culture itself. It is the ministers of evangelization who come from the North American cultural reality who first of all need to be evangelized in relation to the materialism, individualism, and hedonism of North American culture. To the degree that we neglect to evangelize North American culture, we will never truly evangelize the Hispanics in this country. . . . In seeking to offer them life, we will in effect be calling them to death.[9]

The title of Deck's book, the "second wave," alludes to the immense migration of millions of Latin American, Asian-Pacific, and other peoples to the United States since the end of the Second World War. The "first wave" of immigrants of course refers to the millions of Europeans who flocked to the United States in the nineteenth century and also in the first decades of the twentieth. Deck boldly foresees that this "second immigration experience promises to be as significant, if not more significant, than the first one whose memory and meaning is rapidly fading from mainstream U.S. Catholics" and also that "this migration will transform that church by the [twenty-first] century into a predominantly Hispanic American institution just as today it is a predominantly Irish institution."[10] Manifestly, then, the ministry and evangelization of the Hispanics will have an enormous impact on the vitality and effectiveness of the church in the twenty-first century.

Hispanic Theology and Method

The organization of Deck's volume follows carefully the method of Latin American liberation theology, especially the "see-judge-act" approach and the utilization of the social sciences in the first step, to "see" the context or reality. I would judge that he has made more use of these sciences than any of the liberation theologians in this book, and his judicious and intelligent selection and use of them is one of the major features of his work.

Thus, his first chapter provides a broad panorama of the

Hispanic American reality through dialogue with a surprising amount of social scientific literature. In the second chapter, he focuses on the historical and cultural elements that are also part of the context of Hispanics of Mexican ancestry in California. The following chapter presents a broad descriptive profile of current pastoral practices in that region. In the fourth chapter, he delineates the key issues that have percolated to the surface from the previous chapter's pastoral praxis. It also proposes a double socio-cultural analysis—of the dominant U.S. culture and also of the dependent Hispanic culture—and stresses the urgent need of a critical attitude toward both cultures.

Finally, the last chapter spotlights again the pastoral praxis, in order to clarify goals, objectives, and strategies. Roughly, then, the first three chapters emphasize the "see" elements in the pastoral method, while chapter four stresses the "judge" factor, and the last chapter highlights the "act" element.

For those not familiar with the American Southwest, some observations from Deck's social analysis in chapter one of his book may be illuminating. There are, he says, approximately 20 to 22 million Hispanics in the United States, half of them below the age of 25. In the 1970s the Hispanic population increased by 61 percent, while the entire population of the United States increased by 11.5 percent. The majority of the Hispanics are concentrated in only five states, California, Texas, New York, Florida, and Illinois, while 60 percent—or twelve million—of all Hispanics are of Mexican descent. The second largest group comprises 1.5 million Puerto Ricans, while Cuban Americans and, recently, Dominicans are both third with approximately one million.

Also of significance is the fact that 88 percent of Hispanics live in cities (only 6 percent are in agricultural work), which is second only to Asian immigrants, who have 91 percent of their population in the cities. Unfortunately, though, the educational level of Hispanics is the lowest of any group in the nation, with 56.7 percent lacking a high school diploma and with the smallest percentage of those with at least a college degree. Finally and deplorably, ". . . the Mexican origin population receives the lowest wages of any group in the country. The median annual income of white males, for example, is

$13,029; for Mexican origin males, $8888. Especially notable is the median annual income of Mexican origin females, which is $4556. Only the Puerto Rican females have a lower annual median income."[11]

As a liberation theologian, Deck is meticulous in clarifying his method and approach to the social sciences. In interpreting the data, he first discusses the functionalist approach that is strongly entrenched in the social sciences in the United States. His cautious statement on functionalism is of great importance for understanding his entire book:

> This approach does not highlight the perduring negative features of the Hispanic reality, nor does it posit structural root causes for ongoing discrimination and injustice that are real features of the reality of Hispanics and other minorities in the U.S. Many social scientists study discrete phenomena and show no interest or ability in placing the phenomena in the broader cultural perspective needed to effect change in society. . . . Functionalist social science is suited to the more individualistic, capitalist society that tends to absolutize the status quo as the best of all possible worlds.[12]

Although Deck sees some values in a Marxist analysis (perhaps he would revise even that statement in a new edition), he criticizes it for presenting sweeping and general conclusions instead of more detailed analyses of the context or reality. He quotes a conference that took place in Colombia in 1977 where the social scientists voiced considerable dissatisfaction with key characteristics of Marxism, including its dogmatic tendencies, its exclusion of the people being analyzed from the process, and treating the poor as objects rather than subjects of transforming action.

As a result, the conference adopted a method proposed by the distinguished sociologist, Orlando Fals Borda, and called "investigation and participative action," which moved beyond both Marxism and functionalism. "At some point, then," Deck maintains, "a vision of God and humanity, an appropriate hermeneutic, a *utopia*, must be applied to even the most 'objective' efforts to grasp reality as a first step in the formulation of an effective pastoral praxis."[13]

History and Culture

In chapter two, "Searching for Roots and Reality," Deck presents a survey of pre-Columban history, the Conquest, and the Spanish colonial history. During the latter period, the church managed to create a Constantinian relationship with the *conquistadores* and an identification with the status quo that led many to an ambivalent attitude toward it. This situation has led to a longstanding paradox that a strong anti-clericalism "coexists in Mexican culture along with a strong, traditional Catholicism. The roots of these seemingly antithetical currents are to be found in Mexico's colonial experience."[14]

The author discusses at some length the literacy of the English settlements versus the orality of the Spanish colonies. As a consequence, the English (who had arrived a century later than the Spanish) were by and large literate, while the Spanish never succeeded in making Mexico a predominantly literate country, even in the twentieth century. Deck points to another very important difference:

At the root of the Anglo-American experience is a marked prejudice against peoples of color. This prejudice led practically to the extermination of the Indians. There never was any significant miscegenation between the English and the Indians of North America, while the Spaniards, in contrast, set about begetting a new *mestizo* race.[15]

Pastoral Planning

The third chapter of the book is concerned with what Deck describes as Hispanic ministry or "the whole range of pastoral services and care by the Church."[16] He begins by insisting that "pastoral care for the majority of Mexican Catholics is whatever sustains, nourishes, and promotes their popular Catholicism, which is the only Catholicism they know."[17] The clergy, moreover, tend to dismiss the popular religion as primitive superstition and as alienating:

. . . historically the clergy *in Mexico* have clashed with the people in the effort to put more order and reason into this mythic, symbolic, and instinctive religiousness. The result, after centuries, seems to be a standoff. A fortiori, the clash between this primary religiousness and the standard norms and procedures of North American Catholicism is greater.[18]

Deck then divides the "pastoral realities" into seven crucial areas: 1) the parish, whether national, Americanized, or multi-ethnic; 2) apostolic movements, *cofradías* (religious confraternities), Catholic Action, nocturnal adoration, the *Asociación Guadalupana*, *cursillos* (a type of retreat), and charismatic prayer groups; 3) the base ecclesial communities (BECs), which are modeled on the small Christian communities throughout Latin America, as well as the RENEW program for parish revival, which has led to the formation of thousands of faith-sharing groups throughout the country; 4) catechesis and adult education programs, which are widespread throughout California; 5) ministry to urban immigrants; 6) pastoral care for undocumented immigrants; and 7) rural ministry, especially to the migrant workers in California, which has the largest population of migrant workers in the United States.

The author concludes with a survey of the diocesan, regional, and national structures that are concerned with Hispanic ministry. The Secretariat for Hispanic Affairs was established by the U.S. Catholic bishops in 1971 as a department of the U.S. Catholic Conference. In addition, there is a regional Office of Hispanic Affairs in Sacramento, California, and six other regional offices throughout the nation. A proposal was also made to the U.S. bishops for funding a regional, pastoral, and cultural center called the Catholic Hispanic Institute of California (CHIC).

Furthermore, the Secretariat for Hispanic Affairs has organized three national meetings of Hispanic Americans in what are called *encuentros*, which have taken place in 1971, 1977, and 1985. The third meeting involved more than 200,000 Hispanic Catholics in lengthy reflections on their realities and needs, and published an outline of a pastoral plan, or *pastoral de conjunto*. There is also a brief discussion of mass media and the Hispanic. As regards their utility for evangelization, Deck is positive but cautious: "The privatized world of living room or automobile is not the context within which evangelization as understood in the church can take root. Mass media can be supportive and complement more fundamental efforts that take as their point of departure communities of faith, worship, and service. But media approaches cannot substitute for the building of viable, concrete communities."[19]

Deck is quite aware in chapter four that he is moving to the second and more challenging part of his book. It is at this point that the structure of what I would call Deck's North American liberation theology becomes readily apparent. For he is reflecting on the many pastoral contexts already discussed in terms of *four key issues:* 1) inculturation, or the evangelization of culture; 2) the promotion of social justice, or structural transformation; 3) modernity and secularization; and 4) popular Catholicism and religiousness. His approach is to explain general ideas on each topic, and then show their implications for the Hispanic church.

What Is Evangelization?

A first response to this question may be discovered in a succinct statement of Pope Paul VI: ". . . the church evangelizes when she seeks to convert, solely through the divine power of the Message she proclaims, both the personal and collective consciences of people, the activities in which they engage, and the lives and concrete milieux which are theirs."[20] But difficulties have cropped up concerning the relationships and priorities between evangelizing and structural change, which Deck attempts to clarify:

> . . . There are two poles, then, within evangelization—one focused on the human heart; the other focused on the milieu, the material structures that influence both the individual and society. The term inculturation or evangelization is conceived of as impacting personal values, feelings, customs, and thought, while liberation is conceived of as relating more to the transformation of the social order, the achievement of a more just society.[21]

Deck avers that there has been a serious division instead of a synthesis between these two poles among pastoral agents. Some stress the personal element, prayer, and morality, while others emphasize socio-political action for change. The author responds to this critical problem in a sentence that could stand as the basic thesis of his entire book: "The proper evangelization of the Hispanic communities of the United States cannot occur until and unless the gospel message is proclaimed in such a way that changes take place in *both* the personal and the social/structural dimensions of the Hispanic people and the larger North American society of which they are only a part."[22]

With regard to the evangelization of culture, Deck proposes two somewhat general definitions of culture: "the meanings, value, thoughts, and feelings mutually shared by a people" and even more broadly, "the specific, concrete ways in which a person is human."[23] He also provides a wide definition of inculturation as the relationship between faith and culture, a theory and practice that has dramatically challenged and changed missionary activity throughout the world:

> The demise of colonialism encouraged reflection on the importance of European culture versus the autochthonous ones. This decline relativized the norms, values, customs, and worldviews of European as well as Anglo-Saxon culture. The newfound sensitivity to the question of culture has had immense practical repercussions on the church in liturgy, pastoral care, missions, preaching, and lifestyle.[24]

There is a very important corollary to this sweeping statement that is even more significant and comprehensive. Inculturation is *not* confined to missiology and the third world; only a relative minority in the church has an active interest in the missions. This corollary then applies to the *universal* church, including the mission countries:

> Nor is the impact of inculturation felt only in these practical areas and in the field of missiology. *All of theology has been shaken to the foundations in the sense that a new, long, and arduous journey has begun.* The journey consists precisely in discovering the interplay between faith and culture at work in every aspect of the Church's life and thought over the centuries.[25]

In regard to inculturation, or the relationship between faith and culture in the United States, one immediately encounters a host of complexities and challenging questions. A major problem is the undeniable fact that the United States, with its technology, capitalist liberal ideology, and mass media, has become in many significant areas the *normative* culture of the West and to a considerable extent of the East. Thus, one can admit that "[m]odernity, understood as culture . . . is largely indistinguishable from Americanization."[26]

Because of this dominating culture, there exists very little awareness in the general public of the considerable *differences* that persist between the first world cultures (or "Christian" cultures) and the message of the New Testament, with the very baneful or even catastrophic result that "the Church's understanding of the gospel message continues to be mediated by first world culture and ideology" and "culturally specific norms and attitudes are confused with the gospel message itself."[27]

In short, the cultural hegemony of the United States presents a background that makes it extremely arduous for pastoral agents to create the cultural critique that is essential for evangelization. They are torn between accommodating to the culture and showing deep sympathy for it, or keeping their distance while criticizing the culture, "because the gospel is, in important respects, always transcultural and countercultural."[28] Deck, moreover, stresses the *absolute necessity* for pastoral agents to continually develop this critique:

> They must somehow break away from the comfortable truths, the prevailing attitudes, expectations, values, and feelings characteristic of their society if any kind of a significant evangelization is to take place. Yet ironically they must be experts in their culture, know its values in a reflective manner, grasp the symbols that express its deepest understanding of itself, and know how to effectively communicate them, nuance them, and even transform them at the service of the gospel to be portrayed.[29]

As if this were not enough, the situation is even greatly exacerbated with regard to the evangelization of Hispanics *within* the U.S. culture. For one thing, North Americans and many Hispanic Americans are convinced that the North American culture is superior to the Hispanic American cultures. Furthermore, the immigrant tradition of the United States creates a strong impetus to assimilate the dominant culture in everything except external details. Finally,

the U.S. is a dominant culture which is based on a strongly individualistic worldview which does not mention much less practice
a worldview of solidarity.

One must then be amazed at the realization that Deck, despite
the gargantuan and complex problems that are involved, audaciously presents a solution. It involves a critique of American culture, in such works as John Kavanaugh's *Following Christ in a
Consumer Society*, stressing that the "effective proclamation of the
gospel occurs when the prevailing cultural values are critiqued and
new, more radical gospel values are proposed in place of them."[30]
Equally important is the recognition that to try to evangelize
Hispanics *without* tackling the larger issue of evangelizing the
North American culture is impossible and counterproductive, "rem-
iniscent of Penelope's spinning her loom by day only to undo her
weaving by night." As Deck expresses it:

> The first elements of an explicit gospel-based critique of North
> American culture are available in two outstanding pastoral letters
> issued by the U.S. bishops, one on war and peace, the other on the
> U.S. economy in 1983 and 1986 respectively. . . . These pastoral let-
> ters, however, have not been communicated or engaged to any
> considerable extent by the leadership in Hispanic ministry
> throughout the country. Pastoral planning based on an awareness
> of the interrelationship between the dominant, North American
> Catholic milieu and the Hispanic Catholic milieu has not been
> pursued. The end result is a fragmented, confused, and ultimately
> ineffective evangelization of culture.[31]

Two corollaries of this excerpt include a critique of Hispanic culture—and much more of the necessary studies in this regard—and a
greater clarity with regard to the gospel of Jesus Christ. Thus, the final problem is that "discerning the core message of the gospel from
the relative, historically and culturally determined expressions of
that core is formidable indeed."[32] Though fraught with challenging
tasks, Deck's liberation theology and overall pastoral plan provide
the best road map so far for the continuing pilgrimage of Hispanic
people in the United States of America—and at the same time for
the pilgrimage of all Americans toward the transformation of their
own nation into a community of justice and solidarity.

Equal Justice Under Law?

In addition to inculturation, Deck envisions transformative action and structural change as the second critical element in the mission of evangelization. He quotes the famous statement of the Extraordinary Synod of Bishops in 1971 that "[a]ction on behalf of justice and participation in the transformation of the world fully appears to us as a constitutive dimension of the preaching of the Gospel or . . . of the Church's mission for the redemption of the human race and its liberation from every oppressive situation."[33] Deck clarifies the church's political dimension (which is often maligned by its own adherents) by stating that its "mission in inextricably involved in political action, not in a narrow, partisan sense but in the sense of participation in the processes by which public policy is formulated and carried out."[34] He admits that, if Christians inordinately concentrate on inculturation and personal conversion, they can contribute to a privatized or individualistic version of the gospel; on the other hand, though, those who focus on social justice can also focus too much on this issue, while confusing ideologies with the faith or manipulating people's beliefs for partisan or oppressive purposes. Let us hope that many more Hispanics will be successful in navigating their voyage between that strait of Scylla and Charybdis.

Concerning the Hispanic community, there exists a strong awareness of the bishops, clergy, and laity *in their documents* for social justice as well as for both personal and social conversion. Despite these pastoral letters and other communications, however, Deck is convinced "that neither the evangelization of culture nor action on behalf of justice has become the characteristic mark of the church's pastoral activity with Hispanics in the U.S. Rather, the predominant pastoral approach reflects the priorities of the period before Vatican II, namely, the maintenance of the people's traditional Catholicism through the dispensation of the sacraments."[35]

What accounts for this strange abyss between the theory and the practice of Hispanic Americans with regard to social justice? Deck holds that Hispanics, especially the Mexicans, possess a deeply religious, sacramental worldview rooted in pre-Columban times, and in Spanish medieval and baroque spiritualities. It includes a cyclic view of history, or lack of history, in sharp contrast to a biblical, linear view, which is completely open to conversion and social transformation. Consequently, ". . . the notion persists that everything remains the same and will be repeated. The task of humans is to shield themselves the best they can from fate. The *mestizo* peoples of Mexico seldom have experienced 'progress,' that is, substantial change in the socioeconomic and political conditions of oppression that have been their lot from time immemorial."[36]

It must also be kept in mind that the Latin church had a history of close alliance with the ruling classes, and opted for the *ancien régime* when Latin America achieved its independence in the early nineteenth century. Thus, ". . . the church and its ministers have been tainted by the errors and sins of the past related to their role in defending their status quo, the rich and the powerful, those autocrats and caudillos of which Latin American history is full."[37]

Again, because of the numbers of Latinos who are of Mexican descent, the author stresses centuries of oppression and manipulations that have birthed a profound cynicism regarding politics:

> The revolution of 1910 was no insignificant *coup d'état*. It was a major upheaval in which more than a million Mexicans died. . . . By the 1940s it became clear that the revolution had failed. Perhaps no other people in Latin America have had such a bitter and disillusioning experience of revolution. Hence it stands to reason that Mexicans should be cautious, if not skeptical, about revolutionary plans.[38]

This skepticism therefore applied also to Marxist utopias and to leftist rhetoric from the single ruling party. Furthermore, it applied to relations with the United States, for "there is considerable awareness in Mexico about the very serious harm, the injustices, violence, disregard of human rights, discrimination, prejudice, and arbitrariness that has characterized U.S.-Mexican relations since the beginning. . . .the United States is truly the principal foreign enemy that Mexico has had in this century."[39] From this has come the proverb or bitter joke: "Poor Mexico—so far from God and so close to the United States!" Finally, there exists in Mexico a notable absence of foreign missionaries, who could be bolder in preaching social justice because they could always appeal to their embassy or home countries to protect them, while the local clergy has nowhere to turn in disputes with their own government.

On a more general level, the author maintains that Catholic social teaching does not provide a *positive* vision for the future, since it has criticized—often caustically—both liberal capitalism and socialism, *without* proposing an alternative, the amorphous "third way." Because of this, Deck concludes that "the thrust toward structural change as a content of evangelization has remained vague and elusive in the context of injustice in Mexico and other Latin American nations."[40]

With regard to the United States, the bishops and clergy paid little attention to the criticisms against liberal capitalism, which have resounded again and again in papal social teaching, but they have communicated to their people the absolute necessity of a crusade against Communism. This stunted social analysis is hardly in favor of structural change, but buttresses the conventional wisdom that the U.S. is basically a just society, with faults that can be overcome by fine tuning in the economy and polity. Deck rises to the attack on this attitude: "Even worse, such an omission reinforces the perception—not justified by the documents—that anticommunism is a higher priority than the transformation of the global economic order. The result of all this is that there is little or no interest in the development of a critical consciousness regarding social, political, and economic structures among North American Catholics, *including Hispanics*."[41]

Deck follows the lead of Juan Luis Segundo that some ideology or ideologies is necessary for policies and strategies for social change. But the key question is whether these ideologies are tested in the fire of social teaching and the lens of the gospel "which contributes something new and altogether unexpected to the often fixed, absolutized, and sinful perspectives provided by the prevailing ideologies of left or right." Thus the magisterium and the gospel bring the faith into their equation and so are "critical of systemic visions rooted in either the *philosophical* materialism of collectivism and certain forms of socialism or of the *practical* materialism characteristic of capitalism."[42]

Deck also warns the church to avoid manipulation by the left or right (or center, where most Americans comfortably reside) and by all means to evade the loss of its own independence. He is blunt about how to achieve this: "Hence the importance of the people of God seeing themselves as a universal community rooted in local contexts and historical moments but never totally identified with one people, race, economic system, ideology or nation. Such a position undoubtedly leads to tension. Popular movements rooted in powerful ideologies and nationalisms tend to demand a total allegiance."[43] Once again, without a critical sense and the promotion of social, political, and economic change, all efforts at evangelizing the Hispanic and Anglo peoples of the U.S. will become futile and even counter-productive.

In all of this, Deck appears to believe that there is a package or "deposit" of gospel values that are clear to everyone and only need to be applied to modern societies in order to achieve a Christian inculturation. Can we overlook the fact that the incredibly changing world technosocieties of today are light years away from a backwater, largely rural province of the Roman empire where Jesus lived? Do we not have to, in the Spirit of Jesus, create new values, more creative ideologies, and more imaginative policies for Anglo, Hispanic, and all the world's cultures? My response is yes to both questions.

Secularization and Popular Religion

The third and fourth key issues—secularization and modernity, and popular religion—are the subjects of fierce debate and an enormous literature. Deck analyzes these themes in a very nuanced and compressed manner, and I will present only some of the highlights that appear most significant for both Anglo and Hispanic cultures.

The first highlight concerns the distinction between premodern and modern cultures or societies. First of all, let us look at the premodern or nonmodern society: "There is a clear-cut pattern of behavior and social organization, an holistic attitude toward life in its physical-material and spiritual dimensions. This society is hierarchically structured and characterized by continuity and permanence. It is closer to nature and has developed less control over it."[44]

Modern society, however, is the exact opposite of this, and the United States is a perfect model of it: "It is basically fragmented and egalitarian. It is distanced from nature and ecology by science and technology. There is a preference for democratic approaches in modern culture. In the modern society, science—not religion or myth—provides the majority of answers, and there is a movement away from transcendent views of God and humanity toward more immanence."[45]

This clash of two cultures is of extreme importance for the evangelization of U.S. Hispanics, most of whom come from a premodern culture. Both systems contain various aspects of the teachings of the gospel, and other characteristics of the exact opposite. This is further complicated by a contemporary discovery of the *postmodern* period, or postmodernity, which concentrates on the severe crisis of science, technology, and the myth of progress and liberation from all forms of slavery.

What should be the approach to evangelization and inculturation as we gaze at these and many other possible variables? It cannot be achieved by retreating into the easier and more secure past, and it should not be "a way of assimilating Hispanics into an American Catholic mainstream that is inexorably drying up." Once again, Deck provides an answer that is bold but expressed in very general terms:

> . . . it must be a process whereby persons and communities of Hispanic origin are provided a gospel message that is understandable and accessible yet challenging and relevant to the postmodern period coming into view. The failure to discover this new way of being Catholic and North American is the result of a dichotomous approach to evangelization in which the Anglo church goes its way and the Hispanic church goes its. The timely evangelization of U.S. culture depends upon there being a prolonged, serious dialogue between the two. *That dialogue, however, has not yet occurred to the extent justified by the reality of the massive Hispanic presence.*[46]

As regards popular religion, Deck discusses the theories of the Argentine theologian, Juan Carlos Scannone, and the Indian writer,

Raimundo Panikkar. Without entering into this conversation, certain characteristics of popular religion should be noted. At one point, Deck points out that popular religion has an important role to play in promoting liberation from oppressive material conditions, because "popular religiosity is one of the more powerful *cultural resistance*" and has been "a special sphere of power that thrives and prospers even in persecution or especially in persecution."[47] Furthermore, it is religious at its very core, as the Puebla Document expressed it: ". . . the religiosity of the people is a storehouse of values that offers the answers of Christian wisdom to the great questions of life."[48] Finally, it must be kept in mind that, since inculturation of the gospel has already taken place in popular culture and religion, what one is trying to achieve is a species of reculturation. "If these tenets are true," Deck continues, ". . . the pastoral practice of many priests and other ministers in the United States must be revised." And thus he concludes:

> In an immigrant nation like the United States . . . the evangelization of culture becomes extremely complicated. For it must take into account both the cultural nucleus of the mother culture as well as that of the new (receiving) culture. At *this* point of mutual contact, the gospel message must be brought to bear through dialogue, evaluation, and critical consciousness. The goal is a new way of being church in an Hispanic and North American milieu that is in gestation.[49]

Finally, it should be emphasized that Deck does not believe that creating a Latin American Catholic subculture is a real option, since it is clear that Hispanic Americans are being assimilated with great rapidity into mainstream of U.S. Catholicism.

Praxis Makes Perfect

In the final chapter of *The Second Wave*, Deck engages in what all the liberation theologies point toward, and that is praxis, the continuous dialectic of theory and practice, which he calls "searching for pastoral objectives and strategies." With his accustomed clarity, he combines a critique of present pastoral objectives and strategies, while briefly and persuasively presenting his own positive vision for the future. The following, then, are the most frequently cited objectives for Hispanic ministry, which are often explicit and at times implicit: 1) sacramentalization, 2) conscientization and empowerment, 3) the formation and nurture of base ecclesial communities (BECs), 4) parish renewal, 5) the promotion of strong and ongoing conversions, 6) the formation of lay leadership, 7) youth ministry, and 8) coordinated pastoral planning *(pastoral de conjunto)*.

First of all, *celebrating the sacraments* is of course a basic objective, and this openness to the sacred is fundamental to evangelization, in spite of the strong cultural tide toward secularization in the North American milieu. It should also be noted, however, that "there is some discomfort with the degree and extent to which this kind of sacramentalization absorbs the energies of the Church's pastoral ministers," and that "energies that are expended in providing this service may effectively eliminate other options and objectives in pastoral service."[50]

Nevertheless, Deck concludes that "the persistent premodern tendencies of Hispanic, especially Mexican, Catholicism are not a problem; rather, those institutions are part of the solution," and that "Hispanic communities in the United States, precisely because they are still grounded in premodern sensibilities, are key players in the elaboration of a postmodern Catholicism."[51] This kind of support for popular religion should also entail repercussions in the efforts at conscientization and in the struggle for justice.

The second objective is concerned with *conscientization*, or consciousness-raising, *and empowerment,* ideas that have been disseminated on the world scene by the Brazilian educator, Paulo Freire. They refer to the process by which marginalized people have become aware of the reality in which they are living and have entered into activities to change or overcome the oppressive situations they encounter. This inevitably leads to politicization of the people, a questioning of the status quo, and opposition from governments (Freire himself has been exiled by a number of countries in Latin America).

In the context of the United States, a similar approach, "community organizing," was created by activist and theorist Saul Alinsky.[52] His approach was in some ways more conservative than Freire's, emphasizing criteria and techniques to achieve very specific goals. Deck also places great stress on the importance of "advocacy" communities in achieving social justice, for example, in providing legal help for refugees or undocumented workers:

> Their "underground" status, inability to communicate effectively in English, and lack of political experience make it necessary for others to speak on their behalf. This aspect of advocacy, however, is always somewhat problematic in that it is obviously better for people to speak for themselves than depend on others. A certain paternalism toward the poor and the powerless can sometimes insinuate itself in these kinds of situations.[53]

The third strategy concerns the creation and nurture of *base ecclesial communities* (BECs; in some countries BCCs for "basic Christian communities"), which were developed in the 1950s in Brazil, then spread to other Latin American countries, Africa, Asia, and the United States and Canada. In a careful study of the existing data on the BECs in the U.S., Deck concludes that they are not as widespread as some enthusiasts seem to believe.[54] He is convinced, though, that they are uniquely appropriate for effective evangelization and are a model for all U.S. pastoral strategies: ". . . it is in the context of a community and mutual support that the gospel message can take roots in a people. In the impersonal and somewhat isolated context of the large urban parish, it is impossible to create the conditions needed for evangelization. . . . That is why these communities continue to receive a great deal of attention among Hispanic Catholic leaders in the United States."[55]

This brings us to the fourth strategy, *the parish,* which Deck asserts is the backbone of the U.S. church and also the critical location where Hispanics will come into contact with the gospel. Mere business as usual there, however, must be supplemented in other ways, and the author lavishes special praise on the RENEW process that has been adopted by numerous American parishes. "No other process or movement," he states, "has succeeded in initiating as many ongoing small faith-sharing communities in the United States among Anglo American or Hispanic communities. They number in the thousands." It may be helpful here to sketch the characteristics of this movement:

In this process the effort to establish ongoing small faith-sharing communities is integrated into a broader process of parish and diocesan renewal. . . . Considerable time is given to articulating a clear, simple, and up-to-date theology of evangelization adequate to the systematic renewal of all aspects of church life: liturgy, preaching, prayer, service, and even decision making. The process is expressed in terms of sound biblical theology and takes as its point of departure the Second Vatican Council, never moving too far beyond its theological and disciplinary parameters.[56]

The next strategy, an emphasis on *ongoing conversion,* is often linked with the *cursillo* movement, which is a brief but intense retreat for lay people and which was established in Spain soon after the end of the Second Vatican Council. Deck observes that this has a special appeal to second and third generation Mexican Americans, or Chicanos, because they have an experience of confusion and rejection: "They are not totally accepted by their parents because they are 'different,' nor are they accepted by the new culture for similar reasons."[57] A profound experience of God's unconditional love in the *cursillo* aids them in strengthening their identity and acceptance by others, which is the first stage of conversion.

The author describes also the *ongoing* conversion: "The conversion experience personalizes the faith and provides a foundation *other than custom and tradition* for Christian life. That foundation is an adult, personal encounter with Jesus Christ mediated in a new way through the dynamics of a weekend retreat or prayer group."[58] He further defines the ongoing conversion not as something miraculous but as a progressive change where there "are strong moments of conversion experience deeply felt."[59] Deck concludes his treatment by strongly endorsing an evaluation of "every movement, organization, agency, catechetical, liturgical, educational, and social program of the church among Hispanics in terms of the five stages of conversion and the magisterium's complete concept of evangelization which those levels of conversion complement."[60]

With regard to formation in leadership, the author notes that the very word "leader" is somewhat problematic for Hispanics, since in their native countries they have been accustomed to dictators and rigid hierarchies. A study of Mexican parents recently disclosed that one of the least important qualities to be promoted in children was leadership training. Despite many difficulties, however, Deck insists that leadership training "is essential, a form of ministry whereby the life of the Christian community is structured, and takes on form and substance."

Another, more basic, point is the "frustration among Hispanic laity due to the resistance of some priests and bishops to allowing the laity to truly function as leaders. . . . There continues to be considerable concern about the sincerity and seriousness of the call for lay leadership when sometimes those leaders are not accepted by the hierarchical ministers and their role is minimized, ignored or eliminated."[61] Clearly, there is an urgent need at this point to reflect upon and clarify the very *meaning of ministry*—for both the ordained and non-ordained.

With respect to *youth ministry*, the seventh strategy, it is first of all essential to realize that the Hispanic population is the youngest of any ethnic group in the U.S. (43 percent under the age of 25); therefore, youth has to be given more attention than is given to any other Catholic group. Deck places great emphasis again on the difference between Anglo and Hispanic cultures: "In the Anglo-American context the socioeconomic and cultural pressures are on prolonging the period of youth, while in the Hispanic context they are on shortening the period of youth. Consequently it becomes difficult to relate youth ministry as it is conceived and practiced in Anglo American and middle-class environments with the needs of Hispanic youth, especially the immigrant youth."[62]

Perhaps the most important point that the author makes in this strategy is with regard to Anglo education, where, he says, "the point is that comforting youth rather than challenging them became the function of youth ministry."[63] Here he quotes Michael Warren to the effect that the most urgent need of youth ministry for both Anglos and Hispanics is *politicization*, and also Gregory Baum who insists that it "is necessary to uncover the myths and illusions in which society brings up young people to disguise from them the inequality, the injustice, exploitation, and violence that characterize the present age. Faith is here first a critique of culture."[64]

Deck summarizes a youth program thus:

... youth ministry must be integrated into all the other ministries in some manner through sound pastoral planning. Given the urgent pastoral, sociopolitical, and economic needs of Hispanics and their youthfulness, finally, a vigorous youth ministry must take as its point of departure the Church's understanding of evangelization. It must challenge youth to a change of heart and to struggle for change of unjust structures.[65]

The final strategy, *organized pastoral planning,* was one of the many significant results of the Medellín conference of Latin American bishops in 1968. It is described by the Secretariat for Hispanic Affairs as ". . . co-responsible ministry involving co-ordination among pastoral agents of all the elements of pastoral life, and the structures of the same in view of a common goal: the Kingdom of God."[66]

A very important point that Deck calls attention to is that pastoral planning in the United States usually has a strong pragmatic approach, and is not generally concerned with *transformative* action. This is quite different from the structural analyses of the Latin America *pastoral de conjunto,* which Deck appears to prefer: "Pastoral planning, therefore, in the context of the U. S. Hispanics and other marginated groups promotes a critique of the status quo and stresses evangelization as struggle for socioeconomic and political change."[67]

The author ends with a description of the teamwork that is essential for the success of any pastoral planning:

The planning is coordinated and reflects a commitment to co-responsible action on the part of all those concerned in the process. In an atmosphere of rigid authoritarianism such a climate simply cannot exist. Dialogue, the give and take of vigorous discussion, and a certain level of pluralism are indispensable elements in *pastoral de conjunto.* Finding the path for that creative revision of priorities and means while simultaneously affirming the hierarchical qualities of the church is not easy.[68]

In a brief conclusion, the author bluntly notes that while his book has tried to attend to the concrete needs of Hispanics it was hindered by three sets of circumstances. The first was a lack of serious social analyses on the Hispanics in terms of their relationships to the church. Surprisingly, the second hindrance was the very word, "Hispanic," which was inadequate to cover so many diverse communities. And, in a parting shot at Anglo theologians, "the lack of theologians and theological studies that take the concrete existence of U.S. Hispanics as their point of departure."[69] Deck also hopes his own book will advance a critical dialogue with open discussion and controversy. His final words should be imprinted indelibly on all those who are concerned with the future of the Catholic church in America: "The important thing is that Hispanic ministry be recognized as one of the most crucial elements of the U.S. church's life as it enters the twenty-first century. Much needs to be done if the response to this monumental challenge is to be at once intelligent, loving, and effective."[70]

MUJERISTA THEOLOGY

One of the most glaring omissions in the book of Allan Figueroa Deck is his failure to study and to integrate *Hispanic women* and indeed Hispanic feminists into his otherwise excellent volume. Only on the last page of his book does he advert to the fact that important issues have been omitted, such as "the role of Hispanic women in the forging of the new U.S. Catholic." Then, with a large dose of paternalism if not patriarchy, he expresses his hope "that Hispanic women will take the issues and points raised here and critique them from their unique perspectives."[71] A better suggestion might have been to have the women produce their own reflections on their own experience as Hispanic women, and then to invite Deck and other males, Anglo or Hispanic, to ponder *their* conclusions. As if this were not enough, Deck also confesses that he has treated the critical role of the family for Hispanics "only tangentially," and that a "rigorous concept of family and data clarifying Hispanic family concerns ought to figure prominently in *future studies*."[72] But certainly *some* data could have been used to focus on the crucial role of the family in Hispanic culture; this is a serious lacuna in an otherwise carefully researched volume.

The Method of *Mujeristas*

At this point, then, I wish to listen to and reflect upon the writings of two Hispanic women, Ada María Isasi-Díaz and Yolanda Tarango, especially their carefully researched and thoughtfully written book, *Hispanic Women, Prophetic Voice in the Church: Toward a Hispanic Women's Liberation Theology.*[73] My major effort will be to hear and understand their experience as U.S. Hispanics, women struggling to balance and to integrate two very different cultures. Also *mujerista* is similar to the term "womanist" discussed in the previous chapter on black theology for women. It came into frequent use, to my knowledge, from an article by Ms. Isasi-Díaz entitled "Mujeristas: A Name of Our Own."[74]

The two women are quite direct in their understanding of theology:

> Our lived experience has pointed us in the direction of being theologians. We see no conflict in being both theologians and activists; this follows our understanding of the intrinsic unity between what has been classically referred to as systematic theology and moral theology or ethics. This will become obvious as we clarify what it means for us to *do* theology.[75]

Another important aspect is their predilection for a *communal* process in theology, whereas male theologians usually prefer to shine as distinct stars in the theological firmament. The ones, moreover, who are engaged with them in the struggle for liberation are their primary audience, dialogue partners, and community of accountability.

Although they are deeply committed Catholics, the women are quite blunt in their recognition of that institution as playing a powerful role in their oppression, since it sanctifies patriarchy in society by being itself patriarchal. On the other hand, if "the church were to denounce patriarchy, it would be an important moment in the process of the liberation of women."[76]

Another important stress by the two authors is placed upon the cultural differences between Hispanic women and men, which are largely based on the sexism of both Anglo and Hispanic cultures. They also view themselves as victims of classism or economic oppression as well as ethnic or racist discrimination. The authors describe it thus: "This coming together of oppressions does not mean that we suffer two, or at times three, different kinds of oppression. It is rather a compounding into one multilayered oppression."[77]

Hispanic women's liberation theology, as seen in the subtitle of their book, ties together feminist theology, cultural theology, and liberation theology. "These three perspectives," the women state, "intertwine to form a whole; they critique and challenge each other, they inform each other. Hispanic women's liberation theology is more than the sum of its parts; it is a synthesis that gives birth to new elements, to a new reality."[78]

As regards Hispanic *culture*, the authors stress the importance of the African American and Amerindian threads, and the need for them and their religiosity. It is very interesting to note that their critique is directed against feminism and Latin American liberation theology, elements of which we are striving to identify in this book:

> This insistence critiques the racism/ethnic prejudice to which feminism and Latin American Liberation Theology seem to be prone. Both have failed to take into consideration the experiences and understandings of racial/ethnic persons. At best, feminism in the United States and Latin American Liberation Theology have attempted to adapt and incorporate into their movements the racial/ethnic understandings that *they* consider important. However, neither of them have been willing to accept the contributions of racial/ethnic persons as intrinsic elements of their theologies.[79]

This is a very trenchant and important critique, and a much more serious dialogue should be initiated and continually developed between the *mujeristas* and white U.S. feminists as well as with Latin American theologians, who are overwhelmingly male.

The *feminist* perspective, moreover, in *mujerista* theology stresses personal experience as the starting point of the process of liberation and thus of doing theology. It also believes it has key elements to contribute to methodology, such as the rejection of any form of the dualism and hierarchy to be found in classical theology: "Both are constructs of patriarchy and, in rejecting them, feminism critiques the sexism in both Latin American and other Third World Liberation Theologies as well as the sexism in Hispanic culture."[80]

Finally, the *liberation* approach of Hispanic women provides insistence on real liberation, conscientization, and the social, political, and economic aspects of all forms of oppression. Furthermore, it "critiques the elitism often present in feminism and denounces the tendencies of Hispanics to lose themselves in the Anglo world, to buy into its dominant culture, to seek an individualistic way out of oppression."[81]

A New Vision of Authority

One of the most important questions that Isasi-Díaz and Tarango have experienced while writing their book is the subject of *authority*. As part of their method, then, the authors state clearly and succinctly in three theses what is truly authoritative in the experience of Hispanic women.

1. The first thesis states that "the sense of security that authority has given us all is found not in what others say, but in struggling to be self-defining." This recalls the conscientization process of Paulo Freire, as well as the priority of conscience in ethical decisions.

2. The next thesis elaborates on the self-defining struggle: "Right and wrong are evaluated/defined in terms of the common good; that is why orthopraxis and not orthodoxy is key. The common good of Hispanic women cannot be defined apart from the common good of other communities of struggle."

3. Perhaps the most significant thesis is the third: "Scripture and Christian tradition are not rejected but rather seen through the lens of Hispanic women's experience. What is rejected is the patriarchal institutional lens of the church as the only or most important normative lens."[82] This is an important statement, for it clarifies what is often overlooked, namely, that every theologian, consciously or unconsciously, chooses topics and illustrations from scripture and tradition that are congenial to his or her experience.

Another key aspect of method was developed after a great deal of consultation and thought, namely, to transcribe verbatim the actual words of Hispanic women as a first step:

Hispanic Women's experiences and how they understand those experiences are at the core of Hispanic Women's Liberation Theology. That is why Hispanic Women's voices, their very own words, are at the heart of this book. Therefore, we have purposefully dedicated at least half of this book to recording their words verbatim. The rest—the analytical chapters—are complementary, suggestive, and understandable only in view of this verbatim material.[83]

Still another important methodological question concerns *objectivity*. The authors state firmly that they "do not believe objectivity is a value; we question its feasibility. Because we believe that nothing escapes historical conditioning, subjectivity is a day-to-day reality."[84] Therefore, the women clearly identify their own subjectivity and compare it with that of others who are in the community of struggle. Objectivity, on the other hand, is defined as "openness to others' history and to the critical claims that history bears and also the ability to learn from others' historical experience." At the same time, they voice their hope that their theology "will always be a 'passionate language' because our survival is indeed at stake."[85] The two women fittingly conclude their prologue by referring to a virtue that is often overlooked: "Joy is an intrinsic part of the work for justice and peace. Joy is an expression of hope, which gives a most important spark to our struggle. As a joyful community we express our belief in the presence of the divine among us and in us, a presence that pushes us on because, in our being fulfilled, divinity is fully revealed."[86]

Praxis and Survival

At this point, I will present some further features of *mujerista* theology. In Chapter 1 the authors provide more ideas on praxis and theology: "Because Hispanic Women's Liberation Theology is praxis, it demands three very clear and concrete commitments: to *do* theology; to do theology from a *specific* perspective; to do theology from a specific perspective *as a communal process*."[87]

The *doing* of theology requires that it be freed from the exclusive grip of the academy, and understood as concerned with the problems of human existence and not just beliefs. "To do theology," they

assert, "is to validate and uphold the lived experience of the oppressed, since the dominant cultures and countries not only deny its
validity, but even question its very existence."

To do theology from a *specific* perspective requires that one clearly identify the daily struggles of those who are doing it. There are
many theologies and the singular word "theology" is "acceptable
only as a heuristic device that provides a 'space' in which the different theologies can meet to discuss their commonalities and differences in order to deepen their understandings."[88]

Finally, to do theology as a *communal process* is based on three
main reasons. First, since theology is based on personal experience,
it must also share the experience of the community, lest it lapse into
solipsism. Second, theology is an intrinsic aspect of the action of liberation, and therefore must be communal just as liberating action is
communal. And third, the community is one of the all-pervasive realities in Hispanic culture:

> *La comunidad* is the immediate reality within which Hispanics find
> their personal identities and function. In concrete terms, the sense
> of community revolves around the *familia* (family) and the *barrio,
> barriada* (neighborhood). Certain aspects of the *iglesia* (church)
> also provide an important focus for the development and main-
> tenance of the sense of community among Hispanics.[89]

All of these elements are especially important in establishing a distinct communal identity against the dominant Anglo culture of the
United States.

An important feature of the book, moreover, is devoted to dialogue with Hispanic women of very diverse backgrounds, in order
to reach a better understanding of their lived experience, whether
existential, religious, or cultural. Isasi-Díaz and Tarango emphasize
throughout their book that the major concern and all-embracing
concern of Hispanic women is *survival*: "Survival starts with sus-
taining the physical life, but it does not end there; being or not being has to do with the social dimension of life. Hispanic women
need bread, but they also need to celebrate. Today they need a roof
over their heads, but they also need to have possibilities of a better
future for themselves and their children."[90]

In their constant struggle for survival, there is a great need for praxis, for the kind of action that helps them with their struggle. As a result, they show esteem for religious functions or beliefs insofar as they produce actions that help them to survive: "Whether these religious understandings and beliefs are sanctioned by the 'proper' church authorities is irrelevant to Hispanic Women."

The authors move on to state that Hispanic women are deeply religious, but it is a specific type of Christianity which is made up of Amerindian and African beliefs as well as Christian ones. Hispanic theology deals with these two religious strands the same as Hispanic women do: "It takes from each of them what is life-giving, what is important for the struggle for survival, and leaves aside what is not relevant or is harmful."[91]

Also, although the Bible is not rejected, it is not given much attention, because it is not part of the daily experience of struggle for the women. Somewhat surprising, too, "a noticeable number of Hispanic women either do not believe that Jesus was divine, or they do not consider him or his divinity something meaningful in their lives."[92] The question immediately arises, then, as to whether the women are really Christians. The authors reply that the popular religiosity of Hispanic women is not antithetical to the core gospel message of justice and love and, on the other hand, syncretism has always been part of Christianity from the beginning.

It seems apparent to me, however, that a deeper evangelization is possible and even necessary for these women. And this has actually occurred throughout Latin America by the creation of base Christian communities and conscientization, whereby thousands of peasants, women and men, have learned to esteem the Bible as well as to accept the centrality of Jesus Christ in the Christian religion.

In summary, then, I have already mentioned the complete absence of Hispanic women and Hispanic feminists in the book of Allan Figueroa Deck, so much so that the *The Second Wave* might rather have been titled *The Second Half-Wave*. In a future edition, I sincerely hope the ideas and contributions of *mujeristas* will be profoundly integrated into all five chapters of Deck's very valuable book, and not relegated to the final chapter or to footnotes.

Furthermore, so that a genuine dialogue among Hispanics may

continue to flourish and reach new heights, the Hispanic women might take up Deck's suggestion that they should critique the "issue and points" that he raised in his book. It should, however, be reciprocated by Deck entering the dialogue to *listen to* and to critique the "issues and points" that have been raised by Hispanic feminists such as María Pilar Aquino, Ada María Isasi-Díaz, and Yolanda Tarango.

Like all Hispanics, the *mujeristas* are daily confronted by the need to straddle or juggle *two cultures*, the Hispanic and the Anglo. Obviously, they are confronting a situation that is challenging and creative, but at the same time continually threatening and disorienting. From this shaky perch they must continue to dialogue with and critique U.S. feminism and Latin American theology for their "racism/ethnic prejudice," as the two women theologians have stated above.

Let me end by emphasizing positively and very strongly that the dialogue and critique must not be allowed to degenerate into quarrels and rancor, but rather be the occasion of constant growth as well as the stimulation of ideas and praxis in all partners of the dialogue. Here I refer to those in this chapter as well as all the liberation theologies around the world. I hope that this book will deepen and strengthen their bonds, their "liberation network," in order to advance the kingdom preached by Jesus of Nazareth and to inflame the hunger and thirst for global justice throughout our common home, Earth.

QUESTIONS FOR REFLECTION AND DISCUSSION

1. The Hispanic people in the United States are now creating their own study centers and theological organizations. Are you in favor of these? Will they divide the Catholic church? Are you or your friends acquainted with Hispanics?

2. In a bold move, Allan Figueroa Deck states that the very core of the challenge to Hispanic ministry is the evangelization of North America itself, and of its materialism, individualism, and hedonism. Do you think that this can be achieved, considering the enormous wealth and power of the United States?

3. In his social analysis, Deck adopts a method called "investigation and participative action," and moves beyond American functionalism and Marxism. Describe these three methods and provide your own choice for social analysis.

4. In Deck's North American liberation theology, he emphasizes four key issues that dominate the book: 1) evangelization, 2) social justice, 3) secularization, and 4) popular Catholicism and religiosity. Which of these do you consider the most important? Can you think of any issues that might be more urgent?

5. Deck delineates "two poles" within evangelization. Which does he proclaim as the more important for Hispanic liberation theology? Which one would you choose? Why?

6. The core of Deck's evangelization stresses that the gospel occurs when the cultural values are critiqued and more radical gospel values are proposed in place of them.

Could this be possible when the reigning cultural U.S. values are so powerful throughout the world? What steps could be taken at the present time?

7. A very important outline of eight objectives for Hispanic ministry is presented by Deck (pages 144-150). Which of the objectives do you think are the most important? Why? Are there other objectives that are overlooked?

8. Describe some of the specific "stresses" or "aspects" of the theologies of Ada María Isasi-Díaz and Yolanda Tarango. What is their major critique of U.S. feminists and Latin American liberation theology? Do you agree with these critiques or not?

9. The *mujeristas* believe that authority is one of the most important questions in their book. What are the three theses they propose that state clearly what is truly authoritative?

Do you agree with this new vision of authority? Or do you see weaknesses in their proposal?

SUGGESTED READINGS

Costa, Orlando E. *Liberating News: A Theology of Contextual Evangelization.* Grand Rapids: Eerdmans, 1989.

Deck, Allan Figueroa, ed. *Frontiers of Hispanic Theology in the United States.* Maryknoll, NY: Orbis Books, 1992.

Elizondo, Virgilio. *The Future Is Mestizo: Life Where Cultures Meet.* Bloomington, IN: Meyer Stone, 1988.

Goizueta, Roberto. *Foundations of Theology: An Hispanic-American Perspective.* Maryknoll, NY: Orbis Books, 1994.

González, Justo L. *Mañana: Christian Theology from an Hispanic Perspective.* Nashville: Abingdon, 1988.

Guerrero, Andrés G. *A Chicano Theology.* Maryknoll, NY: Orbis Books, 1987.

Isasi-Díaz, Ada María. *En la Lucha/In the Struggle: An Hispanic Women's Liberation Theology.* Minneapolis: Fortress, 1993.

Pérez, Arturo. *Popular Catholicism: A Hispanic Perspective.* Washington, DC: Pastoral Press, 1988.

Recinos, Harold J. *Hear the Cry! A Latino Pastor Challenges the Church.* Louisville: Westminster/John Knox, 1989.

Sandoval, Moises. *On the Move: A History of the Hispanic Church in the United States.* Maryknoll, NY: Orbis Books, 1988.

Stevens Arroyo, Antonio. *Prophets Denied Honor. An Anthology of the Hispanic Church of the United States.* Maryknoll, NY: Orbis Books, 1980.

Villafañe, Eldín. *The Liberating Spirit: Towards an Hispanic American Pentecostal Social Ethic.* Lanham, MD: University Press of America: 1992.

CHAPTER FIVE

THE AGONY OF AFRICA

African Liberation Theology

The black church will succeed to be a servant of liberation when it responds creatively to the process of liberation, when the black church becomes accountable to the black community. . . . The black church becomes relevant to the process of liberation when it rejects its distorted white image and its theological foundations which support the status quo and discovers its liberating task exemplified in the life of Jesus Christ.

Bonganjalo Goba
An Agenda for Black Theology 65

It goes without saying that, along with formulating a relevant christology, women would also need to be on the alert, and to be critical of any "versions" of christology that would be inimical to their cause. They would have to reject, like others before them, any christology that smirks of sexism, or that functions to entrench lopsided gender relations. Only in so doing would African women be able confidently to confess Christ as their liberator, as a partisan in their search for emancipation.

Teresa M. Hinga
The Will to Arise: Women, Tradition, and the Church in Africa 192

In short, Black Theology is a theology of liberation *par excellence* which issues a passionate call for all people to be free. To be sure, Black Theology is addressed to the oppressed Black people, but it hopes that Whites too will hear its message and therefore be saved and liberated from the tendency to oppress, so that they could become reconciled to their fellows as free selves.

Simon Maimela
Proclaim Freedom to My People 70

THE REASON FOR THE TITLE OF THIS chapter, *The Agony of Africa*, may be discerned by some comments from a recent book on preparations for the twenty-first century.[1] The author describes the quandary of Africa: "Recent reports upon the continent's plight are extraordinarily gloomy, describing Africa as a 'human and environmental disaster area,' as 'moribund,' 'marginalized,' and 'peripheral to the rest of the world,' and as having so many intractable problems that some foreign development experts are abandoning it to work elsewhere."[2] He proceeds to point out that Africa's economy is in a far worse condition now than it was at the time of independence and asserts that "the most startling illustration of its plight is the fact that 'excluding South Africa, the nations of sub-Saharan Africa with their 450 million people have a total GDP [Gross Domestic Product] less than that of Belgium's 11 million people'; in fact, the entire continent generates roughly 1 percent of world GDP."[3]

If we compare this performance with another part of the third world, that is, East Asia, the conclusions are also bleak. In 1965, sub-Saharan Africa produced *0.4 percent* of world trade in manufactures, which is an important key to economic health. In the same year, the Asian NIEs (Newly Industrialized Economies) had a share of 1.5 percent in world trade in manufactures. By 1986, however, sub-Saharan Africa had lapsed to *0.2 percent* of manufactures, while the "Asian tigers" had escalated astonishingly to 8.5 percent of world manufactures. In the same time frame, then, the African share of manufactures decreased by 50 percent, while the East Asian countries increased their share by over 560 percent. These startling figures are crucial to understanding the context of liberation theology in Africa.

BÉNÉZET BUJO

One of the pioneers in the search for a truly African theology is Fr. Bénézet Bujo, a diocesan priest from Zaire, Africa. At this writing, he holds the chair of moral theology at Freiburg, Switzerland, and is a prolific writer in all areas of theology. My comments will include the origins of African theology, and also a framework for such a theology. His major work, in my opinion, is *African Theology in Its Social Context*,[4] which will be my major resource for African theology.

Background to Theology

In a preface to his book, Bujo provides a brief question that resonates like a symphonic theme throughout the volume: *"In which way can Jesus Christ be an African among the Africans according to their own religious experience?"*[5] This approach to christology, he continues, will also lead to a truly African ecclesiology, with all its charisms and rights. At the same time, the author modestly admits that his work is only a beginning, to provide material for more profound reflection.

In his introduction, Bujo points out that there are two tendencies or approaches in African theology at the present time. The first tendency exclusively emphasizes the cultural heritage of Africa, while it ignores the contemporary African context. This approach has received a number of criticisms, especially that it culminates in a bourgeois Christianity, and also that it has been the baneful result of an African inferiority complex with regard to Western culture.

The second tendency is more complex. A distinction must be made from the beginning between the "Black Theology" of South Africa, and the liberation theology that has arisen in various forms in the rest of Africa. South African theologians have established a close affiliation with the black theology of the United States (see Chapter Three of this book), which emphasizes the question of racial discrimination and the need to establish a just society for all. On the other hand, the preoccupation of the liberation theology group is the struggle against dictatorships and domination of all kinds.

As regards Bujo's own position, he opts for the second position, *provided* that African culture is included in the analysis, and refers to his approach as an "African theology in a social context." He also insists that the "whole tradition of Black Africa treats religion as something essentially liberating. This dimension of liberation persists through all social, political and economic changes."[6]

A Panoramic View

It will be helpful at this point to provide an overall perspective of Bujo's theology. He divides his work into two major areas, a long discussion of the preliminaries and origins of an African theology (Part One), and a systematic study of the elements of such a theology (Part Two). Furthermore, Part One concentrates on three areas: 1) the liberating dimension in *traditional* African society and culture; 2) the impact of the colonial period and the arrival of foreign missionaries on these traditional elements; and 3) the influence of African secular authors and theologians, leading to the birth of an African theology.

Part Two also provides a three-part structure with regard to a systematic African theology. First, it analyzes the theology of the ancestors as a starting point for a new christology, that is, Jesus understood as the Proto-Ancestor. Second, it uses the ancestors as a starting point for a new ecclesiology as well as a new christological-eucharistic vision of the church. Finally, the third section discusses two consequences of the new christology-ecclesiology, that is, 1) a spirituality of marriage in Africa, and 2) pastoral care for the dying in an African context with the support of the clan community. In discussing all of this, I will concentrate on the theological statements of Bujo, and treat the many cultural elements only in their relation to theological understanding.

The Birth of African Theology

In Part One, a major liberating element in traditional African society is that God is the source of all *life*, and that life itself maintains a privileged place in the ancestor cult. As Bujo explains it:

Long before the arrival of any missionaries, most of the tribes of Africa worshipped one God and God alone. The novelty of Christianity for Africans did not consist of its proclamation of one God, but rather in the more complete and definitive proclamation of that one God, whom Africa already knew, and who is also the

God of Jesus Christ. It showed more clearly than the African tradition was able to, how this one God wishes to be, and can be in fact, better known and loved.[7]

This life is understood to exist above all in the ancestor cults, where Africans seek an increase in the life-force, which is present to the mystical body of themselves and of their ancestors. This relationship to the ancestors contains both eschatological and salvational elements. Bujo describes this in a succinct paragraph:

> Salvation is the concern of both the living and the dead members of society, for all affect each other and depend upon each other. The dead can only be happy when they live on in the affectionate remembrance of the living; nevertheless, they are stronger than the living on whom they exercise a decisive influence, since the living cannot hope even to survive unless they render due honour to their dead and continue faithfully along the track laid down by them.[8]

These key concepts will appear again later on as essential girders in Bujo's theological structure. Bujo then presents many details on various rites, such as funeral rites, initiation rites, hunting ceremonies, and others, and also devotes attention to the African ethic, which revolves around God, life and taking life, sexuality, transmission of property, and the abomination of lying.[9]

In a historical section, Bujo summarizes the crimes of the colonizers, and devotes special attention to the deeds and misdeeds of the foreign missionaries. "It is hardly an exaggeration," he states, "to say that the missionaries adopted an attitude of blanket condemnation of African culture in all its aspects. African converts were required to turn their backs on the whole of their tradition and the whole of their culture."[10] The quintessence of this approach was the belief that African names were unworthy of the Christian faith and must be rejected, so that Africans had to adopt the names of foreigners. The sad thing about this was that Africans were inculturated to accept the foreign titles, and even condemned their traditional names as pagan. Bujo is almost mocking when he writes:

The Roman breviary, divided into the four seasons of spring, summer, autumn and winter was simply placed ready-made into the hands of the African clergy, for whom such seasons had no meaning. Africans learned Christmas carols full of references to snow and frost. The Holy Eucharist is still celebrated with bread and wine, although the ordinary African Christians have no idea what wine is and cannot imagine how it can bring them into a closer relationship with Christ.[11]

This brainwashing by the entire colonial system, it must be noted, was first opposed by secular authors, and it was only later that the theologians would follow in their footsteps.

The Impact of *"Négritude"*

The secular African writers who rose up to oppose the cultural destruction of Africans began with the very important concept of "négritude," or blackness. The three best known authors were Léopold Sédar Senghor, Aimé Césaire, and Léon Contran Damas. These writers had studied together at the Sorbonne in Paris during the 1930s, and they agreed on the essentials of the new movement: "Négritude is an act of faith in Africa, in its past and in its destiny. The three pioneers wanted to think and write as Africans, believing that only in this way could they recover their identity and their freedom."[12]

When Senghor was later attacked on the grounds that *négritude* was merely racism in reverse, he denied this vehemently, and insisted that the people of Africa should break out of their cultural ghetto and join in a universal dialogue with all men and women in the human family. Bujo, however, did note that "there can be no denying that the whole négritude enterprise did involve redefining black people vis-à-vis white people. We can understand why black people felt the need to speak out loudly and clearly, and especially why they gloried in, and thanked God for, those features which were mocked by white men: the shape of the head and nose, the thick lips."[13]

The movement of negritude accomplished its goals and at present has been superseded. Bujo claims that it "never managed to get beyond the stage of an antithesis against colonialism's thesis" and goes so far as to assert that in the present situation of neo-colonialism "the heroes of negritude have not seldom themselves turned into the new oppressors."[14] At any rate, the key question to-day is whether Africans can discover Christian categories in order to advance further than the exponents of negritude.

The First African Theologians

As ironic as it seems, the first African theologian was *not* an African, but rather a Belgian missionary, Rev. Placide Tempels, who worked in the then Belgian Congo (present-day Zaire). An example of his expansive views is as follows:

> Tempels realized that the African quest for life, for fertility (fatherhood and motherhood) in its most comprehensive form, the yearning for communion with other beings, was not an aspiration confined to the Dark Continent. We were dealing here with a fundamental human instinct, common also to Europeans. It went deep into human nature itself, and the uncovering of an African philosophy could therefore help white people too to discover themselves.[15]

Tempels also related his teachings concerning the African "life-force" with the teaching of John the Evangelist that Jesus had come in order to bring life to human beings and to bring it in abundance (Jn 10:10). Although he was a foreigner, Tempels nevertheless came to believe that in "seeking to christianize these peoples, missionaries must put aside their own Western culture, repudiate it even, in order to adapt themselves to their people of adoption. This is the price they must pay in order to win the people to whom they are sent."[16]

During his investigation of African culture, Tempels also founded the Jamaa Movement. In Swahili "jamaa" is the word for "family," and Tempels understood it as a Christian spirituality, "a vital religious experience of the church as a living community of priests and people. It is neither a sect nor a confraternity nor a new movement, but nothing more nor less than the church itself."[17] At any rate, Bujo has no qualms in referring to this foreigner as "the Father of African Theology," who laid the foundations for the legions of

African theologians in the contemporary world.

According to Bujo, moreover, the first *African* theologian was Vincent Mulago, a Catholic priest in the then Belgian Congo. Mulago studied in the Urban University in Rome, and in 1956 published his thesis on community in the Bantu people.[18] Also in 1956 a priest from Rwanda, Alex Kagame, published a book on Bantu philosophy.[19] In the same year, a very influential book was written regarding the urgent questions of black priests in Africa.[20] The well-known missiologist, Robert Schreiter, published his views on the latter book in his foreword to Bujo's volume: "Modern African theology began in 1956 with the publication of *Les Prêtres noirs s'interrogent*. In that volume a group of young African theologians raised questions about how theology was being done in Africa and whether or not things could be different—both theologizing in a more genuinely African way and dealing with topics important to Africans."[21]

I would say that Bujo and not Schreiter is correct regarding the beginning of African theology, since Bujo referred to all the books written in the historic year of 1956. As he expressed it, "with all their limitations, these early African theologians laid foundations which were to be of great importance for the future of Christianity in Africa."[22]

Conflicts and Consensus

In January 1960, a passionate conference on the meaning of "African theology" took place among the faculty of theology of the Louvain University in Kinshasha, capital of Zaire. The major protagonists included the dean, Alfred Vanneste, and a student, Tharcisse Tshibangu, who was later to become an auxiliary bishop in Kinshasha. Tshibangu maintained steadfastly that the Africanization of the church was not merely a question of African personnel, or of reform of the liturgy and of parish structures, but was rather an issue of an African theology working alongside African research in general. As guiding principles, he proposed life-force, symbolism, and intuition, which were essential to Africa's outlook on life, its philosophy of life. Moreover, religion held precedence over all else, and it was the task of missionaries to uncover the "seeds" in the culture that would be a preparation for conversion: "The religious life of the African contained many elements which could be considered as 'latent theological seeds.' If these 'seeds' could be purified, they could be used as 'religious analogues' to illuminate theological problems. At least, they could serve as the foundations of purified African religious categories capable of theological formulation."[23]

Dean Vanneste vigorously counterattacked, insisting that Christianity must maintain a theology that extends to all cultures and all races.[24] The most recent theologians, he insisted, had aimed at a true "universality," just as modern philosophy does. Vanneste also stressed the need to distinguish between theology and pastoral catechesis. Thus, he maintained that "it was not the function of theology to lay down the route which adaptation had to take. Theology operated at a higher level, at the level of the whole church, and method in theology resembled method in the sciences, where apparently useless and quite disinterested research resulted in almost miraculous technical progress."[25]

Vanneste then moved on to a very controversial issue, namely, that Western-educated Africans could not be expected to return to the primitive concepts that they had long outgrown: "Furthermore, society was evolving, and it was more than likely that the African culture of the future would be more like the culture of Europe than that of ancient Africa."[26] Vanneste, it seemed, could not conceive that African culture would be radically different from the future of the culture of Europe.

In a parting shot, he accused African theologians of retreating into their own small world, and relegating themselves to becoming second-rate scholars, if that. The majority of the theologians, however, rejected the arguments of Vanneste and supported the position of Tshibangu. Bujo also saw deficiencies in the work of Tshibangu, in that he "became an official administrator so soon after completing his studies in Louvain that he was unable to pursue further theological research. He was totally taken up with an endless round of journeys, meetings, congresses, continually being asked to give lectures and to write forewords for books."[27]

A Renewal of African Theology?

Responding to this question, Bujo sees two forms of criticism directed toward a renewal of theology in Africa. They have been treated under two theological approaches: 1) theology and African tradition, and 2) inculturation and liberation theology.

With regard to the African tradition, two writers are especially prominent at the present time, John Mbiti and Charles Nyamiti, although there are a number of lesser figures working in this field.[28] Mbiti has concentrated on research on parallels between African concepts and the message of the Bible. Bujo, however, judges that his "effort was admirable, but it cannot be said that the attempt to incarnate Christianity in the African context was a success."[29]

Nyamiti's work provides a much broader perspective, since he systematically analyzes the Catholic dogmatic tradition, comparing it with the concepts of African tradition and also the results of ethnological research.[30] Bujo also has difficulties with Nyamiti's approach: "Indeed he takes the propositions of European scholastic and neo-scholastic thought as his starting point. It is impossible to avoid the impression that Nyamiti simply wants to rebuild the scholastic or neo-scholastic edifice, but using African rather than scholastic or neo-scholastic terminologies."[31]

In opposition to these authors, Bujo prefers an approach that begins by uncovering the key elements of the African culture and the African soul: "Once the African heritage has been clearly understood, then it can be placed alongside the biblical and patristic traditions, and progress will be possible."[32] He admits that many Africans no longer know their traditions and indeed that the African values are gradually disappearing; however, he does not propose a solution for this crucial problem. Or rather he appears to move from theology as such to the more important role of catechesis:

> What Africa needs today is an enlightened catechesis which knows how to distinguish between traditions which are still alive in the hearts of men and women, even if only implicitly, and those which have truly died. The catechesis needs to be able to discriminate so that it may be seen which traditions should be maintained, or perhaps recalled from a kind of cultural limbo into which they may have fallen.[33]

With regard to the second critical area, inculturation and liberation theology, Bujo maintains that it has become far too academic and even irrelevant: "What are we to say of an African theology which never gets beyond the lecture halls of universities and congresses, mostly outside Africa? No one could take seriously a theology which preached the necessity of inculturation, but simply ignored the surrounding social misery."[34]

Of course, Bujo acknowledges that some church groups are active in attempting to alleviate the terrible poverty of Africa. Nevertheless, he insists, "the church of Africa has been a silent church. Personal witness has certainly not been its strong point."[35] Bujo declares further that the hierarchy should take the side of the poor, relinquishing their palaces, vacations, expensive cars, and travel expenses from political leaders "which serve only to enslave them to governments and alienate them from the people."[36]

Bujo closes this section somewhat pessimistically when he avers that the failure to incarnate the church in Africa is almost complete. As regards theology, also, there has been a great deal of talk, but it can only be said to have cleared the ground upon which a genuine African theology might be constructed. Obviously, Bujo feels that his own outline of an African theology in Part Two of his book is at least a very promising beginning.

Jesus as Proto-Ancestor

Only in this second part of his book does Bujo move into the arena of systematic theology as such; the previous reflections were important but, in his own term, "preliminaries." This is clear in his first paragraph:

> The incarnation of Christianity in Africa can only come about when it has been shown to the people of that continent that the message of Jesus, far from destroying the liberation which traditional religion sought, provides it with a new, purifying and total stimulus. . . .our task must be to bring together the fundamentals of both Christian faith and the African tradition, so that the Africans may find their own way in the resulting Christianity and feel at home therein.[37]

His first step, therefore, involves reflection on Jesus Christ as the "Proto-Ancestor." To understand this, it is of the utmost importance to understand the role of the ancestors: "The particular words, actions and rituals associated with the ancestors, and with the elders in general, have a deep meaning in the life of the African people. They constitute a rule of conduct for the living, and they must be continually repeated."[38] With this background, Bujo asks,

> . . . could not the recognition of the place which the ancestors and the elders occupy in the life of Africans stimulate theologians to construct something new? In particular, could we not use this cultural phenomenon to find a new "Messianic" title for Jesus Christ and work out a new theological way of speaking of him? I would like to suggest that such a new way of speaking would be to give Jesus the title of "Ancestor Par Excellence," that is, of "Proto-Ancestor."[39]

Bujo places great stress on the historical life and teaching of Jesus of Nazareth and takes pains to stress its similarity with the ancestor ideal. Jesus is, moreover, "not only the African ancestor-ideal in the highest ideal, but one who brought that ideal to an altogether new fulfillment."[40]

To buttress his assertions, Bujo emphasizes that this title of Proto-Ancestor will have far greater significance and existential meaning than *Logos* (Word) or *Kyrios* (Lord), which were found to be meaningful in cultures in the past that are foreign to the culture of Africa. He even goes further, noting that "the African's sensitivity is not touched by [these terms], and of course the modern European or American may be in much the same situation."[41]

Since Bujo's specialty in theology is in the field of moral theology, his next step is to demonstrate that Jesus Christ the Proto-Ancestor also provides a model of morality for African men and women. He lauds "the goal of the absolute commitment of Jesus of Nazareth to the restoration of human dignity. He vigorously defended the rights of the weak, of women, of children, and identified himself with outcasts and sinners."[42] From all of this, the author highlights other elements in African culture that Jesus endorses, such as hospitality, sense of family, and care for the elderly, the orphaned, and the unfortunate.

On the negative side, Bujo is concerned about correcting and complementing traditional African morality, which should not be limited to friends or clan but rather open out to the whole human race: "The history of the Crucified One must be subversive for the customs and practices of both traditional and modern Africa. From the standpoint of tradition, the remembering of Jesus is a challenge to conscience, urging the elimination from life of those mistakes which might be labeled 'the specific errors of African group life.'"[43] For example, Bujo refers to the practice of fertility, which has often turned into an absolute that has brought suffering to childless couples. The practice has also brought discrimination against celibates, and led to scorn and contempt for the celibacy of the priesthood.

Bujo then turns his attention to what he calls "modern African sins" that are disastrous plagues on the continent: "Corruption in public service is holding back human development and human progress in Africa. The same is to be said of the way authority is exercised, and of political takeovers which only means enriching oneself and exploiting the weak."[44] To overcome these plagues, modern Africans should see in Jesus not some tyrant but rather the Proto-Ancestor who left behind a legacy of love and the conquest of inhumanity wherever it occurs. Thus Bujo concludes:

> This new ethic will no longer be limited to the customs of the ancestors but will also have the difficult task of addressing the modern problems of development. At the same time, confrontation with new problems will breathe new life into the ancient customs. Only a theology which takes account of both the traditional and the modern is capable of producing an original and effective model for Christianity in Africa today.[45]

Ancestors and a New Ecclesiology

The second major pillar of Bujo's African theology is the theology of the ancestors as the starting point for a new ecclesiology, which is based on the christology just analyzed and the traditional African understanding of life. The author also emphasizes that the Eucharist must be understood as the very life of the church and the true source of its development: "When we try to construct an ecclesiology from this point of view, we see that the Eucharist as the proto-ancestral meal must be the foundation-stone of a church which is truly African. A church constructed on such a basis can have important prophetic consequences for the whole social and community life of modern Africa."[46] Bujo's model of church also explicitly seeks to be Spirit-centered: "It is this same joyful vital power, uniting Father and Son, and constituting the inner strength of the Trinity, which now creates a new community of initiated 'clan' members."[47]

The Eucharist and a New Ecclesiology

At this point, Bujo emphasizes the need to go beyond theoretical positions and to aim at a conversion process for every level of the church as the People of God. The conversion would entail drawing the practical conclusions that all Christians must adopt in following Jesus the Proto-Ancestor.

The first level is concerned with the clergy, that is, bishops and priests, who obviously have an important role and responsibility in the eucharistic assembly. Bujo warns right from the beginning: "Their position however is not simply one of privilege, bringing honour to the occupants. It is rather a matter of service, of *diakonia*. Bishops and priests are at the service of the ecclesial life."[48] Their responsibility is to transmit the fuller life of Jesus the Proto-Ancestor and even to give their own lives for the sake of their people. Bujo continues:

> A truly eucharistic vision of ministry leads to the destruction of all clericalism and all episcopalism, so to call it, and to the abandonment of the pyramid model of the church in which the laity are treated as mere consumers and in which the proto-ancestral life of the Mystical Body cannot circulate. We cannot speak of "a living Christian community" when the laity are systematically excluded from any part in decision-making in their own Church....[49]

Bujo continues to speak bluntly with regard to the clergy: "A priest or a bishop can turn into a lifelong oppressor of the ecclesial community, effectively dechristianizing it. Priests and bishops act like people who cannot be corrected 'from below,' since their very vices and mistakes are presented as 'holiness' and offered to the people as virtue to be imitated!"[50]

This leads the author to a discussion of class distinctions, which comprise a very serious problem in Africa. The causes of this classism are listed as the bourgeois aspirations of the people, the rule of dictatorships, and colonial influences from abroad. An offshoot of this is the natural temptation to see the priesthood and the episcopacy as stepping stones to advancement in the social order, rather than in terms of transmitting the ancestral life of Jesus. Bujo attacks this temptation by calling for an option for the poor:

> This temptation must be strenuously resisted, and a eucharistic ecclesiology can help by encouraging church leaders really to enter into the sufferings of the poor and oppressed so that they may ease [sic] them in the name of Christ. It is time to do away with a bourgeois Christianity in which the clerical office, in all its degrees, is treated as a source of material benefits, while everyone ignores the misery that dehumanizes the whole society.[51]

The author clarifies this option, insisting that it is not enough to be the voice of the people, but that the clergy must live among the poor and oppressed and *work* for their benefit. Furthermore, they must not be content to give alms to the poor, but also to work for the eradication of poverty.

Bujo emphasizes the crucial importance of this attention to the poor by posing some unambiguous and blunt questions to the clergy:

> How far do the bishops and priests really take the side of the oppressed peasants and seek to protect them against exploiters. . . ? Is our position so clear and so radical that we are willing to sacrifice our precious advantages and privileges when circumstances demand it? If not, we shall become stubborn defenders of our own titles and clerical prerogatives, accomplices in a system which despises the poor, and yet on which we pin all our own hopes for survival.[52]

These and other questions are paramount not only for the clergy, but for all of the inhabitants of the poorest continent in the world, a poverty that continues to sink to ever deeper depths.[53]

The Role of the Pope

Bujo begins by noting that the Petrine ministry has not been a subject of discussion in African theology, but that it is an issue that cannot be avoided, especially in the third world. Once again, he turns to the ancestors and the African understanding of life-force in order to elucidate the problem. He also takes for granted the fact that a privileged position exists for the pope and the church of Rome; what remains to be seen is the meaning of this privilege. Once again, Bujo turns to the African concept of the ancestor and the "heir":

> The Petrine ministry resembles that of the heir in the African tradition. When a son is appointed as his father's heir, he assumes responsibility for increasing the ancestral life-force among the members of the family and in the clan community generally. He must see to the just distribution of the inheritance, but he must also be attentive to all family affairs which contribute to a meaningful life for all.[54]

An example of this is the "eldest son" who receives the inheritance of the family cow, and has the responsibility to use this for the benefit of all; thus, a calf from the cow may be assigned to each of the other sons. The important point is that the eldest son "may not behave in an arbitrary or authoritarian manner, or deny the rights of others."[55]

Bujo suggests that the pope acts as the eldest son, the patriarchal church of Rome is the family cow, and the calves stand for the local churches that have come of age. An important step is that the calves separate from the mother cow and the elder brother, but the elder brother still keeps his position as mediator and is responsible for the other members of the family who lead their own independent paths. Consequently, says Bujo:

> According to this model, an ecclesiology rooted in the African tradition would suggest that the Pope . . . may not interfere in the affairs of the local church in an authoritarian or paternalistic fashion. . . . The Pope is the eldest son, he has the presiding place. But this does not mean that he is a reincarnation of the dead father. He must rather accept that the other brothers too have received the life-force of the same father, and not exercise his

presidency as if he were the only one with a claim on the life-force which is the common inheritance of all.[56]

The author then raises certain questions to be asked of Rome. For example, are the local African churches treated as responsible adults, or are their episcopal conferences under the thumb of the Papal Nuncio, which seems to be the case? Bujo believes that the nuncio "behaves like a ruler and pretends that he represents the Pope in diocesan matters; whereas in reality the local bishop must have more to say in local affairs than the Pope."[57]

Bujo moves from these to another vexed question, the arbitrary appointment of bishops in Africa. Although in Europe, a person of a different culture or language than the people would never be appointed as bishop of a diocese, all over Africa complete strangers have been appointed, so that "the result is almost intolerable tension between the bishop and his new diocese."[58] The author also notes that African bishops do not possess the confidence to protest these appointments, even when such a response is called for. Again, he states frankly that one reason for this is "clearly that such opposition would mean turning off the Roman tap and the consequent drying up of funds."[59] Bujo ends that analysis by stating unambiguously that the task of an African ecclesiology must be "to call upon Rome to incarnate the Petrine ministry in the African tradition. Such an incarnation could constitute a contribution to the discussion about the papacy and could benefit the whole church."[60]

Priests for the People?

The next element in an African ecclesiology concerns the painful issues of the choice and education of candidates for the priesthood. Bujo immediately asserts that current priestly training is still modeled both on the Council of Trent and on the theology and lifestyle of Europe. In such a setting, the very mention of African theology arouses suspicion and fear. Furthermore, isolation in European-style seminaries over the years tends to erase many features of their African culture and religion. How to respond to this situation? Bujo audaciously calls for a complete overhaul of the seminary curriculum and lifestyle:

Biblical interpretation, systematic theology, moral and pastoral theology: all should be connected with the actual situation in Africa. Even the courses in canon law and church history should take that situation as their starting point. On what grounds are Africans still subject to a canon law based on the European-Roman constitution and without any reference to the Black African legal situation? As for church history, it has for centuries been expounded and interpreted by Europeans. It must today be written and taught from the African point of view.[61]

Bujo also proposes that the seminarians live and work with their own people, whether they are located in urban or rural areas. He also focuses on the fact that many "vocations" are based on the need of security and upward mobility, and many seminarians are obsessed with material possessions. "In truth," says Bujo, "in many African countries no citizen is as secure as the priest."[62] To avoid these temptations, the author believes that a Proto-Ancestor theology can bring about a "new spirituality which will prepare seminarians for a future ministry in which they will see themselves not as mercenaries eager for profit, but as shepherds called to give their lives for the sheep."[63] As for priestly celibacy, Bujo argues for two options, a celibate and a married priesthood, especially in view of the great value that African culture bestows on the married state.[64]

The Treasure of Prophecy

Bujo also provides surprising reflections on the urgent need for "genuinely African, non-episcopal religious communities, that is, communities founded by bishops and in a certain way controlled by them."[65] He explains this as follows: "The special prophetic charism of religious orders is that they constitute an 'evangelical' opposition to the institutional bishop-controlled church. The members of a religious order or congregation must be free vis-à-vis the pyramidically-structured church precisely so that they can serve it by their beneficial but radical criticism."[66]

Bujo proceeds further, insisting that the prophetic ministry is not merely directed toward the church community, but must extend to every facet of African life. These communities have a special mission to the millions of Africans who are refugees, shanty-dwellers, and villagers. If necessary, new "African religious orders must be founded to dedicate themselves together to the basic communities of the outcasts and deprived."[67] He explains the urgent need:

> The existence of veritable palaces belonging to pitiless exploiters alongside subhuman slums must be a challenge to the Christian conscience and provoke a healthy shock which will lead to the founding of specific groups to call attention to the multiple problems of African countries. The witness, the commitment, and the criticisms of such groups before an inhuman bourgeoisie would be an invaluable service to modern Africa as it searches for the ancestral life.[68]

Bujo also describes the plight of the villagers, and lists the myriad areas where religious orders could help these people, who are now "helpless victims to persons of power."[69]

Are Missionaries Needed?

Bujo emphasizes that missionaries—whatever countries they come from—are not to be seen as strangers, but as members of the Mystical Body of the Proto-Ancestor: "All belong by right to the clan of the Risen One."[70] At the same time, missionaries have obligations and must act like trustworthy blood brothers and sisters to the people of Africa. Some of them bring with them visions of educating uncivilized people, and others "treat an African diocese like a piece of cake which they can share out as they please without reference to the African clergy."[71]

The author moves on to distinguish three kinds of missionaries:

> Some devote themselves without reserve to the welfare of the local church. These are a small minority, and for the most part they are regarded by their colleagues as a nuisance and even as traitors. A second group, the majority, take refuge in silence and refuse to take sides in current disputes. . . . A third group behaves unashamedly like masters and are concerned only with the interests of their own religious family. They have a wide audience and alienate the local people.[72]

Bujo also notes that some mission congregations seem to want to stay indefinitely even if their contributions are no longer needed. Others occupy important posts that could be turned over to the local clergy, but do not train Africa successors "on the grounds that no one is competent to succeed them."[73] Missionaries, he contends, also recommend candidates for the episcopate who will favor the mission organizations, so that they will continue to have a secure base and permanent home in Africa. Little heed, then, is paid to the desires and needs of the local churches in the selection of bishops. Bujo once again presents a prophetic alternative to this situation:

> Missionaries must stop behaving like neo-colonialist bosses. They must be, not oppressors, but liberators, who bring good news. If they are to win a welcome for their message, they must study deeply the culture of their new homeland and seek a truly fraternal relationship with the local people. Only then can their word really take flesh and contribute to the advance of the proto-ancestral life, and only then can we have a truly African church.[74]

Role of the People

It is quite obvious to all that the vast majority of the members of the church are the laity, with a minuscule number of priests and bishops who exist to serve this people of God. Bujo, unfortunately, is quite negative in his remarks to lay persons, expressing an outlook for the future that carries more darkness than light. He first cautions that the great African virtue of hospitality ought not to be abused and even changed into a form of parasitism. He is even more incensed regarding the somber state of solidarity in Africa:

> The real meaning of African solidarity is to be found in the building up of the ancestral Mystical Body. Today however this solidarity is wrongly understood, and it becomes an instrument of oppression. People in influential positions use their power to procure exclusive privileges for their own kinspeople and clan community at the expense of outsiders. It often happens that doctors are only interested in their relatives, and may demand exorbitant bribes from people they know. Politicians may channel development to their native villages or districts when other areas are in much greater need.[75]

Bujo does not hesitate to designate these and other similar situations as a cancer eating at the heart of Africa. He retrieves the ancestral African tradition of the importance of the clan community, but also emphasizes that "members of the clan were expected to concern themselves unreservedly also with strangers, for these too had the right to increase of life."[76] This wider perspective of a vastly enlarged clan, however, also entails more profound and radical demands:

> We Africans should be ashamed of waiting for more highly-organized countries to help our suffering neighbors when we could quite often come to their rescue ourselves. We do not seem to feel any sympathy for our suffering fellow-Africans who are oppressed by Marxism, capitalism, racism, imperialism, and so many other "isms." South Africa may be cited in this connection. We were accomplices in apartheid by our silence, and by leaving protests to Europeans and North Americans.[77]

Thus, Africans are exhorted to live in solidarity with all the suffering peoples of the world, including Asia and Latin America. One person among the Africans, moreover, who has a special responsibility for solidarity is the chief, the bearer of a very ancient tradition. Bujo insists that the chiefs "must exercise their authority, not for their own benefit, but for the sake of all. The chief has no right to operate as a kind of lone ruler, apart from the people."[78]

Happily, Bujo concludes this discussion of the laity on a more positive note: "The role of the ordinary people is indispensable in building up the church in Africa. The leaders of this ecclesial community should make use of a suitable catechesis to help everyone to play their part in bringing about a community which is ever more creative and forward looking, and a vibrant sign of the health of the eucharistic assembly."[79]

Bujo adds a very brief epilogue to his book that expresses very well his vision of liberation theology for the future well-being of all of Africa. It also serves as an epilogue for the first part of this chapter:

> I have tried to show that African religion is essentially liberating, and that any modern African Christian theology must therefore

also have as its goal the liberation of men and women. I am not speaking of some sociopolitical liberation to be achieved by revolution, but of liberation in all its aspects, personal as well as social. People should enjoy fullness of life at every level.[80]

MERCY AMBA ODUYOYE

The name Mercy Amba Oduyoye may not be a household name in Europe or North America, but she does enjoy a wide following in her native Ghana, in the rest of Africa, and in many nations throughout the third world. A Methodist, she holds degrees in theology from the universities of Ghana and Cambridge, and is at present a senior lecturer in theology at the University of Abadan in Nigeria. Her book, *Hearing and Knowing: Theological Reflections on Christianity in Africa,*[81] continues to draw much attention in the areas just mentioned.

My intention is to emphasize some of her most significant reflections, especially with regard to the experiences of an African woman in what is unquestionably a sexist society. Her book is divided into two main parts, the first of which is concerned with the history of African theology, the missionary movement, Africa's primal religions, and African culture and indigenization. The second part is devoted to themes in African theology, including feminism, and this is where I will devote most of my attention.

An Introduction to African Theology

Oduyoye's introduction is important, since she is not attempting to produce a systematic theology in the manner that is expected in Western universities. First of all, her primary interest is not in Western theology, but in "third world theology," which she describes as an unhappy but unavoidable term. Her description:

> Combined with the word 'theology,' 'Third World' refers to the world of the oppressed, the majority of whom are to be found in the areas defined by the Bandung [Indonesia] Conference of 1955 . . . Because of the intricate nature of oppression throughout the world, the concept of the Third World is not limited by geography. All who do theology from the context of injustice and unrighteousness—feminists, for example—find themselves at home among the Third World theologians.[82]

All of these theologies, therefore, are considered to be "contextual" theologies.

The author also notes that liberation had arrived in mission lands, followed by the liberation of Christian theology. Not until the publication of Juan Luis Segundo's *The Liberation of Theology* (1975),[83] however, was this position publicly proclaimed. This is how Oduyoye describes the result: "Theologians throughout the world who felt a call to speak more relevantly to their age and generation freed themselves from dogmatic and systematic theology and focused on life issues. Instead of telling people what questions to ask and then furnishing them with answers, theologians began to listen to the questions people were asking and then to seek the answers."[84] Segundo's book, says Oduyoye, along with Gustavo Gutiérrez's book, *A Theology of Liberation*,[85] and the 1968 Medellín conference "brought what was christened 'liberation theology' to the attention of theologians and theological schools everywhere."

Another key event for the author was the founding of the Ecumenical Association of Third World Theologians (EATWOT), which was born in Africa in August 1976, at Dar es Salaam, Tanzania, with theologians in attendance from Asia, Latin America, and the United States, as well as many from Africa.[86] The author is somewhat jubilant that whatever "names they call themselves or may be called by others, those who have joined the Ecumenical Association of Third World Theologians can all be called 'liberation theologians.'"[87]

An African View of Missions

In a later chapter, Oduyoye offers penetrating observations of the contributions and effects of the foreign missionary movement on the continent of Africa. For instance, she notes that in the 1940s and 1950s when she was growing up, the missionaries' understanding of Christian fellowship meant living with other Europeans, so that "the isolation of the missionaries from the people was more noticeable even than that of the British administrators."[88] She takes a dim view also to the missionaries' "theology of soul-snatching"[89] and their motto of "come apart and be saved" in Christian enclaves.[90]

Odudoye also berates the missionaries for their individualistic approach to evangelization:

The emphasis . . . was on the individual—the context from which people came did not matter and was not seriously studied. The story of the missions is built on personalities, not on the transformation of communities. To effect the transformation of a whole community demanded more knowledge of the community than the missionaries could muster or their collaborators were willing to supply.[91]

Another very important area that the author delineates at some length is the practice of racism, which she sees as the central problem between Africans and Europeans and as firmly based on the twin pillars of ethnocentricity and greed. Closely related to this was a great deal of injustice; Africans were allowed to oppose their tribal leaders, but it was strictly forbidden to protest any actions of the missionaries or even the colonial administrators. As a result:

Although the missionaries were involved in charitable acts, they were not equipped ideologically to protest, let alone work against, incipient racism, exploitation, and other injustices. They accepted the structure of Western society as a given and did philanthropic work to alleviate the results of its injustices. A good deal of this benevolence was performed in the condescending manner we now call paternalism.[92]

After this, Odudoye devotes a chapter to traditional, or as she prefers, "primal" African religions and another chapter to such concepts as acculturation, inculturation, and "indigenization." She prefers the latter phrase despite its aroma of jargon and people's general resistance to neologisms. She also adopts the description of the Nigerian theologian, I.B. Idowu, who argues forcefully that "the church should bear the unmistakable stamp of the fact that it is the church of God in Nigeria, not an outreach or colony of Rome, Canterbury, or Westminster Central Hall, London, or the vested interest of some European or American missionary board."[93]

Feminism in Africa

In the second part of Oduyoye's book on the themes of African theology, I believe the most important contribution is the chapter on "Feminism: A Precondition for a Christian Anthropology." As a beginning, the author provides a number of descriptions of feminism in Africa. Two of these appear to have a special significance on different levels of meaning. On the first plane, she states that feminism "is the proclamation that women's experience should become an integral part of what goes into the definition of being human. It highlights the woman's world and her worldview as she struggles side by side with the man to realize her full potential as a human being."[94] On another level she insists that

> feminism is not the word of the female; it is the word of all who are conscious of the true nature of the human community as a mixture of those things, values, roles, and temperaments that we divide into feminine and masculine. . . . Feminism then is part of the whole movement liberating the human community from entrenched attitudes and structures that can only operate if dichotomies and hierarchies are maintained.[95]

Oduyoye moves next to the experience of African women, and it is undeniable that they are dominated by the role of mother or of wife. Recent research indicates that even university students today in Africa understand themselves and are viewed by males as "somehow owned by their men who support them. They are economic attachments to men; their wage is seen as supplementary."[96]

Another researcher's study of the traditional rites for Ndemba girls demonstrates that African women are usually treated as "pawns in sociopolitical games and alliances."[97] As for traditional religious rituals, women are forbidden to participate and are sometimes even prohibited from viewing the rites. A rather shocking statement is that the "supposed ritual impurity of the menstruating woman places her outside full involvement in religious ritual for almost half her life."[98]

Furthermore, concerning economic matters, both men and women are expected to be economically productive; however, immediate differences crop up repeatedly: ". . . women make pots that are sold cheaply; men make ritual objects and carvings that are highly regarded. Men plant yams; women have to be content with cassava. The technology that modifies men's labor is welcomed; the modernization of women's work is viewed with suspicion—*African women*

still grind and pound the hours away."[99] These and many other examples are ample evidence that the continent of Africa has been
charged and convicted of the all-pervasive social sin of sexism.

With regard to women's experiences in the churches, one African
woman expressed her feelings very succinctly: "The women are
very much concerned about the church, but the church is not so
much concerned about women."[100] Oduyoye also reveals her own
experience: "The church has never tried to build a dynamic community of women and men. I never cease to be astonished at how
little we have actually accomplished in community-building."[101]
With regard to the African sisters' congregations, Ancilla Kupalo
emphasizes the tensions between the mother superiors and the bishops, and observes that a recognition of equality and equal responsibility is a long way off. As an example, some bishops believe
that the sisters' obedience must be "like the civil servants who always go wherever they are appointed without questioning, without
consultation."[102]

As for the neuralgic issue of the full ordination of African wom-
en, Oduyoye takes aim at the many ruses, excuses, and red herrings
that abound, for example, "We have deaconesses and that's
enough," or "We don't want to jeopardize Roman Catholic and
Orthodox relationships," and so forth. Women themselves are even
brought up as opponents: "Women themselves don't want to be ordained" and "Women do not like women ministers." The author
concludes: "That women are 'afforded' sufficient room for ministry
was already asserted at the Amsterdam assembly. The question is,
what opportunities? what training? and at what price? Above all,
who decides the limits of these opportunities? The assumptions
upon which these opinions are based have to be challenged."[103]

Oduyoye also provides many other instances of gender stereo-
typing, some of which are quite fascinating. For example, the male
African is programmed never even to think of cooking food for
himself, since nature has given this task to females. Sometimes
problems arise for the man because the society does not have res-
taurants and women are not allowed to touch food at the time of
menstruation. How is the problem solved? The African male resorts
to polygyny, that is, multiple wives, since the different wives will

presumably have their periods at different times of the month.

Another stereotype holds that African women should not be allowed a Western education, because that is not profitable for their families: "She will get married and the benefits that come from the investment will accrue to her husband. That the education will be of benefit to *her as a person* is not considered because only the biological aspect of her Being is important."[104]

Summing up, then, these male/female labels, or stereotypes, are accepted as decreed by God both by individuals and entire communities. Oduyoye attacks these assumptions head on:

> The authority of tradition can only be binding when, upon examination and testing, it is found to be the best we can have at the moment. Feminists (and others who feel their oppression) do not believe that the present order of human relations furthers our ultimate good. Sexist criteria cripple rather than enable, and their tendency to subsume the woman under the man suggests that we believe the needs of the male are more important than those of the whole community.[105]

This line of reasoning leads Oduyoye to the acceptance of our "brokenness" both in the whole society and in the churches. As late as 1980, women were being encouraged not to leave the home, but to "go back to nature" and to "housekeeping." At the same time, the man's absence from home and family is accepted as the normal situation. The author notes that women who object to these relationships are subjected to ridicule. Nevertheless, she perseveres:

> . . . the human personality is fractured into objective and subjective, rational and emotional, and the head is given prominence over the heart. We have thus destroyed the mutuality that must exist in order to evolve an integrated community enriching to all. To work toward such a community requires that we face our brokenness in a realistic manner, but this is resisted by many, both women and men.[106]

In this feminist search for full humanity and community, another crucial issue is the role and source of authority, which needs reexamination: "In what measure or on what basis do we allow the demands of authority, continuity, and stability to shape our potential of turning to good or evil? Where or what is the ultimate source of authority for the human community and how do we receive this authority?"[107] In the final paragraph of her chapter on feminism, despite all of the problems, ignorance, hatred, and apathy, Mercy Amba Oduyoye utters her own lyrical ode to the future:

> Happy and responsible in my being human and female, I shall be able to live a life in doxology in the human community, glorifying God for the gifts I receive in others and for the possibility I have of giving myself freely for the good of the community while remaining responsible and responsive to God. It is only then that I can say I am fully human.[108]

A Prophet from South Africa

At the end of this chapter, I have divided the lists for further reading into two categories, one concerned specifically with the country of South Africa, and the other that embraces the entire continent of Africa. The importance of the transformations that have occurred in South Africa is known throughout the world and is the object of deep concern for all people committed to that struggle. And, since both whites and blacks in South Africa have struggled for liberation of their country, an enormous literature on liberation theology has developed.

In my opinion, the recent book of John de Gruchy on *Liberating Reformed Theology*[109] is the most significant contribution thus far to a theology of liberation in South Africa, as well as a model and enrichment for churches around the globe. The author is professor of Christian Studies at the University of Cape Town, and has already published a number of books on South African issues.[110]

Since this book contains such a wealth of historical and theological scholarship as well as passionate commitment to his country and his church, I will not try to cover de Gruchy's many theological advances, but will focus on his method and goals. The author locates his own church in the "Reformed tradition" of the church in South Africa, which derives from the Protestant Reformation, especially as it developed in Switzerland under the influence of John Calvin.

He is strongly convinced that liberating Reformed theology is "best understood as a liberating theology that is catholic in its substance, evangelical in principle, and socially engaged and prophetic in its witness. At the same time the title [of the book] intentionally reflects an ambiguity in Reformed theology and the Reformed tradition more broadly. For while they may be liberating in intent, they have also been guilty of legitimating oppression in practice."[111] In order to achieve the liberating potential of Reformed theology and tradition, de Gruchy intends Reformed theology to enter into dialogue with the various liberation theologies present in the contemporary church.

He admits that it may appear strange to go back to sixteenth century Calvinism in seeking to create a theology for contemporary South Africa. "They are," he says, "literally worlds apart. . . . Why not simply be a liberation theologian?"[112] In response, de Gruchy emphasizes that every Christian belongs to some historical tradition, and must work within that tradition with all its strengths and weaknesses. A second reason for "liberating" his or her tradition "is the fact that for many black Reformed Christians in South Africa, Reformed theology, and especially Calvinism, is regarded as in some significant way responsible for their oppression."[113] This profound suspicion simply cannot be ignored, and it is most important to develop the prophetic and liberating aspects of Reformed theology.

De Gruchy then moves on to some astonishing comments about liberation theology and the Reformed tradition. The research that he undertook in the writings of Calvin and Karl Barth led him to the

> discovery of the extent to which the reforming labors of Calvin in sixteenth-century Geneva correspond to those of some Catholic theologians, not least Catholic liberation theologians in Latin America. On reflection this should not be surprising because Calvin was not a Protestant in the first instance but a Catholic lay theologian committed to the Catholic church and its witness.[114]

Thus, the author concludes, that as it is possible to be a Catholic liberation theologian, so is it possible to be a Reformed liberation theologian.

He also makes a very important point at the end of his introduction, that Reformed theology also has contributions to make to liberation theology. Rightly pointing out that Reformed theology has been around for a much longer time, he emphasizes concerning the latter theology that "whatever its failings, and however much it may need to be liberated from its various forms of captivity, it has both a critical and constructive contribution to make to the liberating and prophetic witness of the church today."[115]

In my view, the most important contribution of de Gruchy is not only that of the Reformed church, although that is extremely significant. Rather, his carefully constructed synthesis provides a model, a paradigm, by which any Christian church and Christian tradition can be renewed and revivified by profound dialogue and creative praxis with the many already existing liberation theologies. De Gruchy is keenly aware of this, as may gleaned from his observation that liberation theology

> is equally challenging to all historic traditions because it radically questions the social location, material interests, and consequences of those traditions and their theologies, and not simply their intentions. In this respect, the Reformed tradition stands together with the other historic traditions under the searchlight of liberation theology's critique.[116]

Although de Gruchy does not expand on this, it seems that the same critique may be applied with equal rigor to the world's many non-Christian religious traditions and their theologies. And, to widen the spaces of the *oikomene* (inhabited Earth) to its widest parameters, liberation theologies can and should impact those secular persons, communities, and nations that are committed to the protection and enhancement of human beings and their habitat with all its species.

At the end of his book, de Gruchy turns to Max Weber and Ernst Troeltsch, who both correctly discerned a kind of "restlessness" in true Calvinism and Reformed theology. It was not a restlessness concerning one's eternal destiny, nor one that comes from a lack of faith, hope, or love, but a restlessness "that derives from a deep concern for the redemption of the world, its liberation from oppression in all its dimensions."[117] Therefore, the Christian, along with others in the churches, is finally one who "is called to respond in faith, active in hope and love, to God's redemptive activity, so that the whole of creation can be liberated by grace from the bondage of sin and oppression and can be restored to full life in Jesus Christ, through the Spirit, to the glory of God."[118]

Reflections

It would be superfluous to attempt to summarize or to evaluate in depth the very articulate visions of Bujo, Oduyoye, and de Gruchy. De Gruchy proposes a profound and integrated revitalization of the Dutch Reformed church in its dialogue with liberation theology, as well as significant contributions to liberation theology. For the immediate future, it would appear that his contribution is the most valuable, since his liberated Dutch Reformed church is a large and influential community, not merely individual theologians and other Christians. It would be most interesting to read an account of that church's influence on the continuous struggles for justice in South Africa.

Perhaps even more difficult than overcoming apartheid is the long march of South Africans toward a truly democratic, multiracial, and stable nation. We may speculate that de Gruchy and his community will devote prodigious energies to these goals for decades ahead; they may also be preparing for oppression and suffering, even to the crown of martyrdom.

Turning to Bujo, he provides a useful sketch of the origins of African theology and a stimulating outline of Africa's "Old Testament" in its religious past. Although he criticizes liberation theology in Africa for indulging in too much speech and too little action, he himself is a genuine liberation theologian. Throughout his book, he sharply criticizes the bishops, the diocesan priests, the missionaries, and the African churches for not devoting themselves to a crusade for social justice for the poor in this teeming, suffering continent. Whether his suggestions for the adoption of Christ the Proto-Ancestor and its accompanying ideas for Africa will be successful seems to me to be dubious; but that must be decided by the Africans themselves.

Mercy Amba Oduyoye also emphasized the need for social justice and the option for the poor. Most poignant for me, however, is her detailed litany of horrors that has accompanied African women over the centuries. To an outsider, this cruel, brutal oppression of women appears to loom as an unconquerable obstacle at the present time. Yet her riveting voice, speaking with the deep candor and anger of the prophet, does give one hope against hope that, just as in my own nation, "we shall overcome some day."

Finally, I return to the beginning of this chapter with the condition of Africa's political economies, as described by Paul Kennedy and many others. Paul Kennedy's last remarks about Africa continue to be ominous: ". . . the coming decade will be critical for Africa. Even a partial recovery would give grounds for hope; on the other hand, a second decade of decline, together with a further surge in population, would result in catastrophe."[119]

As a contrast to Kennedy's view, one of the most momentous events in the entire history of the African Catholic church occurred in April and May 1994, with the First Synod of the bishops of all Africa and Madagascar, which promulgated a "Final Message of the Synod for Africa" on May 6, 1994, which has immense importance.[120]

In that document, the bishops stressed that they "received from Christ himself its profound significance, namely, the synod of resurrection, the synod of life" (#2). They conclude that paragraph by reiterating that they "want to say a word of hope and encouragement to you, family of God in Africa, to you, the family of God all over the world: Christ our hope is alive; we shall live!"

An accompanying motif throughout the entire document is the need for inculturation of the church in Africa. The bishops view their culture as in a serious crisis and "the fundamental need is for prophets to arise and speak in the name of the God of hope for the creation of a new identity. Africa has need of holy prophets" (#15). The synod also gave a great deal of attention to the serious socioeconomic and political problems that plague the continent. In answering these issues they state:

> The Savior has bestowed on us those two great gifts of the kingdom of God which he is in person: justice and peace. The synod

demands greater justice between North and South. There should
be an end to presenting us in a ridiculous and insignificant light
on the world scene after having brought about and maintained a
structural inequality and while upholding unjust terms of trade (#
32).[121]

One last time, the bishops plead for saintly politicians and saintly
heads of state: "They will be men [and women] who love their people to the end and who wish to serve rather than be served. It is
their duty to work for the restoration of dignity to our countries and
to promote brotherhood" (#35).
   I close with their final prayer (#70):

Make of us
the church family of the Father,
the brotherhood of the Son,
the image of the Trinity,
anticipating the reign of God
and working with all for a society
that has God as its builder,
a society of justice and of peace.
Amen!

QUESTIONS FOR REFLECTION AND DISCUSSION

1. Which do you think is more important for the future of Africa,
its traditional heritage or its contemporary context? Provide reasons
for your choice.
   2. From his experiences as an African, Fr. Bujo does not hesitate
to present a strong critique of the foreign missionaries who have
worked in Africa. Do you agree with this, or do you know of positive accomplishments of the missionaries? Have you met and
talked to missionaries?
   3. What is you judgment of the debate in Kinshasha between the
Dean Alfred Vanneste and the student Tharcisse Tshibangu? Were
there elements of truth in the positions of both men? What is your
view?

4. A key element in Fr. Bujo's christology is his emphasis on Jesus' title of "Proto-Ancestor" or "Ancestor par Excellence." Do you think that this will replace the traditional titles? Would it be something similar to the title of "Jesus the Liberator" in Latin America?

5. What is your reaction to Fr. Bujo's call for both a celibate and a married priesthood, especially since the African people have such a high esteem for marriage?

6. Ms. Odudoye as a feminist liberation theologian is shocked at the role of African women as mere pawns and economic attachments to men. What is your opinion of the remedies she proposes for this clearly unjust situation?

7. John de Gruchy sees resemblances in the theology of Calvin in the Dutch Reformed church to the Catholic liberation theologians in Latin America. Have you read about the beliefs of Calvin or met people from the reformed church in the United States? Have you seen any resemblances?

8. Does it seem that John de Gruchy will be successful in his efforts to affect real, profound changes in the Dutch Reformed church? What are your reasons?

9. A "Final Message of the Synod for Africa" was promulgated by the African bishops in their meeting in May 1994. Have you read about this or heard about it from others? From the synopsis of the meeting, do you think it will have much of an impact on the "agony of Africa"?

SUGGESTED READINGS

A. South African Theology

de Gruchy, John W. *Liberating Reformed Theology: A South African Contribution to an Ecumenical Debate.* Grand Rapids: Eerdmans, 1991.

Hopkins, Dwight N. *Black Theology USA and South Africa: Politics, Culture, and Liberation.* Maryknoll, NY: Orbis Books, 1990.

Logan, W. *The Kairos Covenant: Standing with South African Christians.* Chicago: Meyer-Stone, 1986.

Mosala, Itumeleng, and Buti Tlhagale. *The Unquestionable Right to Be Free: Black Theology from South Africa.* Maryknoll, NY: Orbis Books, 1986.

Tutu, Desmond. *Crying in the Wilderness: The Struggle for Justice in South Africa.* Grand Rapids: Eerdmans, 1982.

Villa-Vicencio, Charles. *Between Christ and Caesar.* Grand Rapids: Eerdmans, 1986.

B. African Liberation Theology

Christensen, Thomas G. *An African Tree of Life.* Maryknoll, NY: Orbis Books, 1990.

Dickson, Kwesi. *Theology in Africa.* Maryknoll, NY: Orbis Books, 1992.

Elá, Jean-Marc. *West African Theology.* Maryknoll, NY: Orbis Books, 1990.

Mbiti, John S. *Concepts of God in Africa.* London: SPCK, 1979.

Muzorewa, Gwinway. *The Origins and Development of African Theology.* Maryknoll, NY: Orbis Books, 1985.

Sanneh, Lamin. *West African Christianity: The Religious Impact.* Maryknoll, NY: Orbis Books, 1983.

CHAPTER SIX

THE HEART OF ASIAN RELIGION

Asian Theologies of Liberation

Our task as Indian women is clear—to search for a feminist hermeneutic which will carry all women and the whole church towards becoming a new and living community in Christ.

Aruna Gnanadason (India)
We Dare to Dream: Doing Theology as Asian Women 125

The Bodhisattva [Enlightened Ones, *Kwan-Non* in Japanese] are like well-equipped ambulances, ever ready to come and help. All technological devices are at the command of mercy and concern. . . . Is this not a beautiful image within the Buddhist tradition? It asks us to use our vast technical skills and powers in the service of humanity, not in the destruction of humanity.

Kosuke Koyama (Japan)
Three Mile an Hour God 144

Due to the cultural and religious background, and due to Asia's semifeudal system, Asian people and especially women are generally apathetic to anything political. However, Asian women are now getting involved in political actions that will improve their lives. This is a trend that will grow and have far-reaching consequences. Asians are beginning to realize that to do nothing is to give silent consent to the oppressors to continue doing harm to them.

Christine Tse (China)
With Passion and Compassion:
Third World Women Doing Theology 97-98

THE IMMENSE EXPANSE OF ASIA, WHICH enfolds in its enormity more than half the people of this planet, also possesses a vast panorama of venerable religions. The Asians themselves, I presume, would prefer to designate these ancient beliefs as a dazzling panoply of gifts of the gods, far surpassing the religious riches of the West. In one brief chapter, however, I will not be so bold as to attempt to comprehend these ancient faiths, which legions of brilliant Eastern and Western scholars have scrutinized for many centuries. Instead, I will confine my attention to the major topic of this book, and concentrate on some of the *liberation theologies* that have recently flowered on the fertile soil of Asia. Again, I will be unable to enter dialogue with *all* of these latecomers to the feast, but only with those who in my opinion bear the greatest promise and hope for the future of Asia and planet Earth. The three theologians I have selected have certainly committed themselves to the hunger and thirst after justice, the touchstone of all liberation theologies.

ALOYSIUS PIERIS

A concise biography of Aloysius Pieris is essential for understanding his theology. He was born in 1934 in Ampitiya, Sri Lanka, a nation formerly known as Ceylon. In 1953, he entered the Society of Jesus (or Jesuits), and was ordained a Roman Catholic priest in 1965. From the beginning of his career, he manifested a passionate interest in the relationships between Christianity and Buddhism, which has had a long and venerable tradition in Sri Lanka. To create a bedrock foundation for his life work, he earned a B.A. in Sanskrit and Pali from the University of London in 1961, and an S.T.L. degree (Licentiate in Sacred Theology) from the Pontifical Theological Faculty in Naples in 1966.

Afterward, he encountered much difficulty in further studies in

Buddhism because of the frequent clashes and misunderstandings covering many years that had occurred between the much-esteemed Buddhist monks and the Christian missionaries from the West. He pursued his course, nevertheless, and became the first Christian ever to be awarded a doctoral degree in Buddhist philosophy at the University of Sri Lanka in Colombo. Furthermore, in order to penetrate more profoundly into the deepest heart of Buddhism, he submitted himself to become a disciple at the feet of a Buddhist monk, and became extremely proficient in Buddhist meditation and lifestyle.

At the present time, Pieris is the director of the Tulana Research Center, which is situated north of Colombo. The motivation and goals of this institution are focused on *dialogue* between Buddhists and Christians in three specific areas: 1) the experience of popular religion; 2) philosophical and textual studies; and 3) pastoral reflection in the area of social transformation. He also serves as Professor of Asian Religions at the East Asia Pastoral Institute in Manila, and has taught in universities and seminaries throughout the world, including a course at Union Theological Seminary in New York City.

A Liberation Theologian?

To answer this question expeditiously, I am convinced that Pieris is a liberation theologian, with the caveat that he has also created his own version of liberation theology from his Sri Lankan and Asian experiences, and differs from many of his colleagues in Latin America, Africa, and even in Asia and parts of the first world. These differences have occurred precisely because his *context*, or reality, differs from theirs. Thus, he has presented sharp challenges to these other theologies as well as to the traditional understandings of the Christian faith in the West; however, as a man committed to dialogue, he has also been open to learning from the contexts of other liberation theologians that differ from his.

The inner core of Pieris's Asian liberation theology may be found at the very beginning of his essay on that topic in his book *An Asian Theology of Liberation:*[1]

Any discussion about Asian theology has to move between two poles: the *Third Worldliness* of our continent and its peculiarly *Asian* character. More realistically and precisely, the common denominator linking Asia with the Third World is its overwhelming poverty. The specific character defining Asia within the other poor countries is its multifaceted religiousness. These two inseparable realities constitute in their impenetration what might be designated as the *Asian context*, the matrix of any theology truly Asian.[2]

From this, Pieris concludes that any theology that displays no urgent concern for the poor of Asia, or any theology that attempts to eradicate poverty while ignoring its religious background, are both doomed to failure. But how does this differ from the experiences of other third world nations or continents? The author replies by locating three different characteristics that set out the "religio-cultural" boundary lines of Asia within the third world. These features include: 1) linguistic heterogeneity; 2) integration of cosmic and metacosmic aspects of the religions of Asia; and 3) the existence of non-Christian soteriologies.[3]

Features of Asian Theology

As regards *heterogeneity*, Pieris mentions the seven major linguistic zones in Asia, far more than in any other continent. There is a theological implication here that demonstrates the nuances of Pieris's thought, for he notes that each language is a distinctively different way of "experiencing" reality: "I think it is only partially true to say that religion is an 'experience' of reality, and language its 'expression'; the converse is closer to the truth: *language is the 'experience' of reality and religion is its 'expression.' Religion begins with language.* Would it be wrong to say that language is a *theologia inchoativa*—an incipient theology?"[4]

Pieris holds, therefore, that the task of the Asian theologians is far more complicated than those of his colleagues in Europe and Latin America, where there are Indo-Germanic or Iberian languages that enable them to think, speak, and act along similar lines. Aside from the fact that there are many Amerindians in Latin America who speak different languages, Pieris makes a good case: "It is . . . regrettable that Asians are not able to consult each other's hidden theologies except in a *non-Asian idiom, thus neutralizing the most promising feature in our methodology.*[5] It is regrettable, then, but certainly necessary, that most Asian theologians think, read, and even pray in English.

With regard to the *cosmic* and *metacosmic* elements of Asian religion, they are complementary, with a cosmic religion and a metacosmic soteriology, or system of salvation. The cosmic religion in Asia, as in Oceania and Africa, is often referred to as "animism," but Pieris sees it as a subconscious mechanism to understand the mysteries of life: "These mysteries relate to cosmic forces—heat, fire, winds and cyclones, earth and its quakes, oceans, rains, and floods—which we need and yet fear. Such forces serve as ambivalent symbols of our own subconscious powers, symbols freely employed in ordinary speech and in sacred rites, expressing our deepest yearnings."[6]

This cosmic religion in the Asian continent does not usually appear in its primordial form, but has been domesticated and synthesized into the three metacosmic soteriologies of Hinduism, Buddhism, and to some extent Taoism. The highest good is to be found in a transphenomenal "beyond" that is sought through gnosis, or knowledge, which makes necessary sages and wise men. "Hence," Pieris states, "these metacosmic soteriologies are never found in the abstract 'textual' form but always 'contextualized' within the worldview of the cosmic religion of a given culture, creating a twofold level of religious experience, each level well integrated into the other."[7]

At this point, the author makes a very important statement about his choice of Buddhism as the best way of understanding Asian religiosity:

> If my choice falls on Buddhism, it is not only because I am familiar with it, but even more because it is the one religion that is *pan-Asian* in cultural integration, numerical strength, geographical extension, and political maturity. Though an integral part of Indian heritage . . . it had penetrated every linguistic zone, even the Semitic, for a brief time. In other words, Buddhism is not limited to one language or national group—as in the case of Hinduism and Taoism.[8]

If this is not sufficient reason for choosing Buddhism as the best way of understanding Eastern religiosity, Pieris continues at length, and I will merely list some of his observations on Buddhism: 1) twenty national territories in Asia where Buddhism is the official religion or very influential, 2) the only Asian religion that can boast of Asia-wide and worldwide ecumenical alliances, 3) politically the most resilient Asian religion with a major role to play in the liberation of Asia, and 4) no Asian theology of liberation able to be created without consulting Asian Buddhism.

As a concluding statement on the importance of Buddhism, Pieris asserts:

> Although Buddhism does not exhaust the whole phenomenon of Asian religiousness, it will nevertheless serve as a paradigm to demonstrate how the interplay of cosmic and the metacosmic levels of religious experience give a new point of departure for the politico-social change and technocratic advancement in the very process of Asia's liberation—something that neither Western technocracy nor scientific socialism has sufficiently appreciated, and something that Asian theologies dare not underestimate.[9]

With regard to the overwhelming *presence of non-Christian soteriologies*, this is the most important characteristic of Asian theology and its major difference from Latin American and African theologies. Note that after more than 400 years of evangelization only about three percent of the Asian masses have accepted Christianity. This insignificant minority drops sharply to one and a half percent, if we do not count the Christian nation of the Philippines. This church, Pieris states frankly, has lost its Asian roots, and is now merely a larger version of the Christian communities that were dispersed in the "Asian diaspora." Paradoxically, Pieris envisions this seeming failure as the greatest potential for the creation of a true third world theology that will be radically different from the Latin American and African theologies. He then inserts a statement that is controversial but plausible and very important: "Asia, as circumstances clearly indicate, will *always remain a non-Christian continent.*"[10] Although this situation is ambivalent, to say the least, Pieris insists that it affords immense possibilities for a Christian presence in Asia "by humble participation in the non-Christian experience of liberation."[11]

Theological Perspectives

At this point, Pieris moves on to an effort to absorb from Buddhism what he calls the "Asian style" of being, thinking, and acting. Concentrating on the issue of soteriology, he recalls both the cosmic and metacosmic features in Asian religion that we have just discussed, and points out how these are centered around the *sangha*, or monastic, community, which comprises both the central institution and the spiritual apex of Buddhist society.

The monks serve the cosmic activity of human beings by teaching them the metacosmic goal of perfection, or *arahatta* in the Pali language, which consists in the absence of acquisitiveness and greed, the absence of oppressiveness and hate, and the presence of perfect knowledge. Furthermore, the basic foundation of the *sangha* is the renunciation of wealth and family to embrace poverty; at the same time, the laity support the monks and are "entrusted with the task of advancing material (technological) progress and socio-political well-being."[12] Pieris states that this religious system can best be understood by the bipolarities of 1) wealth and poverty, 2) state and church, and 3) scientific knowledge and spiritual wisdom, which we will now discuss.

With regard to *wealth*, it must be emphasized that its opposite is not poverty; rather, the opposite is acquisitiveness or greed. Consequently, the fundamental concern is not overcoming poverty, but the "struggle against mammon—that undefinable force that organizes itself within every person and among persons to make material wealth antihuman, antireligious, and oppressive."[13] In fact, Christianity's continuing alliance with Mammon, that is, commercialism and colonialism, and its refusal to accept the spirit of the *sangha* was one of the reasons for Christianity's failure in Asia. This policy exists even today, with the emphasis on immense development programs, which force the huge non-Christian majority to become ever more dependent on a tiny Christian minority. The dire consequences follow: "This use of mammon, imposingly and manipulatively present in Asia, is a continuation, albeit in a new way, of the missiology of conquest and power characteristic of the colonial era. When a revolution rises against such establishments, the churches speak of themselves as being persecuted—when in reality they are only being trampled upon, like salt without flavor (Mt 5:13)."[14]

With regard to the monks, wealth remains a constant paradox: the holier and poorer the monk becomes, the more the laity showers him with donations. Of course, this is true of the monasteries as a whole, which are confronted by the same paradoxes, even being defended and pressed with lavish gifts from rulers. We turn now to the relationship between *religion and the state*, which is an essential feature of the Buddhist worldview.

The *sangha*, the monastic community, has never been neutral with regard to political authority, and, especially in Southeast Asia, often has legitimated the state in turn for the same courtesy by the state. On the other hand, the monks have also opposed governments: "This is why it has often suffered both persecution and purification at the hands of the state, but has also at other times initiated political revolutions against the state."[15] Pieris has expressed this concisely: "The dialectics between withdrawal from the world and involvement in the world—or contemplation and action—illustrative of the mutuality between the cosmic and the metacosmic, is nowhere so clearly attested as in the political role that spiritual persons play in a Buddhist culture."[16]

With regard to *scientific knowledge and spiritual wisdom*, Pieris notes the desacralizing process of technology in modern society, which could be interpreted as a needed liberation from religious superstition. However, since technology is deeply ambivalent, its haphazard use could also enslave human beings in the traps of pollution, consumerism, materialism, and many other ills. Pieris points to the way out of these traps:

> It took a wise man in the West—Pope Paul VI—to appeal for reciprocation between the technician busy with scientific progress and the wise person who could guide the technician from a contemplative distance. Thus, the patriarch of the Western church has recognized the need for a bipolarity between secular knowledge and spiritual wisdom. Asia has taught this for centuries in its religious view of material progress.[17]

Pieris's description, then, of what technology should and could be is "an induced cosmic process, which is at once a conscious continuation of biological evolution, and which, like it, becomes humanized only by a metacosmic orientation."[18] In this respect, he observes that "Latin American liberation theology, the *only* valid model of theology for the Third World today, also lacks a perceptive understanding of this monastic ideal." Another quote will be helpful in order to comprehend the difference between these two major schools of liberation theology: "The Asian religious attitude to poverty, even in the context of its march to economic progress, differs from the Latin American attitude as a *psychological* differs from a *sociological* one. In the former, voluntary poverty is a spiritual antidote; in the latter it is a political strategy."[19]

The "Asian Sense"

To accept the "Asian sense" into our Western Christian consciousness, Pieris suggests that we shed our inhibitions and enter into the *third world point of view in general* and the *Asian point of view in particular*. What he is interested in is the Asian style of doing theology, and not so much in its content.

With refreshing candor, Pieris acknowledges that the Asian *church* has no theology, although its host culture is overflowing with all sorts of theology. The church, though, has two imported theologies to choose from: "The first is the classic European theology, which, in its various brands, is officially taught in all major institutions of the Asian church. The second is the Latin American liberation theology, which is also making itself felt in certain circles. These theologies, of course, are diametrically opposed to each other."[20]

The author refers to a so-called breakthrough in European theology in the 1960s proposed by Mark Schoof,[21] but he rejects this interpretation. The achievements of the Europeans, he insists, were "only a mild reform" compared with the achievements of Latin Americans in those years. As Pieris sees it, the "liberationists effected a complete reversal of method. They seem to have done to European theology what Feuerbach did to Hegelian dialectics. They put theology back on its feet. They grounded it on theopraxis."[22] He also goes on to say that, although liberation theology is thoroughly Western, it was thoroughly renewed by its contact with the third world outside of Latin America, especially through the efforts of the Ecumenical Association of Third World Theologians (EATWOT). Finally, the Asians are in agreement with the Latin Americans in holding that liberation theology is not a new theology but a *new method* of doing theology as well as the *correct method* for doing theology anywhere.

Even though he is discussing the "Asian sense" of theology, Pieris makes use of a study by another Jesuit, Jon Sobrino of El Salvador,[23] for a deeper understanding of theological method, but says that he is choosing those aspects that are particularly relevant for Asians. Sobrino holds that Kant liberated *reason* from *dogma,* "whereas the Marxist attempt to free *reality* from *oppression* did not receive theological attention in Europe until the Latin Americans made an issue of it."[24] Furthermore, the Latins employ the social sciences rather than philosophy, in order to *change* and *not merely explain* the world of suffering and injustice, a direction that was not pursued by the Europeans, either Protestant or Catholic.

Thus, there exists a primacy of praxis over theory, and Sobrino insists that spirituality "is not the practical conclusion of theology but the radical involvement with the poor and the oppressed, and this is what creates theology."[25] A third feature is that the following of Jesus involves the way of the cross, which is the basis for all theological knowledge, and that the kingdom grows not progressively but by sharp contradictions and transformations, phenomena he refers to as the "epistemological break."

Fourth, it is not a "theology of development" that is needed, which would merely justify the values of a consumer society, but a "liberation theology" that promotes an asceticism of renunciation and a poverty that rejects greed totally: "What it inculcates is not merely a passive solidarity with the poor in their poverty and oppression, but also a dynamic participation in their struggle for full humanity—indeed, a dynamic following of Christ!"[26]

Finally, the dialectic of grace and liberty is understood as the obligation to use all one's powers to bring about the kingdom, all of which remains the gratuitous gift and grace of God. "This," Pieris asserts, "explains the liberationist's political option for socialism—that is, for a definite social order in which structures are changed radically, even violently, in order to allow every person to be fully human, the assumption being that no one is liberated unless everyone is."[27] In summarizing his position, Pieris emphasizes that "the mutuality of praxis and theory that defines the Asian sense in theology is the missing ingredient in the theology of religions, which its practitioners have uncritically accepted and which hampers their task of acquiring the Asian style."[28]

An Asian Theology

Pieris completes his article by enumerating seven conclusions from his study of Asian liberation theology. The first asserts that Asian theology is a way of doing things, as in the struggles of the people for spiritual and social emancipation. Next, he stresses that in his culture God-talk for its own sake is utter nonsense, and is made relative to God-experience. In the Buddhist paradox, it "is wordlessness that gives every word its meaning."[29] Third, the same harmony exists between *God-experience* and *concern for humanity*, so that one is not prior to the other: "It is . . . the mutuality between wisdom and love, gnosis and agape, *pleroma* [fullness] and *kenosis* [emptying]," or as the Buddhists have put it, between "knowledge that directs us to Nirvana and the compassion that pins us down to the world." For liberation-praxis is at once a withdrawal into the metacosmic and an immersion into the cosmic.[30]

The fourth conclusion mentions the subtlety of the relationship between freedom and authority, since authority does not make external claims and it is "competence to mediate liberation." Fifth, Pieris concludes that the church in Asia must abandon its alliances with power. It "must be humble enough to be baptized in the Jordan of Asian religion and bold enough to be baptized on the cross of Asian poverty. Does not the fear of losing its identity make it lean on Mammon? . . . The theology of power-domination and instrumentalization must give way to a theology of humility, immersion, and participation."

The sixth conclusion is that the search for the Asian face of God can only be successful if we participate in the Asians' own search for it in the "abyss where religion and poverty seem to have the same common source: God, who has declared mammon to be the enemy (Mt 6:24)."[31] Finally, Pieris asks where is the locus of this praxis. He concludes that it is certainly not Christian life within the church in the presence of non-Christians, but rather it is the God-experience of God's people living beyond the church. The author ends with a cryptic and ambiguous statement: "It is among non-Christians that the church is called to lose itself in total participation. That is to say, *theology in Asia is the Christic apocalypse of the non-Christian experiences of liberation.*"[32]

Perspectives on Christology

I take it for granted that any Christian theology must be centered on the person, teaching, and actions of Jesus the Christ, which brings us to a serious reflection on christology. Also, as a background for the discussion on christology in Asia, one must recall that Jesus himself was Asian, and yet "Gautama the Buddha and Muhammad the Prophet are household names in the East, but Jesus the Christ is hardly invoked by the vast majority (over 97 percent) of Asians."[33] How, then, can we explain the fact that the first Asians who listened to Jesus made significant inroads into the West but failed to enter into the many complex cultures of Asia?

Pieris answers this question by noting that the Philippines (an Asian country) did accept Christianity, but it was precisely because none of the other Asian religions had arrived earlier and sunk their roots into that culture. Thus he concludes: "The rapid rate of christianization in South America, contemporary Africa, and Oceania, in contrast to Asia's persistent defiance of the Christian kerygma, confirms my thesis: *The door once closed to Jesus in Asia is the only door that can take him in today, namely, the soteriological nucleus or the liberative core of various religions that have given shape and stability to our cultures.*"[34]

To be sure, Pieris stresses that there is a sinful and enslaving side to Eastern religions as well as the liberating dimension, so that the authentic core of the religion must be discerned from the sinful elements. He uses H. Richard Niebuhr's categories to describe two approaches, the Christ-against-religions school and the Christ-of-religions group. His own contextual approach stresses that "religion and poverty in their coalescence provide both the *cultural* context and the *liberationist* thrust required in any Asian christology. Besides, are they not the two perspectives along which Jesus himself revealed his divine sonship to his first Asian followers?"[35] Pieris also believes that there is a trinitarian or "triune mystery" in many religions which makes up its soteriological core. He then proceeds:

> The significance of speaking of the "Son of God" in such a context depends on the discovery of the *sensitive spot in the Asian heart* where Jesus, by making us retell his story, will find the proper idiom to communicate his unique identity within that tridimensional mystery. This sensitive spot can be recovered by retracing the steps that Jesus himself took in his effort to reveal his person in the Asian context of religion and poverty.[36]

Pieris then points out that Jesus evolved his self-understanding by two prophetic immersions, a first prophetic baptism in the Jordan and his final prophetic baptism on Calvary. Thus, he made a choice at the Jordan to adopt the *"politically dangerous brand of prophetic asceticism"* that John the Baptist had practiced. "It was," he asserts, "when he stepped into the Jordan to identify himself with the religious poor of the countryside and sought initiation under this great Asian guru [John] that he manifested his own salvific role to the people: the lamb/servant of God, the beloved Son (of God), the Word to be heard, the Giver of the Spirit, as the culture of the day phrased it."[37]

The second baptism at Calvary also demonstrated that there could be no authentic religion without taking part in the painful conflicts of poverty, the struggle against Mammon, that led to the cross. If the human event of Jesus is to be manifested unambiguously for Asians, "then that event is, preeminently, the trajectory that *today* links the Jordan of Asian religion with the Calvary of Asian poverty. If this is done, the Asian cultures will open their repertoire of titles, symbols, and formulas to express their new discovery; the Asian church will sing not one but a thousand new canticles to its Spouse and Lord."[38]

At this point, Pieris turns to what he considers the first meaningful christological formula, one that would make sense to Christians and non-Christians alike. Rather surprisingly, he maintains that this formula would be "an authentically Asian church." Equally surprising is his evaluation of the church as it exists now in Asia as an esoteric community, "ranting as it does in the occult language of colonial founders to be understood only by the initiated." Thus, he cries out for an ecclesiological revolution, when the church would enter the baptismal water of Asian religion and would also experience the baptism of passion and death on the cross of Asian poverty. Until this revolution occurs completely, "there will be no Asian christology."[39]

Fortunately, however, the ecclesiastical revolution has already been initiated on the fringes of the church in Asia, where "little laboratories of hope" are struggling to be born and are known as "basic *human* communities," that is, with persons from different religions. Pieris notes ironically that they may appear to be on the fringe, but are truly at the heart of the Asian reality. He describes their earnest efforts "to fuse politics with asceticism, involvement with introspection, class analysis and self-analysis, the Marx *laborare* with the monastic *orare*, a militant repudiation of Mammon with a mystic relationship with Abba their Father has plunged them into the liberative streams of both religion and poverty."[40]

Aside from these communities, who have what the author calls a "participation-explication" to Asian christology, he also calls for a search for the heart of Asian religiosity:

> My suggestion is that non-Christian sages be encouraged to tell *their own* story of Jesus. I am not referring to intellectuals and their "theory of religions. . . ." I speak rather of those *religious* seekers who have opted to be *poor* in their search for the saving truth and who, during their pilgrimage, encounter Jesus within their own soteriological perspectives.[41]

These religious seekers are not a figment of the imagination. Since about 1820, many committed Hindus gave a great deal of reflection to the figure of Jesus, and even included trinitarian speculations in their rudimentary "christologies." What is needed, then, is an in-depth dialogue between the basic human communities and the non-Christian disciples of Christ "trying to retell the story of Jesus to one another in terms of the one, absolute, triune mystery of salvation." [41]

Jesus and the Buddha

We have seen that Pieris completely accepts a theology of liberation for Asia, provided it derives from the context of Asia, which he has summarized as a marriage of profound religiosity and extreme poverty (imposed poverty rather than voluntarily accepted poverty). Also, he views the church ideally as the true presence of God in Asia, that is, a church that follows Christ into a baptism among the poor, and a baptism of suffering and death because of his prophetic/religious commitment.

It seems appropriate at this point, then, to compare the deepest core of both Buddhism and Christianity, and to explore the possibilities of a more profound core-to-core dialogue. As a beginning step, Pieris achieves clarity by pointing out three major obstacles to the dialogue:

> 1) The *language barrier*, which can be overcome with a certain amount of psychological adjustment; 2) the inevitability of a *communio in sacris* [communion in ritual] in a core-to-core dialogue, which implies a new understanding of religions; and finally 3) the most challenging difficulty that arises when Christology is confronted with the competing claims of Buddhology.[42]

The "core" of any religion may be described as the liberating experience that brought it into being and made it available to successive generations by the creation of its own particular means of communication. By this mediation the core experience is able to recreate the *psycho-spiritual* "mood," at the same time transmitting its own particular quality to the *social* and *cultural* manifestations of the religion involved.

In Buddhism, then, this core experience is understood as *gnosis*, or "liberating knowledge," while in Christianity it is clearly manifested as *agape*, or "redemptive love." Each of the experiences is salvific, that is, an act of self-transcendence that profoundly transforms the person who undergoes the experience. But it is of the utmost im-

portance to keep in mind that contrasts and differences exist between the two religions, as is epitomized in the *contemplative* calm of
the *mystic* Buddha beneath the tree of knowledge, and in the *agony*
of the *prophetic* Jesus on the tree of the cross, which reveals the cost
of love.

It is crucial, also, to keep in mind that both the *gnosis* of
Buddhism and the *agape* of Christianity prove to be inadequate
without each other, both for experiencing and expressing our relation to the Source of Liberation, as well as mediating "salvation"
to others. Also, there should be no language barrier, since the
Buddhists recognize the complementarity of *prajna* and *karuna*,
which are the equivalent of the Christian "wisdom" and "love or
compassion." The real "language barrier," then, "is the prejudice
that each party has toward the other's epistemology. More bluntly
said, Christian thinkers are all too often antignostic and Buddhist
intellectuals anti-agapeic, in their 'official' positions."[43]

At this point, Pieris once again boldly proposes four reflections
addressed mainly to Christians that give promise of overcoming the
antipathies just enunciated. First of all, the Christians have a history
of various gnostic aberrations, such as docetism, Manicheism,
Jansenism, quietism, and many others, which serve as an impedi-
ment for the acceptance of Christian gnosis. Pieris does admit that
there is a genuine gnosis, but "the heretical gnoses were only the
embroidery along the orthodox line of Christian gnosis."[44] This also
applies to Buddhist intellectuals, who have experienced pathological deviations and erotic extremism in the affective spiritualities in
many cults and thus developed an aversion to agapeic language.

Next, both Buddhists and Christians have unfortunately been
blissfully ignorant of the positive elements in both religions.
Christians have tended to categorize Buddhism as a "world-
denying asceticism" (to use a Weberian term), whereas that religion's very survival is based on the fact that it was actively involved in movements for social and political change. On the other
hand, Buddhists, as mentioned above, are suspicious of *bhakti* (love
or agape) elements in Buddhism, which they transfer to the basic
theme of agape in Christianity. Pieris waxes eloquent in opposing
this view and calling upon Buddhists

to acquire an unbiased view of agape—namely, that it is a creative force in the history of Christianity—something that transforms rather than enfeebles persons; that it is a kind of love that blooms into justice, bringing peace through the conflict of the cross, raising us from the terra firma of infantile innocence to the insecure heights of spiritual maturity, as the lives of many Christian saints testify.[45]

Pieris's third observation is concerned with genuine and aberrant gnosticism in the two faiths. We have already discussed that theme, and I will turn to his last reflection, which he sees as a summary. Basically, he contends that there is a Christian gnosis that is also agapeic, and a Buddhist agape that continues to be gnostic. Thus, "deep within each one of us there is a Buddhist and a Christian engaged in a profound encounter that each tradition . . . has registered in the articulation of each religion's core experience. What seems impossible . . . has already taken place within Christianity and within Buddhism."[46] If we accept this fact, the major obstacle to a core-to-core dialogue has been overcome. This victory has taken place, however, in theory; the high mountain of praxis has yet to be scaled.

An Asian Spirituality

All of the theologies in the liberation network contain a "spirituality" as an essential element of their understanding of Christianity. This is true even in the cases where the dimension of spirituality is implicit amid the different themes that are treated explicitly. Indeed, a strong case for the latter approach could be justified as more effective and fruitful in the long run, since it avoids the centuries-long *separation* of spirituality from theology and even from the daily activities of a person or community that are living in the Spirit of Jesus. For example, *A Theology of Liberation by* Gustavo Gutiérrez is drenched with spirituality from beginning to end (and only mentioned explicitly in the final pages).[47] Yet this book has been much more effective and influential as a kind of theology/spirituality than Gutiérrez's later books, which are explicitly devoted to spirituality. The same may be said of the works of Jon Sobrino. [48]

At any rate, Pieris also articulates a spirituality of liberation explicitly, even though it is implicit in all his writings. It cannot be called a comprehensive treatment, but it does illustrate a rare capacity to illumine the major, crucial elements of Christian spirituality at a time when many theologians manifest an instinct for the capillary.

From the very beginning, Pieris emphasizes the need to avoid the narrow view of spirituality as merely contemplation, an approach that has appeared in various forms for centuries, "without which 'liturgy' and more especially the Christian 'commitment' to the paschal transformation of the world would be unspiritual."[49] The narrow view of "spiritual life," then, ends up in a triple dichotomy: 1) *liturgy* versus *spirituality*; 2) *spirituality* versus *secular involvement*; and 3) *secular involvement* versus *liturgy*. Pieris insists that "the refusal to see all these three elements as mutually inclusive dimensions of one authentic Christian life creates an insoluble circularity in all the attempts made so far to overcome any 'spiritual crisis,' as will be explained below."

Here, he goes on to stress, liberation theology presents a robust synthesis that identifies the exact point where the three elements intersect; these include: 1) the liturgy of *life*; 2) the theology of the *cross*; and 3) the *historical Jesus* and his humanity. Pieris notes that this framework is not that of any single one of the liberation theologians, but that it reflects his "own personal assessment of the ever-new and yet ever-ancient principles of spirituality that seem to be emerging from the ecclesial life of basic communities in Latin America."[50]

Pieris turns first to the opposition between *liturgy* and *spirituality* on a historical level. He adverts primarily to the teaching of Vatican II's Constitution on the Sacred Liturgy, where the liturgy and especially the Eucharist are referred to as the source and summit (*fons et culmen*) of the whole of Christian existence.[51] This total integration of spirituality and liturgy was unparalleled in Christian history, and the exuberant liturgists had high hopes that such a *liturgical* renewal would lead to a great *spiritual* renewal of the whole church.

Pieris insists, though, that the spiritual renewal did not take place, because what happened most of the time was a change of *rite*, and not the essential change of *life*. What, then, were the reasons for this monumental failure? Pieris provides a blunt and succinct re-sponse:

> . . . the Roman church has, somewhere in the course of its history, devalued the most crucial dimension of spirituality—the *liturgy of life,* which is the matrix of all sacramental expressions, for it is the context of a living encounter with God in Christ. Sacramental life and mysticism cannot be artificially reconciled if they are both up-rooted from their natural environment, which is the paschal Mystery of Christ continued in the (secular) lives and struggles, in the deaths and triumphs of his members. . . .[52]

The author believes that a kind of clericalism is responsible, be-cause the clergy did not give full liturgical emphasis to the priest-hood of the people (that is, the liturgy of life). Finally, from a historical perspective, he proceeds to a discussion of baptism and the eucharist. The eucharist, he states, "was a 1) *sacramental* 2) *mys-ticism* of 3) *secular* commitment . . .* , the last element being the focal point of the first two. For sacrament and mysticism are intensive moments (the one being ecclesial, the other personal) of the *life of self-sacrifice lived in accordance with the gospel.*"[53] Thus, if sacraments and mysticism are uprooted from the day-to-day struggles of the people, that is, from the liturgy of life, they will never be able to come together.

Pieris then turns to the *second dichotomy,* that of spirituality ver-sus secular involvement. After discussing the history of these con-cepts, he fastens on the "contemplative in action" spirituality of Ignatius of Loyola. Loyola, he states, was convinced that the crucial test of authentic spirituality was located in *self-abnegation,* flowing from the *crucified* (and exalted) *Christ*: "Once there is self-abnegation, he taught, it would not take long to find God!"[54] Pieris is convinced that this precious teaching of Western spirituality should be retrieved as the genuine criterion of any authentic spir-ituality.

Furthermore, the christological foundations of this doctrine are of capital importance, namely,

1) that in the person of *God-Man* Jesus, God and humanity have

been so reconciled as to form one indivisible mystery of salvation, and 2) that this reconciliation is effected through the kenosis of the cross, which makes visible and accessible the initial kenosis of the incarnation, and consequently, 3) that the crucified Christ provides, so to speak, a link between the divine and the human, so that one can always touch God in humanity, and touch humanity in God, provided one opts for the cross where alone love for God and love for humanity are convertible.[55]

Pieris is also convinced, finally, that it was liberation theology that restored the theology of the cross to the universal church after the Second Vatican Council.

This brings us to the final dichotomy, that of secular involvement versus liturgy. Pieris begins with a reference to the theology of Edward Schillebeeckx with regard to secular life as worship: "Jesus did not give his life in a liturgical assembly. . . .in an obvious secular context, colored though it was by religion, he was faithful to God and [people] and gave his life for his own in a secular combination of circumstances."[56] Schillebeeckx is convinced that through Jesus cult has acquired a new meaning, namely, that human life itself is experienced as liturgy and the worship of God.

What about the teaching of Vatican II that church liturgy is the "source and summit" of the liturgy of life? Pieris believes this is a remnant of an approach "that germinated in the monastico-clerical ethos of the pre-Vatican II liturgical renewal." He adopts a liberationist perspective and stands the question on its head, that is, "we presume that the liturgy of the official church would originate and culminate in the *liturgy of life*, which is the primary guarantee of salvation/sanctification, and not the other way around!"[57] In short, then, there must be an "ecclesiastical revolution" that subordinates church liturgy to the liturgy of life.

Pieris places a strong emphasis on the humanity of Jesus, without of course neglecting his divinity. He states that a non-liberationist theology could produce "devotions" to Jesus, but "a liberation theology stimulates commitments to Jesus who is God-become-our-neighbor. It is a shift from the Christ of contemplation to the Christ with flesh and blood."[58] He even points out that the devotion to the Sacred Heart could become pathological unless there existed a

Christ who was really capable of suffering and therefore in need of reparation.

From a positive point of view, the human Christ corresponds to Christian humanism today, which "enlighten[s] us about the hidden roots of dehumanization, proposes an alternative model of society where human growth rather than profit-accumulation (mammon) is the motivating force, and spells out a process of discernment not different from the classical method: identification of the enemy, choice of strategy, and struggle for the kingdom with confidence and hope in divine grace."[59]

One final aspect of a modern spirituality in Pieris's book is to be found in an entire essay on poverty.[60] Pieris holds that any contemporary spirituality must have two essential directions: spirituality as a struggle to *be poor* and spirituality as a struggle *for the poor.* His final paragraph is a brilliant compendium of the entire essay:

> Whoever dares to be with God on the side of the poor must renounce all hope of being a hero. It is the criminal's fate—the cross—that Jesus holds out as the banner under which victory is assured. The disciple is not greater than the master. If the master is the victim-judge of oppression (Mt 25:31-46), disciples too must become victims of the present order or else they have no right to denounce it. The struggle for the poor is a mission entrusted only to those who are or have become poor.[61]

RAIMUNDO PANIKKAR

Perhaps the most prolific and successful author in the dialogue between East and West is Raimundo Panikkar, now professor emeritus in the religious studies department of the University of California in Santa Barbara. He has published 30 books and about 300 major articles on philosophy, comparative religions, theology of religions, and indology.[62] Also, he was ordained as a Roman Catholic priest in 1946.

Will the Three Rivers Ever Meet?

Faced with this abundance of intellectual treasures, I uttered a profound *eureka!* when I happened upon this sentence in an article of his: "In this chapter, I should like to present a general picture of what I have been doing and saying for almost half a century regarding the question of what it means to be a Christian."[63] Equally intriguing is a brief sentence in italics before the text that contains explosive material for all the Christian churches: *"Does one need to be spiritually a Semite or intellectually a Westerner in order to be a Christian?"*[64]

Panikkar's selection of the three great sacred rivers is intended to symbolize the major streams of the Christian tradition with regard to other world religions. The baptism of Jesus occurred in the Jordan River, and Christianity is indelibly stamped with its Jewish origin, since Jesus, the apostles, and the evangelists were all Jews. Panikkar then proposes some preliminary questions: "Can there be a single universal spirituality—that is, a basic human attitude that is both universal and concrete? Does a Jewish-based spirituality offer such a possibility?"[65]

In similar fashion, the Tiber River in Rome also was indelibly impressed on Christian tradition, as the place where the apostles Peter and Paul were martyred, so that Christianity is incomprehensible without Rome. Thus, the author concludes, "Present-day Christianity is a more or less blended complex of Jewish heritage with Helleno-Roman-Gothico-Western elements."[66]

The major issue, furthermore, is whether these two rivers should mark the boundaries of Christianity or whether they should be allowed to flow peacefully into the Ganges in India. Panikkar then summarizes the twofold question: "Must Christians recognize that they cannot—and should not—conquer the world, because they represent only one phylum in human history, and thus should not claim the universality of being the only true religion? Or is there something specifically universal in the Christic fact: Is Christ a universal symbol?" Panikkar adds that he uses the mother river of the Ganges as a symbol not only for religions and traditions in Hinduism, Buddhism, Jainism, Sikhism, and primordial religions, but also for all other religions and traditions in Asia, Africa, and Oceania.[67]

He also acknowledges the dilemma that many Christians experience. They feel that they are betraying their deepest beliefs if they do not accept that Jesus Christ is meant to be a universal symbol. At the same time, however, they are gradually becoming painfully conscious of the fact that the claim to universality is an imperialist claim and a thing of the past; on the other hand, the adherents of other religions charge that such claims are insulting and a threat to their very existence. The author himself tries to solve the dilemma metaphorically by saying that the three rivers do not flow into each other on Earth; however, they do meet in the heavens where their vapors rise and intermingle, "which eventually will pour down again into the valleys of mortals to feed the religions of the earth."[68]

In more theological discourse, furthermore, Panikkar maintains that the Christ principle is neither a separate event nor a universal religion. It is, he says, "the center of reality as seen by the Christian tradition. But this vision is only the Christian vision, not an absolutely universal one. It is the *christic* universal vision."[69] At this point, he turns to a historico-empirical approach, which will consist in an analysis of five historical periods of the Christian phenomenon as well as a theological critique of these periods.

Five Moments of Kairos

According to Panikkar's typology, the various periods have interpreted Christianity in different ways and they also overlap in different ways. Therefore, he refers to the epochs as kairological moments (times of decisive change), rather than chronological history.

The first era, which ended with the fall of Rome to Alaric and the Visigoths in 410 C.E., is characterized by the word "witnessing." The characteristics of this witness are these: "[The early Christians] witnessed to a fact that transformed their lives and, although soon interpreted in different ways, remained a kind of transhistorical event. . . . They could fearlessly face death. They were martyrs, witnesses to an event. Fidelity was paramount."[70]

The second period, which lasted until the early Middle Ages, is marked by an emphasis on *conversion:* "One becomes a real Christian not because one adheres to a religion but because one undergoes a change of heart. . . . The authentic Christian may tamper with the emerging political order or be allured by Christian social power, but the real criterion is style of life, purity of heart."[71]

Gradually, however, Christianity becomes a religion joined with the Roman empire, and conversion takes on political connotations. The conflict with Islam, moreover, gave rise to a third attitude.

"Crusade" dominated Christian understanding from the eighth century to well past the fall of Constantinople in 1453 and until the victory over the Turks in the battle of Lepanto in 1571. Christendom is well established, and Christian life is dominated by the dark spectre of Islam. At this *kairos*, the "Christian has to a be a soldier, a 'militant,' a word that will be used until our times. The superiors of the new religious movements are no longer called fathers, abbots, or mothers, but generals—and the movements become 'orders.'"[72]

Protestantism also adopts the features of the crusade: "Christianity is a demanding enterprise; it requires courage, faith, decision. . . . You need to be a hero; you have the sacred duty of conquering or reconquering for Christ the life within and the life without."[73] Christianity also begins to embrace the idea that it is the only true religion and all the others are false; thus, the meaning of Christianity shifts from authentic religiousness to joining the one true salvific institutionalized religion. This period ends with the "discovery" of the New World, the gradual dissolution of Christendom as a world order, and the recovery of Christianity as a religion.

The fourth period of *mission* takes its place as the major feature from 1492 up to the end of the modern age. Even though the Amerindians constituted no real threat, an urge to conquer prevailed, the conquest of the souls of the inhabitants of the New World. "Bartolomé de las Casas defends the *Indios*. Francisco de Vitoria tries his best, but the triumphant ideology is that Christians have the duty—in a word, the *mission*—to proclaim, convert, and thus to save the Amerindians. This ideology spreads steadily. The true Christian is a *missionary.*"[74]

Despite this approach of spiritual conquest, Christians like Matteo Ricci and Roberto de Nobili unearth the treasures in these new religions and strive to integrate them with Christianity. Nevertheless, this kairotic moment in the history of the church was not grasped, and many such efforts were stifled because Christian institutions found them threatening to the dynamism of the times—

that is, to the political expansion of the European states, which, because they declared themselves Christian, could not allow other interpretations that might undermine their power."[75] The age of the missions is over, as we enter the contemporary age.

Panikkar gives the least space to the fifth and final period of *dialogue*, which has come about after the demise of colonialism. Still, he compresses a great deal into his discussion of the contemporary situation:

> Many Christians no longer want to conquer, not even to convert; they want to serve and to learn; they offer themselves as sincere participants in an open dialogue. . . . Christians are beginning to say that dialogue is not a new strategy, but an open process of mutual enrichment and better knowledge of each other. Christendom has little prospect; Christianity is in crisis, but the Christ-symbol remains effective.[76]

Lessons of History

Panikkar proceeds to place these five periods in the framework of the three rivers mentioned earlier. The first period is still influenced by the Jordan, since Christians are spiritually Semites. The second, third, and fourth epochs are nourished by the Tiber in Rome, and Christians are intellectually Europeans, culturally linked to the nations of the Mediterranean. Historically speaking, the Americas are only colonies of Europe, even though they manifest their own characteristics. It is only the fifth period, nurtured by the Ganges, that rejects the Mediterranean culture and "aspires to bathe, together with other believers, in the waters of the Ganges and all the other rivers of the world. Christians discover that those rivers are real rivers that do not belong to them."[77]

At this point, the author delineates four lessons from history from the survey he has just sketched. The first is that our reflections are deeply influenced by historical circumstances. We can assert then that "[d]ialogue has not sprung out of pure speculation. It has been almost forced upon Christians by circumstances. Praxis conditions theory."[78] The second lesson stresses liberation both from unidimensional supernaturalism and also dialectical materialism. The transformation of Christian attitudes is not merely divine providence, nor is it purely the plotting "of institutional churches hoping to remain in power and continue dominating purses and consciences."[79] Using the gospel parable, the wheat and the tares must be allowed to grow together until the end of the world.

The third lesson teaches the relativization of all our efforts, including theology and other intellectual achievements, and thus that we are living and working in a limited and provisional situation. "We are," asserts Panikkar, "as much a passing phase as our ancestors were. If we have to beware of ethnocentrism, we should equally guard against chronocentrism."[80]

The fourth lesson is one that I was delighted with as a professional theologian, since it stresses the *creativity* and *freedom* of authentic theologizing. Panikkar expresses it briefly but accurately:

> Theology does not merely repeat past doctrines or only draw implicit consequences from them. It also creates something new. . . . Theology is not only exegesis, it is also praxis, not simply a matter of drawing conclusions, but also of establishing new premises and creating new situations. . . . it is the fruit of a series of factors, many of which are free movements of the human and divine spirit.[81]

Panikkar next treats at some length the geographical and theological differences that are to be found as the background of the three rivers, and which are expansions of the five kairotic periods discussed above.

Basic Christian Attitudes

The author moves on to "situate the specific challenge and problems of a pluralistic Christian self-understanding for our times."[82] He begins with an analysis of "Christian," which can have three meanings: 1) a civilization, that is, Christendom; 2) a religion, that is, Christianity; and 3) personal religiousness, or Christianness. He outlines this as follows:

> During the period of the so-called Christian culture of the high Middle Ages, one could hardly be a Christian without belonging to Christendom. Until recently, one could hardly confess oneself to be Christian without belonging to Christianity. Now persons

increasingly envisage the possibility of being Christian as a personal attitude without adhering either to Christendom or Christianity as institutional constructs.[83]

Panikkar appears to be primarily interested in the third understanding or attitude of Christianness, although he does not deny some aspects of the first two attitudes. He defines Christianness as confessing a personal faith and adopting a Christlike attitude, with Christ representing the central symbol of one's own life.

The author provides examples in the Roman church, where an enormous number of people consider themselves "good Catholics" and yet blithely ignore the teachings of their church regarding the use of contraceptives. In some countries, the same thing is happening with regard to divorce, abortion, euthanasia, and so forth. Another example is the growth of base Christian communities in Latin America, which have developed a true Christianness within the existing Christianity. Panikkar also notes that the Christianness of the past century was usually pietist and individualistic, while today "Christianness presents a more personal and political commitment, and so poses a challenge to Christianity."[84]

Undoubtedly, Panikkar insists, there is a profound crisis regarding Christian identity in the world today, and the solution is to be found in Christianness, which he describes in simpler terms: ". . . a substantial number of contemporary Christians want to be religious, believers, and even Christian—but without the 'contaminations' that they feel have been attached to those names. They aspire to recover their roots in order to grow in another soil unspoiled by the manure of ancient times, the graftings of the Middle Ages, the pesticides of the modern age, and the radiation of modernity."[85]

In summary, the spirituality of the Jordan is close to Christianity, the spirituality of the Tiber resembles Christendom, and the Ganges stands as a symbol for Christianness, all representing the complexity of the Christian phenomenon today. Nevertheless, "the increasing awareness of Christianness offers a platform from which the dilemma of exclusivism or inclusivism may be solved in favor of a healthy pluralism of religions that in no way dilutes the particular contribution of each human tradition."[86]

Problems and Conclusions

Panikkar judges that the present time is ripe for adopting a pluralistic attitude, "a plunge into the Ganges."[87] He points out that pluralism does *not* consider unity to be an indispensable goal; it accepts the irreconcilable elements of religions as well as their commonalities, and does not expect at the *eschaton* that all will be united. In a rather intricate way, Panikkar uses Western logic to arrive at Eastern thought: "Pluralism affirms neither that the truth is one nor that it is many. If truth were one, we could not accept the positive tolerance of a pluralistic attitude and would have to consider pluralism a connivance with error. If truth were many, we would fall into a plain contradiction."[88]

In brief, the author holds that pluralism is non-dualistic and defends the pluralism of truth because *reality itself* is pluralistic. Furthermore, the "mystery of the Trinity is the ultimate foundation for pluralism" and the "pluralist attitude tries to reach intelligibility as much as possible, but it does not need the idea of a total intelligibility of the real."[89]

Panikkar also holds a necessary attitude of pluralism in Christian theologies, so that they "cannot be put under one common umbrella as a supersystem." These theologies may use the term "Christ" in a central role, but each may be using it in a different way or meaning. Thus, vis-à-vis the religions of the world, the pluralist will affirm the Christian beliefs by saying, I believe that this is true, but *not* that this belief is true. Thus he holds that "this means that Christian self-understanding is a function of the all-embracing myth reigning at a particular time and place. This unifying myth is not constant."[90]

The author ends his essay with a series of twelve conclusions regarding a Christian reflection on pluralism, and I will mention only the major ones. His first four propositions are concerned with a *new context:* "The new context entails both new elements, which were not there before, and a transformation of the old context. It is a new context that embraces, corrects, and supersedes the old, but keeps a certain continuity with it. Nevertheless, this new context is equally limited and concrete."[91]

Other conclusions are concerned with the world religions: "Each religion is unique with the uniqueness of every real being. . . . Each one represents the whole of human experience in a concrete way."[92] Finally, he concludes by asserting that Christians find in Christ the source of union, understanding, and love with all human beings and the whole cosmos, and also "the kenotic experience of Christ, which entails acceptance of and openness to the Spirit."[93]

At the end of his work, Panikkar adopts a mystical tone that returns again to the theme of Christianness and presents an encapsulation of his essay:

> Christianness stands for the life of Christ within ourselves, insight into a communion, without confusion, with all reality, an experience that "I and the Father are one," that labels do not matter, that security is of no importance, and that reflection also is a secondary source (although a primary tool). It is with hesitation that I use the phrase "mystical experience" but perhaps there is no better way of saying it. Not without a certain bias I chose the mystical Ganges as the symbol.[94]

CHUNG HYUN KYUNG

Chung Hyun Kyung is a Korean Christian woman who studied for a doctorate in systematic theology at Union Theological Seminary in New York City. Her article, "'Han-pu-ri': Doing Theology from Korean Women's Perspective," was published in the *Ecumenical Review* and in the collection entitled *We Dare to Dream: Doing Theology as Asian Women.*[95] In my view, she is a gifted writer as well as a creative theologian.

Art and Theology Merge

Chung begins her essay in New York City, where a collection of recent Korean woodcut prints was being exhibited that featured the struggles of the Korean people. When she entered the exhibition hall, she was overwhelmed by the power of the art and burst into tears: "I cried because I could see the opening of a new horizon in these prints, something I had been longing for in my theological work for a long time: discovering, naming, claiming, and creating our own reality. I could not see any apologetic attitude in these prints. They simply said what they felt, with confidence. They trusted their experience."[96] The Korean art critic who had brought the prints told her that Korean artists were breaking out of the Western style they were taught and creating art that portrayed the everyday lives of the people and their struggle for liberation. She also had noted something similar in an exhibition in Korea where an artist summarized the transformation in people's art: ". . . it was the artists' belief in their own feelings as opposed to a need for approval from their teachers or Western standards."[97]

Chung refers to these artists and herself as "second-generation liberationists." Her teachers, she says, were the first-generation liberationists, who were reacting against colonialism and absorbed subconsciously in proving themselves to the colonizers. She continues with this interesting analysis:

> Our teachers clearly knew what they did not like but they did not know where they should go in their own work. We members of the second generation owe a lot to our teachers because they gave us the colonizers' tools and the space to create. We second-generation liberationists are not unaware of the neo-colonial power surrounding us but we also know our own power. . . . We believe in our experiences and are not intimidated by outside authorities any more.[98]

Another important step occurred with regard to the feminist perspective of a third world woman. Kyung's teachers were compelled to prove their theological competence to (in descending order) white male theologians, white feminist theologians, and finally Korean male theologians, in order to prove the quality of Korean women's theology. But Chung and her generation begin by taking ownership of their own feelings and experiences, and realizing that they must reject foreign criteria while accepting their own gut feelings. The author is quite eloquent on this point:

> If we do not permit ourselves to fully experience who we are, we will not have the power to fight back and create our own space. We have to touch something really real among and around us in order to meet God. Just as young Korean artists from the people's movement find their aesthetics in ordinary people's everyday lives, so we emerging women theologians find God's revelations in our ordinary everyday experiences.[99]

Chung ends this section by stating that she will not try to articulate Korean women's God-experience from biblical or other traditional theological sources, but will name their experience "within our cultural context of suffering and life-giving using our traditional symbols and metaphors in an organic way."[100] Only after that will she attempt to establish connections between the experiences of Korean women and the Christian tradition.

The Many Ghosts of Korea

The author turns next to her own experience, and rather surprisingly states that her childhood was filled with haunting ghosts of every possible kind: "As a young girl, It was difficult for me to live with so many ghosts. . . . These ghosts were the spirits who could not rest because what had happened to them in their earthly lives was too cruel and unjust to forget or forgive."[101] All of this was connected with the worship of ancestors and shamanistic rituals described as "Kut."

Fortunately, there was a more joyous side to the land of the ghosts, for some of them were their ancestors: "Many relatives gathered together, prepared meals and had big feasts. We opened up all the windows and doors to let our ancestors into the house. Ancestors were friendly ghosts. Most of them had families to take care of their tombs and to remember them. They were not wandering ghosts. They rested in paradise and visited us annually on the ancestor worship day."[102] Chung recalls, however, that only the males in the family took part in the worship. As a child of five or six years, she cried so loudly and long that her father allowed her to go with him to the worship. But the older women who prepared all the festive meals were never allowed to engage in the worship.

Chung also greatly enjoyed the shamanistic rituals of "Kut," even though her mother, who was a Christian, forbade her to attend them. Betraying early signs of being a feminist, she "had to go there without my mother's knowledge. There was always music, dancing, and excitement in Kut. . . .The shaman wore beautiful, colorful dresses and sang and danced until she reached a state of ecstasy."[103]

A turning point in Chung's young life occurred in high school, where she was introduced to the pragmatism of John Dewey and brainwashed into believing that all ghosts were mere fantasies. As the author expressed it: "It was an age of enlightenment and independence. I could sleep alone and go to the bathroom courageously by myself!"[104] In college, moreover, the ghosts returned to haunt her as she read Korean history, which was scarred by wars, invasions, and exploitation both by foreigners and domestic elites. She was stunned by the vast numbers of people who had died unjustly in Korean history, and thus had become wandering spirits without any place of eternal rest. She summed up her feelings: "Since my college days wandering ghosts have not been objects of fear for me. I started to believe that these ghosts were the voices in the wilderness which could unveil and proclaim all of the injustices in our history. I must listen to their voices because they must clearly contain God's voice as it resonated throughout our history."[105]

Theology of "Han" and "Minjung"

At this point, Chung analyzes some theological terms that are unique to Korean theology, the concepts of "Han" and "Minjung." Several meanings are attributed to the term "Han." It is "the suppressed, amassed and condensed experience of oppression caused by mischief or misfortune so that it forms a kind of 'lump' in one's spirit." Again, it is "a sense of unresolved resentment against injustice suffered, a sense of helplessness because of the overwhelming odds against . . . a feeling of acute pain of sorrow in one's guts and bowels making the whole body writhe and wiggle, and an obstinate urge to take 'revenge' and to right the wrong all of these constitute."[106] Finally, the feeling of Han is described as the people's "root experience" or "collective consciousness," which "comes from the sinful interconnectedness of classism, racism, sexism, colonialism, neo-colonialism, and cultural imperialism."[107]

The second major term, "Minjung," is translated as "people," but it means a very specific people. The Korean Minjung theologian, Suh Kwang-Sun, describes this people as "the oppressed, exploited, dominated, discriminated against, alienated and suppressed politically, economically, socially, culturally, and intellectually, like women, ethnic groups, the poor, workers, and farmers, including intellectuals themselves."[108]

This Minjung theology shares many ideas with Korean women's theology, but the women go further and say that they should be seen as "the minjung within the minjung." This does not discourage Korean women, as can be seen in this statement by Chung Hyun Kyung: "Korean women have taken within their whole being the poisons of injustice and suffering in our history and have survived. She was at the bottom of the oppressive system but has not always been a passive victim. The Korean woman is also an agent of liberation. She has given birth to a new life and hope for our country."[109]

The Curse of Women's Han

In this section, Chung proposes to discuss the *specific* aspects of women's Han, since both Korean men and women have suffered oppression over the centuries. In ancient Korea, in fact, men and women enjoyed more or less equal status, with traces of a matriarchal society. Since Korea organized into rigid religious and social systems, and especially after the Yi dynasty, women have been the object of oppression and exploitation. The Yi dynasty established Confucian ethics, which established the male as the authority in the family, while the others obeyed for the sake of harmony, and an ideology of female chastity and obedience developed. For example:

> Widows' remarriage, it was thought, made the blood of the family unclean. Women are responsible for the purity of the family's blood. When a widow got married, she was punished along with her parents, new husband, and children by blocked social advancement. Even a 10-year-old girl who was engaged through her parents' arrangement had to keep to her widowhood in the in-laws' house if her future husband died before marriage.[110]

The remnants of this are seen even today when an unmarried woman who remains single is discouraged, and/or when widows are discouraged, from remarriage. "Korean women," Chung states emphatically, "have endured such social, cultural, and religious control over their lives. But they have also actively fought against double standards in our cultural and religious life by creating and sharing songs, poems and stories among women."[111]

A particularly vicious example of women's Han under colonialism occurred when 100,000 poor, rural Korean women were
forced to be official prostitutes for the Japanese army during World
War II. Many of the Korean women died of venereal diseases or
were killed when the Japanese soldiers retreated. Also, some
"Korean women survived this hell. Many of them could not return
to Korea, however, because they were ashamed of themselves and
'virtuous' Korean morality would not accept these 'dirty' women
back. . . . The Japanese government deliberately destroyed the reports of these Korean women. Their pain could thus be erased permanently from history."[112]

Chung also provides evidence of women's Han under neo-
colonialism. "Behind the rapidly increasing GNP of Korea in the
1970s," she asserts, "there were many women who worked under
miserable conditions in the textile industry. These companies provided the main materials for Korean export."[113]

There were also many examples of women's Han under military
dictatorships. Kwon In-Sook, a 23-year-old labor activist, was arrested in June 1986 as a subversive. She was raped and tortured
when she would not reveal the names of her compatriots. She ad-
mitted that she considered suicide because of extreme shame and
humiliation; however, she decided to let the world know what happened and she accused her torturer. When her request was ignored,
the men and women in the prison all took part in a hunger strike.
Finally, "Ms. Kwon broke the culture of silence on violations of
women's sexual and personal integrity which were prevalent in
Korea under the military government."[114]

Finally, Chung turns to another term that is in the title of her essay, that is, "Han-pu-ri," which means a release from Han and is the
main purpose of doing women's theology in Korea. The term comes
from Korean shamanistic religion, where the Kut ritual permits the
ghosts to express their stories of Han either by eliminating the cause
of oppression or by being comforted. Chung points out that Han-
pu-ri has provided a situation where the ghosts and their communities can experience repentance, group therapy, and communal
healing.

The author then emphasizes that the Han-pu-ri is very fascinating because of three characteristics: "1) The majority (65-70 percent) of Shamans who play the role of the priest/ess of Han-pu-ri Korean society are women. 2) The majority of people who participate in the Han-pu-ri Kut in Korean society are women. 3) The majority of characters in ghost stories are women."[115] Since it was stated earlier that women were not allowed at Korean shamanistic worship, I must presume that the Han-pu-ri was an exception. Ms. Chung appears to hold that position when she says that "Han-pu-ri became one of the few spaces where poor Korean women played their role without being dominated by male-centered religious authorities. Han-ridden women got together and tried to release their accumulated Han through Han-pu-ri Kut."[116]

Chung explains the important steps in the Han-pu-ri. The first is *speaking and hearing,* where the shaman allows the persons or ghosts to express their Han publicly for the entire community. The second step of *naming* is allowing the ghosts or persons with the help of the shaman to name the source of their oppression. The final step is *changing* the unjust situation by actions so that the persons or ghosts can achieve peace and serenity.

Reflections on Feminist Theology

The author notes that the Korean Association of Women Theologians (KAWT) follows steps that are similar to the Han-pu-ri, although she admits that this is her personal view of the methodology and not the official position of KAWT.[117] The women theologians listened to the stories of poor women first, then constructed a social analysis of the situation with the help of social scientists. They then reflected as theologians with the questions that came up, and returned to the poor women to find out if their theology was helpful to them and actually empowered them. The final step of action included demonstrations and protests with KAWT to alleviate women's Han.[118]

In the emerging theologies of Korean women, Chung has located four primary sources.

The most important source for Korean women's theology is the Korean women's lived experience. However, this experience is not the universal, abstract, and standardized human experience as alluded to by some traditional European male theologians. The specific historical experience of Korean women is manifested in their experience as victims and agents of liberation, and through the experience of Han and Han-pu-ri.[119]

The second source is critical consciousness, which is an engaged subjective reason that takes sides and uncovers the ideologies of domination.

Tradition as the third source uses all our traditions, including Shamanism, Buddhism, Confucianism, Christianity, and political ideologies, but also employs a women's perspective to use them critically: "We distinguish from a specifically women's perspective the liberative traditions from the oppressive traditions. We women learn from our experiences that male-defined liberation did not always include women's liberation. We use liberative traditions to empower women and use our critical analysis of the oppressive traditions to name the source of oppression."[120]

Finally, the fourth source is scripture, that is, the Old and New Testaments as well as the texts of other traditional religions, and the women selectively choose liberating messages from all the texts.

With this methodology and sources, the question may be raised concerning the *norm* of Korean women's theology. The author responds:

> If a theology entangles the Korean women's Han and liberates us from bondage, it is a good theology. If a theology keeps us accumulating our Han and staying in our Han-ridden places, it is a bad theology no matter how important church unity, the authority of the Bible, and church traditions are. If a theology has a life-giving power to Korean women and empowers us to grow in our full humanhood, that is a good theology.[121]

In summary, the two norms are liberation (Han-pu-ri) and life-giving power. Can a Korean women's theology be a Christian theology with those norms? I will let Ms. Chung end her essay with this response: "For us, the gospel of Jesus means liberation (Han-pu-ri) and life-giving power. In that sense we are Christians. Where there is genuine experience of liberation (Han-pu-ri) and life-giving power, we meet our God, Christ, and the power of the Spirit. That is good news."[122]

Conclusion

These three Asian theologians—Pieris, Panikkar, and Chung—are only three examples, but very important ones, of the many creative theologies that are being produced in the vast reaches of the Asian continent, where more than half of the human race lives and struggles for liberation. For Christians outside Asia who find their approaches and new concepts to be aberrant or even shocking, we must strongly emphasize their *uniqueness* and the *peculiar challenges* that loom before them. This is due to the enormous fact that, aside from the nation of the Philippines, Asian Christians constitute less than one and one-half percent of its teeming millions—a mere toehold on an endless land mass. That is the Asian *context*—in contrast to all other liberation theologies around the world. Neverthess, its tiny voice continues to expand and its light to gleam, as we have seen in the work of the three Asian theologians.

In this context, we in the West, I believe, should not engage in a hasty critique of these many faces of God at the present period of history. Our task is simple: to listen profoundly to our Asian sisters and brothers, and to open our hearts in wonder. At some time in the future, on some unknown path, we *will* walk together and help one another in the quest for liberation, the advance of the Reign of God, and the hunger and thirst after justice.

Questions for Reflection and Discussion

1. Aloysius Pieris defines Asia's specific characteristics as its overwhelming poverty and its multifaceted religiousness. Can you think of other characteristics of modern Asia besides these?

2. Fr. Pieris describes the importance in Buddhism of the *sangha*, or community, of monks. Do these monks have political alliances similar to the Christian churches in the West? Try to contrast the two religions in this respect.

3. Fr. Pieris states that it is "among the non-Christians that the

[Christian] church is called to lose itself in total participation." How do you understand this statement and would you agree with it?

4. He also sees a number of similarities and differences between the world churches of Christianity and Buddhism. Which of the similarities and differences do you think are the most important ones and why? Do you think this might bring the religions closer together?

5. Raimundo Panikkar states that Christians are becoming more and more aware that their claim to universality is an imperialist approach that is a thing of the past. Give your views and your reasons for them.

6. Fr. Panikkar places much emphasis on a spirituality which he refers to as "Christianness," and which he believes is the only viable spirituality for the Christian church. Give your views on this statement.

7. In the article of Chung Hyun Kyung, she integrates elements of the "Ghosts of Korea" to her Christian theology. Is this a dangerous syncretism or is it a fruitful integration? Give reasons for your view.

8. In Korean traditional theology, the principal concepts are called "Han," "Minjung," and "Han-pu-ri." After you grasp the meanings of these, which are somewhat subtle, can you see anything similar in Christian theology and in Christian customs? Does it also have similarities to the other world religions?

SUGGESTED READINGS

Amaladoss, Michael. *Making All Things New: Dialogue, Pluralism, and Evangelization in Asia.* Maryknoll, NY: Orbis Books, 1990.

Choan-Seng Song. *Third-Eye Theology: Theology in Formation in Asian Settings.* Revised ed.; Maryknoll, NY: Orbis Books, 1991.

Chung, Hyun Kyung. *Struggle to be the Sun Again: Introducing Asian Women's Theology.* Maryknoll: Orbis Books, 1990.

Cobb, John B. *Beyond Dialogue: Toward a Mutual Transformation of Christianity and Buddhism.* Minneapolis: Fortress, 1982.

Corless, Roger, and Paul F. Knitter. *Buddhist Emptiness and Christian Trinity.* New York: Paulist, 1990.

Esposito, John L. *Islam in Asia: Religion, Politics, and Society*. New York: Oxford University Press, 1987.

Fabella, Virginia, and Lee Sun Ai Park, eds. *We Dare to Dream: Doing Theology as Asian Women*. Maryknoll, NY: Orbis Books, 1990.

Ingram, Paul O., and Frederick J. Streng. *Buddhist-Christian Dialogue: Mutual Renewal and Transformation*. Honolulu: University of Hawaii Press, 1986.

Katoppo, Marianne. *Compassionate and Free: An Asian Woman's Theology*. Maryknoll: Orbis Books, 1980.

Koyama, Kosuke. *Mount Fuji and Mount Sinai: A Critique of Idols*. Maryknoll, NY: Orbis Books, 1984.

Küng, Hans, and Julia Ching. *Christianity and Chinese Religions*. New York: Doubleday, 1989.

Panikkar, Raimundo. *The Unknown Christ of Hinduism: Towards an Ecumenical Christophany*. Maryknoll, NY: Orbis Books, 1981.

Tracy, David. *Dialogue with the Other: The Inter-Religious Dialogue*. Grand Rapids: Eerdmans, 1990.

CHAPTER SEVEN

AN OPTION FOR THE POOR?

Liberation Theology in the First World

Social change, social criticism, and cultural growth have been largely ineffectual in American society and in the American churches because of the dangerous separation of spirituality and faith from society and justice. Social activists, bereft of the sources of spirit, commitment, lifestyle, and resilient faith, most often fail to bring any total vision or long-haul commitment to social programming and change.

John F. Kavanaugh
Still Following Christ in a Consumer Society 168

My experience of crossing class and culture boundaries reveals first of all the superiority complexes that come with being American and middle-class. It shows me sides of evil and oppression that I could never see within my own secure circles. Likewise, it manifests the extraordinary virtues that are fired within the daily task to survive. Above all it teaches me how to cope creatively with the inherent conflicts of difference rather than ignore or obliterate them.

Katherine E. Zappone
The Special Nature of Women? (Concilium 1991/6) 93

AS WE TURN OUR ATTENTION TO THEOLOGY as it is produced in the first world (or the nations of the West), I would like to reflect on several important facts that are of the utmost importance for the next stage of human history. In the twentieth century, history has been dominated by two world wars and five decades of the cold war; only in the last few years has Mars, the god of war, ceased to stalk and threaten the entire globe, although smaller wars continue to spread humanity's greatest plague. With the demise of the cold war, the East-West protagonists, Russia and its allies versus the United States and its allies, appear to have abandoned their antagonisms and the East-West axis has ceased to exist. It must be remembered, however, that it was only after torrents of blood (usually in proxy wars) had been spilled, and trillions of dollars and rubles squandered prodigiously rather than serving the desperate needs of humanity.

North, South, and Theology?

Another fact of the greatest significance is that a new axis has entered into human consciousness and into a new stage of history. This is the North-South axis, or conflict, between the wealthy nations of the northern hemisphere, where most are obsessed by losing weight, and the southern hemisphere, where most are haunted by hunger and subsequent death. Considering the global explosion of telecommunications, so that the poor can gaze with their own eyes on this horror, it is patent that such a spectacle cannot continue without continual eruptions, rebellions, disorder, famine, and more deaths for the poor. In my view, this gross inequity is now and will continue to be the central issue for the Christian churches both today and throughout the twenty-first century.

In the face of this glaring reality, we might expect the theologians and Christians of the Western nations to recognize and interpret these "signs of the times" as a true revelation of the Christian God of the poor. Not only that but that they would take action, ring the alarms, and storm the barricades of suffering and untimely death in every corner of the world.

In fact, however, I would judge that at the present time only very scant attention to these overwhelming realities may be found in the avalanche of theological tomes, articles, speeches, and lectures that are annually produced in the United States, Canada, Europe, and Australia, that is, in the first world. Whatever disasters menace and afflict most of humanity, the vast preponderance of Western theology continues to choose and produce topics that painstakingly support the status quo of church and state, that are carefully chosen to insure tenure and promotion, and that succeed in keeping good Christians in the first world tranquilized and pacified, despite the screams from all over the globe.

Sometimes I imagine this vast production as a great supertanker, with its engines at full speed, that is extraordinarily difficult to stop and even to turn. Indeed, perhaps the oceans of theological output comprise in themselves an *immense ideology*, which unconsciously keeps students, doctoral candidates, professors, and ordinary Christians totally *occupied* with the impossible task of consuming and digesting this prodigious output. Thus, they have neither the time, energy, or interest to turn their eyes to the vast geography of suffering in the world, even in their own nominally Christian countries. I do not know how to change the course of this theological supertanker, but I think it would be fruitful to examine some of the few but creative and courageous white theologians who produce liberation theology in the first world.

JÜRGEN MOLTMANN

The past two decades, the distinguished Lutheran theologian, Jürgen Moltmann, has been engaged in a dialogue that verged on a love-hate relationship at times with some theologians in Latin America. Although he has demonstrated more than any other European his solidarity with the Latin Americans and pledged his dedication to their cause, he has often been the object of sharp criticism from the south. In 1975, for example, José Míguez Bonino, a leading Methodist theologian from Buenos Aires, published a book entitled *Doing Theology in a Revolutionary Situation,*[1] in which he voiced strong criticism of the theology of Moltmann.[2] At the same time, however, he referred to Moltmann as "the theologian to whom liberation theology is most indebted and with whom it has the closest affinity."[3] As soon as Moltmann read Míguez's diatribe, he launched a missive (or missile) of his own, an "Open Letter to José Míguez Bonino, " in an American periodical,[4] with a strong defense of his own position together with a counter-criticism of Míguez's own theology and social analysis.

Liberation Theology or Political Theology?

Without going into further details in this matter, I pose the question of what relationship actually exists between Moltmann's European "political theology" and "liberation theology" as it is produced in Latin America. Although I find some of Moltmann's writings to be highly rhetorical, he has recently published a speech he gave in Mexico City on the very topic of European and Latin American theologies, which is both succinct and illuminating.[5]

Moltmann begins by emphasizing that he speaks as one involved in this topic and not as a neutral observer. He also notes that he has been involved in such a dialogue from the beginning, but that at present it is necessary to begin it anew because of the elimination of the second world and the realignment between first and third worlds. Furthermore, his context is Europe and, within Europe, Germany, while his intention is to speak about liberation theology from the perspective of political theology. He also bluntly states the problem:

> Many liberation theologians share the judgment of Gustavo Gutiérrez that there exists a "break" between the "progressive" theology of the modern world and the liberation theology of the world oppressed by this modern world. European political theology would be an academic theology, while Latin American liberation theology would be a theology of the people.[6]

Moltmann reacts strongly against this analysis and insists that he "will describe the history of political theology, in order to show that it is exactly *not* a question of the liberal 'progressive' theology of the rising bourgeois, but rather that it is a political and social critique of the victims of the first world, and therefore it can be the natural ally of the liberation theology of the third world."[7]

The author lays out his rationale for this thesis in four parts: 1) beginnings and origins of the theologies, 2) developments in European political theology, 3) an evaluation of political theology at present, and 4) open questions in the new situation. In the first part, he states rather apodictically that both theologies arose in the years 1964-1968,[8] but in different circumstances: liberation theology from among the poor in Latin America (North-South axis), and political theology from the cold war in a divided Europe (East-West axis).

Quest for Origins

As regards liberation theology, Moltmann states that the Cuban revolution in 1958 was a *señal luminosa universal*, that is, a universal, luminous signal for mobilization of the people in many Latin American nations. But the powerful and learned strata of the population followed the example of development of the first world, and theologians spoke of a *theology of development*. Nevertheless, insofar as it became apparent that the development of some was achieved at the expense of others, a *theology of revolution* was announced in a Geneva conference in 1966, which was aided in praxis by the sacrifice of Camilo Torres's life, a revolutionary priest in Colombia.[9]

This movement was further impelled forward in 1971 by the publication of the epoch-making book of Gustavo Gutiérrez, *A Theology of Liberation*.[10] The *sitz-im-leben* (life situation) of this theology, according to Moltmann, is the context of the suffering of vast masses of the poor, leading to a stress on action (orthopraxis) for the liberation of the poor, and with the churches adopting a "preferential option for the poor." Liberation theology also utilized the social sciences as instruments to reveal the causes of poverty. Liberation theologians, moreover, contributed greatly to the Medellín (1968) and Puebla (1979) bishops' conferences, which located the church itself within the transformation process that was taking place in Latin America.[11]

Turning to Europe in the 1960s, some key events were the escalation of the cold war due to the construction of the Berlin wall in 1961, and the continuing increase of nuclear weapons on both sides of the iron curtain (more than 12,000 weapons on each side). The only signs of hope were to be found in Willy Brandt's social democracy and Alexander Dubcek's "socialism with a human face" in

Czechoslovakia. At this point, political theology appeared not only in the work of Moltmann, but also in the writings of Johannes Metz, Helmut Gollwitzer, Dorothee Sölle, and Jan Lochmann, and it viewed itself as a theology aimed at ideological and social criticism. But why the name "political" theology? This theology arose in Germany above all under the horrendous impact of Auschwitz and the other death camps, so that the concrete situation of theology was always the looming shadow of the Holocaust, the period of "after Auschwitz." This *locus theologicus* not only constituted a political and moral crisis for the German people, but it also emerged as a theological crisis for the entire Christian faith: *Why*, except in a few scattered cases, did Christian people and Christian leaders *keep silent* in the face of the Holocaust?[12]

Moltmann points to answers to this critical question in the privatization of religion, and the division of religion and politics as a result of the Lutheran doctrine of the two Kingdoms, which limited religion and conscience to the church. Although Moltmann does not say so, these answers hardly touch the face of evil in this matter. But at any rate, the new political theology reacted by stressing the *public* testimony of faith, as well as the *political* following of Christ. It did not seek to "politicize" the church, as critics charged, but rather to "christianize" the political existence of the churches and of Christians along the lines of the Sermon on the Mount. Moltmann also narrates political theology's involvement in the Christian-Marxist dialogues beginning in 1965, in the Russian takeover of Czechoslovakia in 1968, and in the persecution of theologians, including Moltmann himself.[13]

Developments in Political Theology

In this second part of his speech, Moltmann notes that political and liberation theologies are not monolithic, but rather comprise a great diversity of concepts and activities. Thus, his outline of the main developments of political theology is solely from his own point of view and *not* that of all political theologians. These developments are: 1) socialist theology, 2) a theology of peace, 3) ecological theology, 4) a theology of human rights, and 5) feminist theology.

With regard to a *socialist theology*, Moltmann refers to the year 1968, when student revolts exploded around the world in Paris, Berlin, Berkeley, and Tokyo, and a new socialist movement came into being. A constant theme, therefore, revolved around the evils and contradictions of capitalism, along with the need for a socialist revolution. As a result, German theologian Helmut Gollwitzer became a chaplain and friend of students committed to socialism, and also wrote several books on the topic. Moltmann sees Gollwitzer's writings and actions as excellent examples of political theology.[14]

The year 1968 was also the beginning of a worldwide movement against the war in Vietnam and for a *theology of peace*, which also occurred in Germany and many parts of Europe. When it was apparent in 1973 that the Americans had lost the war in Vietnam, attention was turned again to disarmament in Europe.[15] This reached a peak in the late 1970s when the Americans began installing Pershing-2 missiles and cruise missiles in Germany and other European nations, while the Russians were also positioning the deadly SS-20 missiles in East Germany. Moltmann reflects on these events:

> At that time political theology took concrete shape in the theology of peace, providing theological justification for the protest movements and actions of civil disobedience. . . . In a situation of "structural violence" as in Latin America, they responded to the question of violence in a distinctive way. But in Europe the only credible actions were nonviolent. Only strict nonviolence in the German revolution brought about the defeat of the brutal socialist system in East Germany.[16]

The Turn to Ecology

A third development in political theology was concerned with the *ecology movement*. Moltmann believes that it is not known when the consciousness of the environment and the European "green" movement began. At the end of the 1960s Rachel Carson's book, *The Silent Spring*, led to the formation of investigative committees in the United States, while the Club of Rome's *The Limits of Growth* in 1972 created universal interest in the problem. Especially after the catastrophic meltdown at the nuclear power plant in Chernobyl in

1986, movements for the protection of the environment arose on all sides, such as "Greenpeace" and the "green" parties of Europe.

This issue was posed starkly for the churches of the world by the Australian biologist, John Birch, at the conference of the World Council of Churches at Nairobi, Kenya, in 1975: "Due to the fact that modern scientific and technological civilization began the destruction of nature four hundred years ago, and based this on the biblical justification that man was the 'lord of Earth,' western Christianity is an accomplice of this occurrence. Only a revolution in religious and moral values can save nature and assure the survival of humanity."[17]

According to Moltmann, the first "ecological theology" was published by John Cobb, a process theologian from the United States, and Gerhard Liedke, an Old Testament scholar, who in 1979 published a book with the title of *The Belly of the Fish: Ecological Theology*.[18] This was followed by a series of ecclesiastical pronouncements calling for "reconciliation with nature" and a new style of spirituality vis-à-vis the created world. Moltmann himself produced a book on ecological theology, *God in the Creation*[19] in 1985. He ends his ecological reflections with these words:

> In the same way as the theology of socialism and the theology of peace, ecological theology attempts to inspire Christians to participate in the aforementioned movements, and to create their own personal visions. On the other hand, like them it brings the problems of society inside the Church, so that the Church may be present in the contradictions and sufferings of humanity and of nature.[20]

Human Rights for All

Political theology's fourth development is related to theological reflection on *human rights*, which is said to be less well known than the others but extremely important. Many declarations have been made by church bodies since the Second World War, all of them based on the inalienable and indestructible "human dignity" created in the image of God, thus linking faith in God with respect for the human person. Moltmann also stresses the connection with the United Nations:

All of [the declarations] seek an equilibrium between individual human rights, as they were defined in the *General Declaration on Human Rights* in 1948, and social and economic rights, as they were accorded by the *Agreements on Human Rights* in 1966. The practical consequences are that the three documents encourage the union of politics (both domestic and foreign) with human and civil rights.[21]

Largely because of the dictatorships that flourished in Latin America and the nations of eastern Europe, a great variety of human rights groups sprang up everywhere. And the result has been, asserts Moltmann, "human and civil rights became the constitutional foundations of the 'common European home.'"

Christian Feminism

Perhaps the most interesting and important development is that of *feminist theology*, which also must be understood as a "political theology." Moltmann views the women's movement as originating in the United States "in favor of the liberation of women from the oppression of patriarchy and for the full recognition of the human rights of women."[22] He refers to many conferences and ecclesiastical statements on this issue, beginning in Europe in the late 1970s, and then comments on feminism:

Feminist theology is political insofar as it signifies the theological vision and reflection for a global cultural revolution, which at present has been taken up by women. . . . Also, it is a movement in favor of the human and civil rights for women in society and in the church. Finally, it both motivates Christian women to participate in the general feminist movement, and also prepares the way for these questions in the churches, which are even more dominated by patriarchy than the society is, not to mention the rejection of women for ordination in the Roman Catholic church.[23]

Evaluation of the Present

With regard to a balance sheet on political theology, Moltmann stakes out *six areas* for treatment. He insists first that political theology is not purely academic, but is related to the expectations and experiences of activist groups and people's movements in the nation of Europe. Thus, he concludes that political theology is "related by marriage" to Latin American theology, *even though their circumstances are completely different.*[24]

Second, Moltmann takes pains to demonstrate that his political theology is *not* "progressive" theology, either in the liberal Protestant or in the modernist Catholic versions. "My differences and conflicts," he maintains, "with the protestant liberal Wolfhart Pannenberg, or the difference between the political theologian Johann Baptist Metz and the progressive post-modernist Hans Küng, are obvious and well known. They have not participated in our movements and conflicts, but have even frequently attacked us."[25] *Liberal theology,* he continues, was and is the theology of the rising bourgeoisie, while *political theology* has its roots in the anti-bourgeois theology of Karl Barth and the experience of the Confessing Church. His political theology, therefore, is not progressive but *dialectical:* "A theology of contradiction and of hope, of the negation of the negative, and of the utopia of the positive."[26]

Next, the author holds that the political theology of the first world has always argued *critically* against the self-justification of the powers that be: ". . . in the name of the victims, we always attempt to strip away the legitimacy of those who dominate by violence. We discuss on a critical level with 'political religion,' with 'civil religion,' with the ideologies of 'patriotism,' about 'the Christian West,' and about 'anticommunism.' We try to 'demystify' the political and economic centers of power."[27]

In fourth place, Moltmann continues, political theology has always championed the *victims of violence* and has become the public exponent of those without a voice. He then lists many of the victims in Europe itself. Next, he makes a very important contrast: "If liberation theology has one theme, that is, the liberation of the poor, then political theology has various themes, but it is always the question of the *liberation of the victims and the indictment of those who are culpable.*"

The fifth evaluation of political theology notes its presence among the aforementioned activist groups and its realizing of the *revolutionary traditions* of the Bible and of Christian history: "This is the good news of Jesus regarding the *Kingdom of God,* which will arrive with the poor and the children in this world, and not at the summits of human 'progress,' but with the victims of human brutality. . . . Even today political theology attracts human beings to Jesus and brings Christians to the victims of this society."[28]

Thus, the Sermon on the Mount is the fundamental law of the Kingdom of God in this world, which offers a path of peace in a world of violence. "In summary," Moltmann insists, "the intention of political theology is undoubtedly to transform human beings from being *objects* humiliated by the violence of others to becoming free *subjects* of their own lives." His final note is that this kind of transformation actually took place in East Germany in 1989, and we hope to live out that new freedom "in the people who suffer the violence of a 'free market economy.'"[29]

The final evaluation notes that it is correct to theologize in *one's own context*, in order to remain in the concrete situation. Some contexts are Latin American, therefore, and some are European. But here Moltmann makes a very important statement for this chapter and, indeed, for this book. It is false, he emphasizes, to partition theology, for example:

> Liberation theology is good for Latin America; political theology is good for Europe. Black theology is good for blacks; feminist theology is good for women. Every theology is conditioned by its *context*, but every theology is theology and therefore *universal*, and must be accepted seriously everywhere. Moreover, every context is connected with every other context, whether by a unilateral form of domination or by a reciprocal form of true community. . . . *In this, liberation theology is as global as political theology strives to be.*[30]

The final question, then, is how these theologies are related, which we will now discuss in the last section.

New Situation, New Questions

Part of the new situation, according to Moltmann, is the fact that the modern world in the North Atlantic has since 1492 lived at the expense of nature and of the peoples of Latin America. "That is true," he says, "with regard to the exploitation of the raw materials of nature, as well as the exploitation of a cheap source of labor and leading the nations into indebtedness."[31] Political theology is a part of the internal critique of the contradictions of the "modern world," which is the principal cause of the suffering that is occurring in the third world. Here he poses the major open question: "After the elimination of the second world, the internal critique of the first world must be united with the protest of the suffering peoples of the third world, in order finally to bring justice to the world economic system. But, where can we discover the alternatives and the utopias?"[32]

Another way of asking this question is to pose it on a more concrete level: How can we create the same living conditions in wealthy West Germany and impoverished East Germany? The unification of Germany and Europe will have to be realistic about the wave of humanity that surges from east to west. Moltmann is blunt: "Without social justice there will be no peace in Europe. If the common free market promotes its proper function well, it will still leave social inequalities. The future tasks of the Churches and political theology will be found there."[33]

The author also clarifies the tasks as publicly critiquing capitalism in the name of the victims of the free market economy, and creating justice for human beings and for nature by means of a social and ecological political order. He is also confident that both the social teaching of the Catholic church and the strength of the religio-social movements in evangelical Christianity will have great potential for these critiques.

Moltmann admits that there is not a base community movement in the churches, but stresses that there have been strong servant churches for the last 150 years. The major part of social services toward children, invalids, the sick, and the elderly is in the hands of the churches. However, he also emphasizes strongly that it would be an abuse of *Christian service* toward the victims of the free market economy, if it were not accompanied with a *prophetic criticism* of those who are responsible and of the system that produces those victims. Moltmann himself ends this section with a rather foreboding prophecy: "Despite the disappearance of the 'communist threat,' I foresee that conflicts will necessarily arise between church and state as well as between Christianity and society."[34]

He then takes up a second situation, namely, that the *ecological conflict* with the natural environment will be at least as threatening as the one mentioned above. Here he says that ecological theology defends the violated and destroyed creation of God, and protests against those who are culpable and the system that produces these victims: "Ecological theology is at the same time a *Christian service* with regard to suffering nature and a *prophetic critique* against the violence that produces this suffering."[35]

Finally, Moltmann notes that European political theology from the beginning was *ecumenical*, developing relationships with Latin America, Asia, and Africa. In the new circumstances of Europe, however, there has also arisen a new *eurocentrism* among the Europeans. The author attacks this eloquently:

> Today nationalism is on the rise in Europe. But we call for *ecu-menical solidarity*, that it will become more powerful than a national and European loyalty! This is not only a moral task, but it is the only reasonable one. Without social justice between the first and third worlds, peace will not exist. And without peace with the third world, the North Atlantic world will self-destruct.[36]

That, he continues, is because a humanity divided by violence and injustice will destroy this *one Earth* on which all of us live.

Political theology is said to be the internal critique of the modern world, while liberation theology is the external critique. Both speak on behalf of the victims. Moltmann concludes with a penetrating question: "Must we not arrive at an alliance between critical theology in the first world and liberation theology in the third world?"[37]

At this point, I would sum up and state that any objective reader can see that Moltmann's European political theology is actually a liberation theology in the context of Germany and Europe. But the "labels" of various theologies are insignificant; what is of the utmost importance is that both of these theologies have placed themselves squarely and unambiguously on the side of the poor and the victims. Thus, both theologies not only supply the essential critique of modernity and postmodernity, but they also stake their lives in concrete praxis on behalf of the poor and the victims. No more honorable, dangerous, and desperately needed alliance can be imagined in today's world.

ROBERT MCAFEE BROWN

Robert McAfee Brown is truly an extraordinary man, an authentic blend of scholar and prophet in a culture that pays homage to neither. His many books, articles, lectures, and praxis of liberation theology over three decades surely deserve accolades and a ranking as the foremost liberation theologian in the United States and perhaps in the entire first world. (Jürgen Moltmann may be the major competitor.) His writings and lectures are uniformly perceptive and stimulating. At the same time, he is a truly ecumenical person, not only with regard to other Christian denominations but to all men, women, and children of the human family, and to their home, mother Earth. At present, he is Professor Emeritus of Theology and Ethics at the Pacific School of Religion at Berkeley, California.

A New Way for Us?

In this chapter I will concentrate on Brown's recent book, *Liberation Theology: An Introductory Guide*,[38] and emphasize his ideas with regard to the meaning of liberation theology. This quote encapsulates the challenges and the difficulties that many North Americans experience as they confront liberation theology in the first world. It is also an excellent example of his concise and forceful style:

> Liberation theology is about "the God of the poor"—and we are not poor. It's about "the view from the poor"—and we're on top. It's about "good news to the poor"—and that's bad news to the rich. It's about the third world—and we live in the first world. It's about social structures as carriers of evil—and those same social structures are very beneficial to us. It's about "subversion"—and that's simply an unacceptable word in our circles.[39]

Given this general context, Brown asks the reader to stop and *look* more closely at the meaning of these assertions: "Looking south from the United States, for example, we see a vast area that for centuries was under the political, economic, and ecclesiastical domination of Spain, and is now under the more recent but rapidly growing domination of the United States."[40] If any nation to the south tries to escape this violation of their sovereignty, there are many responses that have been and are now being used. There is always recourse to sending in the marines, as happened many times in Central America and the Caribbean, as well as financing and directing military coups. Another strategy is to provide "covert" military aid, as in the case of the contras in Nicaragua, and still another that doesn't even stop at assassination attempts, as in the case of Fidel Castro. Even more lethal is the fact that we "engaged in *direct military invasion* of small countries who were not willing (in President Reagan's phrase) to 'say uncle' to Uncle Sam, as, for example, in the case of Grenada and Panama, a tactic that was always being threatened against Nicaragua."[41]

Besides military and political assaults, however, the most powerful influence of all has been economic pressure and economic domination:

> Through a variety of instrumentalities who offered "funding," many countries in Latin America ended up hopelessly in debt to the United States and other powers in the northern hemisphere, who in the 1970s made loans at interest rates impossible for poor and struggling nations to meet. . . . Economic pressures have also been exerted through restrictions on trade, high tariffs, and direct economic blockades. . . .[42]

Whether or not we know all the causes of these examples of domination, Brown insists, the point for Christians is to open our eyes and see that this is happening, and that it must be taken seriously and responsibly.

The Third World Around Us

Once again, Brown calls upon readers to open their eyes to a second reality, a phenomenon that exists in all our cities, even if their worst neighborhoods are kept out of sight. Although we ordinarily think of the third world, the world of the poor, as thousands of miles away, the truth is that this world is right in our midst; the third world of poverty really exists in the United States and the rest of the first world. Brown presents a shocking portrait of the contrasts in the two worlds in all our cities:

Not far from our museums are the substandard and decaying housing units; not too far from our schools are the drug rings and, barely in their shadow, the drug lords who consider life cheap; not too far from our parks are the skid rows reserved for an abandoned humanity; not too far from our libraries are the sweatshops where workers (mostly women) receive far below the minimum wage; not too far from our skyscrapers (symbols of corporate power) are the soup kitchens.[43]

At this point Brown stresses again that the third world is on your block or just around the corner. Since liberation theology is created and developed by the poor and the oppressed, therefore, it is often overlooked that all of the oppressed communities have developed their own unique liberation theologies in many varied patterns. Brown alludes to black theology, feminist and womanist theologies, gay and lesbian theologies, the theologies of native Americans, Filipino-Americans, Hispanic-Americans, Asian-Americans, and a wide spectrum of other ethnic and racial groups. The constructive results of this are that they "have discovered their distinctiveness, and the consequent need to find new ways to articulate the gospel from a variety of backgrounds and perspectives."[44]

The Ambiguity of Power

A third reality, to which the author devotes a great deal of attention, is the *issue of power*. Obviously, this draws attention to a very large group not mentioned above, that is, to communities of *white, male* Americans, whom the other groups regard as quintessential oppressors. Brown points out, first of all, that we white males "must accept the truth of the charges that we have been overbearing, destructive, insensitive, sexist, and racist" and that ". . . we must begin to find ways to redress the wrongs we have committed. This will be a lifelong undertaking, because one does not shed the role of 'oppressor' in a fortnight."[45]

Secondly, Brown continues, the indictment of white males is easily proven because, for whatever historical reasons, white males have enjoyed the reins of power and also have verified the axiom of Lord Acton that "Power tends to corrupt and absolute power corrupts absolutely." Still speaking of white males, the author continues:

Is it not true that the abuse of power, as least as much as skin col-or or ideology, has fueled our unenviable track record? Furthermore, we have been able to mold social structures in such a way that they become our means of retaining power for our-selves, and are skewed to make it difficult for others to dislodge us. Thus, race, gender, and class become intertwined with struc-tures of power.[46]

This analysis, however, is not quite as coherent as it appears to be, since persons of other classes, gender, race, and nationality are also prone to abuses of power, so that white males do not have a monopoly of the use and abuse of power. "This," Brown declares, "makes it impossible either to confer unblemished sanctity on any racial, social, or class group or to deny the possibility of virtue to such groups."[47]

Those who oppose social change and strive to retain their own power often use the excuse that "the oppressed, when they get pow-er, always become oppressors." The key word in this ideology is the word "always," and the author correctly reasons that such a situa-tion is *possible*, but not *inevitable*. He also stands the maxim of Santayana on its head: "Those who cannot remember the past are condemned to fulfill it" takes on a more Christian cast as "those who remember the past are privileged to redirect it." The author then presents a compact view of political power:

The special task of the church in such situations is to *remind* all participants in the power struggle that whoever gains power will be tempted to abuse it, and also *challenge* all participants to re-member that the acquisition of power can sometimes be a way to advance the common good. . . . Power is not evil per se; it is nec-essary to any ordering of society, and it is not wrong to seek it.[48]

Brown believes that the United States (led by white male policy-makers) is unwilling to share power with other nations, even the smallest. This will consequently lead to social conflict and division among nations. The solution he proposes is often rejected, but gets to the core of the matter: "To struggle for the common good—a minor-ity position in the conventional marketplace of ideas—is an extremely important act of 'liberation' for power-conscious white males."[49]

As regards the Christian churches in this matter, Brown emphasizes that all Christians belong to a worldwide fellowship, and that our sisters and brothers in the third world are trying desperately to make contact with church members in the United States regarding U.S. policy. He describes this concisely: "I believe they are trying to communicate to us that as things stand now, *we are part of the problem rather than part of the solution.* We are perceived (sometimes in despairing and sometimes in strident tones) as being direct contributors to the plight of the poor, and when we hear them we have to acknowledge the truth of what they are saying."[50]

Signs of the Kingdom

As an example of these attempts, the author refers to a document called *Kairos Central America*, written by Christians in Central America.[51] These people state that they are searching for "signs of the kingdom," and that the major one they have discovered is that the poor have become agents of their own history: "They join Mary in proclaiming that the mighty will be cast down from their thrones and the poor lifted up. They announce that God is on the side of the oppressed and will help them in their ongoing bid for freedom."[52]

On the other hand, the writers of the document have also experienced many "signs of the *anti*-kingdom," when the will of God is clearly violated and God's people are oppressed. Once again, Brown produces a short litany of what third world Christians are saying to us:

> They see the hand of our nation at work in such things as the legitimization of conquest and genocide; the equation of faith with domination and oppression; puppet governments that falsely represent themselves as something other than what they are; forms of transnational capitalism that exploit rather than help the poor; and claims that Christians should be "above politics," which means in their situation giving silent approval to tyrannical regimes.[53]

The writers admit that they, too, have at times advanced the anti-kingdom and are in need of constant self-criticism. Nevertheless, all Christians are called upon to recognize the great sign of the kingdom today, that is, an option and commitment to the cause of the poor. As the document expresses it, you "are on the side of the people or you becomes an accomplice of their oppressors; you are on the side of the poor or you are with the Empire; [you are] with the God of Life or with the idols of death."[54]

A Time of Decision

Brown then focuses his attention on the Greek word, *kairos*, which is an important biblical concept, used by Jesus Christ in his first preaching that the "*kairos* is fulfilled and the kingdom of God is at hand" (Mk 1:15). Brown's description of the word is concise and to the point: the *kairos* is "a special time, a time of decision, a time when things may hang in the balance and what we do (or don't do) will have far-reaching consequences."[55] Thus, it differs from *chronos*, another Greek word for time, which refers to "clock time," the succession of seconds, minutes, hours, etc.

Thus, a *kairos* occurs when new possibilities emerge and unexpected events occur. This is abundantly manifest in the experience of the Central Americans:

> Never before in our history have the poor felt themselves so moved by the Wind of the Spirit to be effective instruments for the purposes of the God who is Creator of all. Never before have the churches of Central America felt themselves so engaged and challenged by the God of the poor. Never before has the Empire [i.e., the first world and especially the United States] had to turn so irrationally to "might makes right." . . . This is the moment. The hour is decisive.[56]

Another way of expressing this is as an either-or situation: ". . . either we close the door on the possibility of hope for the poor for many years, or as prophets we open up a new Day for humanity and thus for the church."[57]

A Kairos for the United States?

Brown titles another chapter with the phrase "our own liberation theology," which went through many drafts as he made his way through the Scylla and Charybdis of being too harsh in his writing or being too bland. The major question he proposes throughout is no longer the *kairos* of Central America or of South Africa but of the United States: "Is it *kairos* time for us?"[58] The writers of the *kairos* documents, he asserts, all shared in one characteristic, a "searingly honest self-scrutiny." That same searchlight should examine our own awareness and honesty as we attempt to discern the *kairos* of the church in the United States.

Brown immediately presents his own choice for a *kairos* in the United States: the beating of Rodney King by four white policemen in Los Angeles, the verdict of not guilty, and the torrent of rioting and violence that flooded the streets of that sprawling city. He sees it as a defining time in American history—"a time when the veneer around the American way of life was stripped away and white middle-class people discovered something that African Americans and other minority peoples have known all along: that we are a racist society and also a violent society."[59] The author continues his *j'accuse*:

> At the same time that we have been denying these truths about ourselves, we have consistently denied equal educational opportunities to minorities and have thus shut them off from the possibility of meaningful employment. They become trapped in cycles of poverty from which they cannot escape, and each generation can only cast its frustration and anger on the next. If there ever was a *"kairos* time," this is it.[60]

Unfortunately, Brown continues, there is a failure in both political parties to articulate a sense of purpose and to provide the leadership that such a crisis demands, so that the people lose faith in their leaders and a sense of national malaise sets in. It is not that the people do not believe in God, but that they have many gods to worship. The author does not hesitate to identify his own view of this idolatry:

> If we do try to name the chief idol in our national pantheon, it is undoubtedly some form of "nationalism." What has at times been a healthy pride in our heritage and its contributions to the entire human venture has degenerated into a crabbed insistence not

only that because of our heritage we behave better than any other nation but that we also have a right to determine how other nations shall behave.[61]

Brown goes beyond Theodore Roosevelt and insists that Americans both speak loudly *and* carry a big stick. If other nations fail to accept our agenda, we bash them either economically or militarily, as (most recently) in the cases of Grenada, Panama, and Iraq. The unspoken assumption is that the U.S. is always right. Consequently, in "order to assume unchallenged preeminence in the bashing department, we create inordinately expensive (and increasingly superfluous) weapons systems, at the cost of the decay of our schools, our social services, our infrastructure, and, increasingly, our environment."[62] Clearly, everyone loses as a result of this nationalism, and the author is blunt in emphasizing that only by overthrowing the idol of nationalism can we turn this nation around.

Precautions in the Crisis

In responding to the crisis, Brown recalls that hope is always alive in Christianity, even though there are at the same time myriad problems and dangers. In weathering the storm, he comments on three precautions: 1) "embracing the flag"; 2) responding with anger, but not hatred; and 3) discerning the difference between the oppressor and the oppressed.

As regards the first caution, Brown, not known as an admirer of ex-President George Bush, notes that he used the phrase "embrace the flag" as a major political gambit in the 1988 presidential election. His understanding of this motto appears to have meant "uncritical and unambiguous adulation of all things American."[63] Brown quotes the poet Wendell Berry, who also employs the term "embrace the flag," but with incisive irony:

> Berry here suggests that the "free republic" is not yet a present achievement, and thus never to be equated with existing structures, but only a future possibility—perhaps occasionally, but only occasionally, realized in fragmentary form in the present. In both cases, the tension between what is and what ought to be is

maintained—a crucial safeguard against an idolatry that is exhibited whenever the sole injunction is to "embrace the flag."[64]

The caution against hatred, Brown states, is given because this always leads to the dehumanization of the recipient: ". . . to dehumanize another is to dehumanize oneself in the process. The exercise is never even a win-lose situation, but always lose-lose."[65]

Anger, on the other hand, needs to be claimed as a virtue, "for if we can remain psychically undisturbed by evil, we are letting indifference go bail for responsibility."[66] Once again, the author names the reasons for anger with a prophetic fervor:

> We will discover much—in our own domestic life, in our country's international relations, in the ugliness of dictatorships, in the frightful ubiquity of torture—that should fill us with anger, revulsion, righteous indignation, and *should* be angered by the specter of hungry children, by the destructiveness of war, by the way the economic system sucks the lifeblood out of the poor, by the reality of nations (our own included) using "food as a weapon."[67]

In short, there is a severe human deficiency in a person who is not angered or has not been angered by the profound evils of this century.

The third precaution is concerned with distinguishing between oppressor and oppressed. Brown has claimed throughout his book that the oppressed must be the ones who bring about their liberation, and that those who oppose them are the oppressors. Unfortunately, however, when we seek out who the oppressors really are, it becomes "disturbingly clear that they are likely to be the sort of people who read this sort of book—reasonably well off, at least moderately comfortable, and on the whole satisfied with the way things are."[68]

The author points out, however, that both white women and white men at times play the role of the oppressor and also of the oppressed in our society. Karen Lebacqz, a feminist theologian, admits that she is part of the *oppressor* class as regards brown or black third-world women: "She has many advantages denied to them, and has access to comforts that her culture makes available to her at the cost of exploiting women elsewhere."[69] At the same time, she lives in a male-dominated culture and is denied many opportunities; therefore, she is also one of the *oppressed*. Ms. Lebacqz is thus in an ambiguous situation, but employs her experience of oppression as something that provides her with greater sensitivity to the voices of the oppressed.

Surprisingly, too, the North American *males* who have been accused of oppressing all others

> are frequently oppressed by the socioeconomic situation in which they find themselves, with pressures abounding to make them conform to such things as striving for upward mobility, competing ruthlessly for jobs, responding to siren calls to "comfort" as the expected fruit of daily labor, checking their consciences at the entrance to the workplace, and so on—in short, worshiping the idols exposed in the *kairos* documents we have already examined.[70]

Renouncing the idols may entail great cost and sacrifice. It is very interesting to note that Brown refers to our first author on this topic, Jürgen Moltmann. Moltmann movingly describes the experience of being labeled a "traitor to one's class," since class is a major idol, and the renunciation that must be squarely faced, perhaps for a lifetime. Those who sincerely seek "liberation" from the gods of their culture will have their sincerity tested when they are asked to transform their words into actions for justice.

Creating a Liberation Theology

In order to overcome the idols, the individual must be aided and guided by other Christians. Utilizing the work of Jack Nelson-Pallmeyer (a prolific first-world liberation theologian), Brown proposes three steps to create a liberation theology in the locale where we are living. These include the following: 1) We must consciously form communities of committed Christians; 2) as people of faith, we must be willing to speak the truth to one another and to the dominant community; 3) we must take risks.

With regard to community, the author recalls that a solitary Christian is a contradiction in terms. While thinking, worshiping, and acting together in a liberation community, a first step is to take part in *social analysis*, "learning where the real sources of power are, the actual means available for change, the ways in which our immediate society responds to challenge, and so forth—all in clear and hard-headed fashion."[71] A second step is reflection on the Bible deriving further insight to understand our present history in a new way. The final step is *action*, letting our analysis and biblical reflections issue in challenging the world around us.

An excellent description of the dialectical nature of these three steps may be found in Nelson-Pallmeyer:

> These components function together, forming a continuous interactive circle that should not be broken. The purpose of bible study is to encourage discipleship, not simply to know more about Jesus; the goal of social analysis is transforming action, not simply to know more about difficult social problems. Social actions are then evaluated and reformulated in the context of further bible study and social analysis.[72]

This theological method is a familiar one in the base communities of the Latin American church, which are mainly characterized by impoverishment and oppression. Obviously, on the other hand the communities in the United States are generally middle class and well off. Although our churches have collective faults, Brown stresses that "the churches are one of the few places left in our society from which impulses for liberation and change might be effectively harnessed and strengthened," and where a "spirituality of liberation" may be created and developed.[73]

The second step for a liberation community is a willingness to speak the truth to one another and also to the dominant society. Brown is attempting to overcome what many experience today as an almost universal culture of lying and deceit, from the government on down. Thus, it is an urgent necessity for Christians to speak the truth to each other "so that we have our facts straight, learn from one another the most effective ways to speak the truth, and are buttressed by the fact of shared convictions, assuring us that we are not off the wall in our individual appraisals."[74]

In speaking to the dominant community, it is very important to have assurance that we are not alone and that there are others who will support us and substantiate our concerns. Brown also warns that the dominant community will always oppose those who threaten their power and authority, and it is fierce in fighting to maintain the status quo: "Those to whom the truth is addressed never want to hear the truth. Speaking the truth to the dominant community will at least not be dull."[75]

The last step for a liberating community is learning to take risks, which Brown says has been required for authentic Christians since 30 A.D. We have learned from the churches in the third world that the risks to be taken are high and that they are often fatal. Although it would be sick to search for suffering, at times it must be accepted in witness to the faith. It is important, then, to discern what kind of witness is appropriate to Christians in the United States and in the rest of the first world.

Brown begins with an individual approach, and this may entail

a vastly simplified lifestyle, or a sharing of tools among neighbors, or limiting consumption, or engaging in tax resistance as a protest against expenditures to the military, or refusing to accept induction into the armed forces, or committing oneself to nonviolence as a consistent way of life, or continuing to challenge the power structures, or refusing to build a big new church and instead making the money available for low-cost housing.[76]

The same holds true for the communal level, where communities will have to make decisions to choose God or mammon, God's will or America first. Will the various religions join together "to demand that an agenda for social justice be created? Will we collectively allow wage discrimination to flourish, or will we flex our collective muscles in defense of 'equal pay for equal work?'"[77]

Servants in Pharaoh's Court?

In the conclusion of his North American liberation theology, Brown returns to a favorite biblical treasure trove revolving around the Exodus and accompanying symbols, especially the escape of the people of Israel from the domination of the pharaoh of Egypt. Oppressed people everywhere hail the Hebrew slaves as models of

God's intervention for themselves at the present time in their history. The author also notes that "[c]ontemporary women discover new possibilities when they read how the Hebrew midwives outwitted the pharaoh and weakened his power over them."[78]

The question arises as to how Christians in the first world interpret this story as they strive for social justice, but are not victims of serious oppression. Rather than the dramatic and exhilarating narration of the exodus, Brown focuses behind the scenes and envisages us in the U.S. as *the servants in pharaoh's court*. These are lower level people, certainly, but are also card-carrying members of the establishment, with their eyes fixed on advancement. And this is true whether

> our pharaoh is the current resident in the white house, the CEO of the corporation that employs us, the chairperson of the university department in which we are trying get tenure, or the head of the real estate agency where we are still working only on commission. How do we relate to the society around us? How do we change it (if we wish to change it)? How, in other words, do we function as human beings?[79]

The author provides a list of five options for his readers to reflect upon. The first and easiest one is to accept what we have and be grateful. However, if "the pharaoh says 'Jump!' we'll ask, 'How high?' and if, in another situation, he says something like 'Crack down on the Jews,' we'll ask, 'How hard?'"[80] Brown looks upon this option as selling one's soul to the highest bidder.

The second option allows the first world Christian to use her or his position to do something for others, as long as it doesn't get them in trouble. For example, if they come across people near us who are lacking in food, shelter, or jobs, they will devote volunteer time from their busy schedules in shelters and job agencies and soup kitchens. Often the pharaohs applaud this at annual banquets, which makes everybody feel good.

Brown interprets this as merely adjusting things cosmetically, and not really bringing about change in *anything*. Despite our kindness at the soup kitchen, "people are going to be hungry again in a few hours, and the soup kitchen (while, of course, necessary for to-

day) won't ever solve the long-range problems of unemployment or unfair wage scales, which are what make the soup kitchens necessary."[81]

In the third option, the author discusses the explosive issue of radical social change or revolution. After a careful dissection of the issues, Brown leaves the choices open for his readers:

> The price that is paid for embracing the revolutionary option is that the attempt might fail and the last state be worse than the first, from failing to "count the cost" ahead of time, or making overly romantic assessments of what was desirable in relation to what was possible. The price for *not* embracing the revolutionary option is that evil, unchallenged, may be able to dig its way even more firmly into ongoing and unjust power structures.[82]

Option four entails leaving pharaoh's court and devoting oneself to creating a better model of community, a sectarian solution that has often taken place in the past and that is still "a more excellent way" for some Christians today. Brown also points out that there are negative elements in this option, since "disengagement from pharaoh's court removes one from the possibility of immediate effective action within the court and allows the power of others to go unchallenged. Any impact will be long-run rather than short-run."[83]

Finally, the last option is to stay inside the court of pharaoh, and to attempt to act as the loyal opposition. Brown elaborates on the recent Gulf War, where the vast majority of Catholic and Protestant leaders opposed the arms buildup and the subsequent war, thus "speaking truth to power." Power in the person of George Bush did not heed their message, but that does not mean they must cease from constant prophetic witness.

This is clearly Brown's own option. Furthermore, he cautions that the time may come, and probably will, when a total break with the pharaoh is necessary in order to witness from the outside. On the other hand, there exists the "danger of selling out too soon to what is expedient or what the public will tolerate, and ending up as accomplices of evil."[84]

Brown correctly leaves it up to his readers in the first world to choose one or more of these options, but the last word is "in any showdown, being loyal to God means increasing opposition to pharaoh."[85]

Observations

In this chapter, I have not included women liberation theologians, since we have already surveyed the writings of three first-world women in Chapter Two of this book. These include the works of Elisabeth Schüssler Fiorenza, Rosemary Radford Ruether, and Elizabeth A. Johnson. We have also listened to the voices of minority women who live in the United States in other chapters. Finally, I highly recommend a book on Catholic women feminists, who are located in the first world of Western Europe, *The Voice of the Turtledove: New Catholic Women in Europe*, edited by Anne Brotherton.[86] Excellent surveys are provided for women in Belgium, England, France, Germany, Ireland, Italy, The Netherlands, and Spain. Brotherton, associate professor of sociology and ministry as well as director of experiential education at the Jesuit School of Theology at Berkeley, is also a member of the Sisters for Christian Community. Her final words are eloquent:

> . . . hope endures in the people of God who see, even through darkness, that something profound is indeed happening—that a new age in the history of the Catholic Church lies ahead, that the authentic and beloved tradition will be recovered in a renewed community of faith. And it is this hope which is especially nourished by the thousands of Europe's new Catholic women, who continue faithfully (though at times with a faith which exacts a high price) to claim their Catholic identity and to serve the people of God in the name of that faith.[87]

Most of my observations on theology in the first world have already been proposed in the first pages of this chapter with regard to the theological supertanker that exists in the United States, and I will not repeat my comments here. I do wish to repeat my admiration for the prolific work of Moltmann and Brown, who have spoken out fearlessly and creatively in their respective countries over a span of many years. *Ojalá*, as the Latin Americans say, that many other women and men theologians in the first world will follow in the paths that they have blazed, with courage and great fortitude. To be blunt, they are foremost among the few prophets that inhabit the first world.

With regard to the writings of Moltmann, I believe that Latin American or other liberation theologians who separate themselves from "progressive" Europeans and the new political theology in Europe are making a serious mistake. I hope it is evident in Moltmann's article that liberation theology and political theology have the same goal, that is, the cause of the poor and the oppressed. They do have different "contexts," but it is the essential method of all liberation theologies to speak from their own context and their own experiences. That there are "differences" or "contexts" is therefore absolutely necessary for authentic liberation theologies. I would also emphasize that the enemies (covert or overt) of the poor and the oppressed are legion, almost limitless. Thus, it ill behooves the committed allies of the poor to quarrel over theological niceties; they are natural *compañeros* in an immense struggle, or *lucha*, together.

While reflecting on the ideas of Moltmann and Brown, I was constantly reminded of a conversation I had with Jon Sobrino, a theologian in the Jesuit university in San Salvador. Over a decade ago, Sobrino visited Washington, D.C., and stayed at the Jesuit residence where I was living. Before his departure, I questioned him concerning his ideas about liberation theology and its role in the United States, using a tape recorder. After over an hour, I turned off the machine, with great satisfaction and gratitude for a plethora of profound ideas.

As I walked away, Jon stopped me and stated that there was one more thing to say, really the most important thing. If the dominant classes in your country applaud your work and shower you with awards, honorary degrees, prestigious chairs, etc., beware—you can be sure you are on the wrong track. A hermeneutic of suspicion should be put into practice, since you may very well have become a tool, a weapon of the dominators. That thought, beyond all the others of Jon, has lived in the shadows of my mind for all the intervening years.

QUESTIONS FOR REFLECTIONS AND DISCUSSION

1. At the present time, very few theologians in the first world have turned their attention to the plight of the wretched in the third world. What is your own reaction to this situation? What steps can be taken to change it?

2. Gustavo Gutiérrez has stated that the Latin American theologians have produced a "theology of the people" while the European political theology is academic and for the bourgeois. After reading some of the theology of Moltmann in this chapter, do you think this statement is correct? Why or why not?

3. In his efforts in Germany, Moltmann has led demonstrations and other activities concerning the movements for peace and the preservation of Earth. Would you consider this to be a German liberation theology? Could you suggest other ways to advance these two movements in the United States?

4. At the end of his article, Moltmann emphasizes that his political theology has developed ecumenical relations with churches in Latin America, Asia, and Africa. Can you suggest any theologians in the United States who are committed to such relations? Have you read their publications or heard them speak?

5. Moltmann believes that a great danger to the churches is the resurgence of nationalism. Do you agree with his statements on this matter? Do you believe there is also a resurgent nationalism in the United States that is similarly dangerous?

6. Robert McAfee Brown begins with a sharp critique against the U.S. in Central America and the Caribbean. Do you agree with his politics and his view of America? Be specific.

7. Brown also stresses forcefully that the "third world" of dire poverty is everywhere in the United States and that liberation theologies have developed in those areas. Have you experienced this in your own town or city? Have you ever thought about a profession or vocation to change these situations?

8. According to Brown, a kairos or crucial time of decision is taking place in the United States. He sees the beating and trial of Rodney King as his own personal kairos. Do you agree with his own choice? Can you discern such a kairos in your own area? If there is one, have you committed yourself to it?

9. Brown has made a call for "liberation communities" in the United States, where the members speak the truth to their own members and to the dominant society. Do you think his plan is feasible? Do you belong to or hope to form such a community?

10. Brown believes that most American Christians are "servants in Pharaoh's court." He proposes five options to choose within this situation. Which of the five options do you think you would choose if you had to make a choice? Give specific reasons.

SUGGESTED READINGS

Bayer, Charles. *A Guide to Liberation Theology for Middle-Class Congregations.* St. Louis: CPB Press, 1986.

Birch, Bruce C., and Larry L. Rasmussen. *The Predicament of the Prosperous.* Philadelphia: Westminster, 1978.

Brown, Robert McAfee. *Saying Yes and Saying No: On Rendering to God and Caesar.* Philadelphia: Westminster, 1986.

Coleman, John. *An American Strategic Theology.* New York: Paulist, 1982.

Crosby, Michael H. *The Dysfunctional Church: Addiction and Codependency in the Family of Catholicism.* Notre Dame, IN: Ave Maria Press, 1991.

Folk, Jerry. *Doing Theology, Doing Justice.* Minneapolis: Fortress, 1990.

Fourez, Gerard. *Liberation Ethics.* Philadelphia: Temple University Press, 1982.

Hennelly, Alfred T. *Theology for a Liberating Church: The New Praxis of Freedom.* Washington, DC: Georgetown University Press, 1989.

Lindberg, Carter H. *Beyond Charity: Reformation Initiatives for the Poor.* Minneapolis: Fortress, 1992.

Mahan, Brian, and L. Dale Richesin. *The Challenge of Liberation Theology: A First World Response.* Maryknoll, NY: Orbis Books, 1980.

Pattison, Stephen. *Pastoral Care and Liberation.* New York: Cambridge University Press, 1994.

Sanks, T. Howland, and John A. Coleman. *Reading the Signs of the Times: Resources for Social and Cultural Analysis.* New York: Paulist, 1993.

Schubeck, Thomas. *Liberation Ethics: Sources, Models, and Norms.* Minneapolis: Fortress, 1993.

CHAPTER EIGHT

SAVING AND CULTIVATING CREATION

An Ecotheology of Liberation

Being rooted in love for our real communities and for our common mother, Gaia, can teach us patient passion, a passion that is not burnt out in a season, but can be renewed season after season. Our revolution is not just for us, but for our children, for the generations of living beings to come. What we can do is to plant a seed, nurture a seed-bearing plant here and there, and hope for a harvest that goes beyond the limits of our powers and the span of our lives.

Rosemary Radford Ruether
Gaia & God: An Ecofeminist Theology of Earth Healing 273-74

As we see, *moyo* [life], *unmunthu* [fullness of life], community, justice, nature, and the power of life are inseparable. Together they represent the bondedness of life. This notion of the bondedness of life has informed some African Christian thinking where that thinking has attempted to transcend the mechanistic views imposed on Africa by the West, where that thinking has drawn upon the rich heritage of Africa itself. But such life-centeredness could also serve as a vital basis for all Christian thinking and action, as a guide and empowering vision for the Christian movement to al-

leviate the suffering and exploitation of living creatures worldwide.

Harvey Sindima
Liberating Life: Contemporary Approaches to Ecological Theology 146

ALTHOUGH I WAS BORN IN MANHATTAN,
my parents (Irish immigrants) moved as soon it was possible from a
noisy, frenetic apartment in an Irish ghetto on West 90th Street.
Continuing their migration, they crossed the Hudson River to New
Jersey and found the modest home of their dreams, a tiny but deeply cherished piece of their own land. There were also many open
fields nearby to explore and to challenge other local teams in base-
ball and football (without parents in pre-Little League days). As a
young boy, moreover, I spent a great deal of free time on weekends
and summer vacations in the "natural" areas of New Jersey. These
included glistening lakes and the myriad trails (for both humans
and animals) of the Watchung and Pocono Mountains, as well as
the great barrier islands, over a hundred miles of white gleaming
beaches, and the great thundering immensity of the Atlantic Ocean,
known simply to all as the "Jersey shore."

Glimmers of Ecology

This friendship with natural beauty and the cornucopia of flora
and fauna left an indelible imprint on my very soul, which has only
deeply intensified as the years have passed. In those innocent years,
it appeared that the mountains, lakes, and especially the ocean,
were somehow infinite, and that they would always continue to
flaunt and promenade their pristine power, beauty and endless lux-
uriance. All the multifarious species, too, of animals, birds, fish, and
insects were bustling at work and play in this utopia, perfectly
adapted to their home ("ecology" means the "study of the home")
and seemingly destined to continue there forever.

As a theologian, moreover, I always perceived these places as
magical or divine—far better locales for prayer and contemplation
than human homes, churches, and cities. Together with the daily
miracle of the sun and its shadow, the moon, and with the stu-
pendous immensity of stars and endless galaxies, I discovered here

the surest proof of an infinitely knowing and loving God, and not in the pages of theological tomes.

Most of my theological reflection and publications, however, had been devoted for many years to political theology and liberation theology, concerned with human communities and their relation to the kingdom of God. It was only infrequently that my political instincts were deeply disturbed by such works as Rachel Carson's *Silent Spring* and *The Limits to Growth*.[1] Carson's carefully documented description of the deliberate poisoning of Earth especially filled me with disgust and anger. Later, in the 1970s and 1980s, a vast number of books and articles erupted concerning the new science of "ecology." At the same time, many authors have discovered this as a new field for theology, perhaps *the* dominant field in coming decades. In my writings, I refer to this trailblazing area of study as an Ecotheology of Liberation. Once again, I have chosen those who mark the trails for the future. As will be seen, diversity among the authors abounds, just as it abounds in "the peaceable kingdom," but also profound commonalities.

THOMAS BERRY

Thomas Berry must be considered as one of the great pioneers of the ecological movement, and he continues to write and lecture strenuously on his views right up to the present time. He is a Roman Catholic priest of the Passionist order, and has taught at Seton Hall, St. John's, Fordham, and other universities. A major change in his life occurred when he decided to devote full time to ecological study and founded the Riverdale Center for Religious Research, located in the Bronx, New York City. He describes this institution as "a place for studying the dynamics of the planet Earth, and the role fulfilled by human beings within the total dynamics of the universe."[2] In all these tasks, finally, he refers to his own role as that of a "geologian."[3]

Is Unity Necessary?

Thomas Berry is not a prolific writer, but what he does publish is characterized by careful selection of words and ideas, as well as a chiseled succinctness in his prose. An important book on his work,

Thomas Berry and the New Cosmology, presents what are two classic essays, along with Twelve Principles "for understanding the universe and the role of the human in the universe."[4] The editors of the book and experienced collaborators with Berry, Anne Lonergan and Caroline Richards, attest to the critical significance of these three writings for the key ideas of the author. Six other authors have commented on and evaluated Berry's ideas in the book.[5]

I begin with Berry's article on "The Earth: A New Context for Religious Unity."[6] He starts by looking at the present situation of Christianity. The Catholic church, he observes, is less than twenty percent of the population of the world, while the other Christian churches have broken up into a large number of diverse communities. As regards the Catholics, he notes their present context: "A more tolerant secularism is pervasive throughout the entire world and tends to dominate life ideals as well as national and international institutions. In view of all this, the religious situation of the Catholic community has become exceedingly complex. The need for a more formal consideration of the church in its relation to the religious and non-religious world about us is clear."[7]

Berry perceives the non-Christian religions as in a situation of vigorous fundamentalistic renewal at the present time, in direct reaction to liberal adaptations in modern times. With regard to Catholics, he quotes the document *Nostra Aetate* (In Our Age) from the Second Vatican Council, which was devoted to relations of the church with other religions. These other religions, the document states, often reflect "a ray of that truth which enlightens all men," followed immediately by the statement that Jesus Christ is "the way, the truth, and the life in whom men find the fullness of religious life. . . ."[8]

Berry points out that these tenets of Catholic doctrine are not something new, but have been substantially the same for a number of centuries. He robustly rejects this viewpoint, and insists that the other religions do not merely transmit a "ray" of the divine light, "but even floods of light illumining the entire religious life of the human community."[9]

Furthermore, the attitude of the Council and the Christian tradition from the beginning manifests "a powerful sense of unity, a suspicion if not abhorrence of diversity in religious concerns." This attitude is seen to proceed from the oneness of the transcendent God, Yahweh:

> Yahweh absorbs into himself all that divine power generally experienced as diffused throughout the universe and articulated on the planet Earth in the manifold phenomena of the natural world. Associated with this deity is a singular people bound by a covenant expressed in written form which, in its later new covenant expression, is communicated to the peoples of Earth through a divinely established hierarchical church.[10]

This stress on an elect people was somewhat spiritualized in the New Testament era, but the church still maintained its sense of having an exclusive universal role for all of humanity, while other religions were perceived as obstacles, "although the Holy Spirit never failed to be present to well-disposed individuals."[11]

The Need for Diversity

Berry brings Thomas Aquinas into the discussion here as teaching that diversity is the "perfection of the universe."[12] And this law of diversity holds good for the religious life as well as for other areas of being and action. Consequently, the perfection of revelation, spirituality, and sacraments lies in their differentiation and diversity, and "the extent of the diversity is the measure of the perfection."[13]

If we survey the religious traditions and their relations, it becomes obvious that they share certain revelatory patterns in a threefold pattern:

> First there is the primordial experience expressed in written or oral form, the scriptural period. This takes place by an isolation process. Second, there is the deepening of the tradition, a patristic period, when the implications of the original experience are elaborated in contact with the larger life force. Third, there is the period of expansion, of interaction with other religions in their more evolved phase.[14]

Berry then proceeds to demonstrate how these three phases are manifested in the major religions of the world: "In every case these ultimate orientations toward reality and value originate in an interior depth so awesome that the experience is perceived as coming from a transphenomenal source, as revelatory of the ultimate mystery whence all things emerge into being."[15] Berry believes that none of these religions are rivals of each other, although they do need space to cultivate their own inner identity: "Each is supreme in it own order. Each is destined for diffusion throughout the human community."[16]

Returning to the Second Vatican Council, the author focuses on the document concerning Revelation. He believes that it should have been called "Christian Revelation" or "Biblical Revelation," since it does not consider the experience of revelation in other religions. These religions are considered either qualitatively or quantitatively different from Christianity. If qualitatively different, the religion does not have revelation, but rather some "natural" way of knowing; if quantitatively different, then Christian superiority can be demonstrated in "terms of fullness or completeness."[17]

In reply to this, Berry faces the problem head on:

> I am proposing a qualitative difference within the authentic revelatory process itself, a difference that cannot be resolved in terms of fullness or completeness but only by mutual presence of highly differentiated traditions. What is to be avoided is any monoform tendency in the meeting of religions. What is to be sought is a mutually enhancing meeting of qualitatively differentiated religions. . . .[18]

Berry finds another false path in the Christian tendency to call for "one flock and one shepherd," which he sees as an escape or a rejection of reality, as well as a hindrance to human welfare and to the salvific process. "This attitude," he insists vigorously, "has led, in the academic world, to such an aversion toward other religions that nowhere on the North American continent is there a Catholic university where professional studies on these other religions can be done."[19] The challenge and the tension for creativity in the dialogue with the religions is avoided; ". . . the ideal is the greatest tension that the situation can bear creatively." Finally, the realm of the sacred needs more variety, the author insists, than any other aspect of human reality.

Some of the suggestions for resolving the difficulties that Christians experience in accepting the variety of religions are these: One can recognize the qualitative differences in religions and foster this diversity. One can identify the dynamics that take place in relations between the religions, and one can cultivate the New Story of the universe as a context for accepting the diversity of religions.[20]

The New Context

Thus far, Berry continues, we have not yet paid significant attention to the "vast changes in our modern way of experiencing the universe, the human community and the modes of human consciousness. Yet these are powerful determinants in all our religions as well as in all our cultural developments."[21] Obstacles to accepting this new context include the dominant secular culture, materialist views of the world and the universe, and rationalist emphases in much of contemporary thought. Because of these prevalent obstacles opposing religion, ". . . we can hardly believe that the long course of scientific meditation on the universe has finally established the emergent universe itself as a spiritual as well as a physical process and the context for a new mode of religious understanding. We might describe it as a meta-religious context for a comprehensive view of the entire complex of religions."[22]

Instead of the traditional theological, sociological, or psychological approaches, Berry proposes a cosmological-historical approach to the new context, which he discerns in Thomas Aquinas and in the French Jesuit Pierre Teilhard de Chardin.[23] Going beyond these thinkers, he makes the startling statement that it is the universe that instructs us:

> If humans have learned anything about the divine, the natural or the human, it is through the instruction received from the universe around us. . . . In this manner it is clear that the universe as such is the primary religious reality, the primary sacred community, the primary revelation of the divine, the primary subject of incarnation, the primary unit of redemption, the primary referent in any discussion of reality or of value.[24]

It certainly would be difficult to take a stronger position on the centrality of Earth and the universe for Christianity, the world religions, and the entire human community. Berry believes that this community, for the first time, has a single creation myth. This does not mean, however, the suffocation of diversity, as the author delights in stressing: "For the first time we can tell the universe story, the Earth story, the human story, the religion story, the Christian story, and the church story as a single comprehensive narrative."[25]

Berry ends on a more sober note as he returns to the Second Vatican Council and the Catholic church. He cites the thought of Saint Paul and Saint John on the "Christ form of the universe," and repeats the views of Thomas Aquinas and Pierre Teilhard de Chardin cited earlier. Despite their visions, he ends on a note of wistful sadness:

> The choice, however, of the Council was to establish the biblical-redemption story rather than the modern creation story as its context of understanding. In doing so it set aside its own most powerful instrument for dealing with the church, revelation, the modern world, missions, and its relation with non-Christian religions. It will undoubtedly be a long time before such a transition in our thinking will take place.[26]

Economics and Life Systems

Latin American liberation theology from the beginning has stressed the importance of the social sciences as interlocutors and collaborators with theologians. Although he does not claim to be a liberation theologian, Berry adopts his own "social analysis" in his second key article on "Economics: Its Effect on the Life Systems of the World."[27]

The author begins by noting that economics as a religious issue can be approached in different ways. The moral-religious approach begins with a quest for justice, so that the basic necessities of life are available to all. "Such an approach," he observes, "emphasizes our social and political responsibilities to see that the weak and less gifted are not exploited by the strong and the competent."[28] This critique zeroes in on a capitalist market economy that does not fulfill its social responsibilities, so that it is necessary to reverse this by incorporating everyone into the benefits of the economy. Berry comes to the heart of the problem in this approach by asserting that "it brings about only temporary improvement since the more basic difficulty may not be the social issue but the industrial economy *which is not a sustainable economy.*"[29]

A second way of viewing economics as a religious issue is to inquire into the present economy and its deeper implications from within its own functioning and its capacity to sustain itself. The author first describes the basic life systems: "In the natural world there exists an amazing richness of life expression in the ever-renewing cycle of the seasons. There is a minimum of entropy. The inflow of energy and the outflow are such that the process is sustainable over an indefinite period of time. So long as the human process is integral to these processes of nature, so long is the human economy sustainable into the future."[30]

The difficulty, however, occurs when the industrial economy disrupts this natural process and destroys the Earth technologies and their productivity. This leads to all kinds of deficits, the national debt, the budgetary deficit, the trade deficit, the military waste, and so forth.

In Berry's view, furthermore, all of these pale in comparison with another form of deficit, that is, the *Earth deficit.* This, he emphasizes, is "the real deficit, the ultimate deficit, the deficit with some consequences so absolute as to be beyond any adjustment from any source in heaven or Earth. Since the Earth system is the ultimate guarantee of all deficits, a failure here is a failure of last resort. Neither economic viability nor improvement in life conditions for the poor can be realized in such circumstances."[31] The deficit, then, is not only the death of *a* living process, but of *the* living process of Earth itself. Berry believes that this problem is definitively different from that of any other generation or any other historical period: "The immediate danger is not *possible* nuclear war but *actual* industrial plundering."[32]

At this point, Berry turns to what can only be described as an ecological Armageddon: "The air, the water, the soil are already in a degraded condition. Forests are dying on this very continent [North America]. The seas are endangered. The rain is acid rain."[33] Many other aspects of natural destruction like the above provide a litany of horrors throughout an exhausted planet (for example, each year the United States loses over four billion tons of topsoil, and the great aquifers of the plains states have no chance of replenishing their once abundant water). The bottom line for Berry: "An exhausted planet is an exhausted economy."[34]

The author notes that economics texts and corporation practices generally ignore these devastating facts, charging it up to business costs or simply disguising the problems. In response to this, Berry replies shrewdly that "we can be sure that whatever fictions exist in Wall Street bookkeeping, Earth is a faithful scribe, a faultless calculator, a superb bookkeeper; we will be held responsible for every bit of our economic folly."[35]

Thus, he continues, there can be an economics of the human as a species, and an economics of Earth as a functional community. Listing a number of recent books and studies that elaborate this in detail, he summarizes the only possible conclusion:

> We have just begun to consider that the primary objective of economic science, of the engineering profession, of technological invention, of industrial processing, of financial investment, and of corporation management, must be the integration of human well-being within the context of the well-being of the natural world. . . . Only within the ever-renewing processes of the natural world is there any future for the human community. Not to recognize this is to make economics a deadly affair.[36]

Is Economics a Myth?

Economists, Berry continues, believe that they are creating a *wonderworld*, when in fact they are rapidly constructing a *wasteworld*. Thus, they manufacture a myth of "progress," that is the functional basis of the economy: "The GNP must increase each year. Everything must be done on a larger scale with little awareness of the inbuilt catastrophe involved in the exponential rate of increase."[37] Although it claims to be rational, economics is visionary, "supported by myth and a sense of having the magic powers of science to overcome any difficulty encountered when human processes reach their limits."[38]

Berry encapsulates what is happening in this way: "If this assault on Earth were done by evil persons with destructive intentions it would be understandable. The tragedy is that our economy is being run by persons with good intentions under the illusion that they are only bringing great benefits to the world and even fulfilling a sacred task on the part of the human community."[39] Even social reformers, whether socialist or capitalist, seek to help the poor by integrating them into the present system. Moral theologians, on the other hand, have been unable to handle this destruction of Earth; they can deal with suicide, homicide, and genocide, but their moral code cannot cope with biocide or geocide. Finally, church leaders have not organized any sustained counterattack against the catastrophe facing Earth.[40] I will dialogue further with moral theologians and, obliquely, church leaders at the end of this chapter.

A "New Sense" in Economics

Berry paints a broad picture of economics over the centuries, during which it had no inkling of the fact that the Earth system itself was the primary context of life in every area: "Every economic system from the mercantile and physiocrat theories of the seventeenth and eighteenth centuries, to the supply-demand theories of Keynes is homocentric and exploitive. The natural world is considered as a resource for human utility, not as a functioning community of mutually supporting life systems within which the human must discover its proper role."[41]

The new sense, then, is that there must be an awareness that the present system is too destructive to supply human needs in the near future, and that alternate approaches are already being set in motion. "If the moral norm of economics is what is happening to the millions of persons in need, then these more functional economic developments are required not only by those excluded from the present system but by the entire nation community, by the entire human community, and by the entire Earth community."[42]

The Dangers of Religion

At this point, Berry comments on the relationship of religion to the new sense in economics, both of which he sees as threatened by

the disruption of the natural world. Also, he asserts that the ultimate causes for an exploitive economy may be found in the re-
ligious-cultural context in which that economy evolved, leading to a
very important question: "Why did this process develop in a civilization that emerged out of a biblical-Christian matrix? . . . A long
list of answers has been written, a few by theologians, but mostly
brief articles not entirely convincing because of their inadequate
consideration of those dark or limited aspects of Christianity that
made our western society liable to act so harshly toward the natural
world."[43]

Berry next proceeds to outline four religious orientations that have
influenced Western culture to an exaggerated degree, and whose
baneful influence must be eliminated. These include: 1) the biblical
monotheistic deity severely prohibiting any worship of the divine in
nature; 2) emphasis on the redemption experience that diminished
attention to the creation experience; 3) emphasis on the spiritual nature of humans vis-à-vis the physical being of other creatures; 4) and
millennial thinking, a new era when the human condition would be
overcome by the power of God. The author provides more detail regarding these orientations, but a synoptic view suffices:

> While none of these Christian beliefs individually is adequate as
> an explanation of the alienation we experience in our natural set-
> ting, they become convincing in their totality in providing a basis
> for understanding how so much planetary destruction has been
> possible in our western tradition. We are radically oriented away
> from the natural world. It has no rights; it exists for human utility,
> even if for spiritual utility.[44]

Another important religious question is how we have lost connection with the revelation of the divine in nature. Without an exalted sense of God in the universe and Earth, Berry asserts, "we
would be terribly impoverished in our religious and spiritual development, even in our emotional, imaginative, and intellectual development."[45] In addition to this, however, it is important to cherish
the reality and nobility of the world *in itself*, not simply as something to be used or exploited. Once more Berry waxes eloquent on
this topic:

The natural world is the maternal source whence we emerge into being as earthlings. The natural world is the life-giving nourishing of our physical, emotional, aesthetic, moral, and religious experience. The natural world is the larger sacred community to which we belong. To be alienated from this community is to become destitute in all that makes us human. To damage this community is to diminish our own existence.[46]

A Program of New Life

In contrast to the era of "technological entrancement," Berry turns his attention to the task of structuring a human manner of life or, in other words, "'reinventing the human,' since none of the prior cultures or concepts of the human can deal with these issues on the scale required."[47] A number of projects, books, and studies are presented that display models of a human economy and model habitations and communities, and in alliance with these projects "there are the fifty-some ecologically oriented organizations in the United States that joined together a few years ago to defend the North American continent from government supported corporation abuse."[48]

Berry believes that one of the most significant of the social movements and the one with the most efficiency is the Bioregional Movement, which appears to have the most strength in North America. Rather obviously, the different regions of the world are not uniform but exist in many bioregions. These are depicted as "identifiable geographical areas of interacting life systems that are relatively self-sustaining in the ever-renewing processes of nature. As we diminish our commitments to our present industrial context of life with its non-renewing infrastructures, we will need to integrate our human communities with the ever-renewing bioregional communities of the place where we find ourselves."[49] Another characteristic of this kind of communities is that they manifest a primary biological identity rather than a primary political one, while their power lies in the integration of the human in the cosmological process.

Berry ends his essay with a few remarks on the world religions. Although he believes that they are essential with regard to the issues he has raised, he believes that at present they are too remote from the new sense of the universe that is necessary for the great tasks before us. Berry then summarizes the twelve principles that are needed for a new kind of religious orientation. [50]

Twelve Principles for Understanding the Universe
and the Role of the Human in the Universe Process:

1. The universe, the solar system, and planet Earth in themselves and in their evolutionary emergence constitute for the human community the primary revelation of that ultimate mystery whence all things emerge into being.

2. The universe is a unity, an interacting and genetically-related community of beings bound together in an inseparable relationship in space and time. The unity of planet Earth is especially clear; each being of the planet is profoundly implicated in the existence and functioning of every other being of the planet.

3. From the beginning the universe is a psychic as well as a physical reality.

4. The three laws of the universe at all levels of reality are differentiation, subjectivity, and communion. These laws identify the reality, the laws, and the directions in which the universe is proceeding.

5. The universe has a violent as well as a harmonious aspect, but it is consistently creative in the larger arc of its development.

6. The human is that being in whom the universe activates, reflects upon, and celebrates itself in conscious self-awareness.

7. Earth, within the solar system, is a self-emergent, self-propagating, self-nourishing, self-educating, self-governing, self-healing, self-fulfilling community. All particular life systems in their being, their sexuality, their nourishment, their education, their governing, their healing, their fulfillment, must integrate their functioning within this larger complex of mutually dependent Earth systems.

8. The genetic coding process is the process through which the world of the living articulates itself in its being and its activities. The great wonder is the creative interaction of the multiple codings among themselves.

9. At the human level, genetic coding mandates a further trans-genetic cultural coding by which specifically human qualities find expression. Cultural coding is carried on by educational processes.

10. The emergent process of the universe is irreversible and non-repeatable in the existing world order. The movement from

non-life to life on the planet is a one-time event. So too, the movement from life to the human form of consciousness. So also the transition from the earlier to the later forms of human culture.

11. The historical sequence of cultural periods can be identified as the tribal-shamanic period, the neolithic village period, the classical civilizational period, the scientific-technological period, and the emerging ecological period.

12. The main human task of the immediate future is to assist in activating the intercommunion of all the living and non-living components of the Earth community in what can be considered the emerging ecological period of Earth development.

SALLIE McFAGUE

A different but complementary perspective that is deeply theological has been provided by Sallie McFague, Carpenter Professor of Theology at the Vanderbilt University in Nashville. She has published two groundbreaking books on metaphorical theology and theology in an ecological and nuclear age.[51] I will give major emphasis to a more recent article on her work, "Imaging a Theology of Nature: The World as God's Body."[52]

Criteria and Imagination

McFague begins with a compact statement of her own worldview that has many similarities to that of Berry:

> As we near the close of the twentieth century we have become increasingly conscious of the fragility of our world. We have also become aware that the anthropocentrism that characterizes much of the Judeo-Christian tradition has often fed a sensibility insensitive to our proper place in the universe. The ecological crisis, epitomized in the possibility of a nuclear holocaust, has brought home to many the need for a new mode of consciousness. . . .[53]

Continuing this, she proposes that one approach to theology can experiment with models and metaphors of God and the world that will create "a theocentric, life-centered, cosmocentric sensibility in place of our anthropocentric one."[54]

Some criteria for a theology of nature pertinent to the contemporary situation are then proposed by the author. The first is that such a theology "must be informed by and commensurate with contemporary scientific accounts of what nature is." Secondly, it must see that human life is profoundly linked with all other forms of life. Next, it will be both creation-centered and profoundly incarnational, in contrast to an almost total interest in redemption. And finally, it will stress forcefully the links between "peace, justice, and ecological issues, aware that there can be no peace or justice unless the fabric of our ecosystem is intact."[55]

All of these criteria must be suffused with *imagination* of the relation between God and the world in a way that can touch the minds and hearts of people today. Stressing that human behavior is deeply influenced by images, symbols, and narratives, she proposes a striking example: "How would we . . . act differently if we imagined the world to be the body of God rather than considering it to be, as the tradition has, the realm of the Almighty King?"[56]

A Heuristic Method?

McFague recognizes the centrality of method in theology, and states clearly that her method will be "heuristic." Here I will choose some of the major features of her nuanced description of this method. Heuristic in the dictionary refers to "a system of education under which students are trained to find out by themselves."[57] In more detail, heuristic theology is construed as

> one that experiments and tests, that thinks in an as-if fashion, that imagines possibilities that are novel, that dares to think differently. It will not accept solely on the basis of authority but will search for what it finds convincing and persuasive; it will not, however, be mere fantasy or play but will assume that there is something to find out and that if some imagined possibilities fail, others may succeed.[58]

McFague compares her method to hermeneutic theology and constructive theology, asserting that her approach is more congenial with times of uncertainty and rapid change as is the case today.

It is also interesting to see in this important statement that the author explicitly associates her method with that of the other theologies of liberation:

My interpretation is similar to that of the so-called liberation theologies. Each of these theologies, from the standpoint of race, gender, class, or another basic human distinction, claims that the
Christian gospel is opposed to oppression of some by others, opposed to hierarchies and dualisms, opposed to the domination of
the weak by the powerful. This reading is said to be commensurate with the paradigmatic story of the life, message, and
death of Jesus of Nazareth, who in his parables, his table fellowship, and his death offered a surprising invitation to *all*, especially
to the outcast and the oppressed.[59]

The author also devotes attention to a definition or at least a description of metaphors and models. She views the metaphor as "an
attempt to say something about the unfamiliar in the terms of the
familiar, an attempt to speak about what we do not know in terms
of what we do know."[60] This is not satisfactory. I find more illumination in the description of Janet Martin Soskice cited by the
author in an endnote: "Metaphor is a figure of speech in which one
entity or state of affairs is spoken of in terms which are seen as being appropriate to another."[61] A "model," according to McFague, is
a metaphor with "staying power," that is, "a model is a metaphor
that has gained sufficient stability and scope so as to present a pattern for relatively comprehensive and coherent explanation."[62] A
pertinent example is God the *father*, a metaphor which has become a
model with far-reaching implications: ". . . if God is seen as father,
human beings become children, sin can be seen as rebellious behavior, and redemption can be thought of as restoration to the status of favored offspring."

A major problem of the model, asserts the author, is how to know
if the model is true. Acknowledging that one must take a risk or wager in proposing it, McFague stresses the role of praxis and consequences in testing the model:

An adequate model will be illuminating, fruitful, have relatively
comprehensive explanatory ability, be relatively consistent, be
able to deal with anomalies, and so on. . . . in the tradition of
Aristotle, truth means constructing the good life for the *polis*,
though for our time this must mean for the cosmos. A "true"
model of God will be one that is a powerful, persuasive construal

of God as being on the side of life and its fulfillment in our time.[63]

Once again, McFague refers to liberation theology in this key foundational element in her method: "The heavily pragmatic view of truth suggested here is similar to that of some liberation theologians and rests on an understanding of praxis not simply as action vs. theory, but as a kind of reflection, one guided by practical experience."[64] Shortly afterward, she links this to its religious aspect: "While I would not identify my position with the extremes of pragmatism, it is, nonetheless, a healthy reminder that religious truth, whatever may be the case for other kinds of truth, involves issues of value, of consequences, of the quality of lived existence."[65]

God as Mighty King?

After these preliminary remarks, McFague turns to models for the relationship of God and the world, obviously a foundation stone in her theology of nature. She is convinced that the prevalent model has been that of a monarch: ". . . the classical picture employs royalist, triumphalist metaphors, depicting god as king, lord, and patriarch, who rules over and cares for the world and human beings."[66] In the contemporary situation, Gordon Kaufman points out that "God is the king who fights on the side of his chosen ones to bring their enemies down; in more refined versions God is the father who will not let his children suffer. The first view supports militarism; the second supports escapism."[67] Kaufman maintains that neither side attempts to *act* responsibly to solve the nuclear puzzle.

McFague herself also analyzes some major problems she has with the monarchical model as an imaginative framework for a God who loves all creatures and nourishes their fulfillment. First of all, "God is distant from the world, relates only to the human world, and controls that world through domination and benevolence."[68] She continues that a king is *distant* and unapproachable: "It is the distance, the difference, the otherness of God, that is underscored by this imagery. God as king is in his kingdom—which is not of this Earth—and we remain in another place, far from his dwelling. In this picture God is worldless and the world is Godless: the world is empty of God's presence."[69]

A second objection to the monarchical model is that there is no concern for the non-human world and cosmos. The model could have developed as father or parent with associations of care, nurturance, and responsibility, but "under the powerful influence of the monarchical model, the parent becomes the patriarch, and patriarchs act more like kings than like fathers: They rule their children and they demand obedience."[70]

This anthropocentrism is accompanied by dualistic hierarchies such as male/female, spirit/nature, human/non-human, Christian/non-Christian, rich/poor, white/colored, etc. As a result: "The hierarchical, dualistic pattern is so widespread in Western thought that it is often not perceived to be a pattern, but *is felt to be simply the way things are.* It appears natural to many that whites, males, the rich, and Christians are superior to other human beings, and that human beings are more valuable in all respects than other forms of life."[71] This is a very important statement; the first step in abolishing dominating images is to explode the fiction that they are simply the way things are.

The third objection to monarchical models is similar to the statement quoted earlier by Kaufman, regarding the undercutting of human responsibility for the world. McFague extolls the greatly increased responsibility of human beings, and rejects all images or models that oppose such responsibility. She expresses the danger as follows:

> If we are capable of extinguishing ourselves and most, if not all, other life, metaphors that support attitudes of distance from, and domination of, other human beings and nonhuman life must be recognized as dangerous. No matter how ancient a metaphorical tradition may be and regardless of its credentials in scripture, liturgy, and creedal statements, it still must be discarded if it threatens the continuation of life itself. If the heart of the Christian gospel is the salvific power of God, triumphalist metaphors cannot express that reality *in our time,* whatever their appropriateness may have been in the past.[72]

In short, because of the dangerous and destructive nature of the monarchical model, McFague proposes to consider Earth as God's body, a metaphor and model for our present situation.

Does God Have a Body?

McFague finds the roots of this radical image of the world as the body of God in Stoicism, the Hebrew scriptures, Tertullian, and Irenaeus, but it found little support in Platonism and Aristotelianism and thus did not influence Augustinian and Thomistic theology. In recent times it has awakened the interest of process theology, and has been the theme of an impressive book by Grace Jantzen, entitled *God's World, God's Body*.[73]

McFague begins her justification for the body-of-God image by recalling that she is using it in an as-if fashion, precisely because there is no other way of thinking about it. She notes astutely that the monarchical image with regard to the God-world relationship "sounds like sense because we are used to it, but reflection shows that in our world it is nonsense."[74] It is also interesting to note that the king image places too much distance between God and the world, while the body image has the problem of too much proximity. This brings us to the fundamental questions that must be raised if the author's thesis is to be proven:

> Is it better to accept an imaginative picture of God as the distant ruler controlling his realm through external and benevolent power or one of God so intimately related to the world that the world can be imagined as God's body? Which is better in terms of our and the world's preservation and fulfillment? Which is better in terms of coherence, comprehensibility, and illumination? Which is better in terms of expressing the Christian understanding of the relationship between God and the world?[75]

Clearly the author upholds the body image, and begins the task of proving that there are cogent reasons and answers to the questions just enunciated. An excellent start is the recollection (not often adverted to) of the "bodily" tradition in Christianity, such as the resurrection of the body, the body of Christ in the eucharist, the church as the body of Christ, and so forth. There is also an important difference, however, from the traditional understandings of body, because this metaphor applies not only to Christians but to all creatures and to all creation. Aside from these ideas, she also notes the modern holistic understanding of the person and thus the prevalent significance of embodiment. Therefore,

> the thought of an embodied divine person is not more incredible than that of a disembodied one; in fact it is less so. In a dualistic culture where mind and body, spirit and flesh, are separable, a disembodied, personal God is more credible, but not in ours. This is only to suggest that the idea of God's embodiment . . . should not be seen as nonsense; it is less nonsense than the idea of a disembodied personal God.[76]

This body of God, McFague continues, is not just Earth but all that is, the universe or universes that the scientists study. Theologians would say that this body of God is the creation, God's self-expression: ". . . it is formed in God's own reality, bodied forth in the eons of evolutionary time, and supplied with the means to nurture and sustain billions of different forms of life."[77]

Is this, however, a descent into *pantheism*, a form of heresy for Christians? McFague answers that God does not identify completely with the universe any more than humans identify totally with their own bodies: ". . . we may be said to be spirits that possess bodies." But she does admit that more is needed than just the body metaphor in an important statement: "Without the use of personal, agential metaphors . . . including among others God as mother, father, healer, lover, friend, judge, and liberator, the metaphor of the world as God's body would be pantheistic, for the body would be all there were."[78] McFague also carefully states that what she is designating is *panentheism*, that is, "a view of the God-world relationship in which all things have their origins in God and nothing exists outside God, though this does not mean that God is reduced to these things."[79] She also adverts to the fact that distinguished theologians such as Paul Tillich and Karl Rahner have definitions similar to hers, which are included in the endnotes.[80]

Although the author evades the charge of pantheism, she admits that her metaphor puts God "at risk." God appears to become dependent and vulnerable by being bodily: "The world as God's body may be poorly cared for, ravaged, and as we are becoming well aware, essentially destroyed, in spite of God's own loving attention to it, because of one creature, ourselves, who can choose or not choose to join with God in conscious care of the world."[81] Clearly, then, the world as God's body accepts and even stresses God's willingness to suffer. McFague goes so far as to state that this metaphor can "remythologize" the inclusive and suffering love of Jesus of Nazareth on the cross. She asserts that in the past human beings killed their God in the body of a man, and that now we have the power again to kill our God in the body of the world. At this point she stops at the abyss: "Could we actually do this? To believe in the resurrection means we could not. God is not in our power to destroy, but the incarnate God is at risk; we have been given central responsibility to care for God's body, our world."[82]

Critical Questions

At this point McFague plunges into the midst of such questions as: How does God know, act in, and love the world? And how does one understand the meaning of evil in God as body of the world? Of course, the responses to these questions will differ from those that are related to the monarchical model. As regards the first question, God is said to be related to all parts of the world with a knowledge that "is empathetic, intimate, sympathetic knowledge, closer to feeling than rationality."[83] Furthermore, McFague emphasizes the analogy of the human body: "Just as we are internally related to our bodies, so God is internally related to all that is—the most radically relational Thou. God relates sympathetically to the world, just as we relate sympathetically to our bodies. This implies, of course, an immediacy and concern in God's knowledge of the world impossible in the king-realm model."[84]

Also, the action of God in the world is both interior and *caring* through the evolutionary process that began eons ago, although God is not actually reduced to this process but is its agent. Furthermore, the model of Earth as God's body indicates that God *loves bodies*, a notion that the author believes contradicts the long anti-body, anti-matter, and anti-sexuality tradition that has plagued the history of Christianity; she insists "that bodies are worth loving, sexually and otherwise, that passionate love as well as attention to the needs of bodily existence are part of fulfillment."[85] She expresses another very significant aspect of God's caring this way: ". . . the basic necessities of bodily existence—adequate food and shelter, for example—are central aspects of God's love for all bodily creatures and therefore should be central concerns for us, God's co-workers . . . . To love bodies, then, is to love not what is opposed to spirit but what is one with it—which the world as God's body fully express-es."[86]

The second crucial question concerns God's responsibility for evil, whether natural or caused by humans. In the monarchical model, God is not held to be responsible for evil, but neither does God identify with the suffering caused by evil. Precisely that iden-tification *does* occur in the God's body metaphor. McFague faces the problem squarely:

> In a physical, biological, historico-cultural evolutionary process as complex as the one universe, much that is evil from various per-spectives will occur, and if one sees this process as God's self-expression, then God is involved in evil. But the other side of this is that God is also involved, profoundly, palpably, personally in-volved, in suffering, the suffering caused by evil.[87]

The other side of this coin is that God also experiences joy and thus wherever "in the universe there is new life, ecstasy, tranquility, and fulfillment, God experiences these pleasures and rejoices with each creature in its joy."[88]

The question of sin and freedom, obviously related to evil, is also considered: ". . . it is refusal to be part of the body, the special part we are as *imago dei*. . . . it is the desire to set oneself apart from all others as not needing them or being needed by them. Sin is the re-fusal to be the eyes, the consciousness, of the cosmos."[89]

McFague calls also for a revived sacramentalism, that is, "a per-ception of the divine as visible, as present, as palpably present in the world" and a kind of "sacramentalism that is painfully con-scious of the world's vulnerability, its preciousness, its unique-ness."[90] The author reminds one of Teilhardian Earth-mysticism: "The world is a body that must be carefully tended, that must be nurtured, protected, guided, loved, and befriended both as valuable in itself—for like us it is an expression of life—and as necessary to the continuation of life. We meet the world as a Thou, as the body of God where God is present to us always in all times and in all places."[91]

At the end of her essay, McFague stresses the crucial importance of our *images*, especially our religious images, in how we understand God and the world. She calls for many images, not just the one she has proposed, so that we may think differently and perhaps avoid the horror of ecological and nuclear destruction.

MICHAEL AND KENNETH HIMES

Earlier in this chapter Thomas Berry remarked that moral theologians had not devoted much attention, if any at all, to the issues of ecology. In answer to that, I am presenting the views of two well-known theologians who have presented their views on this matter. Rev. Michael Himes is associate professor at theology at the University of Notre Dame, and Kenneth Himes, O.F.M., is associate professor of moral theology at Washington Theological Union in Silver Spring, Maryland. Kenneth Himes has co-edited an introductory volume of 604 pages on Christian ethics, in which, I was disappointed to find, there is not a single article on environmental ethics.[92] Their ideas, then, will be based on a lengthy article published in *Commonweal* a year after this book was published.[93]

Preliminary Remarks

After some introductory comments about how an ecological crisis is looming over our planet, the two authors go right to the heart of the matter: "What does Christianity say to the contemporary ecological movement?"[94] The answer to this question is also forthright: ". . . what it has to say is not primarily advice on public policy or clear moral judgments for settling disputes about economic growth versus ecological protection. In this regard, the Christian tradition is, in the words of Richard McCormick, 'more a value raiser than a problem solver.'"[95]

The values raised are said to be humanity's basic relatedness to nature and an understanding of the created order, one strand of which "is profoundly insightful and potentially transformative of modern ways of addressing the crisis of creation." This, they assert, must replace instrumental rationality, atomized individualism, the consumerist mentality, the myth of progress, and the technological mind-set. But this transformation at the root of the problem is more complex than expected.

Some advocates of the environment, the authors assert, exhibit ideologies of ecological activism and environmental romanticism that approach the anti-human, in which nature is idealized and civilization is rejected. Paradoxically, this is the same approach as that of the technocrats, since both are opposed to nature. Thus "[i]n both cases humanity is set in opposition to the rest of creation. Either alternative is unacceptable from a relational worldview. To separate nature from human culture is environmental romanticism. To consider human culture apart from the nonhuman is to invite the impoverishment of the first and the devastation of the second."[96]

The worldview of Jewish and Christian traditions is seen to be not against nature but as a part of it. We can examine the traditions to see which insights have not been fruitful, but we must above all emphasize constructively how these teachings can be used in promoting the values of environmental wisdom.

The Tradition of Genesis

The authors begin with the two Genesis stories (1:1–2:4a and 2:4b–25), which they frankly admit "have been elaborated into cosmologies and theories of the soul and twisted into ideological support for male-dominance and industrial exploitation."[97] The first story has provided the foundations of both lordship and stewardship images, especially in the phrases "fill the whole Earth and *subdue it; have dominion* over the fish of the sea and the birds of the air and all the living things that move on Earth" (1:26,28). The concept behind both images is one of sovereignty, so that "without such dominion and power over the rest of creation, the human being would not be 'like God.'"[98]

The authors also note that there is another theme, that God is *relational* and is always at work in *creating*, as in the text "in the divine image did God create the human being, male and female did he create them" (1:27). The consequences are profound: "Even in one of its creation myths, the Hebrew tradition envisions God as the God of the covenant, God in relationship. To be the image of this

God, the human being must be relational. Humanity is sexed in order that human beings may be driven into relationship one with another."[99]

This is also a central theme in the second Genesis story. There is a dominion theme in the fact that a human being gave the names to all the animals (2:19), which shows human power over creation. But the context of this is the need for *companionship*, as when God says in the first story that it is "very good" that there is a differentiation between the sexes (1:31). It is even clearer in the second story at the moment of human creation when God proclaims that "it is not good for the human being to be alone" (2:18). However, this companionship extends also to "the various wild beasts and birds of the air," which God created for the good of human beings.

Returning to the dominion images, it is clear that they can be utilized by human beings to dominate and exploit Earth, leading to the need for responsibility and *stewardship*. Yet even this is not enough, according to the Himes brothers: "To be sure, this stewardship image prohibited wanton wastefulness, the mere exploitation of nature by humankind. The world is presented as a garden given into our care to be tended and nurtured. But undeniably the role of stewardship carries the implication that *nonhuman creation is to be used*."[100]

The authors stress that the companionship theme needs to be retrieved, since it has been overwhelmed by the stewardship approach. The essence of their approach may be condensed to the fact that the needed companionship *implies mutuality*: "It excludes the reduction of either side of the relationship to a tool of the other's purposes." There follows a discussion of Martin Buber's "I-Thou" versus "I-It" relationships to illustrate these ideas. But the authors raise another very interesting question: ". . . in what sense can one speak of the nonhuman world as companion to human beings,"[101] given the fact that we do not wish to revive the personification of nature extolled by nineteenth-century poets? To answer this question, the authors move on to other areas of the Catholic tradition.

Augustine and Francis of Assisi

Two important symbols of the Catholic tradition, the authors contend, that can illuminate the theme of companionship are *poverty* and *sacramentality*. They speak of an experience of Augustine, in which he had a vision of the saints in glory and also of the passing away of all creatures, which is a fundamental form of poverty. Later on, Francis of Assisi took up the two central elements of Augustine and built them as the two pillars of his life: *poverty* and *the unity of all creatures*. There exists also a profound unity between these pillars: "True poverty, the poverty of the spirit, is the realization that there is no intrinsic reason for one's being at all. In this fundamental poverty of creatureliness, there is equality. The human person has no more claim to intrinsic being than a plant or an animal, a star or a stone."[102]

This does not mean to deny the role of human beings in the divine plan, but to emphasize that they too are *creatures* as such. Thus, Francis was not merely carried away by a poetic effusion of personification when he spoke to the sun and the moon, Earth and air, fire and water, and all animate and inanimate creatures as his brothers and sisters. "Since everything," the authors stress, "that is exists because of the free act of God—the overflowing *agape* that is the source of all being—then everything is a sacrament of the goodness and creative power of God."[103]

A Vision of Sacramentality

For the Catholic tradition, creation and poverty are brought together in sacramentality. A sacrament has the capacity to reveal grace, which is the loving gift of Godself, just by being itself. The Catholic church has recognized seven key events in the human life span as grace-bearing, but the more fundamental vision is that absolutely every creature can be a sacrament. As the authors express it: "The more richly developed our sacramental vision, the more sacraments crowd in upon us. Francis of Assisi's interweaving of poverty with the brotherhood and sisterhood of all creatures is profoundly Catholic because it is profoundly sacramental."[104]

In an ecumenical gesture, the authors make use of the *Treatise on Religious Affections* by Johnathan Edwards, in which he describes the first of the marks of conversion as affections that "do arise from influences and operations on the heart which are *spiritual, super-*

natural, and *divine*," and "a new inward perception or sensation of their minds entirely different in its nature and kind, from anything that ever their minds were subjects of before they were sanctified."[105] As the authors explain it: "The saints, to use Edwards's term, see reality differently from the unconverted. They do not see things that others do not see; rather, they see what everyone else sees in a different way. They see everything in its relation to God: they see it as creature. . . .one way of describing this 'new inward perception' of the Edwardsean saint is the capacity for sacramental vision."[106]

Thus, the most profound conception of the Himes brothers is to link the earlier companionship theme in Genesis with the sacramental vision, and to offer this as a necessary component for the contemporary problems of ecology. To put it succinctly, the "discovery that every creature, including oneself, is a sacrament of the love of God that causes all things to be provides the deepest foundation for reverencing creation."[107] Above all, the faculty most needed to cherish creation is that of imagination. Here, the authors are more than usually eloquent:

> Since every creature can and should be a sacrament, so every creature can and should be "thou," a companion. But this sacramental vision demands unflinching recognition of the poverty of one's own being —for many too terrible to be true—and joyful acceptance of the absolute *agape* that supports one's own being—for many too good to be true. This requires the *expansion of the imagination.*[108]

Rather than making this kind of imagination a "moral imperative," the authors shrewdly propose that it be called a "Christian aesthetic that needs cultivation." They also point out that the whole praxis of the church is geared for training in the sacramental imagination: "Liturgy and social action, marriage and parenthood, prayer and politics, music and dances and the visual arts, all educate us to appreciate the other as sacramental, worthy companions of our poverty and our engracedness."[109]

A New Christian Ethic?

Michael and Kenneth Himes next present a Christian ethic that utilizes the companionship motif that has been at the core of this essay. Obviously, such an ethic would reject an ethic of individualism which, however, is rampant, at least in the developed countries. The situation is described as follows:

> The exaltation of the individual at the expense of the community, which in its crudest form becomes the "trickle-down" theory of social responsibility, stands in contradiction to this foundational insight of the Jewish and Christian traditions. Not surprisingly, this individualist ethic has debased the image of stewardship from participation in the creative activity of God into cost-benefit analysis.[110]

The companionship model will be one that has its foundations in a relational anthropology, but this has to be seen as an *orientation*, and not a full-blown environmental ethic.

The first point of orientation is the need of a changed context where an environmental ethic can be developed. This requires a rejection of individualist and stewardship images, and the cultivation and nourishment of companionship images that enable the imagination to see the intrinsic good of creation. Also necessary for any ethic is an understanding of the "other" that one will encounter: "The reduction of creation to 'it' has promoted a loss of respect for nature and an attitude of instrumental rationality. Doing justice to the environment becomes difficult when the context of decision making is so one-sided."[111]

On the other hand, an awareness of the poverty and sacramentality of all creation should lessen the tendency to belittle the worth of non-human creation. In short, our "poverty as creatures and our dignity as sacramental mediations of divine grace must be held in tension as twin aspects of our organic connection with all creation."

The second point of orientation is a revised understanding of the "common good." In the encyclical *Mater et Magistra* (Mother and Teacher), issued in 1961, Pope John XXIII defined the common good as "the sum total of those conditions of social living whereby people are enabled to achieve their own integral perfection more fully and easily." To amplify the meaning of the "conditions of social living," he outlined a detailed list of *human* rights.

The succeeding popes, Paul VI and especially John Paul II, have continued in their encyclical letters and other writings to use human rights language when they discourse on the common good. A theologian, David Hollenbach, "suggests that the use of human rights in recent Catholic social teaching is a way of specifying the essential *needs*, basic *freedoms*, and *relationships* with others that comprise the common good and serve human dignity."[112] The authors of this essay hold that, since the created order is an "other" with whom we have a relationship, this relationship is part of the common good, and *non-human creation* is certainly one of the aims of *human* rights.

The writings of Pope Pius XII also make it clear that property rights are secondary rights and not primary ones: "Private property is always subordinate to the more fundamental right of all people to the goods of Earth." And therefore it follows that: "It is humanity's fundamental human right to share in the goods of Earth that is at stake in the ecological issue. Setting this human right in the context of companionship is necessary, however, to prevent the human right to the universal goods of creation from being interpreted according to a narrow mind-set of instrumental rationality."[113]

The third point of orientation is concerned with the *means* by which we can protect and cultivate an expanded version of human rights, as we have just seen. In the encyclical letter *Pacem in Terris* (Peace on Earth), Pope John XXIII used the language of the "universal common good." Thus these issues go beyond the competence of nation-states, especially with regard to issues of the environment. An excellent example of the universal common good that the popes have supported is the Law of the Sea Treaty, but unfortunately narrow national self-interest often ignores the common good, as happened when President Reagan opposed that treaty. Since the United States emphasizes individual liberties and a free market, it has a national responsibility to find ways to enhance the common good of the nation, especially with regard to the environment.

Ecology or Economic Development?

The relationship and tension between ecology and economic development is certainly one of the most important and complex issues that confronts humanity today. The Himes brothers pose the questions on a practical level: "Are ecological concerns to be traded off for the creation of jobs in poor areas? Or vice-versa? Is industrialization to be discouraged in nations with undeveloped economies for the sake of preserving certain animal and plant species?"[114] Pope John Paul II in his encyclical letter *Redemptor Hominis* (Redeemer of Humanity) vigorously opposes an approach to development that is "dilapidating at an accelerated pace material and energy resources, and compromising the geophysical environment." Even earlier, the Synod of Bishops in 1971 stressed that

> such is the demand for resources and energy by the richer nations
> . . . and such are the effects of dumping by them in the atmosphere and the sea that irreparable damage would be done to the essential elements of life on Earth, such as air and water, if their high rates of consumption and pollution, which are constantly on the increase, were extended to the whole of mankind.[115]

The authors go on to point out that it is a form of exploitation for the rich nations to overuse the goods of Earth, for it would be impossible for the developing nations to attain such levels or even, in many cases, to attain a poor but decent existence. The authors do not offer a plan, but point to the present situation: "No consensus yet exists on how to reconcile ecological concerns and developmental needs, but some headway in resolving them is a *sine qua non* if the environmental movement is to make progress.[116]

Conclusions

An important statement is that theology has a leading role in confronting the challenges of ecology, and in creating methods of conscientization that will cultivate a correct understanding of creation. This is not to encourage a back to nature movement, for technology—the creation of human beings—is destined to continue and to develop. The point is to control the development of technology, and not to attempt to eliminate it. A fine summary is provided:

"The primacy of ethics and politics over technology must be asserted. First, we must assess the human goods that technology must serve. Second, the political process is the arena in which many of the moral choices will be worked through and implemented. Effective political action must follow careful ethical reflection."[117]

The authors also warn that the Jewish and Christian understanding of creation should not become captive to any economic ideology, although neither capitalism nor socialism should be dismissed as a partner to environmental change. Both systems must strive for the correct balance between ecology and economic development, with a goal of *sustainable efficiency.*

Finally, the authors caution that we should not forget the quest for social justice, while being strongly committed to the struggle for the ecology. This applies most of all to the developing nations, who comprise more than four-fifths of the world's population:

> Poorer nations will not be willing to forego economic development at the behest of wealthier nations, who have belatedly seen the results of their own assaults on nature in the quest for more and more expansion. To avoid a new imbalance, an environmental ethic must be informed by a careful analysis of the demands of economic justice.[118]

The Himes brothers conclude their minor masterpiece of ethical reflection with another masterpiece in their concluding sentence: "The first task before us, that which theology can assist, is to revision all beings in their createdness, given to one another as companions, sacraments of the 'love that moves the sun and other stars.'"[119]

In conclusion, I have profited from the dialogue on ecotheology from three different but very creative and original approaches. Thomas Berry comes from a Teilhardian background, but molds it to his own experience and study of the cosmos over many years. Sallie McFague states that her interpretation is similar to the liberation theologies, but she transforms that in her own uniquely imaginative approach to the impact and importance of metaphors and models and especially the cosmos as the body of God. Finally, the Himes brothers make brilliant use of the Roman Catholic tradition in creating their own ecotheology, which stresses companionship and opens our eyes to the sacraments that continuously crowd in upon us.

I hope that my readers have benefitted from this dialogue, and that they begin or continue to open their eyes and hearts to the vast riches that can help to create their own ecotheology of liberation in every corner of Earth. Once again, we have all profited greatly from the inspiring leadership of Berry, McFague, and the Himes brothers, as we continue to hunger and thirst after justice and peace for all God's creatures.

Rather than further discussion, I will end on a note of prayer and contemplation, using the reflections of Sallie McFague from her essay:

> This is a form of prayer for the world
> as the body of God that we,
> as lovers and friends of the world,
> are summoned to practice. . . .
> It is a form of prayer
> to help us think differently about the world,
> to enable us to work together with God,
> to save our beleaguered planet,
> our beautiful, vulnerable Earth,
> our blue and green marble in a universe of
> silent rock and fire.[120]

QUESTIONS FOR REFLECTION AND DISCUSSION

1. According to Thomas Berry, other religions than Christianity can illumine the entire religious life of the human community. What is your reaction to this statement and what is your own position concerning it?

2. Berry also believes that the natural world is amazingly rich and self-sustaining, but that the industrial economy tends to destroy it. This leads to what he calls the "earth deficit" or the "ultimate def-

icit." Do you think this is going to happen? If not, what can you suggest some alternatives?

3. The author is forthright about the dangers of religion. He believes that Christianity had an inadequate understanding of Earth and contributed a great deal to its destruction. Do you agree with this? Also do you agree with the four religious orientations he proposes to prove his statement?

4. As regards Berry's famous "Twelve Principles," which of them do you find most promising and helpful? Which do you believe are the least promising? Give reasons for your choices.

5. As regards ecology or ecofeminism, can you discern similarities and also differences in the approaches of Thomas Berry and Sallie McFague? Which of the approaches do you find most congenial to your own experience?

6. Do you agree with McFague's understanding of liberation theology on p. 282 of this chapter? Are there elements missing from her description? Would you agree with her understanding?

7. McFague bestows much attention on the model of God as mighty King. Would you agree or disagree with the three objections she has to this model? In general, do you find this model to be very appropriate or very disconcerting?

8. A major concept of McFague is planet Earth (or the universe) as the body of God. Is this a form of pantheism? Do you agree with her that this is a very appealing and substantive model?

9. The Himes brothers begin with the book of Genesis, where they find the central theme to be need for companionship and not dominion or stewardship. Do you agree with this interpretation of Genesis? Do you see any alternatives?

10. The Himeses present a new form of ethics with special regard to ecology. Which of their proposals do you find appealing and which would you reject? Overall, do you accept the authors' new form of ethics as a useful contribution to moral theology?

SUGGESTED READINGS

Berry, Thomas. *The Dream of the Earth.* San Francisco: Sierra Books, 1988.

Berry, Thomas, and Thomas Clarke. *Befriending the Earth.* Mystic, CT: Twenty-Third Publications, 1990.

Birch, Charles, and John B. Cobb. *The Liberation of Life: From the Cell to the Community.* New York: Cambridge University Press, 1981.

Caldecott, Leonie, and Stephanie Leland. *Reclaim the Earth: Women Speak Out for Life on Earth.* London: Woman's Press, 1983.

Cobb, John B. *Matters of Life and Death.* Louisville: Westminster/John Knox, 1991.

Diamond, Irene, and Gloria Orenstein. *Reweaving the World: The Emergence of Ecofeminism.* San Francisco: Sierra Club, 1990.

Jantzen, Grace. *God's World, God's Body.* Philadelphia: Westminster, 1984.

Moltmann, Jürgen. *God in Creation: A New Theology of Creation and the Spirit of God.* San Francisco: Harper & Row, 1985.

Nash, James. *Loving Nature: Ecological Integrity and Christian Responsibility.* Nashville: Abingdon Press, 1991.

Plant, Judith. *Healing the Wounds: The Promise of Ecofeminism.* Philadelphia: New Society Publishers, 1989.

Ruether, Rosemary Radford. *Gaia & God: An Ecofeminist Theology of Earth Healing.* San Francisco: Harper & Row, 1992.

Shinn, Roger and Paul Albrecht, eds. *Faith and Science in an Unjust World.* Philadelphia: Fortress, 1981.

Toulmin, Stephen. *The Return to Cosmology: Postmodern Science and the Theology of Nature.* Berkeley: University of California Press, 1982.

CHAPTER NINE

THE WORLD RELIGIONS
AS LIBERATORS?

A Liberation Theology
of the World Religions

The great liberation theologies of our day do not mean by history theories of historiography, or mere philosophies or theologies of history. . . . With the prophets, the liberation theologians mean history. They mean the concrete struggles of whole groups, societies and persons, who have been shunted aside by the official story or triumph. They mean, with Gutiérrez, that the central theological issue today is not the question of the unbeliever but the question of the non-person—the forgotten one, living and dead, whose struggle and memory is our history.

David Tracy
Dialogue with the Other 119

Interreligious relationships speak of many different ways on which experience of the divine has been located in human experience and the mutual recognition of these historico-cultural configurations by each other. Feminism speaks of new contexts where the divine needs to be localized. By and large, not only Judaism and Christianity, Islam, and Buddhism, but even ancient tribal religions have not allowed the divine to be experienced in a way defined by women. Feminism looks back at the history of all religions as expressions of male-dominated cultures that have marginalized women to some extent, although women have been more radically and totally marginalized in some religious systems than in others.

Rosemary Radford Ruether
Essay in *The Myth of Christian Uniqueness* 142

IN THE CHAPTER ON AN ASIAN LIBERATION theology, we discussed the question of the uniqueness of Jesus in the light of Buddhism as seen by Aloysius Pieris of Sri Lanka.[1] At the present time, an even more publicized controversy has erupted in the United States in regard to this issue, with the major protagonists being Paul Knitter and John Hick.

PAUL KNITTER

I will begin with some reflections of Paul Knitter from the book, *The Myth of Christian Uniqueness.*[2] Knitter is at present professor of theology at Xavier University in Cincinnati, and is well known for his work on the world religions and his promotion of dialogue among them, as we shall see later on. Furthermore, he refers to trends in his thought recently as "a liberation theology of world religions," or as "a liberation theology of religious pluralism."

The Religions and the Poor

In that book, Knitter emphasizes two phenomena that are particularly urgent at the present time: 1) a profound concern with the *many poor* in the world; and 2) the problem of the *many religions* throughout the world.[3] As a result, the most creative theologies today are the theology of religions with the problem of religious pluralism, and the theology of liberation with the greater problem of suffering and injustice. He goes on to state that his focus will be on what the theology of religions can learn from liberation theology, that is, he hopes to show how principles and guidelines from liberation theology can help us move toward a pluralistic theology of religions. Taken together, they directly address both the suffering and injustice of the vast masses of humanity and also the theology of religions and its great potential of religious pluralism. I will analyze his conclusions, and then suggest some other areas in which liberation theology can contribute to the theology of religions.

A Theology of Religions

Knitter points out to the Latin American theologians that their theological lenses have not been trained on the great world religions, precisely where the vast majority of the world's poor struggle for their very existence: "A purely Christian theology of liberation, in other words, suffers the dangerous limitation of inbreeding, of drawing on only one vision of the kingdom."[4] Thus, a worldwide liberation theology must open itself to the liberating possibilities of Buddhism, Hinduism, Islam, Judaism, and other religions. This is not, it must be stressed, purely for academic reasons, but for praxis and cooperation in a preferential option for the poor and the oppressed all over the globe.

What theologians are called upon to envision is the discharge of the enormous energies and potential of *all* of the religions to create a vast "geotheology of liberation." This would also demonstrate clearly that in the world of today there are really only two kinds of theologies, *liberation* theologies, which strive toward social change and justice, and the many versions of oppressive or *alienating* theologies which, unfortunately, produce ideologies that disguise the many versions that justify the status quo and injustice.

Contributions of Liberation Theology

If this kind of dialogue and cooperation is to be achieved, Knitter continues, it must successfully navigate between pluralism and relativism. To achieve such a voyage, he believes that liberation theology can contribute in four ways: 1) the hermeneutical circle and its companion, the hermeneutics of suspicion; 2) the preferential option (or hermeneutical privilege) of the poor; 3) a "soteriocentric" approach, so that the major stress is given to the soteriologies and not to the theologies of the religions; and 4) an analysis of the *sensus fidelium*, or acceptance of church teaching by its members.

Knitter describes the hermeneutics of suspicion in these words: "All too often the truths that we propose as 'God's will' or divinely revealed is really our own disguised, subconscious will to maintain the status quo or to protect our own control of the situation or our own cultural-economic superiority."[5] Thus, the first step is to open our eyes and hearts to the possibility of clarifying and rejecting our own ideologies and selfish interests. Only then can we liberate ourselves and others and advance the kingdom of God.

In the context of dialogue with the world religions, Knitter proposes a very important point for the theologians of religion:

> How much has traditional theology of religions, especially its christological base, served to cloak or condone an unconscious, ideological desire to maintain superiority, or to dominate and control, or to devalue other traditions culturally or religiously. . . . Certainly it cannot be denied that in the past such doctrines and such christology have been used to justify the subordination and exploitation of other cultures and religions.[6]

The only sure way, Knitter continues, is for the most part to expose oneself to an open dialogue with other cultures and other religions. And it should be noted honestly that Karl Rahner's "anonymous Christianity" and Hans Küng's "critical catalyst" model are seen by other religions as the crypto-colonialism of the religions and the cultural imperialism of the first world.

With regard to the second contribution of liberation theology, the preferential option for the poor, or hermeneutical privilege of the poor, should be able to facilitate a dialogue of the religions and to overcome many of the obstacles and complexities that are involved. Knitter's major supporting argument, which I agree with, proceeds as follows:

> If the religions of the world, in other words, can recognize poverty and oppression as a common problem, if they can share a common commitment (expressed in different forms) to remove such evils, they will have the basis for reaching across their incommensurabilities and differences in order to hear and understand each other and possibly be transformed in the process.[7]

Thus, the beginning and the continuation of dialogue among the religions will be based not only on a mystical-contemplative experience (the path of Thomas Merton) but also and especially an experience and communion of liberating praxis.

The encounter with other religions, therefore, will not begin with the ineffable mystery of God, but rather with the ineffable mystery of salvation or liberation. The least that can be said is that this is less open to ideological distortion, although certainly not completely free from it. As Aloysius Pieris has expressed it, "the common thrust remains . . . *soteriological,* the concern of most religions being *liberation (vimukti, moksa, nirvana)* rather than speculation about a hypothetical [divine] liberator."[8] In another book, Knitter presents a clear picture of how salvation or liberation will come about: "On the basis of this common praxis of political liberation and social transformation, the religions can continue to speak to each other, challenge and criticize each other, as to how their beliefs, their view of the world, of the ultimate and the self, can contribute to removing the evil wrought on human beings and on Earth."[9]

Again, in an article on "A Liberation-Centered Theology of Religions," Knitter referred to the Asian Catholic bishops' conference, who called on Christians to turn to Buddhists, Hindus, Confucianists and "to join together in promoting unity, love, justice, whatever promotes human values, and whatever relieves the afflictions of our time . . . and whatever relieves famine and hunger, natural disasters, inferior education, inadequate housing, and unequal distribution of wealth. This will in turn include organized action and reflection in faith."[10]

Another important and creative analysis concludes Knitter's essay on liberation theology and the theology of religions.[11] In this essay he applies the method and principles of liberation theology to the question of the uniqueness of Christ. Must Christians, he queries, change or even reject their traditional understanding of Christ as the definitive and normative revelation of God? "Can they do this," he asks bluntly, "and still call themselves Christians?"[12] Here I outline his ideas and then comment on them.

Praxis as Origin of Theory

First of all, Knitter recalls the theory-praxis relationship in liberation theology, emphasizing that "praxis is both the *origin* and the *confirmation* of theory or *doctrine.*"[13] He expands this statement for the sake of clarity: "All Christian beliefs and truth claims must grow out of and then be reconfirmed in the praxis or lived experience of these truths. According to liberation theology, one does not first know the truth and then apply it in praxis; it is in action, in doing, that truth is really known and validated."[14]

Applying this to christology, as has been done by the Latin American theologians Leonardo Boff and Jon Sobrino, leads to the conclusion that in order to know Christ one must first follow Christ, that is, "everything we know or say about Jesus must be continually confirmed, clarified, and perhaps corrected in the praxis of living his vision within the changing contexts of history."[15] In short, praxis is both the starting point and the criterion of all christology. Therefore, as Boff concludes in his christology, none of the many titles given to Jesus can be absolutized or made final. An important conclusion from this may be found in Sobrino's christology: "[Jesus'] universality cannot be demonstrated or proved on the basis of formulas or symbols that are universal in themselves: e.g., dogmatic formulas, the kerygma as event, the resurrection as universal symbol of hope, and so forth. The real universality of Jesus shows up *only in its concrete embodiment.*"[16] Therefore the uniqueness of Jesus can only be known and affirmed in the praxis of historical, social involvement. A very important step then takes place, namely, that "unless we are engaged in the *praxis of Christian dialogue* with other religions— following Christ, applying his message, within the dialogue with other believers—we cannot experience and confirm what the uniqueness and normativity of Christ mean."[17]

Knitter then affirms that this type of praxis with other believers has *not* been extensive enough to make the universal claim that Jesus surpasses and is therefore normative for all the religions. He admits that the churches have sent foreign missionaries abroad for centuries, but insists that only in this century has there been real, extensive *dialogue* with other religions. The author concludes:

From the perspective of a liberation theology of religions, therefore, Christians will have to admit that at least at the moment it is *impossible* to make claims for finality and normativity for Christ or

Christianity. This means that we have "permission"—maybe even an obligation—to enter into a dialogue with other believers without making our traditional claims of "no other name" or "one mediator."[18]

This statement is obviously quite controversial. In my view, it is possible and even plausible; however, those who do not accept its foundations in liberation theology may find it shocking and even heretical. I would venture, however, that in a decade or so it will be a commonplace in theology.

The Primacy of Orthopraxis

The second element in Knitter's analysis also utilizes another teaching of liberation theology, that is, the *primacy of orthopraxis over orthodoxy*. Here Knitter insists that not only are claims about the finality of Christ not presently possible, but they are also not *necessary*. His main thesis is:

> The primary concern of a soteriocentric liberation theology of religions is not "right belief" about the uniqueness of Christ, but the "right practice," with other religions, of furthering the Kingdom and its *Soteria*. Clarity about whether and how Christ is one lord and savior, as well as clarity about any other doctrine, may be important, but it is subordinate to carrying out the preferential option for the poor and nonpersons.[19]

Knitter proceeds to emphasize that Christians do not *need* to have clarity and certainty that Jesus is the only savior in order to commit themselves to his liberating message. What they *do* know is that his life and teaching *is* a certain means of bringing about liberation from injustice and promoting the kingdom. He turns to a statement of H. Richard Niebuhr that orthodox "claims about the superiority or normativity of Christ over all religions were not only not necessary for the living out of the Christian Confession; they were, in Niebuhr's prophetic words, 'more destructive of religion, Christianity, and the soul than any foe's attack can possibly be.'"[20]

Option for the Poor

A third element in Knitter's theological edifice is the preferential option for the poor, which he believes could be used as a criterion for evaluating all religions. If this criterion is used, then Christians

> have the means to discern not only whether but *how much* other beliefs may be genuine "ways of salvation"—and further, whether and *how much* other religious figures may be genuine liberators and "saviors." In other words, the soteriocentric criteria for religious dialogue contained in the preferential option for the oppressed offer Christians the tools to critically examine and possibly revise the traditional understanding of the uniqueness of Christ.[21]

The author allows that judgments can be different in this process. Jesus could be seen as the special and unique liberator, even though there are "saviors" in other religions. On the other hand, others might for instance "conclude that the liberative, transformative power of the Buddhist notions of enlightenment, dependent co-origination, and compassion" would appear just as salvific as the symbols of Christianity. It is possible then that Jesus "would be universal savior—with other universal saviors. His universality and uniqueness would be not exclusive, nor inclusive, but complementary."[22]

Acceptance by the People

A fourth element of a liberation theology of religions stresses the traditional theological concept of *sensus fidelium*, that is, acceptance by the people of God: "Reception by the faithful was the final criterion for the validity of the early councils and it remains such a criterion today for popes, councils, and theologians."[23] It is precisely this concept that a number of distinguished theologians believe diminishes the uniqueness of Jesus Christ. For Monika Hellwig and Franz van Beeck, "to claim only that Jesus offers a way of salvation to us which is one among many is to fall short of fidelity to the classics about Jesus in the bible and the tradition."[24] Avery Dulles avers: "If this [Christ's utter uniqueness] is obscured, the Christ event will not elicit the kind of worship and thanksgiving needed to sustain the Christian community in its vibrant relationship to God."[25] Hans

Küng has also stated that although to move in the direction of a non-absolutist christology might be logical, he would not move in that direction for two reasons: ". . . it would alienate him from his faith community and it would tend to diminish the depth and firmness of Christians' personal commitment to Jesus Christ."[26] Knitter then sums up the issue: ". . . if these new christologies have any future within Christian theology, they need a better *ecclesial mediation* in order that they might be 'received' by the faithful."[27]

As part of this mediation, Knitter turns again to liberation theology and its close relationship to the *basic Christian communities*. His argument is this:

> What happens in the basic Christian communities is not simply a reflecting upon Christian beliefs but a sharpening, indeed a transformation, of the sense of the faithful. Liberation theologians consider themselves not only teachers and learners but also, where need be, *prophets*. . . . Especially in this question of the uniqueness of Christ, I have found that congregational fears and hesitations can be overcome—indeed, that many of the faithful are happy someone is finally pushing and challenging them.[28]

It is puzzling that Knitter does not refer here at all to Paulo Freire and his highly developed and widely used technique of conscientization in the context of the base communities, since it would strongly buttress his argument.

Recalling the primacy of orthopraxis over orthodoxy, Knitter insists that Christians who are brought into touch with their own experience through a liberating praxis of the gospel will agree "that the essence of being a Christian is *doing* the will of the Father rather than knowing or insisting that Jesus is the one and only or the best of the bunch."[29] Another rather appealing argument is that the more secure and profound commitment a person has to one's own religion, the more one is open to the riches and truth of other religions. Christians, then, can be helped to see "that neither their commitment to Jesus nor their ability to worship him (the *lex orandi*) need be jeopardized just because there may be others like him. Why, really, must something be 'one and only' in order to merit our devotion and commitment?"[30]

Knitter's final argument for non-uniqueness is that it may be *necessary* at the present time in order to be faithful to the original Christian message, which is the kingdom of love, unity, and justice. His final paragraph sums up the thesis of the book, referring to the kingdom:

> In order to serve and promote that kingdom, we want to dialogue with others and be open to the possibility that there are other teachers and liberators and saviors who can help us understand and work for that kingdom in ways as yet beyond our hearing or imagination. . . . This present volume was assembled with the suspicion and trust that there are others, perhaps many others, *with* Jesus—and many other religious paths, *with* Christianity. Each very different, each unique—but *with* each other.[31]

As I mentioned earlier, Knitter's proposals are plausible, but not absolutely convincing, regarding the possible non-uniqueness of Jesus. I personally believe that his directions will be more and more acceptable, as the global village grows closer and closer together on many levels. But I wonder if it really is necessary to reflect on which savior is unique or not unique. The vast majority of Christians (except for academics like myself) will continue to view Jesus as their unique savior. And the world religions, like Islam and Buddhism, will probably be unanimous in seeing Muhammad and the Buddha as unique savior figures in their religion and culture. Consequently, I believe the major question for the religions and liberation theology is precisely the *dialogue concerning praxis*, and *actual praxis* to advance the kingdom of God and to resist oppression of the poor and oppressed. Thus, I will consider Knitter's views in that area more in detail. A fine condensation may be found in the lecture series mentioned earlier.[32]

The Base Communities

At the end of the series, Knitter discusses the base Christian communities in Latin America and the "basic human communities" in Asia.[33] Here I am in agreement with his position which was not as strong and clear in the previous essay mentioned above:

> . . . the new pluralist theology of religions will be developed and will take hold of the churches just as liberation theology did—from the *praxis* of liberative dialogue on the grassroots level. All the theory that we have considered during these days will be clarified, confirmed, corrected in the actual encounter of Christians with other believers in their shared praxis of confronting human / ecological suffering.[34]

Knitter here links "liberative dialogue" with the religions and "shared praxis" with the religions, and locates both of them in the "base human communities." In these communities, participation is not judged by one's religious beliefs but by their commitment to the relief of human suffering: "And in this common striving, in their shared liberative analysis and praxis, they find not only that they have a new lens to understand their own traditions, but that they have found a new voice for communicating and learning from each other across previously sound-proof religious barriers." In these "interreligious communities of justice," Knitter concludes, "a new age of inter-religious understanding and cooperation is dawning."[35]

HANS KÜNG

Hans Küng is a Swiss Catholic priest, author of many theological volumes, and at present is the director of the Institute for Ecumenical Research at the University of Tübingen, Germany. He became interested in the world religions in his book, *On Being a Christian*,[36] but in my judgment his views at that point were quite superficial, despite huge bibliographies. Since that time, however, he has produced a number of books that burrow more deeply into the world religions and that produce increasingly nuanced and at times profound insights.[37] In this section, I wish to focus on his recent book, *Global Responsibility: In Search of a New World Ethic.*[38] Küng certainly does not consider himself to be a liberation theologian or even a European political theologian like Jürgen Moltmann; in this book, however, he appears to be traveling on parallel tracks with liberation theology and European new political theology.

Possible Strategies

With regard to his major interest in Christianity and the world religions, Küng delineates four strategies that Christians can adopt vis-à-vis the other religions. The first approach, the "fortress strategy," had been adopted by the Roman Catholic church before the Second Vatican Council, based on the dictum that "outside the [Catholic] church there is no salvation" *(Extra ecclesiam nulla salus).* Furthermore, this narrow view is also evident in Protestant fundamentalism in the United States, in German pietists, and in the adherents of Islam up to the present day. Küng's judgment on these is quite grim: "Everywhere there is the same spirit of intolerance, absolutism of truth and self-righteousness which has caused so much misery to people. Associated with this religious imperialism and triumphalism is a self-opinionated theological apologetic which is incapable of learning and causes more problems than it solves."[39]

The second approach to ecumenism is the "strategy of playing down differences." This tactic, Küng stresses, is widespread in the supposedly enlightened nations of Western civilization, and is grounded on two slogans: 1) "The existential problem of 'truth' does not really exist since each religion is equally true in its own way, in its essence," and 2) "Religious 'peace' will not be achieved by ignoring the differences and contradictions."[40] The author also has serious difficulties with this strategy, since anyone who knows the world religions in any depth will be aware of the fact that great dissimilarities exist among them. He points out the difficulty: "This would level out not only the fundamental differences between the basic types of mystical, prophetic and wisdom religion but also all the contradictions between the individual religions themselves. . . . This thoughtless strategy of playing down differences does not do justice to any religion; a religious potpourri is not the solution."[41] In summary, then, a strategy for which all religious positions are equally valid is not a real solution.

The third approach, a "strategy of embrace," is acknowledged to be more subtle beyond question, and has been employed by both Christian and non-Christian religions. The main principles are that 1) only one religion is the true one, but all have a part in the truth of this one religion; and that 2) religious "peace" will be achieved by the integration of the others. This strategy appears to be convincing, since it adopts the standpoint of a generous and tolerant inclusivism. It has been adopted by Christian theologians who see all non-Christians as supposedly "anonymous Christians," and also by religions of Indian origin: "All empirical religions represent just different levels, stages, partial aspects of the universal truth of one's own religion. The other religions, including those of Semitic and prophetic origin, are not regarded as untrue, but as provisional. They are said to have a share in the one universal truth (Hindu, Buddhist or even Taoist)."[42]

The consequence is that any other religion is seen as possessing a lower or partial truth, so that "what looks like toleration in practice proves to be a kind of conquest through embrace, a matter of allowing validity through domestication, an integration through a loss of identity."[43] Consequently, the "strategy of embrace" is not a real solution to the problem of truth and no real contribution to peace among the nations.

The Ecumenical Strategy

The fourth approach, an "ecumenical strategy," is the approach proposed by Küng. As a "presupposition" to this strategy, he strongly emphasizes self-criticism in all the religions. "A criticism of the other position," he declares, "can therefore only be justified on the basis of resolute self-criticism."[44] Küng provides a survey of the various crusades, inquisitions, witch hunts, and so forth, as a "critical mirror" held up to Christianity as well as to the world religions.

The author notes that the vast majority of Christians are totally unaware of how bitterly the world religions criticize Christianity and its adherents. Some of these critiques are the following:

It is said that Christianity, despite its ethic of love and peace, is often exclusive, intolerant and aggressive in its manner and activity: in short, it is loveless and unpeaceful; exaggerates almost pathologically the consciousness of sin and guilt in human beings who are said to be corrupt at heart, so that it can stress all the more emphatically the necessity of their redemption and their need for grace; on top of everything falsifies by its christology the figure of Jesus, who is almost always seen in positive terms in the other religions, so that he is made an exclusive divine figure.[45]

Küng then asks if this is the reason why, after hundreds of years of evangelization in the East, Christianity has succeeded in converting only five percent of the population. According to Aloysius Pieris, as we saw in Chapter Six, the number of Roman Catholics in Asia is only three percent (if the Philippines is not included, one and one-half percent).

Granted the necessary ingredient of self-criticism (no easy task), Küng moves audaciously into the truly formidable task of establishing universal ethical criteria. Also, he is confident that religion has a necessary relationship with the *humanum*: "Religion has always proved most convincing where it has succeeded—long before any modern attempts at autonomy—in effectively establishing what is truly human, the *humanum*, against the horizon of the Absolute. . . ."[46] Examples that are provided include the Decalogue, Sermon on the Mount, Qur'an, Discourses of the Buddha, and Bhagavadgita, all of which must be reevaluated in the changed conditions of the world of today.

At this point, Küng makes the interesting suggestion that Christianity more than other religions has had to undergo truly radical transformations and a painful process of change in this century, and that this is extremely important for the other religions. Thus, for many years the Roman Catholic church actually opposed basic human rights as un-Christian, a situation that completely changed only in the 1960s with the Second Vatican Council. Küng therefore believes that if such wrenching transitions could occur in one church it could serve as a prototype for change in the other world religions.

Furthermore, he observes paradoxically that once the *humanum* had achieved autonomy from religion and the churches "it could finally once again find a home in the sphere of Christianity—above all other religions—though the full realization of human rights (in respect of women, theologians, and dissidents) has still to be achieved in the Roman system itself. . . ."[47] Also, he is much concerned and very positive concerning the need for a *religious foundation* for universal human values. In the struggle for the *humanum*, he asserts that religion can unambiguously demonstrate why morality, ethical values and norms must be unconditionally binding (and not just where it is convenient for me) and thus universal (for all strata, classes and races). Precisely in this way the *humanum* is rescued by being seen to be grounded in the *divinum*. It has proved that only the Unconditioned can itself impose an unconditional obligation, and only the Absolute can be absolutely binding.[48]

At this juncture, Küng compares negative events, such as inquisitions in the Roman Catholic church, *suttee* (the burning of widows) in Indian culture, and numerous reforms in Islam, such as the *jihad* (holy war) and especially the *shariah* (law), which is seen to be in striking contrast to the United Nations Declaration of Human Rights. On a more positive level, he suggests that in the future there will be greater awareness among the world religions, with regard to four central human concerns: 1) the preservation of human rights, 2) the emancipation of women, 3) the realization of social justice, and 4) the immorality of war.[49]

Humanum as Basic Criterion

The *humanum*, or human dignity, or human rights, would seem to be a universal criterion for all men and women. The fundamental question then is: What is good for human beings? And the answer, not as obvious as it seems, is, what helps them to be truly human: ". . . that would be morally good which allows human life to succeed and prosper in the long term in its individual and social dimension: what enables the best possible development of men and women at all levels (including the levels of drives and feelings) and in all their dimensions (including their relationship to society and nature)."[50]

Therefore a religion is true if it serves human beings in its teachings and morals, its rites and institutions, and brings them the identity, meaning, and dignity that allows them to have a significant and fruitful life. A religion is false and evil if it propagates inhumanity by hindering human beings in all the things just mentioned. Küng also views religion and humanity in a dialectical relationship, with the *humanum* as a form of "superstructure" stretching over religions by which they are to be judged or condemned. It forms the minimum requirement of any religion, but also raises the question of why have a religion in the first place. Küng replies:

> True religion is the fulfillment of true humanity. That means that religion (as the expression of all-embracing meaning, supreme values, unconditional obligation) is an optimal presupposition for the realization of the *humanum*: there must be religion, in particular (that is a maximal criterion) where humanity is to be realized and made concrete as a truly unconditioned and universal obligation.[51]

The author refers to the first colloquium on religion sponsored by UNESCO that took place in Paris in February 1989, as a harbinger of the future and concrete examples of the preceding paragraph. In the first place, all of the religious representatives agreed that the *humanum* must be rooted in the Absolute or supreme Reality, however that was understood. Next, all accepted self-criticism as a presupposition for dialogue among the religions, and all agreed that religions have violated human rights, and incited hostility and violence. Third, there was general agreement that men and women in the religions must train for peacemaking; all accepted the overall motto of the symposium: "No world peace without religious peace." Finally, all the representatives of the world religions agreed that humanity could become the foundation of a common ethic in all of the traditions. This agreement, however, led Küng to raise a warning flag: "Is not the identity of the individual religion lost in a dialogue of religions, in so much forming of a consensus?"[52]

Are Dialogue and Steadfastness Opposites?

One answer that Küng proposes to this question is his suggestion that a neglected virtue is sorely needed in the dialogue, namely, "steadfastness," sometimes seen as bravery, constancy, courage, consistency, and stamina. Küng provides his own description, which "in this context is connected to resistance to external powers and those in power; with self-assertion, not giving in, holding firm; with courage, resolution, executive ability—all this with the freedom and responsibility of the individual in view. . . .steadfastness is not a rigid and static reality, but a dynamic reality which proves itself in the processes of life."[53] One cannot help but observe that this "neglected virtue" has loomed large in the entire life of Hans Küng!

At this point, the author is clearly moving closer to the problematic of Paul Knitter, as we saw in the first section of this chapter. Küng asks whether steadfastness in faith is a block to true dialogue: ". . . if one believes in Christ as the way, the truth, and the life, can one then also accept that there are other ways, other truths, that there is other life from transcendence? . . . That is the main question in any inter-religious undertaking."[54] Or in other words, can a Christian accept the truth of other religions without giving up their own religion or their own religious identity? Somewhat testily, he observes that slogans like "indifferentism," "relativism," and "syncretism" are always being hurled at inter-religious dialogue. Küng rejects these charges vigorously, and presents what he refers to as a "critically ecumenical" standpoint, which combines steadfastness and a readiness for dialogue.

There are three elements in this standpoint, and Küng holds that what we must aim at is 1) not indifferentism of equal value for everything, but *more* indifference for the type of orthodoxy that acts as the criterion of human salvation and imposes its truth through power and compulsion; 2) no relativism for which there is not an absolute, but *more* relativism when human beings create absolutes, and *more* relationality, which makes us capable of seeing the relationships in every religion; 3) no syncretism, which mixes together anything and everything, but *more* will for *synthesis,* that is, growing together in the face of religious antagonisms and oppositions, so that peace can prevail over war and strife.[55]

Along with the "critically ecumenical" standpoint, then, the author includes the necessity of "truth in freedom." He is adamant in the assertion that truth may not be sacrificed for the pseudo-unity of a single world religion. "Particularly," he insists, "in the third world, where the history of colonization and the history of mission mixed up with it are still by no means forgotten, this is rightly regarded as a threat to cultural and religious identity."[56] He summarizes his view in this way: "Self-critically, all this means that the Christian, too, has no monopoly of the truth, but does not have the right to dispense with the confession of truth in the form of a random pluralism either. Dialogue and testimony do not exclude each other. Confession of the truth includes the courage to recognize untruth and to say what it is."[57] Küng is also careful to point out that true freedom is freedom *for* other people, the environment, the Absolute, and not a freedom *from* responsibility; thus "true freedom is a freedom for the truth."[58]

Criteria and the Christian Criterion

The next step is the need for criteria between religions, to satisfy the urgent need to distinguish good and bad religion in all the religions. Again Küng provides three criteria: 1) a religion is true and good insofar as it protects and furthers humanity, but does not suppress and destroy it; 2) a religion is true and good insofar as it remains true to its own canon and its normative scripture or figure, and constantly uses them; 3) according to the specifically Christian criterion, a religion is true and good insofar as it shows the spirit of Jesus Christ in its theory and praxis.

At this point I believe the disagreement between Knitter and Küng becomes crystal clear. The latter refers to Knitter's "brand new doctrine," really the revived spirit of Protestant liberalism, which abandoned the normativeness and finality of Jesus Christ and which reduced him to one more prophet among others. Küng in a footnote makes it clear that this "brand new doctrine" is in reference to the writings and speeches of Paul Knitter: "Professor Knitter had an opportunity to present his arguments in a lecture to the University of Tübingen on 20 November 1989 and discuss them publicly with my Protestant colleagues Eberhard Jüngel and Jürgen Moltmann and myself."[59] It is quite clear that he associates Knitter with a failed Protestant liberalism.

Küng repeats that if Christian theologians give up the normativeness and finality of Jesus Christ, this would be abandoning "the central statement of all the scriptures that are normative for them, and which almost two thousand years ago came to form the New Testament, the foundation document of Christianity. Whether it is convenient or not, Jesus is normative and definitive for the whole of the New Testament."[60] In order to avoid "imperialism" or "neo-colonialism," as well as to avoid both absolutist-exclusivist positions and relativist-inclusivist positions, Küng provides his own distinction between the view of religions from the outside and religions from the inside. "Only in this way," he reiterates, "is a differentiated answer to the question of the truth of religions possible."[61]

Outside and Inside Perspectives

Seen from the viewpoint of the study of religions, that is, from the *outside perspective,* there are many different true religions, with different saviors and paths toward the one goal. At times they can overlap, and even exert benign influences on each other.

On the other hand, there is the *inside perspective,* that is, from the viewpoint of believing Christians, like Küng, "there is only one true religion: Christianity, in so far as it bears witness to the one true God as he has made himself known in Jesus Christ."[62] Paradoxically, Küng concedes that this one true religion does not exclude truth in other religions, with qualifications. Also, insofar "as they do not directly contradict the Christian message, other religions can supplement and correct the Christian religion and make it more profound."[63] Rather obviously, Küng has to raise the question: Is this in fact a contradiction?

His answer to this of course is no, and he uses a political analogy in order to show that there can be inside and outside perspectives. Thus, the statesman or constitutional lawyer must agree that the *other* state has its own legitimate polity and laws that effect and bind its citizens. The statesman or lawyer, however, have their own commitments:

> As a loyal citizen of the state among other citizens he or she feel themselves obligated in knowledge and conscience to this particular constitution (and no other); they see themselves as owing a uniquely binding loyalty to this state and this government (and to no other). I think that the best negotiator may be the one who can ideally combine both perspectives: the best possible loyalty to his or her own land (constitution, confession or religion) and a maximal openness to others.[64]

Thus, openness to other religions does not call for the suspension of one's own convictions, as if religious dialogue would require the giving up of one's faith. Although the political analogy is not perfect, I believe that Küng's viewpoint will be more appealing to the majority of Christians and theologians at this time than that of Paul Knitter. Of course, this discussion does not and can not provide an apodictic answer, although I incline toward the approach of Knitter.

Readiness for Dialogue

As I mentioned earlier, Küng and Knitter, while disagreeing on the Christian view of the religions, do find general unanimity in the *praxis* of Christianity and the world religions. Küng, as the title of his book declares, is proposing a "global ethic" for all the religions, while Knitter proposes a "liberation-centered theology of religions," orthopraxis, centering on the kingdom and base human communities. In other words, both men are emphasizing the importance of orthopraxis over orthodoxy (although the latter is also essential), and both are searching for dialogue and other efficacious mediations for the protection and nurturing of the human person, whether religiously affiliated or not.

Finally, one of the areas of orthopraxis that Küng stresses throughout his recent writings is the critical urgency of work for *peace*. "Capacity for dialogue," he declares, "is ultimately a virtue of capacity for peace."[65] He also again and again stresses the importance of a *conversion* to the true peace of Christianity, of the world religions, and of every last person of the human family. Here is how Küng phrases it: "Those who engage in dialogue must have the inner power and strength to sustain dialogue and where necessary to respect the standpoint of others. For one thing is certain: that impatience with dissent which is constantly breaking out all over the world, in all religions, has no understanding of the virtue of a capacity for dialogue. And yet: on this, literally on this, the whole of our spiritual and indeed physical survival will depend."[66]

FRANCIS X. CLOONEY, S.J.

Another well-known scholarly protagonist in the dialogue of the religions is the Jesuit Francis X. Clooney, who is an associate professor of theology at Boston College. Along with his more general

studies, he has recently published academic works in Indian religion such as *Thinking Ritually: Rediscovering the Purva Mimamsa of
Jaimini* and *Theology After Vedanta: An Experiment in Comparative
Theology*.[67] I have chosen a review-article by Clooney that provides a
panoramic view of the debate or, at times, controversy.

Agreement on Basic Issues

The books under review include S. Wesley Ariarajah *(The Bible
and People of Other Faiths)*; Hans Küng and Jürgen Moltmann, eds.
(Christianity Among World Religions); Hans Küng, et al. *(Christianity
and the World Religions)*; Alan Race *(Christians and Religious
Pluralism)*; S. Mark Heim *(Is Christ the Only Way?)*; Vernon Gregson
(Lonergan, Spirituality, and the Meeting of Religions); John Hick and
Paul Knitter, eds. *(The Myth of Christian Uniqueness)*; Paul Knitter
(No Other Name?); John Hick *(Problems of Religious Pluralism)*; M.M.
Thomas *(Risking Christ for Christ's Sake)*; Gavin D'Costa *(Theology
and Religious Pluralism)*; Richard H. Drummond *(Toward a New Age
in Christian Theology)*; and Leonard Swidler, ed. *(Toward a Universal
Theology of Religion)*.[68] This is truly a remarkable collection of world-
class scholars. Unfortunately, however, it appears that few major
women scholars are interested in this field, although there exist collections that are related to the issues.[69]

Clooney begins by acknowledging that there has been a "vigorous discussion" for quite some time on this topic and that "a veritable flood of such works" has erupted without any signs of
abatement. He then moves rapidly to the key questions that have
arisen:

> What are Christians to make of the continuing vitality of non-
> Christian religions, particularly in the light of the minimal success
> of centuries of missionary efforts? If we now desire the peaceful
> cooperation of people of various faiths, what has changed? . . .
> Can a Christian respect other religions and still claim that ul-
> timately the Christian Gospel alone announces the full solution to
> the world's problems?[70]

Clooney also provides a valuable service by identifying his interlocutors and their backgrounds; it is a spectacularly ecumenical

group. Three are from Europe (Hick, Küng, Race), three from Southern Asia (Ariarajah, D'Costa, and Thomas), and four from the United States (Drummond, Gregson, Heim, and Knitter). As regards religious backgrounds, there is also remarkable diversity: four are Roman Catholic (D'Costa, Gregson, Knitter, Küng), while three are Protestant (Drummond, Heim, Hick), two are Anglican (Race, Ariarajah), and one is Orthodox (Thomas).

Clooney then makes the startling statement that this diverse group all agree on four basic issues with regard to pluralism and the Christian understanding of it. These are the points of agreement:

> 1) Christians cannot realistically ignore the many religions flourishing in today's world. . . . 2) respect for these religions and a willingness to learn from them are essential to viable dialogue; 3) faithfulness to the Christian heritage remains essential; 4) the Christian tradition must therefore be read anew in the light of today's situation, so that Christians can responsibly account for the new while remaining faithful to their heritage.[71]

This agreement is remarkable and demonstrates that all of the denominations are being challenged to rethink their theologies of the religions and of Christianity itself. Hans Küng has made the acute observation that "the boundary between true and false today, even as Christians see it, no longer runs simply *between* Christianity and other religions, but at least in part *within* each of the religions."[72]

Exclusivism, Inclusivism, or Pluralism?

Most of the authors reject a position of *exclusivism*, which emphasizes "that other religions are marked by humankind's fundamental sinfulness and therefore erroneous, and that Christ (or Christianity) offers the only valid path."[73] D'Costa and Race defend an *inclusivism* (said to be that of Karl Rahner) that "on the one hand . . . accepts the spiritual power and depth manifest [in the other faiths] . . . on the other hand it rejects them as not being sufficient for salvation apart from Christ, for Christ alone is savior."[74] Knitter and Hick argue for *pluralism*, which D'Costa describes as maintaining "that other religions are equally salvific paths to the one

God, and Christianity's claim that it is the only path . . . should be rejected for good theological and phenomenological grounds."[75] Knitter has stated that his pluralist position was "a move away from insistence on the superiority or finality of Christ and Christianity toward a recognition of the independent validity of other ways."[76]

Some of the authors have more limited goals than those just mentioned. For example, Heim is mainly devoted to rejecting false issues and "retrieving the proper form of the question of the uniqueness of Christ, freed from peripheral issues such as colonialism, etc.—so that the issue of the Gospel's truth can be directly discussed."[77] Ariarajah stresses retrieving biblical ideas from religions at the present time, while Gregson uses Lonergan's ideas in attempting to ground a common epistemology for all the religions.[78] Küng for his part is intent on getting beyond preliminaries and generalities so that he can concentrate on the actual theological content of the other religions.[79]

Clooney believes that beneath these differences are real differences in the understanding of the word *pluralism*. It can mean *de facto* pluralism, that is, Christians recognize the reality of many religions and the need to dialogue with them, but continue to believe in Christianity (also called exclusivism).

A second form of pluralism holds that all truth is partial and fragmentary; thus, there can be no universal truth. This form of religious pluralism is represented by Swidler[80] and especially by Knitter, as may be seen in this quote:

> . . . truth is no longer defined according to the Aristotelian notion of science: "certain knowledge through causes." Rather, "modern science is not true; it is only on the way towards truth."[81] . . . on the personal level truth is no longer seen as the pursuit of certainty but as the pursuit of understanding—ever greater understanding. This means that all "true understanding" will be open to change and revision.[82]

Clooney points out, I would say correctly, that Knitter has gone far beyond issues of the world religions and that much more must be said about contemporary distinctions with regard to truth "in the 'hard' sciences, truth in the social sciences, truth in religions, personal truth, etc., before a particular application regarding religions—truth is plural, religions are plural—is warranted or convincing."[83]

John Hick is also concerned with religious truth claims, and defends his views from the attacks of many critics. Paul Griffiths and Delmas Lewis have participated in this critique of Hick as follows: ". . . religious belief is thus determined exclusively by large-scale cultural variables or small-scale psychological ones, and in any event by historical accident and not by a conscious attempt to apprehend and incarnate a true world-view. . . .the apparently conflicting truth-claims which form an important part of the major religious world-views are not really in conflict because they are not really truth-claims."[84] In Clooney's view, Hick's reply is really an acceptance of the validity of their charges, since he states that divergences in religious myth or doctrine are merely "alternative maps, in different projections, of the universe . . . they are not of great *religious*, i.e., soteriological importance."[85] Such an approach seems to dispose of any serious interest in the world religions or in their soteriological function, which is of great importance to billions of people.

The next group of authors are inclusivists—D'Costa, Küng, and Heim—and they are loath to discard objective truth and its significance for religion. They also believe in the uniqueness of Christ, and insist that it is possible to be loyal to one's beliefs, to take those of other religions seriously, and to make a responsible critique of their beliefs. Clooney makes a cautious evaluation of their contributions to the debate: "Although the inclusivist position at times seems to be an option for compromise and the safe middle ground, its true benefit lies in its respect for the stubborn complexities of religion's context and reason's demands."[86]

Clooney also faults these scholars for not demonstrating how to discern what is true and what is false with regard to religious beliefs. Thus, D'Costa asserts that Christ is the definitive criterion of truth and therefore is able "to trace elements of continuity and discontinuity, truth and error within other religions,"[87] but gives no examples of how this truth and error are discerned. Heim also defends the possibility of "Christian truth claims," but does not show how these will be accepted by those who do not accept the biblical revelation.[88]

Gregson, however, does attempt to synthesize truth and religious experience, using the influential writings of Bernard Lonergan, and proposes that Lonergan's epistemology as ways of understanding is common to all humans, Western or Eastern: "The fundamental human *ways* of knowing and expressing what are known are invariant, and on this reliable basis rests our confidence that talking to one another makes sense. When a person does not attend to this process, and articulates a system which misunderstands the process, any reasonable thinker can legitimately criticize his or her mistake."[89] Clooney rightly approves this valuable contribution, since in the context of pluralism it bolsters a normative meaning with regard to truth.

A History of Pluralism

Clooney then moves on to an historical overview of pluralism, stressing that Europeans recognized peoples with different religions and that many Europeans accepted the validity of their lives and religious experience or spirituality. He then continues:

But most of these same Europeans remained unabashed exclusivists, claiming a superior Christian understanding of truth; this exclusivism, itself true or false, became arrogant precisely when detached from (real or supposed) rational underpinnings and made to rely strictly on some self-evident superiority of Christian revelation, some higher morality of Christian peoples, etc.[90]

Clooney notes that Thomas Aquinas may have been inclusivist or exclusivist, but he certainly could not have been a pluralist, "because he believed that reason was universal, normative for believer and unbeliever alike."[91]

Clooney also states that the Jesuit Roberto de Nobili was an explicit follower of Aquinas when he established missions in southern India in the seventeenth century and he confidently proved the irrationality of basic Hindu doctrines. Clooney acutely observes that we differ from de Nobili not because we are more sympathetic to other cultures but because we place less confidence in the truth of our arguments. Today also, Clooney believes, there is no need for missionaries charging abroad to refute the creeds of the pagans: ". . . the analysis would cut both ways, as theologians on all sides read each other's texts seriously. There is no reason to presume that Christian positions *will appear the more reasonable.*"[92] The explosive last sentence should be required reading for all those who are seriously interested in the Christian-world religions dialogue.

Broadening the Parameters

The attention given to the role of reason has been a benefit, since it destroys the myth that pluralism is a problem in its own right and that it has its own solutions if we only dig deep enough. What is needed are broader horizons into other fields of study such as other areas of theology, as well as the study of religion, the social sciences, and the history of culture. M.M. Thomas, Alan Race, and Hans Küng have already been exploring these areas with very beneficial results.

At present there are developments also that are changing the whole physiognomy of theology. For example, Elouise Fraser, in a response to Paul Knitter's *No Other Name?* has pointed out that we need to retrieve the less heard voices from the past and to scuttle the myth that "the present is superior to the past."[93] For example, the Hebrew Scriptures need to be studied assiduously in their own right and not merely as a prelude to the New Testament. Along the same lines in response to Knitter, Thomas Dean proposes that

> to get at the truth of Christian proposals for a theocentric approach to dialogue [such as Knitter had proposed] we need to take seriously what is being concealed by the current Christian agenda . . . who feels excluded, who feels not spoken for, who is not speaking in his or her own voice, in a theocentric Christology [such as Knitter proposes] and dialogue agenda written by white, male (etc.) intellectuals.[94]

Other examples include the recent work of Rosemary Radford Ruether and Marjorie Hewitt Suchocki, who both place strong emphasis on the need for a coalition between religious pluralism and feminist theology. Suchocki emphasizes the fact that the critiques of sexism and religious absolutism are closely related and allied.[95] Ruether takes a different tack and insists that it is impossible to take the "major" religions seriously without taking into account ancient and modern forms of goddess worship and related practices and doctrines.[96] A final contribution of Paul Knitter that I believe is very important for all of theology is his integration of religious pluralism with liberation theology and the struggle for justice.[97]

On a wider horizon, George Lindbeck has studied inter-religious problems on grids of the "cognitive-propositional," the "experiential-expressivist," and the "cultural-linguistic." He has also voiced a needed cautiousness that is required by those who attempt to translate religious beliefs into terms that are more widely acceptable.[98] From a social science perspective, moreover, Charles Taylor has developed a notion of "perspicuous contrast," in order to be able to avoid the extremes of ethnocentricity (similar to exclusivism) and "incorrigibility" (similar to pluralism), as a means of studying cross-cultural issues.[99] Hans Penner has also made a contribution by analyzing the weaknesses of both "logical positivism" and "cognitive relativism" in a more profound understanding of religion.[100]

Some Critical Reflections

At this point, Clooney moves from an excellent survey of the theology of religions and pluralism by other authors in order to propose some evaluations of his own. A significant lacuna in the works reviewed is that they present so little information about specific religions, leading the author to a key question about this absence: "Can other religions have a role in the development of a Christian theology of religions and the dialogue of religions?"[101] Writers from the religions are not called upon to present their own views about what are, after all, their own religions, nor are they asked to evaluate and critique the views of the Christian theologians. A significant exception is an article by the Hindu Bibhuti Yadav in reply to an essay of the Indian Raimundo Panikkar. Yadav is able to provide "a welcome contribution to the whole discussion, in part because as a Hindu he can from a fresh vantage point notice the fundamentally Christian outlook which pervades Panikkar's writings."[102]

Clooney goes further and states his view that the absence of data from the non-Christian religions is mainly due to the belief that truth is irreducibly plural. Since all approaches are equally valid, there is no urgency to delve more deeply into what the others are actually saying. As Clooney describes it in an example: "Even if a pluralist willingly presumes that Indians have found the theory of rebirth meaningful, he or she may have little incentive to discover what exactly various Hindus, Buddhists, and Jainas have said about rebirth, or whether Indians might be wrong in positing future births—or, conversely, whether Christians might be misled in not doing so."[103] Clooney thus insists on the role of reason as universal in opposition to pluralism, and believes that reason is the driving force that leads Westerners to explore and profoundly study other cultures in the first place.

The author then offers some illuminating ideas on the notion of "dialogue," which is certainly influenced by many historical and cultural factors. Hindus, for example, have distinguished a number of forms of debate or argument that constitute dialogue, "and it can by no means be assumed that the most irenic is the most spiritual or most important." An example may be found in the article of the Sri Lankan, Aloysius Pieris, who criticizes the forms of "export Buddhism," and the different kinds of dialogue that accompany it.[104] At any rate, it seems essential that both parties should be aware of the form of dialogue that they will be entering.

Collections of Essays

Clooney ends his article with a survey of the three collections of essays edited by Küng and Moltmann, by Swidler, and by Hick and Knitter. The first collection is divided into four sections that deal with Christianity in relation to Islam, Hinduism, Buddhism, and Chinese religion. Each of the sections then provides a non-Christian reflection on Christianity, a Christian reflection on the other religions, and a report on collaboration and communication. Clooney was quite impressed by the article of Wang Hsien-Chih on the location of Christianity within the various religions that abound in the island of Taiwan. [105]

Swidler's collection was begun in a conference in 1984 at Temple

University. It is structured around an extensive essay by Swidler, entitled "Interreligious and Interideological Dialogue: The Matrix for All Systematic Reflection Today."[106] This was followed by major responses by Wilfred Cantwell Smith, Cobb, Panikkar, and Küng, and other exchanges by a dozen other very divergent interlocutors. Clooney was much impressed with Swidler's ten ground rules for dialogue, his call for "ecumenical esperanto," or a cross-religious theological language (to me, an impossibility), and his comparison of the stages of readiness for dialogue and Lawrence Kohlberg's stages of development.

Another important conference took place at Claremont, California, in 1986, and the papers produced there formed the substance of *The Myth of Christian Uniqueness*. All of these papers were submitted by those "theologians who were exploring the possibility of a *pluralist* position—a move away from insistence on the superiority or finality of Christ and Christianity toward a recognition of the independent validity of other ways."[107]

The book is divided into three "bridges," or sections, entitled the "historico-cultural," the "theologico-mystical," and the "ethico-practical." Clooney is impressed by some comments of Langdon Gilkey on the difficulty of religious dialogue: "The interplay of absolute and relative—of being a Christian, Jew, or Buddhist, and *affirming* that stance, and yet at the same time relativizing this mode of existence—both stuns and silences the mind, at least mine."[108] Clooney also presents an excellent summary of his own views:

> . . . this attention to paradox reminds us that any irreversible 'progression' from exclusivism to pluralism is unlikely; exclusivists, inclusivists, and pluralists will have to learn to live together. In part, it may be the intractable, stubborn, and unconfinable nature of religion and thinking about religion that makes the volume as a whole less satisfying than its parts, less than convincing as a step toward solidifying the pluralist position.[109]

Clooney's final paragraph notes that all of the books reviewed are worthy, and "a careful reading of any one of them will lead to the others and engage the reader in the larger issues,"[110] which I endorse.

Marjorie Hewitt Suchocki

One of the few women engaged academically both in feminism and the theology of the world religions, Marjorie Hewitt Suchocki has formerly taught and directed the Doctor of Ministry Program at Pittsburgh University, and was the Academic Dean at Wesley Theological Seminary in Washington, D.C. Her books and numerous articles also demonstrate her strong interest in process theology.

In Search of Justice

I found it very interesting to discover the title, "In Search of Justice,"[111] in Suchocki's essay, since justice has been a major theme throughout this book. I have mentioned already the fine article of Paul Knitter, "Towards a Liberation Theology of Religions."[112] Suchocki states her own goal candidly and clearly:

> Liberation theology has pointed to the invidious effects that follow when one mode of humanity is made normative for others. . . . The thesis of this essay is that the principle holds for religion as well: universalizing one religion such that it is taken as a norm whereby all other religions are judged and valued leads to oppression, and hence falls short of the norm that liberationists consider ultimate—the normative justice that creates well-being in the world community.[113]

Suchocki moves on to stress that feminism must accept a radical form of religious pluralism, but at the same time it must employ a critical consciousness on human well-being. In brief, "[j]ustice is thus to be the fundamental criterion of value and the focus of dialogue and action among religions."[114]

Suchocki then voices her acceptance of the uniqueness of each of the religions, while at the same time rejecting the idea of entering dialogue without any judgments being made. What she advocates is "a shift of judgment from ideological ground to ethical ground, along with an open recognition of the conditioned nature of the norm of justice we bring, and a commitment to critical exploration of the norm in the very dialogue wherein it is brought to bear."[115]

Justice as Norm?

After a comparison of sexism and the negative Christian attitude toward other religions (with Küng presented as a perfect example[116]), the author turns her attention to the problems and possibilities of justice as a norm. After exploring the relativism of justice, she states that a basis does exist for justice as a self-critical norm in religious dialogue in a manner that is not imperialistic.

She asserts that one's own well-being is conditioned by personal and social situation, and can be as culturally influenced as much as any other concept. Also, the understanding of well-being can be understood in many different ways in various cultural situations. But the author also insists that:

> There is a certain intransigence to the norm . . . when it comes to fundamental aspects of human existence, such as peaceful access to food, water, health, shelter, work, and community. To use justice normatively in interreligious dialogue implies, first, a fundamental importance accorded to these values for all peoples, and secondly, a commitment to work cooperatively with any religious group toward the creation of such well-being for the various communities of the world.[117]

The author next moves on to the concept of ill-being, which of course could be conceived as well-being in some environments, and even in the Christian religion where eternal damnation and suffering are considered to be an ultimate manifestation of justice. This is attested to by history, as the liberation theologians strongly insist:

> The ill-being of women, blacks, and others outside the dominant culture system has been called well-being within a posited system of order. . . . I, as a feminist, cannot in any way consider these views as functions for dealing with social situations not easily changed. Rather, using justice as an internal basis for criticism, I name such practices evil, and call for their reform.[118]

Another Criterion of Justice?

Despite what has been said, there exists an avenue of dialogue that admits a non-imperialistic criterion for justice. Thus, Suchocki states, "it is possible that each religion's deepest valuation of what physical existence should be lies, not in its coping with the exigencies of history, but in its projection of the *ideal*."[119] If each society looked at its saints and holy ones and their projection of an ideal existence, there could be some unanimity with regard to the value of freedom from suffering.

Suchocki develops this idea further:

> This vision is far more likely to yield agreement on the value of at least the basic forms of justice dealing with physical existence. If so, then the criterion of justice in that minimal mode can appeal to an internal norm within each religion. This mitigates the charge that the norm of justice as a basis for making value judgments concerning religions is as imperialistic as doctrinal norms.[120]

With regard to religious pluralism and justice, then, the author ends her thoughtful essay with what is certainly the virtue of hope: "One vision of justice can temper, criticize, and deepen another, and through dialogue each vision might grow richer in understanding and implementation."[121]

Reflections

It is possible that readers may find these discussions academic and somewhat tedious. Thus, I think it will be profitable to move beyond the "world religions" as mere abstractions and contemplate them as immense numbers of human beings, of individual persons.[122] The figures presented here will be rounded off to the highest millions. If we start with our own faith, there are 1,784,000,000 persons in the Christian churches; of these 1,011,000,000 adhere to the Roman Catholic church, and Orthodox churches comprise 169,000,000 members, with the rest belonging to Protestant and Anglican churches (over 600,000,000 adherents).

Looking abroad, we find that there are 951,000,000 human beings in the Muslim religion worldwide, while a total of 720,000,000 adhere to the Hindu religion, mainly in India. There are also 310,000,000 Buddhists, who are spread over most of Asia. If smaller groups are included, these religions have far more than two billion members. Thus, it can be said that adherents of the world religions comprise far more than half of the world's members (5,500,000,000).

In my view, then, these vast numbers of religious persons would form an enormous constituency if they were able to dialogue together on their beliefs and especially on their praxis for the *protection* and *enhancement* of *all* human beings. This would certainly constitute the greatest peaceful revolution in the history of the world.

Thus, the efforts and writings of our authors are not merely academic, but are intimately concerned with the well-being of billions of human beings. I am very hopeful and concerned that Suchocki can amplify and develop the crucial concept of justice she analyzed, so that it can aid more profoundly in the construction of a modern theology of religions. Küng, also, has published a great deal of valuable material on the world religions and stimulated a number of important dialogues. His "new world ethic" is certainly a valuable contribution, especially in the area of praxis; it seems, however, that he has no defined constituency who will accept and put into practice his global ethics. That appears to me, at least, to be the case in the Americas, if not in Europe.

But I believe that the most important trail for the future continues to be blazed by Paul Knitter, since he has synthesized the *theology of religions* and *liberation theology*. This synthesis appeals to the many who are influenced by one or more of all the liberation theologians we have discussed in this volume and many others, so that Knitter should attract the interest of many diverse and distant persons. May his tribe increase!

In my own view, I tentatively find the pluralist viewpoint interesting, and think that the viewpoint will be part of the development of dogma, much like the development of *nulla salus extra ecclesiam*, (no salvation outside the [Catholic] church), a teaching that was jettisoned after the Second Vatican Council.

My major interest is not theoretical, however, but that the world religions may come together to enkindle a passion for justice and for work together for the betterment of all humans, especially those that are poor and oppressed. A crucial part of that dialogue means *repentance* for all the ideologies that disguised injustice—in each of the world religions for so many centuries. This means, for example, that the U.S. churches have sinned personally and in common, as

Robert McAfee Brown delineated in Chapter Seven of this book. The other world churches must also declare their sins, especially the dehumanizing of girls and women, e.g., in female infanticide, various forms of mutilation, extremely exhaustive work, and many other graphic examples that Mercy Amba Oduyoye presented throughout her remarks in Chapter Five of this book.

In brief, the major discussions of the world religions in the future must squarely face the urgent need to focus squarely on the *protection* and *enhancement* of every person on the globe. Equally important are the graced institutions that must be created and the structures of evil that must be annihilated, that is to advance the Kingdom of God in our generation. In this we are empowered by the Spirit and impassioned by a great and enduring hope in the words of Jesus: "Blessed are those who hunger and thirst after justice, for they shall be satisfied" (Mt 5:6).

QUESTIONS FOR REFLECTION AND DISCUSSION

1. A very important point for dialogue with the world religions, according to Paul Knitter, would be for the theologians of the West to eliminate their attitude of superiority as well as their devaluing of other religions. Have you acted this way in relationships with other religions and their members? How should we Christians find ways to overcome the crypto-colonialism we have toward other religions?

2. Paul Knitter states that at least at the moment it is impossible to make claims for finality and normativity for Christianity. Would you accept the possibility of this position or not? What are your reasons?

3. The author stresses numerous times that orthopraxis is more important than orthodoxy in all the world religions.

Do you agree with that or perhaps prefer a balance between the two? Are there any other approaches you can think of?

4. Paul Knitter has highly approved the approach of small base communities. However, he understands them as basic human communities, not consisting only of Christians. Do you see these latter communities as feasible in the long run? Give reasons for or against.

5. In his studies of world religions, Hans Küng suggests four dif-

ferent strategies Christianity can adopt vis-à-vis the other religions. Which of these strategies do you find most congenial? Also, can you conceive another strategy that would be more appropriate?

6. A great obstacle to dialogue with other religions, says Küng, is the fact that Christians are totally unaware of how strongly other religions criticize Christianity. Can you suggest any strategies to overcome this difficulty? Can we also ask the religions to criticize themselves?

7. Hans Küng has given great emphasis to the importance of universal human rights. In the light of so many cultures, does this have a feasible future? What are possible strategies to promote universal human rights?

8. From his extensive studies of other religions, Francis Clooney concludes that there is no reason to presume that Christian doctrine will appear as more reasonable. Do you think that this statement is acceptable? Why or why not?

9. Marjorie Hewitt Suchocki provides a very important contribution concerning the visions of justice in all religions, and using the saints and holy ones as ideals. Do you agree with this approach or can you think of others more appropriate?

10. Surveying the entire chapter, do you think that as a Christian you are closest to either the exclusive, inclusive, or pluralist position with regard to the world religions? Give your specific reasons for your choice. Finally, perhaps you might be able to conceive other possible positions regarding the religions.

SUGGESTED READINGS

Carmody, Denise Lardner. *Women and World Religions*. Nashville: Abingdon, 1979.

Concilium 183: *Christianity Among World Religions*. Hans Küng and Jürgen Moltmann, eds.; Edinburgh: T. & T. Clark, 1986.

Coward, Harold, ed. *Modern Indian Responses to Religious Pluralism*. Albany: State University of New York Press, 1987.

D'Costa, Gavin. *Theology & Religious Pluralism: The Challenge of Other Religions*. Oxford: Basil Blackwell, 1986.

Ferré, Frederick, and Rita Mataragnon, eds. *God and Global Justice: Religion and Poverty in an Unequal World.* New York: Paragon House, 1985.

Geffré, Claude, and Mariasusai Dhavamony, eds. *Buddhism and Christianity.* New York: Seabury Press, 1979.

Hick, John. *An Interpretation of Religion: Human Responses to the Transcendent.* New Haven: Yale University Press, 1989.

Knitter, Paul F. *No Other Name? A Critical Survey of Christian Attitudes Toward the World Religions.* Maryknoll, NY: Orbis Books, 1985.

Küng, Hans. *Christianity and the World Religions: Paths of Dialogue with Islam, Hinduism, and Buddhism.* Garden City, NY: Doubleday, 1986.

Richard, Lucien. *What Are They Saying About Christ and the World Religions?* New York: Paulist, 1981.

Smith, Wilfrid Cantwell. *Towards a World Theology: Faith and the Comparative History of Religions.* Philadelphia: Westminster, 1980.

Thomas, M.M. *Risking Christ for Christ's Sake: Towards an Ecumenical Theology of Pluralism.* Geneva: World Council of Churches, 1987.

Tillich, Paul. *Christianity and the Encounter of World Religions.* New York: Columbia University Press, 1963.

JUSTICE IN THE NEW MILLENNIUM

TO SOME READERS, THIS BOOK MAY HAVE consisted of a rather arduous journey, somewhat analogous to the popular film, *Around the World in Eighty Days,* but without the humor and dazzling scenery it provided. At any rate, I will be brief and accentuate here only some of the most significant ideas in this epilogue.

Looking back to the prologue of this work, I referred to all of the authors in the nine chapters of this book as liberation theologians, but also as a "new world community of liberation." The new world community of liberation, I insisted, "represents the vanguard, the pioneers, the spearhead, the cutting edge of a new Christianity for a new millennium." Here, at the end of the book, I repeat in even more emphatic terms the importance of this liberation community for the churches and for the world.

It is pellucidly clear, also, that these pioneers are creating their theologies for the present and the future of their countries and of their peoples. On the other hand, they are profoundly aware that the academic theologians, especially in the first world, devote much of their energies to analyzing and reproducing the theology or theologies of the past, and they often import foreign theologies that have no relation to the contexts of their own nations.

As a result, furthermore, the accusation has been made in the first world that the liberation theologians are too "activist," too deeply immersed in the present and the future, and in their own "reality," or context. These theologians are not annoyed or displeased, but joyfully accept this "accusation" and gladly continue their present *reflections* and *practice*. They realize that their work is not confined to seminar rooms and libraries, but consists of a theory and praxis that promise to ameliorate enormously the dismal fate of countless human beings and other creatures of today and tomorrow. They also readily reply that if we briefly glance over the few millennia of the Christian past, it is indubitable that the best theologians were not those who merely repeated the past but those who fashioned a more profound vision and a more vibrant motivation for action for the Christians of their era and context. And the very core of that vision and motivation of the liberation community continues to revolve around Jesus' preaching of the kingdom, or reign, of God and thus a profound option for the poor in every corner of the globe.

Another illuminating perspective on the present and future of the churches and theology has been provided by the sociologist of religion, Catherine Albanese. She has pointed out clearly and succinctly that the Christian religion and indeed all the religions of the world are divided into two kinds. The first type is designated as "ordinary" religion, which reveals itself in the many daily customs and expected mores that are embedded in a culture.[1]

> In other words, ordinary religion is at home with the way things are. It functions as the (mostly unexamined) religion of a community as community. Because it is about living well within the boundaries, it values the social distinctions that define life in the community and respects the social roles that people play. It honors the ranks that they hold and the general institutions of government, education, family, and recreation to which they assent.[2]

On the other hand, there exists an "extraordinary" religion that is not definitively assimilated into the culture. Its religious forms and language clearly and strongly stand out from the "ordinary" culture; these terms "chart the unknown and suggest how it beckons people away from their more ordinary concerns." Furthermore, "extraordinary religion often encourages religious activity not only on the part of the community but also on the part of separate individuals who tune themselves with particular intensity to the message delivered to the community."[3] In short, they become the mystics and prophets of the community.

These mystics and prophets are the same as the liberation theologians who are scattered throughout the nine chapters of this book. Their message is constructed solidly upon the Old and New Testaments and the life and teaching of Jesus Christ. The major project of their lives is the re-creation of that life and teaching in their own lives and in that of their contemporaries around the world. It seems fitting, therefore, to turn to the earliest gospel and reflect on the first preaching of Jesus in Galilee: "The time is fulfilled, and the kingdom of God is at hand. Be converted, and believe in the good news" (Mk 1:15).

NOTES

Prologue: Blazing New Trails

1. Juan Luis Segundo, *The Liberation of Theology* (Maryknoll, NY: Orbis Books, 1976), p. 3. Segundo also stresses that "certain basic points" are held by those he has just mentioned: "They would maintain that the longstanding stress on individual salvation in the next world represents a distortion of Jesus's message. He was concerned with man's full and integral liberation, a process which is already at work in history and which makes use of historical means. . . . They would also maintain that there are not two separate orders—one being a supernatural order and the other being a natural order inside history; that instead one and the same grace raises human beings to a supernatural level and provides them with the means to achieve their true destiny within one and the same historical process" (ibid.).

2. Alfred T. Hennelly, ed., *Liberation Theology: A Documentary History* (Maryknoll, NY: Orbis Books, 1990).

3. I do not mention here the works of the great German Jesuit, Karl Rahner, because he did not have a closed system. Thus, all his writings were appropriately entitled *Theological Investigations*.

4. Elizabeth A. Johnson, *She Who Is: The Mystery of God in Feminist Theological Discourse* (New York: Crossroad, 1992), p. 10.

5. Ibid., p. 12; italics mine. She goes on to note that "enough has been broken through, been struggled over, prayed over, celebrated, and been articulated by astute thinkers and artists with and without academic credentials that the present schema may serve as one way of consolidating gains while preparing advance."

6. See Paul, 1 Corinthians, ch. 15.

7. Segundo, *Liberation of Theology*, p. 3.

8. Harvey Cox, *The Silencing of Leonardo Boff: The Vatican and the Future of World Christianity* (Oak Park, IL: Meyer Stone Books, 1988). Cox notes with simple and profound eloquence: "In the biblical tradition, God is known as the Holy One who speaks to human beings and who expects them to answer. Therefore, to silence someone, it could be said, is a type of blasphemy. It denies that person the opportunity to respond to God's call, and it therefore denies God" (pp. 187-88).

9. Segundo, *Liberation of Theology*, p. 5.

10. Ibid.

11. Jon Sobrino, *Christology at the Crossroads: A Latin American Approach* (Maryknoll, NY: Orbis Books, 1978), p. 232.

Chapter 1: Theology From the Underside of History
Latin American Liberation Theology

1. Quoted in Curt Cadorette, *From the Heart of the People: The Theology of Gustavo Gutiérrez* (Oak Park, IL: Meyer Stone Books, 1988), pp. 93-94. The original text is *Il materialismo storico e la filosofia di Benedetto Croce* (Turin: Einaudi, 1971), p. xvii.

2. James Brockman, "Gustavo Gutiérrez," *Christian Century* (October 19,

1983), p. 933; italics mine. He develops this further: "My aim has never been to publish books. Not that there is anything wrong with publishing. It's just not my vocation, which is fundamentally pastoral. But when I do theology I try to do it as seriously as possible. I regard that as an obligation. *A Theology of Liberation* was carefully thought out, and it confronted modern thought. That's why there are so many references, not to show how much I had read but to expose my thought to those of others" (p. 935). Quoted in Robert McAfee Brown, *Gustavo Gutiérrez: An Introduction to Liberation Theology* (Maryknoll, NY: Orbis Books, 1990), pp. 46-47.

3. Gustavo Gutiérrez, *A Theology of Liberation: History, Politics, and Salvation* (revised ed.; Maryknoll, NY: Orbis Books, 1988), p. 174.

4. The major books of Gutiérrez are: *The Power of the Poor in History: Selected Writings* (Maryknoll, NY: Orbis Books, 1983); *We Drink from Our Own Wells: The Spiritual Journey of a People* (Maryknoll, NY: Orbis Books, 1984); *On Job: God-Talk and the Suffering of the Innocent* (Maryknoll, NY: Orbis Books, 1985); *The Truth Will Set You Free* (Maryknoll, NY: Orbis Books, 1990); and *The God of Life* (Maryknoll, NY: Orbis Books, 1991). For the past several years he has been working on a four-volume study of the life and works of the great champion of the Indians in the sixteenth century, Fray Bartolomé de Las Casas, O.P. This has recently been published as *Las Casas: In Search of the Poor of Jesus Christ* (Maryknoll, NY: Orbis Books, 1993). As usual, he focuses his gaze fixedly on the faces of Christ's poor on the last page of his book: ". . . we are called by them—each of us from his or her cultural world—to make the present our own and to shape and forge the time to come. They both challenge us to write our names, in all haste and urgency, with purpose and determination, on the pages of that history of long duration that is the coming of the Reign of life proclaimed by Jesus" (p. 460).

5. Alfred T. Hennelly, ed., *Liberation Theology: A Documentary History* (Maryknoll, NY: Orbis Books, 1990), p. 64.

6. Ibid. There is also evidence that Gutiérrez was rather dissatisfied with some previous meetings that were not "concrete" enough: "The process of liberation is a sign of the times. It is a call to action at the same time that it is a new theme of reflection, new because it is a global term for the problems contained within it. *Thus there is a certain deficiency in the attempts that are being made with regard to a theology of liberation, which is clearly evident in the conclusions of the meetings at Mar del Plata and Itapoan, both of which leave me dissatisfied*" (ibid.; italics mine). In my judgment, this dissatisfaction provided a major impetus that impacted on the writing of his book.

7. Ibid., p. 63.

8. Ibid.

9. Ibid., pp. 63-64.

10. Ibid., p. 64.

11. Ibid.

12. *Theology of Liberation*, 1.

13. Ibid., p. 3.

14. Ibid. The text reads as follows: "It is necessary to destroy the widely held prejudice that philosophy is something extremely difficult because it is the intellectual activity proper to a certain category of scientific specialists or professional and systematic philosophers. It is necessary, therefore, to demonstrate first that all persons are 'philosophers,' establishing the parameters and characteristics of this 'spontaneous' philosophy proper to 'everyman'" ("Avviamemento allo studio della filosofia e del materialismo

storico, Saggio introduttivo" in *La formazione dell'uomo* [Rome: Editori Riuniti, 1969], p. 217); *Theology of Liberation*, pp. 177-78.

15. *A Theology of Liberation*, pp. 5-12.

16. Ibid., p. 5.

17. Ibid.

18. Ibid., p. 6.

19. Ibid., p. 12. I may add here that Gutiérrez summons up many witnesses in recent times that agree with his approach and thus bolster his thesis. As examples I add here a statement of the distinguished Dutch theologian, Edward Schillebeeckx: "It is evident that thought is also necessary for action. But the Church has for centuries devoted its attention to formulating truths and meanwhile did almost nothing to further the world. In other words, the Church focused on orthodoxy and left orthopraxis in the hands of nonmembers and nonbelievers." (ibid., p. 8). He also speaks of one of his favorite comrades in arms in the field of philosophy and theology: "Maurice Blondel, moving away from an empty and fruitless spirituality and attempting to make philosophical speculation more concrete and alive, presented it as a critical reflection on action. This reflection attempts to understand the internal logic of an action through which persons seek fulfillment by constantly transcending themselves. Blondel thus contributed to a new *apologetics* and became one of the most important thinkers of contemporary theology, including the most recent trends" (ibid., pp. 7-8).

20. Ibid., p. 23.

21. Ibid., p. 24. The major witness the author calls on at this point is Dietrich Bonhoeffer, the Lutheran pastor who was hanged by the Nazis in a prison camp during the Second World War, and who has written: "In the language of the Bible freedom is not something man has for himself but something he has for others . . . It is not a possession, an object, . . . but a relationship and nothing else. In truth, freedom is a relationship between two persons. Being free means 'being free for the other,' because the other has bound me to him. Only in relationship with the other am I free" (ibid.). The text is taken from *Creation and Fall, Temptation* (New York: Macmillan, 1966), p. 37.

22. *A Theology of Liberation*, p. 24.

23. Ibid., p. 25.

24. Ibid.

25. Ibid., p. 29.

26. Ibid., pp. 41-46.

27. Ibid., p. 42. Gutiérrez also appends here the somewhat surprising assertion that "rather than define the world in relation to the religious phenomena, it would seem that religion should be redefined in relation to the profane. . . . This is Bonhoeffer's world come of age, *mündig*, the source of his anguished question, 'How can we speak about God in this adult world?'" The reference is to *Christians Active*, p. 71.

28. Ibid., p. 43. The author also emphasizes that this process of secularization is quite complex, since it is "uneven and combined," a term attributed to Leon Trotsky.

29. Ibid., p. 44.

30. Ibid., p. 74.

31. Ibid., p. 75. My view is that the Eucharist is a major element in creating unity and taking steps to reconciliation of the Christian community. However, its prayer, song, and worship must always issue in real practice.

32. Ibid., pp. 75-76.

33. Ibid., p. 77.

34. There is an addition to the charge as follows: "We often confuse the possession of basic necessities with a comfortable position in the world, freedom to preach the gospel with protection by powerful groups, instruments of service with the means of power."

35. Ibid., p. 79.

36. Cf. ibid., p. 43 ff.

37. Cf. ibid., p. 77.

38. Ibid., p. 91. The author also notes that "when we assert that humanity fulfills itself by continuing the work of creation by means of its labor, we are saying that it places itself, by this very fact, within an all-embracing salvific process. To work, to transform this world, is to become a human being and to build the human community; it is also to save. Likewise, to struggle against misery and exploitation and to build a just society is already to be part of the saving action, which is moving towards its complete fulfillment."

39. Ibid., p. 97.

40. Ibid., p. 118. Gutiérrez continues with a description of the conversion: "We have to break with our mental categories, with the way we relate to others, with our way of identifying with the Lord, with our cultural milieu, with our social class, in other words, with all that can stand in the way of a real, profound solidarity with those who suffer, in the first place, from misery and injustice."

41. Ibid., p. 124.

42. Ibid., p. 129.

43. Ibid., p. 133.

44. Ibid., p. 147.

45. Ibid.

46. Ibid., pp. 148-49. See my remarks on the Eucharist in n. 31.

47. Ibid., p. 150.

48. Ibid., p. 161. This is the author's ecumenical plea: "The call to unity certainly extends beyond the Catholic Church. It extends to all Christians and is the wellspring of the ecumenism to which Vatican II gave such an important stimulus. . . . Among us, as experience has shown, the commitment to proclaiming the love of God for all in the person of the poorest is a fruitful meeting ground for Christians from the various confessions. At the same time, we are all trying to follow Jesus on the path leading to the eternal Father."

49. Cf. *Función de la Iglesia en la realidad rioplatense* (Montevideo: Barreiro y Ramos, 1962); *Etapas precristianas de la fe: Evolución de la idea de Dios en el Antiguo Testamento* (Montevideo: Cursos de Complementación Cristiana, 1962).

50. Cf. Alfred T. Hennelly, ed., *Liberation Theology: A Documentary History* (Maryknoll, NY: Orbis Books, 1990), pp. 29-37.

51. Gutiérrez, *Theology of Liberation*, p. 9.

52. Segundo, *Liberation of Theology*, p. 9.

53. Ibid.

54. Ibid.

55. Ibid., pp. 10-34.

56. Ibid., pp. 39-40.

57. Ibid., pp. 40-47.

58. Ibid., p. 40.

59. Ibid., p. 41.

60. Ibid., pp. 42-43.

61. *Our Idea of God* (Maryknoll, NY: Orbis Books, 1973).

62. Ibid., p. 43.

63. Ibid., p. 47.

64. *Faith and Ideologies* (Maryknoll, NY: Orbis Books, 1982). It is the first volume in the English edition of Segundo's christology, entitled *Jesus of Nazareth Yesterday and Today*. The original edition is entitled *El hombre de hoy ante Jesús de Nazaret* (Madrid: Ediciones Christiandad, 1982), in three volumes. Volume one of the Spanish edition is also entitled *Fe e ideología*.

65. *Liberation of Theology*, p. 97.

66. Ibid., p. 107.

67. Cf. *Funk & Wagnalls Standard Desk Dictionary* (New York: Harper & Row, 1984).

68. *Liberation of Theology*, p. 106.

69. Ibid., p. 107.

70. Ibid., pp. 117-18.

71. Ibid., p. 116. He continues: ". . . we must build a bridge between our conception of God and the real-life problems of history. This bridge, this provisional but necessary system of means and ends is what we are calling *ideology* here."

72. Ibid., p. 117.

73. Ibid., p. 120. A further clarification follows the previous text: ". . . fighting one's way out of bondage in Egypt is one experience and turning the other cheek is another experience. Someone who has gone through both experiences and has reflected on them has learned how to learn; he has multiplied his faith-based information, not subtracted it to a zero."

74. Jn 16:12–16.

75. *Liberation of Theology*, p. 120.

76. Ibid., p. 121.

77. Ibid.

78. Ibid., p. 122. On this page Segundo provides an excellent summary of Paul's interpretation of the Christian's moral obligations in the light of revelation.

79. Ibid., pp. 125-26.

80. Ibid., p. 126. Segundo continues: "That this is a serious problem for liberation theology is evident from the fact that most of the attacks against it stem from a specific conception of the Church and its function as well as from a specific conception of eschatology, that is, of what God is fashioning above and beyond the reaches of history."

81. Ibid., p. 139.

82. Ibid., pp. 149-150.

83. Ibid., p. 150.

84. Ibid.

85. Ibid., pp. 150-51. Segundo adds: "So the catholic doctrine was clearly inadequate insofar as it made the law the object of our liberty, and the Lutheran doctrine was inadequate insofar as it turned faith into a deprecation of human liberty" (p. 151).

86. Ibid., p. 72. Segundo waxes ironic: "Yet curiously enough, except for a few strong reactions against *Populorum Progressio* (in one instance labeled 'warmed-over Marxism'), the popes have not been accused of mixing religion and politics."

87. Ibid., p. 71.

88. Ibid., p. 74.

89. Ibid., p. 75.

90. Elsa Tamez, ed., *Through Her Eyes: Women's Theology from Latin America* (Maryknoll, NY: Orbis Books, 1989). Elsa Tamez is a Methodist from Mexico and the author of *The Bible of the Oppressed* (Maryknoll, NY: Orbis Books, 1982).

91. Bidegain, "Women and the Theology of Liberation," in *Through Her Eyes*, pp. 15-36.

92. The books are *Nacionalismo, Militarismo y Dominación en América Latina; Iglesia, Pueblo y Política*; and *Así Actuaron los Christianos en la Historia de América*. Further information on these books was not included in this volume. Her thesis for the doctorate in historical sciences was entitled "La organización de movimientos de Juventud de Acción Católica en América Latina" (Louvain: Université de Louvain, 1979).

93. *Through Her Eyes*, p. 16.

94. Ibid., p. 19.

95. Ibid., pp. 20-21.

96. Ibid., p. 24.

97. Ibid., p. 25. The movement that influenced them were the Jocists, which was originally created in France as JOC (*Jeunesse Ouvrière Catholique*—Young Catholic Workers).

98. Ibid., p. 27.

99. Ibid., p. 28.

100. Leonardo Boff, *The Maternal Face of God* (San Francisco: Harper & Row, 1987).

101. *Through Her Eyes*, pp. 28-29.

102. Ibid., p. 31.

103. Gustavo Gutiérrez, *Las Casas: In Search of the Poor of Jesus Christ* (Maryknoll, NY: Orbis Books, 1993). The Spanish edition was published in 1992 by Centro de Estudios y Publicaciones in Lima, Peru.

104. Juan Luis Segundo, *The Liberation of Dogma* (Maryknoll, NY: Orbis Books, 1992). The Spanish edition appeared in 1989 by Editorial Sal Terrae, in Santander, Spain.

105. The rather odd Spanish title is *¿Qué mundo? ¿Qué hombre? ¿Qué Dios?* It also was published by Sal Terrae in 1993. The citation is on p. 328.

106. Jon Sobrino, *Jesus the Liberator: A Historical-Theological View* (Maryknoll, NY: Orbis Books, 1993). The Spanish edition appeared in 1991 and was published by Editorial Trotto in Madrid.

107. Ignacio Ellacuría, *Filosofía de la realidad histórica* (San Salvador, El Salvador: UCA Editores, 1990).

108. Ignacio Ellacuría and Jon Sobrino, eds., *Mysterium Liberationis: Fundamental Concepts of Liberation* (Maryknoll, NY: Orbis Books, 1993). According to my count, the English volume had 35 articles, while the two Spanish volumes contained 50 essays.

Chapter 2: The New Copernican Revolution
North American Feminist Liberation Theology

1. Cf. Anne E. Carr, *Transforming Grace: Christian Tradition and Women's Experience* (San Francisco: Harper & Row, 1988), especially "Coming of Age in Christianity: The Women's Movement and the Churches," pp. 5-18.

2. Ibid., p. 10-11. Carr points out: "Most of the insights of contemporary Christian feminism, elements of which have now filtered into the ranks of other church women who do not consider themselves feminists at all, are not really new."

3. Ibid., p. 11.

4. Ibid., p. 13.

5. Ibid., p. 18. Carr stresses also that women "are deeply conscious of the damage that the churches have done to women, in the theologies, the language, and the structures that have kept women in a narrowly defined 'place.'"

6. Elisabeth Schüssler Fiorenza, *In Memory of Her: A Feminist Theological Reconstruction of Christian Origins* (New York: Crossroad, 1988). Also quite helpful is the book *Bread Not Stone: The Challenge of Feminist Biblical Interpretation* (Boston: Beacon Press, 1984). More recent is an expansion relating to the strategies and practices of biblical women: *But She Said: Feminist Practices of Biblical Interpretation* (Boston: Beacon Press, 1992). As she explains this new step: " . . . this book seeks to situate a critical feminist interpretation for liberation *differently*. By problematizing women's voice and agency, by making women the subjects of biblical readings, by asking how feminist biblical interpretations remain implicated in the discourses of the 'Fathers,' and by inquiring into the hermeneutical possibilities of women's ability to interject their 'but' into the hegemonic discourse, I seek to articulate a critical feminist interpretation on feminist political terms" (p. 7). See also *Discipleship of Equals: A Critical Feminist Ekklesiology of Liberation Theology* (New York: Crossroad, 1993) and *Searching the Scriptures, Vol. One: A Feminist Introduction* (New York: Crossroad, 1994). A diminutive but substantive classic in the field is Sandra M. Schneiders, *Beyond Patching: Faith and Feminism in the Catholic Church* (New York: Paulist, 1991).

7. *In Memory of Her*, p. 3.

8. Ibid., p. 6.

9. Ibid., p. 38, n. 50.

10. Ibid., pp. 29-30. Thus "[a feminist reconstitution of the world] not only challenges androcentric reality constructions in language but seeks to move from androcentric texts to patriarchal-historical contexts. While androcentrism characterizes a mind-set, patriarchy represents a social-cultural system in which a few men have power over men, women, children, slaves and colonized peoples" (p. 29).

11. Ibid., p. 30.

12. Ibid., p. 33.

13. Ibid., p. 36. Fiorenza looks also to the church: "Women as church have a continuous history and tradition that can claim Jesus and the praxis of the early church as its biblical root model or prototype, one that is open to feminist transformation" (ibid.).

14. *Sexism and God-Talk: Toward a Feminist Theology* (Boston: Beacon Press, 1983).

15. Ibid., p. 12; italics are mine.

16. Ibid.

17. Ibid.

18. Ibid., pp. 12-13.

19. Ibid., p. 13.

20. Ibid., p. 18.

21. Ibid., pp. 18-19.

22. Ibid., p. 20. Although she does not stress it, Ruether insists that women "must also criticize humanocentrism, that is, making humans the norm and crown of creation." The author has created a much more comprehensive panorama of all of creation in her brilliant book, *Gaia & God: An Ecofeminist Theology of Earth Healing* (San Francisco: Harper & Row, 1992).

23. Ibid., p. 30.

24. Ibid., p. 32. For the dissent to this use of the prophets see Elisabeth Schüssler Fiorenza, *In Memory of Her*, pp. 16ff.

25. Ibid., pp. 33-34.

26. Ibid., p. 38. Ruether emphasizes that ". . . the Christian paradigm continues to be a powerful and formative structure. Its continuing power to provide an interpretive framework for human situations of conflict and struggle for justice is reflected by the fact that modern liberation movements, both in the West and in the third world, continually adopt and make use of this basic pattern in secular form."

27. Ibid., p. 41.

28. Ibid., pp. 44-45.

29. Ibid., p. 126. Ruether elaborates on this: "Behind the argument of the necessary maleness of Christ lies the theological assumption of the maleness of God. The human male can represent both the divine (male) and also the creaturely sides of this hierarchy. Women can represent only the creaturely (female), never the divine (male) side."

30. Ibid., p. 135.

31. Ibid., pp. 136-37.

32. Ibid., p. 137.

33. Ibid., p. 138.

34. Ibid., pp. 153-54.

35. Ibid., p. 155. Ruether shrewdly continues: "This theme grates unpleasantly on the ears of most affluent Christians. . . . They prefer to jump immediately to the idea that God loves the rich and poor alike. This assumes that God loves the rich and the poor, oppressors and oppressed, in the same way, accepting them 'as they are.' . . . salvation has nothing to do with changing this relationship."

36. Ibid., p. 158.

37. Ibid., p. 173.

38. Ibid.

39. Ibid., p. 174.

40. Ibid., p. 182. At the same time, Ruether also accents the enormity of evil: "The system is so much larger than any individual that one could easily imagine oneself totally helpless, the captive of demonic powers beyond one's control. Yet this system is the creation of humans, not of God or fallen angels. We made it. We perpetuate it with our cooperation with it."

41. Ibid., p. 184.

42. Ibid., p. 185.

43. Ibid., p. 186.

44. Ibid., p. 187.

45. Ibid., p. 190.

46. Ibid. Ruether notes that "Jungian psychology provides the intellectual base for this male 'feminism.'"

47. Ibid.

48. Ibid., p. 191.

49. Ibid., pp. 191-92.

50. Ibid., pp. 193-94. The author observes that women often experience great alienation from existing churches: "The discovery of alternative possibilities for identity and the increasing conviction that an alternative is a more authentic understanding of the Gospel make all the more painful and insulting the reality of most historical churches. These churches continue to ratify, by their language, institutional structures, and social commitments, the opposite message."

51. Ibid., p. 204. A scholarly treatment of base communities may be found in the Brazilian Marcello Azevedo, *Basic Christian Communities in Brazil* (Washington, DC: Georgetown University Press, 1987). Since so many women are coordinators of the base communities, one would have expected some treatment of feminism. Alas, there is no sign in Azevedo's book of such a study.

52. Ibid., p. 205.

53. Ibid., p. 207. Professor Ruether has studied at great length a "liberation community" in *Women-Church: Theory and Practice* (San Francisco: Harper & Row, 1987).

54. Ibid., p. 208.

55. Ibid., p. 212.

56. Elizabeth A. Johnson, *She Who Is: The Mystery of God in Feminist Theological Discourse* (New York: Crossroad, 1992).

57. Ibid., p. 10.

58. Ibid., p. 11.

59. Ibid. Note the importance of the South African visit for Johnson: "It is especially the months of teaching in South Africa under the state of emergency, giving lectures that turned into sessions of mutual grappling with the meaning and praxis of faith in situations of massive suffering due to injustice, poverty, and violence, that have honed for me the feminist theological paradigm into liberation contours and given it a global intent."

60. Ibid., p. 13.

61. Ibid., p. 8. As regards equality, Johnson adds: "Women are equally created in the image and likeness of God, equally redeemed by Christ, equally sanctified by the Holy Spirit; women are equally involved in the ongoing tragedy of sin and the mystery of grace, equally called to mission in this world, equally destined for life with God in glory."

62. Ibid., p. 9.

63. Ibid., p. 15.

64. Ibid., p. 18.

65. Ibid., p. 21.

66. Ibid., pp. 20-21.

67. Margaret Farley, "Sexism," *New Catholic Encyclopedia* (New York: McGraw Hill, 1978) 17, p. 604.

68. *She Who Is*, pp. 23-24.

69. Ibid., p. 24.

70. Ibid., p. 26.

71. Ibid.

72. Ibid., p. 27.

73. Cf. Gerda Lerner, *The Creation of Patriarchy* (New York: Oxford University Press, 1986); Peggy Sunday, *Female Power and Male Dominance: On the Origins of Sexual Inequality* (Cambridge: Cambridge University Press, 1981); Rosemary Ruether, *New Woman, New Earth: Sexist Ideologies and Human Liberation* (New York: Seabury, 1975).

74. Ibid., p. 29.

75. Ibid.

76. Ibid.

77. Ibid., pp. 29-30. Johnson also includes a retrieval of systematic theology: "The creation of male and female in the divine image; the sacrament of baptism that recreates women and men in the image of Christ and initiates a new form of community; eschatological hope for a cosmos redeemed in all its dimensions—these and other elements of belief are plumbed to release their

liberating truth, which challenges the churches to become faithful to the best of their own tradition" (p. 30).

78. Ibid., p. 30.

79. See p. 57 in this chapter.

80. Ibid., p. 31.

81. Ibid.

82. Ibid., p. 32.

83. Ibid.

84. Ibid., p. 33. An important issue is the impact on academic theology: "For theology as an academic discipline, it is clear that placing women's experience at the center of inquiry and pressing toward transformation of oppressive symbols and systems are occasioning an intellectual paradigm shift of great magnitude. . . . This is not minor tinkering with the discipline but an effort toward major reshaping of theology and the religious tradition that gives rise to it."

85. Ibid., p. 34.

86. Ibid., p. 35.

87. Ibid., p. 39. There is an interesting antidote for idolatry: "Throughout the Jewish and Christian traditions prophetic thinkers have challenged the propensity of the human heart to evade the living God by taming the wildness of divine mystery into a more domesticated deity."

88. Ibid., p. 40.

89. Ibid., p. 43.

90. Ibid., p. 44. The reference given is to Aquinas following Damascene: *Summa Theologica* I, q. 13, a. 8.

91. *She Who Is*, p. 46. Later she continues: "Images of God are not peripheral or dispensable to theological speech, nor as we have seen, to ecclesial and social praxis. They are crucially important among the many colored veils through which divine mystery is mediated and by means of which we express relationship in return."

92. Ibid., pp. 47-54.

93. Ibid., p. 47.

94. Ibid.

95. Ibid., p. 56.

96. Jacquelyn Grant, *White Women's Christ and Black Women's Jesus: Feminist Christology and Womanist Response* (Atlanta: Scholars Press, 1989).

97. *White Women's Christ*, pp. 5-6.

98. Ibid., p. 8, n. 7.

99. Ibid., pp. 195-230.

100. Ibid., p. 195.

101. Ibid.

102. Ibid., pp. 196-97.

103. Ibid., p. 198. Grant also quotes the interesting comments of Bell Hooks: ". . . many Black women experienced White women as the white supremacist group who most directly exercised power over them, often in a manner more brutal and dehumanizing than that of racist White men. (Even) today, despite predominant rule by White supremacist patriarchs, Black women often work in a situation where the immediate supervisor, boss, or authority figure is a White woman" (*Feminist Theology: From Margin to Center* [Boston: South End Press, 1984], p. 49). See also her book *Ain't I a Woman? Black Women and Feminism* (Boston: South End Press, 1981).

104. Joel Kovel, *White Racism: A Psychohistory* (New York: Columbia University Press, 1984), p. x.

105. *White Women's Christ*, p. 199. C. Eric Lincoln expands this definition as follows: "[f]or racism to flourish with the vigor it enjoys in America, there must be an extensive climate of acceptance and participation by large numbers of people who constitute its power base. It is the consensus of private persons that gives racism its derivative power. . . . The power of racism is the power conceded by those respectable citizens who by their actions or inaction communicate the consensus which directs and empowers the overt bigot to act on their behalf" (*Race, Religion and the Continuing American Dilemma* [New York: Hill and Wang, 1984], p. 11-12).

106. *White Women's Christ*, p. 200.

107. Brenda Eichelberger, "Voice of Black Feminism," *Quest: A Feminist Quarterly* III (Spring), pp. 16-23.

108. Iva Carruthers, "War in African Familyhood," in Roseann P. Bell et al., eds., *Sturdy Black Bridges: Visions of Black Women in Literature* (New York: Anchor/Doubleday, 1979), p. 9. See also the perceptive views of Deborah Hines, "Racism Breeds Stereotypes," *The Witness* 63 (February 1982), p. 7.

109. *White Women's Christ*, p. 201.

110. Ibid., p. 209.

111. Ibid.

112. Ibid., p. 210. The reference is to Hooks, *Feminist Theology*, p. 3.

113. *White Women's Christ*, p. 210.

Chapter 3: American Dream—Or Nightmare?
Black Theology of Liberation

1. James H. Cone, "Black Theology: Where We Have Been and a Vision for Where We Are Going," in *Yearning to Breathe Free: Liberation Theologies in the U.S.* (Mar Peter-Raoul, et al., eds.; Maryknoll, NY: Orbis Books, 1990), p. 48.

2. Ibid., p. 49. Some of the other advice his father gave him was the following: "Don't let anybody buy your integrity, especially white people. Tell them that it is not for sale. Do what you do because it is right and not because of the money involved. And never let yourself be put in a position where you are dependent on your enemies to survive. For God will make a way out of no way, and he will make your enemies your footstool" (ibid.).

3. Ibid.

4. Ibid., pp. 49-50 (italics mine).

5. William K. Tabb, ed., *Churches in Struggle: Liberation Theologies and Social Change in North America* (New York: Monthly Review Press, 1986), p. 33.

6. Joseph Washington, *Black Religion* (Boston: Beacon Press, 1964).

7. *Yearning to Breathe Free*, p. 51.

8. Ibid.

9. Stokely Carmichael and Charles V. Hamilton, *Black Power: The Politics of Liberation in America* (New York: Random House, 1967).

10. *Yearning to Breathe Free*, p. 52.

11. James H. Cone, *Black Theology and Black Power* (New York: Seabury, 1969).

12. James H. Cone, *A Black Theology of Liberation* (Philadelphia: Lippincott, 1970).

13. *Churches in Struggle*, p. 36.

14. Ibid., pp. 36-37.

15. Ibid., p. 37. Cone concludes by observing that black feminist theology "is both a challenge to the sexist orientation of black theology and a deepening of the black struggle against racism" (ibid.).

16. James H. Cone, "A Black Perspective on the Future of African Theology," in Kofi Appiah-Kubi and Sergio Torres, eds., *African Theology en Route: Papers from the Pan-African Conference of Third World Theologians, December 17-23, 1977, Accra, Ghana* (Maryknoll, NY: Orbis Books, 1979), pp. 176-86.

17. *Churches in Struggle*, p. 37.

18. Sergio Torres and Virginia Fabella, eds., *The Emergent Gospel, Theology from the Underside of History: Papers from the Ecumenical Dialogue of Third World Theologians, Dar es Salaam, August 5-12, 1976* (Maryknoll, NY: Orbis Books, 1978).

19. *Churches in Struggle*, p. 38.

20. Ibid., p. 40.

21. Ibid., p. 42.

22. Ibid., p. 43.

23. *Yearning to Breathe Free*, pp. 58-59.

24. Ibid., p. 59.

25. Ibid.

26. Ibid.

27. *A Black Theology of Liberation* (Philadelphia: Lippincott, 1970); *Martin & Malcolm & America: A Dream or a Nightmare* (Maryknoll, NY: Orbis Books, 1991). A Twentieth Anniversary Edition of *A Black Theology of Liberation* was published in 1991. Included in this edition were critical reflections by Gayraud Wilmore ("A Revolution Unfulfilled, but not Invalidated"), Robert McAfee Brown ("Learning from James Cone"), Pablo Richard ("Black Theology: A Liberating Theology in Latin America"), Rosemary Radford Ruether, ("Black Woman and Feminism: The U.S. and South African Contexts"), K. C. Abraham ("Black Theology: A Reflection From Asia") and Delores S. Williams ("James Cone's Liberation: Twenty Years Later"). Allotted an "Afterword" to reply to these reflections, Cone's last words are that black theology "must not . . . seek merely to be an academic discipline, reflecting on intellectual matters interesting to university and seminary professors and their graduate students. Rather, black theology must be the prophetic voice of the church, proclaiming throughout the world what Amos said nearly 3000 years ago: 'Let justice roll down like waters and righteousness as a mighty stream.' Without this voice the church ceases to be the church, and theology ceases to be Christian" (p. 201).

28. Cf. n. 11.

29. Cone, *Black Theology of Liberation*, p. 11.

30. Ibid., p. 22.

31. Ibid., p. 46.

32. Ibid., p. 48.

33. Ibid., pp. 65-66.

34. Ibid., p. 69.

35. Ibid., p. 80; italics are the author's.

36. Ibid., p. 91.

37. Ibid., p. 84.

38. See *Churches in Struggle*, p. 59.

39. Cone, *Black Theology of Liberation*, p. 120.

40. Ibid.

41. Ibid., p. 122. He continues this as follows: "That is why whites are finding and will continue to find the black experience a disturbing reality. White theologians would prefer to do theology without reference to color, but this only reveals how deeply racism is imbedded in this culture."

42. Ibid., p. 183. "Being free in America means accepting blackness as the

only possible way of existing in the world. It means defining one's identity by the marks of oppression. It means rejecting white proposals for peace and reconciliation, saying 'All we know is, we must have justice, not next week but this minute'" (ibid.).

43. Ibid., p. 196.

44. Ibid., p. 203.

45. Ibid., p. 214.

46. Ibid., p. 223.

47. Maryknoll, NY: Orbis Books, 1991.

48. *Martin & Malcolm*, pp. 213-43.

49. Ibid., p. 318.

50. Ibid., p. 61.

51. Ibid., pp. 61-62. The tape and printed copy of King's "Address to the Initial Mass Meeting of the Montgomery Improvement Association" at the Holt Street Baptist Church on December 5, 1955, are located today in the Martin Luther King, Jr., Papers, Center for Nonviolent Social Change, Atlanta, Georgia. Cone proves beyond reasonable doubt that King changed his original text to an emphasis on love and persuasion, *not coercion*, in his book, *Stride Toward Freedom* (New York: Harper & Row, 1958), p. 62.

52. Ibid., p. 63.

53. Ibid., p. 62.

54. Ibid., p. 64. This was published in the *Montgomery Advertiser* (January 19, 1956), p. 4-A.

55. *Martin & Malcolm*, p. 64. "Faith in Man" is the name of this sermon. It was published in the *New York Times* (February 27, 1956), p. 17.

56. *Martin & Malcolm*, p. 64.

57. Ibid., p. 222.

58. Ibid., p. 223.

59. Ibid., p. 225.

60. Ibid., p. 236.

61. Ibid., p. 237. This address is now in King's papers at the Center for Nonviolent Social Change in Atlanta, Georgia. It was also published as an essay in *Ramparts* (January 1967).

62. *Martin & Malcolm*, p. 237. Cone added: "His public condemnation of America for its criminal involvement in Vietnam, however, did not begin with the Riverside address or end with it."

63. Ibid., p. 239.

64. Ibid., p. 274.

65. Ibid.

66. Ibid. Coretta Scott King, *My Life with Martin Luther King, Jr.* (Holt, Rinehart & Winston, 1969), pp. 60, 91.

67. *Martin & Malcolm*, p. 275.

68. Ibid., p. 277.

69. Ibid., p. 278.

70. Ibid., p. 279; Malcolm X, *By Any Means Necessary* (ed. George Breitman; New York: Pathfinder Press, 1970), p. 179.

71. *Martin & Malcolm*, p. 280.

72. Ibid., p. 284.

73. Ibid., p. 285.

74. "Womanist Theology: Black Women's Voices," in *Yearning to Breathe Free*, pp. 62-69.

75. Alice Walker, *In Search of Our Mothers' Gardens*.

76. "Womanist Theology," p. 62.

77. Ibid., p. 63.

78. Ibid.

79. Ibid.

80. Ibid., p. 64.

81. Ibid., p. 65. Another interesting example of the black folk heroine is the following: "Milla Granson, a slave, conducted a midnight school for several years. She had been taught to read and write by her former master in Kentucky. . . . and in her little school hundreds of slaves benefited from her learning. . . . After laboring all day for their master, the slaves would creep stealthily to Milla's 'schoolroom' (a little cabin in a back alley). . . . The doors and windows . . . had to be kept tightly sealed to avoid discovery. Each class was composed of twelve pupils and when Milla had brought them up to the extent of her ability, she 'graduated' them and took in a dozen more. Through this means she graduated hundreds of slaves. Many of whom she taught to write a legible hand [forged] their own passes and set out for Canada."

82. Ibid.

83. Ibid., p. 66.

84. Ibid., p. 67.

85. Ibid. Walker adds an interesting metaphor from African American music: "Multidialogical activity may, like a jazz symphony, communicate some of its most important messages in what the harmony-driven conventional ear hears as discord, as disruption of the harmony in both the black American and white American social, political, and religious status quo."

86. Ibid.

87. Ibid.

88. Ibid., p. 68.

89. Ibid.

90. Ibid., p. 69.

91. Ibid.

Chapter 4: We Are a People!
Hispanic Liberation Theology

1. Allan Figueroa Deck, ed., *Frontiers of Hispanic Theology in the United States* (Maryknoll, NY: Orbis Books, 1992), p. xii.

2. Ibid., pp. xii-xiii.

3. *National Catholic Reporter* (July 17, 1992), p. 4.

4. Cf. *National Catholic Reporter* (August 28, 1992), pp. 3-4.

5. Allan Figueroa Deck, *The Second Wave: Hispanic Ministry and the Conversion of Cultures* (Maryknoll, NY: Orbis Books, 1992).

6. Deck, *Frontiers of Hispanic Theology*, p. xi.

7. Ibid.

8. Ibid.

9. Deck, *The Second Wave*, p. xv. The quotation is from the Foreword by Virgilio Elizondo.

10. Deck, *The Second Wave*, pp. 1-2.

11. Ibid., pp. 11-12. These figures were taken from the Bureau of the Census records for 1980.

12. Deck, *The Second Wave*, pp. 24-25.

13. Ibid., p. 25.

14. Ibid., p. 42.

15. Ibid., p. 44.

16. Ibid., p. 54.

17. Ibid., p. 57.
18. Ibid.
19. Ibid., p. 91.
20. Ibid., p. 93. The reference is to Pope Paul VI, *Evangelii Nuntiandi*, no. 18. For a broader view of evangelization, see David Bohr, *Evangelization in America* (New York: Paulist, 1977) and Kenneth Boyack, *Catholic Evangelization Today* (New York: Paulist, 1987).
21. Deck, *The Second Wave*, p. 93.
22. Ibid., p. 94.
23. Ibid., p. 95.
24. Ibid., p. 96.
25. Ibid. An excellent work on this whole area is Marcello Azevedo, *Inculturation and the Challenges of Modernity* (Rome: Pontifical Gregorian University, 1982).
26. Deck, *The Second Wave*, pp. 97-98.
27. Ibid., p. 98.
28. Ibid., p. 99. Deck goes on to see a cogent example in John F. Kavanaugh, *Still Following Christ in a Consumer Society—Still: The Spirituality of Cultural Resistance* (revised ed.; Maryknoll, NY: Orbis Books, 1991): "He analyzes Christian life as essentially countercultural. It is opposed to consumerism that reduces the human person to the status of an object; it promotes life styles such as Christian marriage, celibacy, and religious life which go contrary to the prevailing cultural norms" (p. 100). A similar work is by Dean Brackley, "Downward Mobility: Social Implications of St. Ignatius's Two Standards," *Studies in the Spirituality of Jesuits*, 2 (January 1988): pp. 1-48.
29. Deck, *The Second Wave*, p. 99.
30. Ibid., p. 101.
31. Ibid., p. 102.
32. Ibid., pp. 103-04.
33. Ibid., p. 104. The text quoted may be found in "Justice in the World," no. 6, Synod of Bishops Second General Assembly, November 30, 1971.
34. Deck, *The Second Wave*, p. 104.
35. Ibid., p. 105. He continues: "The fact that there does not yet exist a critical cultural consciousness of either the Anglo American or the Hispanic cultures nor a mutually agreed upon perception of the core values of the Gospel means that the condition of the possibility of evangelization in its fullest sense does not yet exist."
36. Ibid., pp. 105-06. Deck also contends that insofar "as ideology of either capitalist or socialist origins has influenced the popular masses, it has done so by overcoming a profound state of apathy or anomie with respect to schemes and projects that propose anything more than survival."
37. Ibid., p. 106.
38. Ibid., pp. 106-07.
39. Ibid., p. 107.
40. Ibid., pp. 107-08.
41. Ibid., p. 108. Deck points out that the "notable opposition and/or indifference experienced by the U.S. bishops in the wake of their pastoral letters on war and peace and on the U.S. economy—opposition organized by prominent Catholic laity—may reasonably be interpreted as the logical consequence of not having communicated the social teachings of the Church in an adequate manner. This omission makes it extremely difficult for the average U.S. Catholic, whether Anglo American or Hispanic, to grasp the rich and complex vision of

social order implicit in Catholic social thought."

42. Ibid., p. 109.

43. Ibid. See Marcello Azevedo, *Inculturation and the Challenge of Modernity* (n. 25).

44. Ibid., p. 110. Other characteristics of the premodern society are "that these people were born into a culture that was organically integrated and in which religion and myth provide an explanation for the origin of things. A premodern or nonmodern society is experienced as a totalizing presence in which the interests of the group, not the individual, are paramount."

45. Ibid.

46. Ibid., p. 113. Italics are mine.

47. Ibid., pp. 114-15.

48. Ibid., p. 116. The text is found in the Puebla Document, no. 448.

49. Deck, *The Second Wave,* p. 116.

50. Ibid., p. 121.

51. Ibid., pp. 124-25.

52. Ibid. p. 127. Cf. Saul Alinsky, *Reveille for Radicals* (New York: Random House, 1969) and P. David Finks, *The Radical Vision of Saul Alinsky* (New York: Paulist Press, 1984).

53. Ibid., p. 128. Deck praises the advocacy of the Committee on Migration of the U.S. Catholic bishops' conference "to articulate the justice issues in the long-standing debate about immigration—legal and illegal. . . ."

54. Ibid., p. 130. For example, he relates that "[a] telephone survey of the dioceses of California in March 1987 revealed that there are very few BECs functioning in California. Many of the groups originally initiated have gone out of existence; some have become charismatic prayer groups. A lack of clarity as to what the BEC is and inadequate leadership to accompany and sustain the BECs are given as reasons for their disappearance. Another serious charge is that they sometimes operate outside the parish system and even compete with it or are mistakenly perceived as doing so" (pp. 172-73, n. 48).

55. Ibid., p. 132.

56. Ibid., p. 135.

57. Ibid., p. 141. Deck notes that "it is generally conceded that a large percentage of laity involved in leadership positions including clergy involved in Hispanic ministry are *cursillistas,* having completed the *cursillo* retreat."

58. Ibid., p. 140.

59. Ibid.

60. Ibid., p. 140. The author adds that the "failure to view ongoing conversion in relation to the Church's holistic concept of evangelization is the source of considerable confusion and loss of energies in pastoral ministry across the board, not just in Hispanic ministries."

61. Ibid., p. 143.

62. Ibid., p. 145.

63. Ibid., p. 146.

64. Ibid., pp. 146-47. Cf. Michael Warren, *Youth, Gospel, Liberation* (San Francisco: Harper & Row, 1987), pp. 1-11; the quote of Gregory Baum is from the preface of this book, p. xiv. Warren has also published *Youth and the Future of the Church* (New York: Seabury, 1982). Baum also "proceeds to show how the pastorals of the U.S. bishops reflect a serious effort to do structural analysis along the lines promoted by the magisterium. However, he shows that there is a conflict between that effort and the fundamentally liberal, progressive orientation of many theologians and laity alike in the United States. . . " (p. 151).

65. Deck, *The Second Wave*, p. 147.

66. Ibid, p. 149.

67. Ibid., p. 152.

68. Ibid., p. 153. Deck goes on to emphasize that without "commitment to substantive change in policy and direction on the one hand, and respect for the unifying and coordinating context of comptent authority on the other, pastoral planning will lose its efficacy as a viable instrument of evangelization in the Catholic Church."

69. Ibid., p. 155.

70. Ibid., p. 157.

71. Ibid.

72. Ibid.

73. San Francisco: Harper & Row, 1988. After each chapter of this book, a synopsis is published in Spanish, entitled *Mujer Hispana, Voz Profética en la Iglesia: Hacia Una Teología de Liberación de la Mujer Hispana.*

74. The article is published in Mar Peter-Raoul et al., eds., *Yearning to Breathe Free: Liberation Theologies in the U.S.* (Maryknoll, NY: Orbis Books, 1988), pp. 121-28.

75. *Hispanic Women*, p. ix.

76. Ibid., p. x.

77. Ibid., p. xii.

78. Ibid., p. xiii.

79. Ibid.

80. Ibid.

81. Ibid., p. xiv.

82. Ibid.

83. Ibid., p. xv.

84. Ibid., p. xvi.

85. Ibid., p. xvii.

86. Ibid.

87. Ibid., p. 2.

88. Ibid., pp. 2-3.

89. Ibid., pp. 6-7.

90. Ibid., p. 61.

91. Ibid., p. 66.

92. Ibid., p. 68.

Chapter 5: The Agony of Africa
African Liberation Theology

1. Paul Kennedy, *Preparations for the Twenty-First Century* (New York: Random House, 1993).

2. Ibid., pp. 211-12.

3. Ibid., p. 215.

4. Maryknoll, NY: Orbis Books, 1992.

5. *African Theology*, p. 12.

6. Ibid., p. 16.

7. Ibid., p. 18. Bujo cites a number of volumes in German, French, and English sources to buttress these important statements.

8. Ibid., p. 24. Bujo has published articles on this topic in "Der afrikanische Ahnenkult und die christliche Verkündigung," *Zeitschrift für Missionswissenschaft und Religionswissenschaft* 64 (1980), pp. 293-306, and "Nos ancêtres, ces saints inconnus," *Bulletin de Théologie Africaine* 1 (1979), pp. 165-178.

9. For further study of this, see the entire volume of *African Christian Morality at the Age of Inculturation* (Nairobi, 1990), which contains two articles by Bujo.

10. *African Theology*, p. 45.

11. Ibid., pp. 46-47.

12. Ibid., p. 50. Senghor further clarified the role of writers: "Our renaissance will be more the work of African writers and artists than of politicians. We have seen from experience that there can be no political liberation without cultural liberation" (ibid., p. 51).

13. Ibid., p. 52.

14. Ibid., pp. 53-54. The author goes even further in his denunciation: "So, it has come about that the major preoccupation of the modern advocates of negritude is how best to fill their own pockets. Political independence has turned into a kind of collector's item, beautiful to contemplate, but quite useless as far as ordinary people are concerned" (p. 54).

15. Ibid., p. 57.

16. Ibid.

17. Ibid., p. 58. Tempels developed these ideas and many others in his two-volume work, *Notre rencontre* (Limete/Leopoldville, 1962).

18. The complete title of this book was *L'Union Vitale Bantu, ou le Principe de Cohésion de la Communauté chez les Bashi, les Banyarwanda, et les Barundi* (Annali Lateranensi XX, 1956). He has continued to be a prolific writer of books and articles on these subjects.

19. The book was entitled *Philosophie Bantu-Rwandaise* (Brussels, 1956). I am not aware of any further publications of Kagame.

20. The title was *Les Prêtres noirs s'interrogent* (Paris, 1956).

21. *African Theology*, p. 5.

22. Ibid., p. 59.

23. Ibid. Tshibangu's essay was published as "Vers une théologie de couleur africain?" *Revue de Clergé Africain* 15 (1960), pp. 333-46.

24. Vanneste's article was published as "D'abord une vraie théologie," *Revue de Clergé Africain* 15 (1960), pp. 346-352.

25. *African Theology*, p. 61.

26. Ibid.

27. Ibid., pp. 65-66.

28. See J.S. Pobee, *Toward an African Theology* (Nashville, 1979); E.J. Penoukou, "Réalité africaine et salut en Jésus-Christ," *Spiritus* 89 (1982), pp. 374-92.

29. *African Theology*, p. 67. Mbiti's major work is *New Testament Eschatology in an African Background* (London, 1971).

30. Ibid. Nyamiti's major work is *Christ as Our Ancestor: Christology from an African Perspective* (Gweru [Zimbabwe], 1984).

31. *African Theology*, p. 68.

32. Ibid.

33. Ibid., p. 70.

34. Ibid. Bujo adopts a prophetic stance as he boldly asserts that the "theology of inculturation so often preached triumphantly in African churches, is a pompous irrelevance, truly an ideological superstructure at the service of the bourgeoisie. It may be a cause of some satisfaction that the African hierarchy has adopted a theology of inculturation as its official policy. So far however there have been more words than actions, and one cannot help wondering how serious is the commitment of the bishops to a truly effective incarnation of Christianity in Africa" (p. 71).

35. Ibid., p. 71.

36. Ibid., pp. 71-72. Bishop Kabanga of Lubumbashi spoke in a similar vein in a pastoral letter to his flock: "We are talking about a real descent into Hell on the part of all church leaders—bishops, priests, brothers and sisters, catechists—so that we can meet our people who are still waiting there for the Messiah who will save them" *(La descente aux enfers* [Lubumbashi, 1983]), n. 14.

37. *African Theology*, p. 75.

38. Ibid., p. 77.

39. Ibid., p. 78. Bujo presents a large number of resources and research on these topics on p. 78, n. 9.

40. *African Theology*, p. 79. Specifically, Bujo stresses the following similarities: "Jesus worked miracles, healing the sick, opening the eyes of the blind, raising the dead to life. In short, he brought life, and life-force, in its fulness. He lived his mission for his fellow-humans in an altogether matchless way, and, furthermore, left to his disciples, as his final commandment, the law of love."

41. Ibid., p. 84.

42. Ibid., p. 87.

43. Ibid., p. 90.

44. Ibid.

45. Ibid., p. 92.

46. Ibid., p. 94.

47. Ibid., p. 95.

48. Ibid., p. 96.

49. Ibid., p. 97.

50. Ibid., p. 98. He continues: "It is clear that episcopalism and sacerdotalism, with their reluctance to engage in fraternal dialogue, constitute a kind of cancerous growth which slowly but surely chokes the proto-ancestral life. That life-giving stream which flows from the Proto-Ancestor can be selfishly monopolized by Church leaders and thus prevented from supplying the proto-ancestral Mystical Body with its indispensable nourishment."

51. Ibid., pp. 98-99.

52. Ibid., p. 99. Some of the other questions Bujo raises are just as trenchant as the ones included in the text of this chapter: "These questions are far from superfluous in a society where human beings are obliged to live in slums of indescribable squalor, while priests and bishops are living next door in bourgeois comfort. And we may surely ask if it is right to erect a vast cathedral in the middle of sub-human dwellings made of packing cases and old tin cans. Can this be a suitable place for celebrating the Eucharist in which the Proto-Ancestor gives his life for the poor? Will not then our splendid eucharistic celebrations in Africa be more a sweet poison than the well-spring of life?" (pp. 99-100).

53. See Paul Kennedy, *Preparing for the Twenty-First Century*, pp. 211-15.

54. *African Theology*, p. 100.

55. Ibid., p. 101.

56. Ibid.

57. Ibid., p. 102. Bujo also phrases this another way: "When we see how Rome in fact behaves toward the local churches of Africa, we may sometimes wonder whether this is really the conduct expected of a steward of the proto-ancestral heritage in the spirit of the Proto-Ancestor, Jesus Christ."

58. Ibid.

59. Ibid. Bujo develops these ideas in greater depth in "Déchristianiser en christianisant?" *Bulletin de Théologie Africaine* 4 (1982), pp. 229-242, and "Au

nom de l'Évangile: Refus d'un christianisme néocolonialiste," *Bulletin de Théologie Africaine* 6 (1984), pp. 117-27.

60. *African Theology,* p. 103.

61. Ibid.

62. Ibid., p. 104. Bujo also notes: "When these material advantages are placed in the foreground, it is inevitable that some people enter the priesthood as a career. Some also may see in it a position of power; after all, it may be a stepping-stone to episcopacy, where the prospects of material advantages are even brighter."

63. Ibid., p. 105.

64. Ibid.

65. Ibid., p. 106.

66. Ibid. Bujo explains further: "A religious who is bound to the episcopal authority, either because the bishop was the founder of the community, or constitutes its highest court of appeal, or has the right of veto in its internal affairs, has lost the freedom to speak and is in some sense in thrall to the bishop." For further development of these ideas see B. Bujo, "Les orders religieux de l'époque post-coloniale en Afrique: Espérance ou déception?" *Cahiers des Religions Africaines* 14 (1980), pp. 141-50.

67. *African Theology,* p. 107.

68. Ibid., pp. 107-08.

69. Ibid., p. 108.

70. Ibid., p. 109.

71. Ibid.

72. Ibid., p. 110.

73. Ibid.

74. Ibid., p. 111. Bujo also notes the results of these machinations: "Thus the African church is turned into an instrument for the convenience of missionaries, swimming in their wake and ministering to their interests."

75. Ibid., p. 112.

76. Ibid.

77. Ibid., p. 112.

78. Ibid.

79. Ibid., p. 113. At the end of the book, Bujo discusses a spirituality for marriage, and death and care for the dying in Africa. For various reasons, a discussion of these did not suit my purposes. Those interested in these topics may find them on pp. 115-29.

80. Ibid., p. 130.

81. *Hearing and Knowing: Theological Reflections on Christianity in Africa* (Maryknoll, NY: Orbis Books, 1986).

82. Ibid., p. 2. The author adds: "The term refers to blacks in the Americas, Native Americans, the aborigines of Australia, the Maoris of New Zealand, and the people of the oceanic areas of the world, such as the Caribbean and the Pacific Islands."

83. *The Liberation of Theology* (Maryknoll, NY: Orbis Books, 1976). The Spanish edition was published in 1975.

84. *Hearing and Knowing,* p. 3.

85. *A Theology of Liberation: History, Politics, and Salvation* (2nd ed.; Maryknoll, NY: Orbis Books, 1988).

86. Sergio Torres and Virginia Fabella, eds., *The Emergent Gospel: Theology from the Underside of History* (Maryknoll, NY: Orbis Books, 1978). In December 1977, a conference for African theologians also took place in Accra, Ghana. See

Kofi Appiah Kubi and Sergio Torres, eds., *African Theology en Route* (Maryknoll, NY: Orbis Books, 1979). Professor Oduyoye presented a paper at the latter conference entitled "The Value of African Religious Beliefs and Practices for Christian Theology," (pp. 109-16).

87. *Hearing and Knowing*, p. 7.

88. Ibid., p. 33.

89. Ibid., pp. 37 ff.

90. Ibid., p. 40.

91. Ibid.

92. Ibid., p. 43. The author is quite blunt in this regard: "The contradiction here is that the missionaries did not accept the structure of African society. At every turn what they did worked toward its breakdown; they were virtually bulls in the African cultural china shop."

93. Ibid., p. 74. The quote from Idowu is from his book, *Towards an Indigenous Church* (London: Oxford University Press, 1965), p. 11.

94. *Hearing and Knowing*, p. 121.

95. Ibid.

96. Ibid., p. 122. This research is attributed to Christine Oppong, *Consequences and Concomitants of Change: Issues Regarding the Relations to Family Structure* (Ibadan: University of Ibadan Press, 1976). Oppong also observes that "the traditional norm within which women are expected to earn an income and to provide at least part of their own as well as their children's needs is perpetuated. So is the norm that makes housework the exclusive responsibility of women."

97. *Hearing and Knowing*, p. 122.

98. Ibid., p. 123.

99. Ibid. Italics are mine.

100. Ibid., p. 124.

101. Ibid.

102. Ibid., p. 126.

103. Ibid., p. 127.

104. Ibid., p. 128.

105. Ibid., p. 129.

106. Ibid., p. 134. Oduyoye recalls a World Council of Churches meeting on male/female community in the churches, which unveiled a great deal of male domination: "It has revealed how many lives are lived according to unexamined norms, according to unquestioned assumptions and myths. These reinforce the brokenness that we all live. If no one is hurt, the corporate acceptance of what is, could continue; but if some in the community feel and express a hurt, then the corporate life can only be described as sick. It will remain an ailing body until we each develop a sensitivity toward the full humanity of the other."

107. Ibid., p. 136.

108. Ibid., p. 137. The author expresses this earlier: "Women's experience of the human community unearths many shortcomings arising from sexism's tendency to shape the extent of our being as creative, caring creatures, who, after the image of God, conquer chaos to bring forth good out of a nebulous existence. No one can claim to be in the image of God who is insensitive to the cry of the afflicted, who invests in structures of destruction, or supports them because of vested interests."

109. *Liberating Reformed Theology: A South African Contribution to an Ecumenical Dialogue* (Grand Rapids: Eerdmans, 1991).

110. See *The Church Struggle in South Africa* (2nd ed.; Grand Rapids:

Eerdmans, 1986); *Cry Justice!* (Maryknoll, NY: Orbis Books, 1987); and with Charles Villa-Vilencio, *Apartheid Is a Heresy* (Grand Rapids: Eerdmans, 1983).

111. *Liberating Reformed Theology*, p. xii.

112. Ibid., p. xiii.

113. Ibid.

114. Ibid., p. xv. The author adds: "Certainly I have found that contemporary Roman Catholic theologians who have studied and written about Calvin generally have an insight into his thought not always apparent in the writings of later Protestants."

115. Ibid., p. xviii.

116. Ibid., p. 36.

117. Ibid., p. 281.

118. Ibid.

119. Kennedy, *Twenty-First Century*, p. 218.

120. "Final Message of the Synod for Africa," *Origins* 24 (May 19, 1994), pp. 1-11.

121. The bishops extend their social analysis here: "The unjust price system brings in its wake an accumulation of the external debt which humiliates our nations and gives them a regrettable sense of inferiority and indigence. In the name of our people we reject this sense of culpability which is imposed on us. But at the same time we appeal to all our African brothers who have embezzled public funds that they are bound in justice to redress the wrong done to our peoples."

Chapter 6: The Heart of Asian Religion
Asian Theologies of Liberation

1. Aloysius Pieris, S.J., *An Asian Theology of Liberation* (Maryknoll, NY: Orbis Books, 1988).

2. Ibid., p. 69.

3. Ibid., p. 70.

4. Ibid.

5. Ibid., pp. 70-71. He notes that this is also true with regard to Africans and their many languages.

6. Ibid., p. 71. Pieris extends this also to the process of evolution: "After all, if the theory of evolution is valid, we were once a mountain, the crust of the earth, as well as water and fire, and all that we carry with us as our material substratum, by which we become sacramentally present to others and to ourselves. We cannot be fully human without them."

7. Ibid., p. 72.

8. Ibid.

9. Ibid., pp. 73-74.

10. Ibid., p. 74. Italics in this quote are mine.

11. Ibid.

12. Ibid., p. 75.

13. Ibid.

14. Ibid.

15. Ibid., p. 76.

16. Ibid., p. 77. There is an interesting paragraph of the relation of Buddhism and Marxism: "As Holmes Welch has shown in his ponderous treatise on how Buddhism fared in revolutionary China, Mao Tse Tung did not at first insist on the eradication of Buddhism. . . . His thesis was that religion springs from certain socio-economic structures; when these structures would change, religion

would automatically disappear. Instead of wasting time on eradicating a religion, he preferred to make use of it to change social structures, to expedite thus its own disappearance." See Holmes Welch, *Buddhism Under Mao* (Cambridge, MA: Harvard University Press, 1972), pp. 1-41 and 340-63.

17. Ibid., p. 79. These statements are to be found in Pope Paul VI's Encyclical Letter, *Populorum Progressio*, # 20 (1967).

18. Ibid., p. 80.

19. Ibid.

20. Ibid., p. 81.

21. Mark Schoof, *Breakthrough: The Beginnings of a New Catholic Theology* (Dublin: Gill and Macmillan, 1970). Pieris also quotes Langdon Gilkey, *Religion and the Scientific Future* (New York: Harper & Row, 1970), pp. 76-77.

22. Pieris, *An Asian Theology of Liberation*, p. 82

23. Jon Sobrino, "El conocimiento teológico en la teología europea y latinoamericana," *Liberación y cautiverio: Debates en torno al método de la teología en América Latina* (Mexico City: Comité Organizador, 1975), pp. 177-207. A revised version of the article may be found in Sobrino, "Theological Understanding in European and Latin American Theology," in *The True Church and the Poor* (Maryknoll, NY: Orbis Books, 1984), pp. 7-38.

24. Pieris, *An Asian Theology of Liberation*, p. 82. Italics are mine.

25. Ibid.

26. Ibid., p. 83.

27. Ibid.

28. Ibid., p. 84.

29. Ibid., p. 85. Pieris succinctly provides the cause: "This inadequacy seems to have been introduced by the early fathers of the church who, in their dialogue with non-biblical systems, restricted their interest to the philosophical rather than the religious plane. They further impressed this dichotomy on the Western theological tradition when they took 'pagan' philosophy out of its religious context and turned it into an intellectual weapon serving Christian apologetics against those very religions!"

30. Ibid., p. 86.

31. Ibid.

32. Ibid.

33. Ibid., p. 59. Pieris also points out that "Asia's later disillusion with the 'colonial Christ' no doubt added to this estrangement. But it also revealed that Christ could make sense in our cultures only to the extent that we use the soteriological idiom of 'non-Christian' religions."

34. Ibid.

35. Ibid., p. 62.

36. Ibid.

37. Ibid., p. 63. In other words, it "was by entering into the soteriological nucleus of his culture that he revealed his salvific mission."

38. Ibid.

39. Ibid., p. 64.

40. Ibid.

41. Ibid.

42. *Love Meets Wisdom: A Christian Experience of Buddhism* (Maryknoll, NY: Orbis Books, 1988), p. 110.

43. Ibid., p. 111.

44. Ibid., p. 112. The quote is from Louis Bouyer, ed., *The History of Christian Spirituality, Part 1: The Spirituality of the New Testament and the Fathers* (London:

Burns & Oates, 1963), pp. 15-16.

45. Pieris, *Love Meets Wisdom*, p. 112. It is interesting to note that a Buddhist scholar "regards Buddhism as nonbhaktic religion, and superior to Christianity on that very account." See Gunapala Dharmasiri, *A Buddhist Critique of the Christian Concept of God* (Colombo: Lake House Investments, 1974), pp. 212-13.

46. Pieris, *Love Meets Wisdom*, p. 113.

47. For example, compare *A Theology of Liberation* with *We Drink from Our Own Wells: The Spiritual Journey of a People* (Maryknoll, NY: Orbis Books, 1983). In my opinion, the former book has a more comprehensive and profound vision of spirituality than the second.

48. Compare Jon Sobrino's book, *Christology at the Crossroads* (Maryknoll, NY: Orbis Books, 1978) with his later work, *Spirituality of Liberation: Toward Political Holiness* (Maryknoll, NY: Orbis Books, 1988).

49. Pieris, *Asian Theology of Liberation*, p. 3.

50. Ibid., p. 4.

51. Constitution on the Sacred Liturgy, # 10.

52. Pieris, *An Asian Theology of Liberation*, p. 5.

53. Ibid., p. 7.

54. Ibid., p. 9.

55. Ibid.

56. Ibid., p. 11.

57. Ibid., p. 12. Pieris poses an intriguing question: "How would all this appear in the context of a life-and-death struggle for justice, where 'festal gathering' and 'song of praise' constitute privileged moments of strength and joy, a profound contemplation and joyous celebration of the mysteries revealed in the humanity of Jesus, as is known from the Gospels as well as through one's own personal encounters with Jesus?"

58. Ibid., p. 13.

59. Ibid., p. 14.

60. "To Be Poor as Jesus Was Poor?" pp. 15-23.

61. Ibid., p. 23.

62. His recent books include *Myth, Faith and Hermeneutics* (New York: Paulist, 1979), *The Unknown Christ of Hinduism* (Maryknoll, NY: Orbis Books, 1981), *Blessed Simplicity* (New York: Seabury, 1982), and *The Silence of God* (Maryknoll, NY: Orbis Books, 1989).

63. Raimundo Panikkar, "The Jordan, The Tiber, and the Ganges: Three Kairological Moments of Christic Self-Consciousness," in John Hick and Paul Knitter, eds., *The Myth of Christian Uniqueness: Towards a Pluralistic Theology of Religions* (Maryknoll, NY: Orbis Books, 1987), pp. 89-116 (here p. 89).

64. Panikkar, "The Jordan," p. 89.

65. Ibid., p. 89-90. Panikkar inquires: "Is the Jordan *the* river, as the Egyptians called the Nile?"

66. Ibid. Panikkar also adds: "If *spiritually* Christianity cannot dispense with Judaism, *intellectually* it would collapse without its connection with the Tiber, which I take as the symbol of the West, however broad and multifaceted this mentality may be."

67. Ibid. Panikkar mentions a helpful panorama of these traditions: Hajime Nakamura, *Ways of Thinking of Eastern People* (Honolulu: University of Honolulu Press, 1985).

68. Panikkar, "The Jordan," p. 92. Thus, says Panikkar, the "true reservoir of religion lies not only in the doctrinal waters of theology; it lies also in the transcendental vapor (revelation) of the divine clouds, and in the immanent ice and

snow (inspiration) from the glaciers and snow-laden mountains of the saints."

69. Ibid.

70. Ibid., p. 93.

71. Ibid.

72. Ibid., p. 94.

73. Panikkar notes that "Islam, which is felt as a threat (partly providential, as a warning not to become lukewarm), becomes *the image of all other religions.*"

74. Ibid. Panikkar continues the meaning of missionary "from literally going to preach to the 'infidels' to mystically offering oneself for their salvation, giving an example to the world. Thérèse of Lisieux, secluded in her Carmelite convent, sees—and fulfills—her life as a missionary."

75. Ibid., p. 95.

76. Ibid.

77. Ibid., p. 96.

78. Ibid.

79. Ibid.

80. Ibid., p. 97.

81. Ibid.

82. Ibid., p. 104.

83. Ibid.

84. Ibid., p. 105.

85. Ibid., p. 107. The author further describes those who embrace Christianness: "They do not sponsor a privatization of Christian identity, although sometimes they are almost forced to it. They sponsor an exteriorization of their Christian identity that is the fruit more of inner experience than of historical and doctrinal inertias. More or less consciously aware that the world is undergoing a mutation, they are attempting to live this change at its deepest—that is, at the religious level of their consciousness and consciences."

86. Ibid., p. 107. In a footnote, Panikkar notes that "many 'ex' or 'fallen' Christians who came as 'converted' Hindus to Varanasi on the Ganges in the 1960s and 70s have in the 80s, after they returned to their homes, acquired a Christianness-identity" (n. 23).

87. Ibid., p. 109.

88. Ibid.

89. Ibid., p. 110.

90. Ibid., p. 111. Panikkar adds that "this does not prevent me from affirming that I believe that others are wrong and even that their views are so harmful that I may feel obliged to combat particular errors—although not as absolute evils."

91. Ibid., pp. 111-12.

92. Ibid., 112.

93. Ibid.

94. Ibid., p. 113. Panikkar continues the mystical theme in his final sentence: "It is simply that I do not worship history, nor do I limit reality—not even human reality—to history, nor history to the Abrahamic history. Just as traditional theology speaks of a *creatio continua,* we could by analogy envisage a continuous incarnation, not only in the flesh, but also in the acts and events of all creatures. Every being is a *christophany.*"

95. Virginia Fabella and Sun Ai Lee Park, eds., *We Dare to Dream: Doing Theology as Asian Women* (Kowloon, Hong Kong: Asian Women's Resource Centre for Culture and Theology, 1989). The article, "'Han-pu-ri': Doing Theology from Korean Women's Perspective," is on pp. 135-46.

96. *We Dare to Dream,* p. 135.

97. Ibid.

98. Ibid., p. 136.

99. Ibid.

100. Ibid.

101. Ibid., pp. 136-37.

102. Ibid., p. 137.

103. Ibid., pp. 137-38. Chung also notes that the shaman "called to the ghosts and talked to them. Other times the shaman consoled the ghosts, played with them, or negotiated with them. There were many people who watched the shaman and responded to her."

104. Ibid., p. 138.

105. Ibid.

106. Ibid.

107. Ibid. Chung refers to an article entitled "Toward a Theology of Han" by Suh Nam-Dong in *Minjung Theology* (Singapore: CCA, 1981), p. 65.

108. *We Dare to Dream,* pp. 138-39. Chung refers to Suh Kwang Sun's class lecture given at the Claremont School of Theology in August 1983.

109. *We Dare to Dream,* p. 139.

110. Ibid., p. 140. Even worse, in "some cases a young widow's room was locked and she was prevented from coming out—in order to protect her chastity. The young girl's sexual desire was the object of the family's fear. In the worst cases, the young widow was encouraged to commit suicide or she was secretly killed to keep the family reputation intact."

111. Ibid. Reference is given for concrete examples in Lee Oo-jung, "Korean Traditional Culture and Feminist Theology," *The Task of Korean Feminist Theology* (Seoul: Korean Association of Women Theologians, 1983), pp. 63-78.

112. *We Dare to Dream,* pp. 140-44. References are provided in *Prostitution: Study on Women* (No. 2; Seoul: Korean EYC, 1984), especially pp. 13-14.

113. *We Dare to Dream,* p. 141.

114. Ibid., p. 142.

115. Ibid., p. 143. Chung is very clear about the treatment of women: "Korean women have been the embodiment of the worst Han in our history. They did not have the public channels to express their Han. This developed a sense of impassibility among Korean women. Many of them died without releasing the sense of impassibility in their lives. That is why there are so many women ghosts in our traditional stories."

116. Ibid.

117. See note 17, p. 146.

118. *We Dare to Dream,* pp. 143-44.

119. Ibid., p. 144.

120. Ibid.

121. Ibid., pp. 144-45.

122. Ibid.

Chapter 7: An Option for the Poor
Liberation in the First World

1. Philadelphia: Fortress Press, 1975.

2. *Doing Theology in a Revolutionary Situation,* pp. 144-50.

3. *Doing Theology in a Revolutionary Situation,* p. 144.

4. *Christianity and Crisis* (March 29, 1976), pp. 57-63. This may also be found in Alfred T. Hennelly, ed., *Liberation Theology: A Documentary History*

(Maryknoll, NY: Orbis Books, 1990), pp. 195-204.

5. *La función de teología en el futuro de América Latina: Simposio International* (Mexico City: Universidad Iberoamericana, 1991). Moltmann's article was entitled "Teología Política y Teología de la Liberación," pp. 258-70. In this work, I have translated all Spanish citations into English.

6. *La función*, p. 258.

7. Ibid.

8. I have shown, I believe convincingly, in my book that liberation theology began in the middle and late 1950s, not in 1964-68, and that therefore Moltmann's statement is false. See Hennelly, *Liberation Theology: A Documentary History*, pp. 1-37. To my knowledge, he is correct concerning the origin of European political theology.

9. *La función*, p. 259. See Hennelly, *Liberation Theology: A Documentary History:* "Torres had left the priesthood and joined guerrilla forces as a sign of true Christian love, and died in battle in the Santander mountains of Colombia on February 15, 1966" (p. 42).

10. The English translation was published by Orbis Books in 1973. A revised edition was published on the fifteenth anniversary of the book in 1988, again by Orbis Books.

11. *La función*, p. 259.

12. Ibid., p. 260.

13. Ibid., p. 261.

14. Ibid., p. 262.

15. Ibid., p. 263.

16. Ibid., pp. 263-64.

17. Ibid., p. 264.

18. Moltmann notes that the book was published in Stuttgart.

19. This book is said to be published in Munich.

20. *La función*, p. 265.

21. Ibid.

22. Ibid., p. 266.

23. Ibid.

24. Ibid. The italics are mine, since it clear that they are natural allies and should cease to waste time on internal feuding. There are many genuine enemies on all sides, and their energy and time should be expended in those battles.

25. *La función*, p. 266.

26. Ibid., p. 267.

27. Ibid.

28. Ibid.

29. Ibid., p. 268.

30. Ibid. The italics are mine in this very important text of Moltmann.

31. Ibid.

32. Ibid.

33. Ibid., p. 269. Moltmann also states that, with the end of the cold war, Mikhail Gorbachev's plan for a "common European home" presents enormous possibilities.

34. Ibid.

35. Ibid., pp. 269-70.

36. Ibid., p. 170.

37. Ibid.

38. Robert McAfee Brown, *Liberation Theology: An Introductory Guide*

(Louisville: Westminster/John Knox, 1993).

39. *Liberation Theology*, p. 89.

40. Ibid., p. 92.

41. Ibid., pp. 92-93. Other examples were the "overthrow of the democratic Arbenz government of Guatemala in 1954, and U.S. help in overthrowing the democratically elected Allende government in Chile in 1970, replacing it with the ruthless dictatorship of General Pinochet, whose bloodbath reprisals took thousands of innocent Chilean lives, lives whose blood is on our hands."

42. Ibid., p. 93. As regards the economic squeeze of debt, Brown sorrowfully narrates that it "was not uncommon for the interest due each year to exceed the entire budget of a country."

43. Ibid., p. 94.

44. Ibid., p. 95.

45. Ibid., p. 96.

46. Ibid.

47. Ibid., p. 97.

48. Ibid.

49. Ibid., p. 98.

50. Ibid., pp. 98-99.

51. Ibid., p. 100. The document may be found in Robert McAfee Brown, ed., *Kairos: Three Prophetic Challenges to the Church* (Grand Rapids: Eerdmans, 1990).

52. *Liberation Theology*, p. 100.

53. Ibid., p. 101.

54. *Kairos Central America*, par. 40.

55. *Liberation Theology*, p. 102.

56. Ibid., p. 103. This and the next quote are from the Central America Kairos Document.

57. *Kairos Central America*, par. 85-86. See *Kairos: Three Prophetic Challenges*, p. 96.

58. *Liberation Theology*, p. 108.

59. Ibid., pp. 108-09.

60. Ibid., p. 109. Brown continues: "We are in the midst of what Kierkegaard called 'the midnight hour when all must unmask,' and when this happens we may not even recognize who we are."

61. *Liberation Theology*, p. 110.

62. Ibid.

63. Ibid., p. 112.

64. Ibid., p. 113. Berry's poem, "Manifesto: The Mad Farmer Liberation Front," is found in his book, *The Country of Marriage* (New York: Harcourt Brace Jovanovich, 1973).

65. *Liberation Theology*, pp. 113-14.

66. Ibid., p. 113.

67. Ibid.

68. Ibid., p. 114.

69. Karen Lebacqz, *Justice in an Unjust World* (Minneapolis: Augsburg, 1987). Brown recommends especially chapter one of this book.

70. *Liberation Theology*, p. 115.

71. Ibid., p. 116. Brown repeats this theme for emphasis: "A central theme of the New Testament is that we are not isolated individuals but part of a community. To be 'in Christ' means 'to be in the Christian community.'"

72. Jack Nelson-Pallmeyer, *Brave New World Order* (Maryknoll, NY: Orbis Books, 1992), p. 147.

73. *Liberation Theology,* p. 117.

74. Ibid., p. 118.

75. Ibid.

76. Ibid., p. 119.

77. Ibid. Brown concludes: "Both lists are as long as the human imagination."

78. Ibid., p. 120.

79. Ibid., pp. 120-21.

80. Ibid., p. 121.

81. Ibid., p. 122.

82. Ibid., p. 124. Brown adds: "To back the oppressors rather than the oppressed must be one of the worst things a Christian can do."

83. Ibid., p. 125.

84. Ibid., pp. 126-27.

85. Ibid., p. 127.

86. Anne Brotherton, ed., *The Voice of the Turtledove: New Catholic Women in Europe* (New York: Paulist, 1992).

87. Ibid., p. 215.

Chapter 8: Saving and Cultivating Creation
An Ecotheology of Liberation

1. Rachel Carson, *Silent Spring* (Boston: Houghton Mifflin, 1962) and Donella Meadows et al., eds., *The Limits to Growth* (New York: Universe Books, 1972). Another early book that I discovered only much later was Paul Ehrlich, *Ecoscience: Population, Resources, Environment* (San Francisco: W.H. Freeman, 1970).

2. Anne Lonergan and Caroline Richards, eds., *Thomas Berry and the New Cosmology* (Mystic, CT: Twenty-Third Publications, 1987), p. 3.

3. Ibid.

4. Ibid., pp. 107-08.

5. The authors are Donald Senior, C.P., Gregory Baum, Margaret Brennan, James Farris, Stephen G. Dunn, C.P., and Brian Swimme. An editor, Caroline Richards, also provides the final chapter in the book.

6. *Thomas Berry,* pp. 27-39.

7. Ibid., p. 27.

8. Ibid., pp. 28-29. Berry remarks: "This assertion betrays a certain anxiety lest any admission of authentic revelatory experience outside the Christian tradition lead to a diminution of the Christian claim to the integral revelation of the divine to the human community."

9. *Thomas Berry,* p. 29.

10. Ibid. Berry speculates on the reason for this: "The sense of an elect people as exclusive bearers of a universal salvation either originated in or was powerfully reinforced by the feeling that as a small people they had an important destiny that was constantly threatened by surrounding political powers. The more threatened the elect people felt, the more intensely they experienced their own significance as a people destined to be the instrument of divine rule over all the nations of the earth" (ibid., pp. 29-30).

11. *Thomas Berry,* p. 30.

12. *Summa Theologica* (Part I, Question 47, article 1).

13. *Thomas Berry,* p. 31.

14. Ibid.

15. Ibid., p. 32.

16. Ibid., p. 33.

17. Ibid., p. 34.

18. Ibid.

19. Ibid., p. 35.

20. Ibid.

21. Ibid., p. 36.

22. Ibid.

23. Berry quotes from a book by Pierre Leroy, *Letters From My Friend: Teilhard de Chardin* (New York: Paulist, 1980).

24. *Thomas Berry*, p. 37.

25. Ibid., pp. 37-38.

26. Ibid., p. 38.

27. Ibid., pp. 5-26.

28. Ibid., p. 5.

29. Ibid. Italics are mine.

30. Ibid., p. 6.

31. Ibid., p. 7.

32. Ibid.

33. Ibid.

34. Ibid., p. 8.

35. Ibid., p. 9.

36. Ibid., pp. 9-10.

37. Ibid., p. 10.

38. Ibid. He sees this visionary approach in such phenomena as "the new surge of the industrial economy, the rising level of stock market quotations, the shifting of currency values, the formation of the great conglomerates, the giant corporation mergers, the new mystique of the entrepreneur."

39. Ibid., pp. 11-12. Berry makes an interesting proposal with regard to the media: "This mythic commitment to continuing economic growth is such that none of our major newspapers or magazines considers having an ecological section in each issue—equivalent to the sports section, or the financial section, or the arts section, or the comic section, or the entertainment section—although the ecological issues are more important than any of these, even more important than the daily national and international political news. The real history that is being made is inter-species and human-earth history, not international history. Our real threat is from the retaliatory powers of the abused earth, not from other nations" (p. 11).

40. Ibid., p. 12.

41. Ibid. Berry acknowledges the pioneers in the "new sense" as: Nicholas Georgescu-Roegen, *The Entropy Law and the Economic Process* (Cambridge, MA: Harvard University Press, 1971), and Rachel Carson, *Silent Spring* (Boston: Houghton Mifflin, 1962).

42. *Thomas Berry*, p. 13.

43. Ibid., p. 15.

44. Ibid., p. 17. Another good description of the process is the following: "Because the human condition was not overcome by spiritual power or divine intervention, humans have since the time of Francis Bacon been determined to bring this better world into being through the scientific, technological, industrial, and corporative enterprise. If this requires the total despoiling of the earth to achieve such transformation, so be it."

45. Ibid.

46. Ibid., p. 18.

47. Ibid., p. 19.

48. Ibid., pp. 20-21.

49. Ibid., p. 23.

50. Ibid., pp. 24-26.

51. Sallie McFague, *Metaphorical Theology: Models of God in Religious Language* (Philadelphia: Fortress Press, 1982); and *Models of God: Theology for an Ecological, Nuclear Age* (Philadelphia: Fortress Press, 1987).

52. Charles Birch, William Eakin, and Jay McDaniel, eds., *Liberating Life: Contemporary Approaches to Ecological Theology* (Maryknoll, NY: Orbis Books, 1990). The article of Sallie McFague is on pp. 201-27.

53. *Liberating Life*, p. 202.

54. Ibid., p. 203.

55. Ibid.

56. Ibid.

57. Ibid, p. 205.

58. Ibid.

59. Ibid., p. 221, n. 9. McFague continues: "It is a destabilizing, inclusive, nonhierarchical vision of Christian faith, the claim that the gospel of Christianity is a new creation for *all* of creation—a life of freedom and fulfillment for all."

60. Ibid., pp. 206-07.

61. Ibid., p. 222, n. 12. The reference to Soskice is her book, *Metaphor and Religious Language* (Oxford: Clarendon Press, 1985), p. 96.

62. *Liberating Life*, p. 207.

63. Ibid., p. 208.

64. Ibid., p. 222, n. 17.

65. Ibid., pp. 222-23, n. 17.

66. Ibid., p. 208. Ian Barbour has concluded that the *"monarchical model* of God as King was developed systematically, both in Jewish thought (God as Lord and King of the Universe), in medieval Christian thought (with its emphasis on divine omnipotence), and in the Reformation (especially in Calvin's insistence on God's sovereignty). In the portrayal of God's relation to the world, the dominant western historical model has been that of the absolute monarch ruling over his kingdom" *(Myths, Models and Paradigms: A Comparative Study in Science and Religion* [New York: Harper & Row, 1974], p. 156).

67. *Liberating Life*, p. 209. The reference is to Gordon Kaufman, *Theology for a Nuclear Age* (Philadelphia: Westminster, 1985), p. 39.

68. *Liberating Life*, p. 209.

69. Ibid. McFague also adds: "Whatever one does for the world is not finally important in this model, for its ruler does not inhabit it as his primary residence, and his subjects are well advised not to become enamored of it either" (pp. 209-10).

70. Ibid., p. 210.

71. Ibid. Italics are mine.

72. Ibid., p. 211.

73. Philadelphia: Westminster, 1984. Theologies of nature have also taken up this topic; see, for example, Clause Stewart's *Nature in Grace: A Study in the Theology of Nature* (Macon, GA: Mercer University Press, 1983).

74. *Liberating Life*, p. 212.

75. Ibid.

76. Ibid., pp. 212-13.

77. Ibid., p. 213. McFague adds: "*We* give life to others of our own species,

but God gives life to *all* that is, all species of life and all forms of matter."

78. Ibid.

79. Ibid.

80. Ibid., p. 224, n. 26. The references are to Paul Tillich, *Systematic Theology*, (Vol. 1; Chicago: University of Chicago Press, 1963), p. 324; and Karl Rahner and Herbert Vorgrimler, *Kleines theologisches Wörterbuch* (Freiburg: Herder & Herder, 1961), p. 275.

81. *Liberating Life*, pp. 213-14.

82. Ibid., p. 214.

83. Ibid.

84. Ibid. Other authorities who propose this understanding of the knowledge of God in the world as God's body include Charles Hartshorne, "Philosophic and Religious Uses of 'God,'" in Ewert Cousins, ed., *Process Theology: Basic Writings* (New York: Newman Press, 1977), p. 109; in the same volume, Schubert Ogden, "The Reality of God," p. 123; and Grace Jantzen, *God's World*, pp. 81 ff.

85. *Liberating Life*, p. 215.

86. Ibid.

87. Ibid., p. 216. For a much more nuanced treatment of God's role in evil, see the lengthy footnote on pp. 224-25, n. 30. Her concluding sentence: "In sum, divine suffering for the cosmos (including each sparrow that falls) must not obscure human responsibility for a tiny corner of it—our earth."

88. Ibid., p. 216.

89. Ibid., p. 217.

90. Ibid.

91. Ibid.

92. Ronald Hamel and Kenneth Himes, eds., *Introduction to Christian Ethics: A Reader* (New York: Paulist Press, 1989).

93. Michael Himes and Kenneth Himes, "The Sacrament of Creation: Toward an Environmental Theology," *Commonweal* (January 26, 1990), pp. 42-49.

94. "Sacrament of Creation," pp. 42-43.

95. Ibid., p. 43.

96. Ibid.

97. Ibid.

98. Ibid.

99. Ibid.

100. Ibid., p. 44. The italics are mine.

101. Ibid.

102. Ibid., p. 45.

103. Ibid.

104. Ibid.

105. Ibid.

106. Ibid.

107. Ibid., pp. 45-46.

108. Ibid., p. 46. Italics are mine. Paul Ricoeur is quoted as saying that "we too often and too quickly think of a will that submits and not enough of an imagination that opens itself."

109. Ibid. A brief bit of a poem by Gerard Manley Hopkins is extremely appropriate at this point: "These things, these things were here, and but the beholder/Wanting." The authors quip: "At present, 'beholders' are desperately wanted."

110. Ibid.
111. Ibid.
112. Ibid., p. 47.
113. Ibid.
114. Ibid.
115. Ibid., pp. 47-48.
116. Ibid., p. 48.
117. Ibid.
118. Ibid., p. 49.
119. Ibid.
120. McFague, *Liberating Life*, p. 219.

Chapter 9: The World Religions as Liberators? A Liberation Theology of World Religions

1. Aloysius Pieris, *An Asian Theology of Liberation* (Maryknoll, NY: Orbis Books, 1988), and *Love Meets Wisdom: A Christian Experience of Buddhism* (Maryknoll, NY: Orbis Books, 1988).

2. John Hick and Paul Knitter, eds., *The Myth of Christian Uniqueness: Toward a Pluralistic Theology of Religions* (Maryknoll, NY: Orbis Books, 1988). Other books of Knitter include: *No Other Name? A Critical Survey of Christian Attitudes Towards the World Religions* (Maryknoll, NY: Orbis Books, 1985); edited with Roger Borless, *Buddhist Emptiness and Christian Trinity: Essays and Explorations* (New York: Paulist, 1990); editor, *Pluralism and Oppression: Theology in World Perspective* (Lanham, MD: University Press of America, 1991).

3. Knitter, *The Myth of Christian Uniqueness*, p. 178. David Tracy has recently followed the same line: "This new hermeneutical practice become living theology can best be described as 'mystical-prophetic.'. . . How then can we think such two different modes of religiousness otherness together? That is the question towards which much serious theology today strives," *Dialogue with the Other: The Inter-Religious Dialogue* (Grand Rapids: Eerdmans, 1990), p. 6.

4. *The Myth of Christian Uniqueness*, p. 180.

5. Ibid., p. 182.

6. Ibid.

7. Ibid., p. 187.

8. Ibid., p. 187, n. 32.

9. Knitter, *No Other Name?* p. 229.

10. Paul Knitter, "A Liberation-Centered Theology of Religions," in *Dialogue and Liberation: Foundations for a Pluralist Theology of Religions* (Madison, NJ: Drew University Press, 1988), p. 47.

11. *The Myth of Christian Uniqueness*, pp. 191 ff.

12. Ibid., p. 191.

13. Ibid.; italics are the author's.

14. Ibid.

15. Ibid. See Jon Sobrino, *Christology at the Crossroads* (Maryknoll, NY: Orbis Books, 1978), pp. 346-95; Leonardo Boff, *Jesus Christ Liberator* (Maryknoll, NY: Orbis Books, 1978), pp. 32-48 and 264-95.

16. *The Myth of Christian Uniqueness*, p. 191. The italics are those of Knitter.

17. Ibid., p. 192. Sobrino, *Christology at the Crossroads*, pp. 9-10.

18. *The Myth of Christian Uniqueness*, p. 192.

19. Ibid., p. 192. In other words, orthodoxy "becomes a pressing concern only when it is necessary for orthopraxis—for carrying out the preferential option and promoting the kingdom."

20. Ibid., p. 193. See H. Richard Niebuhr, *The Meaning of Revelation* (New York: Macmillan, 1962), pp. 39, 41.

21. *The Myth of Christian Uniqueness*, p. 193.

22. Ibid., p. 194. In other words, Knitter holds that "whether such discernments about uniqueness and finality are eventually made or not is, in the final analysis, not that important—as long as we, with all peoples and religions, are seeking first the kingdom and its justice."

23. Ibid.

24. Ibid. See Monika Hellwig, *Jesus the Compassion of God* (Wilmington: Glazier, 1983), p. 133; Franz van Beeck, "Professing the Uniqueness of Christ," *Chicago Studies* 24 (1985), pp. 17-35.

25. *The Myth of Christian Uniqueness*, p. 194. See Avery Dulles, *The Resilient Church: The Necessity and Limits of Adaptation* (Garden City: Doubleday, 1977), p. 78.

26. *The Myth of Christian Uniqueness*, pp. 194-95. These comments were made personally to Paul Knitter.

27. Ibid., p. 195.

28. Ibid. See also Paul Knitter, "The Impact of World Religions on Academic and Ecclesial Theology," *Catholic Theological Society of America Proceedings* (1985), pp. 160-65.

29. *The Myth of Christian Uniqueness*, pp. 195-96.

30. Ibid., p. 196.

31. Ibid., p. 197.

32. Knitter, "A Liberation-Centered Theology of Religions" (see n. 10).

33. Ibid., pp. 46-48.

34. Ibid., pp. 46-47.

35. Ibid., p. 48.

36. *On Being a Christian* (Carden City, NY: Doubleday, 1976).

37. See especially *Christianity and the World Religions: Paths of Dialogue with Islam, Hinduism, and Buddhism* (Garden City, NY: Doubleday, 1986).

38. New York: Crossroad, 1991.

39. *Global Responsibility*, p. 78. Küng criticizes the World Council of Churches for affirming dialogue in principle and still not making a decisive move to true ecumenism.

40. Ibid., p. 79.

41. Ibid., pp. 79-80.

42. Ibid., p. 80-81.

43. Ibid., p. 81.

44. Ibid.

45. Ibid., p. 82.

46. Ibid., p. 86.

47. Ibid., p. 87. Küng also notes that the Vatican, "the last absolute monarchy in Europe," has not yet signed the declaration of human rights of the Council of Europe. He also muses on how *glasnost* and *perestroika* will affect this last monarchy.

48. Ibid., p. 87.

49. Ibid., p. 88.

50. Ibid., p. 90.

51. Ibid., p. 91.

52. Ibid., p. 93. In other words, does "not the capacity of dialogue basically mean the absence of a standpoint?"

53. Ibid., p. 95.

54. Ibid., p. 96.
55. Ibid., pp. 96-97.
56. Ibid., p. 97.
57. Ibid.
58. Ibid.
59. Ibid., p. 155, n. 109. See J. Moltmann, *Evangelische Theologie* 49 (1989, vol. 6), on *Dialog der Religionen*.
60. Ibid., p. 99.
61. Ibid.
62. Ibid.
63. Ibid., pp. 99-100.
64. Ibid., p. 100. Küng adds: "This makes it clear that a maximal theological openness to the other religions in no way calls for the suspension of one's own convictions in faith."
65. Ibid., p. 104. Küng here also expands the importance of working for *peace*: "There can be no peace among the nations without peace among the religions. There can be no peace among religions without dialogue between the religions. There can be no dialogue between the religions without research into theological foundations."
66. Ibid.
67. Francis X. Clooney, S.J., *Thinking Ritually: Rediscovering the Purva Mimamsa of Jaimini* (Vienna: Indological Institute of the University of Vienna, 1990); and *Theology After Vedanta: An Experiment in Comparative Theology* (Albany: State University of New York Press, 1993).
68. More details on these books may be found at the end of this chapter. The reference to Clooney's review-article is "Christianity and World Religions: Religion, Reason, and Pluralism," *Religious Studies Review* 15 (July 1989), pp. 198-204.
69. For example, see Paula M. Cooey, William R. Eakin, and Jay B. McDonald, eds., *After Patriarchy: Feminist Transformations of the World Religions* (Maryknoll, NY: Orbis Books, 1991).
70. Clooney, "Christianity and World Religions," p. 198.
71. Ibid., p. 199.
72. Hans Küng, *Christianity and the World Religions: Paths to Dialogue with Islam, Hinduism, and Buddhism* (Garden City, NY: Doubleday, 1986), p. xviii. Küng is here incisive, too, on dialogue: ". . . it must be a critical dialogue, in which all religions are challenged not simply to justify everything, but to deliver their best and most profound message. In short we need a dialogue in *mutual* responsibility and in the awareness that none of us possesses the truth 'ready-made,' but all are on the way to the 'ever greater' truth."
73. This is described by Gavin D'Costa, *Theology and Religious Pluralism* (Oxford: Basil Blackwell, 1986), p. 52.
74. Alan Race, *Christians and Religious Pluralism: Patterns in the Christian Theology of Religions* (Maryknoll, NY: Orbis Books, 1985), p. 38.
75. D'Costa, *Theology and Religious Pluralism*, p. 22.
76. Knitter, *The Myth of Christian Uniqueness*, p. viii. The author also noted the gravity of his step: "Such a move came to be described by participants in our project as the crossing of a theological Rubicon." He also notes that Langdon Gilkey considers it "a monstrous shift indeed . . . a position quite new to the churches, even the liberal churches."
77. Clooney, "Christianity and World Religions," p. 199.
78. Heim, *Is Christ the Only Way?*; Ariarajah, *The Bible and People of Other*

Faiths; and Gregson, *Lonergan, Spirituality, and the Meeting of Religions.*

79. Küng, in both *Christianity in World Religions* and *Christianity Among World Religions.*

80. Swidler, ed., *Toward a Universal Theology of Religion,* especially pp. 7-13.

81. This quote is from Bernard Lonergan, "Dimensions of Meaning," in *Collection* (New York: Herder and Herder, 1967), p. 259.

82. Knitter, *No Other Name?,* p. 32.

83. Clooney, "Christianity and World Religions," p. 200.

84. Griffiths and Lewis, "On Grading Religions, Seeking Truth, and Being Nice to People," *Religious Studies* 19, pp. 75-80 (pp. 76, 78).

85. Hick, *Problems of Religious Pluralism,* pp. 95, 94.

86. Clooney, "Christianity and World Religions," p. 200.

87. D'Costa, *Theology and Religious Pluralism,* p. 133.

88. Heim, *Is Christ the Only Way?,* p. 38.

89. Gregson, *Lonergan,* p. 200.

90. Clooney, "Christianity and World Religions," p. 200.

91. Ibid.

92. Ibid., p. 201.

93. Elouise Fraser, "Thinking about Theocentric Christology," *Journal of Ecumenical Studies* 24 (1987), pp. 34-35. Fraser was responding to some of the ideas of Paul Knitter in his *No Other Name?*

94. Thomas Dean, "Thinking about Theocentric Christology," *Journal of Ecumenical Studies* 24 (1987), p. 31.

95. Marjorie Hewitt Suchocki, "In Search of Justice," in *The Myth of Christian Uniqueness,* p. 150.

96. Rosemary Radford Ruether, "Feminism and Jewish-Christian Dialogue," in *The Myth of Christian Uniqueness,* pp. 147-48.

97. Paul Knitter, *Dialogue and Liberation: Foundations for a Pluralist Theology of Religions* (Madison, NJ: Drew University Press, 1988). Especially important is Chapter 3, "A Liberation Centered Theology of Religions," pp. 33-48.

98. George Lindbeck, *The Nature of Doctrine: Religion and Theology in a Postliberal Age* (Philadelphia: Westminster, 1984), pp. 129-30.

99. Charles Taylor, "Understanding and Ethnocentricity," in *Philosophy and the Human Sciences* (Cambridge: Cambridge University Press, 1985).

100. Hans Penner, "Rationality and Religion: Problems in the Comparison of Modes of Thought," *Journal of the American Academy of Religion* 54 (1986), pp. 645-71.

101. Clooney, "Christianity and World Religions," p. 201.

102. Bibhuti S. Yadav, "Anthropomorphism and Cosmic Confidence," in L. Swidler, ed., *Toward a Universal Theology of Religion* (Maryknoll, NY: Orbis Books, 1987), pp. 175-91. Yadav also critiques Panikkar from the viewpoint of Buddhism on pp. 183-91.

103. Clooney, "Christianity and World Religions," p. 201. The author rephrases his point: "If the belief in rebirth is no more than a cultural artifact, it is not likely to make a claim on our attention."

104. Aloysius Pieris, "Buddhism as a Challenge for Christians," in Hans Küng and Jürgen Moltmann, eds., *Christianity Among World Religions* (Edinburgh: T. & T. Clark, 1986), pp. 60-66.

105. Wang Hsien-Chih, "The Co-Existence between Christians and the People on Taiwan," in *Christianity Among World Religions,* pp. 90-95.

106. Leonard Swidler, *Toward a Universal Theology of Religion,* pp. 5-50.

107. Hick and Knitter, eds., *The Myth of Christian Uniqueness,* p. viii. Knitter,

who wrote the preface, goes on to explain his goal: "Part of the purpose of this book is to 'expose' this new approach, to bring it out into the open so that other theologians, together with the Christian community at large, might better evaluate its content and coherence, and judge how adequate it is to human experience, how appropriate and faithful to Christian tradition."

108. Ibid., p. 47. Gilkey's own solution is that "it is in praxis that we uncover a *relative absoluteness.*"

109. Clooney, *Christianity and World Religions*, p. 203.

110. Ibid.

111. Marjorie Hewitt Suchocki, "In Search of Justice: Religious Pluralism from a Feminist Perspective," in *The Myth of Christian Uniqueness*, pp. 149-61.

112. Paul Knitter, "Toward a Liberation Theology of Religions," in *The Myth of Christian Uniqueness*, pp. 178-200.

113. Suchocki, "In Search of Justice," p. 149.

114. Ibid.

115. Ibid., p. 150.

116. Hans Küng, *On Being a Christian* (Garden City, NY: Doubleday, 1976). Suchocki comments on the book: ". . . its clear intent, from page 1 to page 602, is to demonstrate the superiority of Christianity over against other modes of being human, whether secular or religious" (p. 152). She also quotes Küng's final conclusion, after 602 pages of argument: "The Christian element therefore is neither a superstructure nor a substructure of the human. It is an elevation or—better—a transfiguration of the human, at once preserving, canceling, surpassing the human." In all fairness, it should be pointed out that Küng wrote those words almost two decades ago, and that since that time he himself has experienced a Copernican revolution with regard to the world religions (although I do not agree with all his present positions).

117. Suchocki, "In Search of Justice," p. 157.

118. Ibid., p. 158.

119. Ibid., p. 159.

120. Ibid.

121. Ibid., p. 160.

122. *Almanac Atlas & Yearbook 1993* (46th ed.; Boston: Houghton Mifflin, 1993), p. 408. See also *The World Almanac and Book of Facts* (New York: Pharos Books, 1993).

Epilogue: Justice in the New Millennium

1. Catherine L. Albanese, *America: Religions and Religion* (Belmont, CA: Wadsworth Publishing, 1981).

2. Ibid., p. 6.

3. Ibid., p. 7.

Index